*BLAZE OF GLORY*

# NEW ORLEANS CAMPAIGN
## 1814-1815

500 MILES

10.95
B + 9.

**TERRITORY**

ALABAMA RIVER

JACKSON FROM THE CREEK WAR

FORT STODDERT

Y THE UNITED STATES, 1813

PERDIDO R.

1814
JACKSON'S
TEMPORARY
HEADQUARTERS,
TO NOV. 21.

Mobile

JACKSON

**SPANISH
EAST
FLORIDA**
TO 1819 AND 1821

PASCAGOULA R.

JACKSON

Pensacola

MOBILE BAY

ST. ROSE I.

CAT ISLAND

SHIP ISLAND

ISLE A'CORNE

DAUPHINE I.

FORT BOWYER

1814-15
BRITISH FLEET
ANCHORAGE
DEC. AND JAN.

1814
COCHRANE'S BRITISH
FLEET CONVOYS
PAKENHAM'S ARMY
FROM JAMAICA,
NOV. AND DEC.

CHANDELEUR
ISLANDS

Mobile    Pensacola

New
Orleans

G U L F    O F
M E X I C O

Havana

**NEW**

CUBA
(SP.)

VE
DE

Balize

JAMAICA
(BR.)

NEGRIL
BAY

**SPAIN**

SOUTHEAST
PASS

SOUTH
PASS

**BRITISH
ROUTE**
FROM JAMAICA

500 MILES

SAMUEL CARTER III

# *BLAZE OF GLORY*

The Fight for New Orleans, 1814-1815

St. Martin's Press   New York

St. Martin's Press
175 Fifth Avenue
New York, N.Y. 10010


AFFILIATED PUBLISHERS: Macmillan & Company, Limited, London
—also at Bombay, Calcutta, Madras and Melbourne
—the Macmillan Company of Canada, Limited, Toronto.

To
CHARLES W. FERGUSON

# Contents

# *Acknowledgments*

Thunderstorms over Jackson Square in New Orleans, and they are frequent, are like thunderstorms nowhere else in the United States — seemingly more sudden, violent, supercharged with lightning flashes, ear-splitting thunder-claps, and rain that spatters the pavements like spent bullets. Standing in what was formerly the *Place d'Armes,* flanked by its ancient Cathedral buildings and rows of balconied nineteenth-century homes, one hears again the roar of cannon from the fields below, sees the flashes of mortar and rockets down the river, smells acrid gunsmoke in the mist that swirls around the trembling earth: in short, one is recalled through time to the sights, the sounds, the sharp impressions of that battle which, in January 1815, sealed the independence of America.

Surely the Chamber of Commerce is not responsible for this phenomenon. But the experience serves as a fortuitous reminder that here in the center of the *Vieux Carré* the siege itself is still alive, still viable and pulsing. Here within a few square miles is the richest source of material on the Battle of New Orleans that can be found in the United States. For the Crescent City is proud and acutely conscious of the conflict which molded American history, has cherished its memory and kept its documents and memorabilia in tender care.

Almost everyone in New Orleans is an authority. The cab driver who took me to the battlefield and Chalmette monument discoursed at length and with intelligence on the event, even suggested books and sources of material, and, after putting his flag down to stop the meter, insisted on showing me landmarks and points of interest I had not intended to investigate. Such is the surviving interest of the city and its population. The bellboy, the waiter, the man behind the bar and the barber who cuts your hair, will, given the opportunity, throw in his bit of legend or opinion. Anyone interested in the siege of New Orleans should attend that city with receptive ears and eyes, and the battle becomes as recent and real as yesterday.

Here, too, are the fountainheads of information, documentary and otherwise. On Chartres and St. Anne streets, off the northeast corner of the Square, is the library of the Louisiana State Museum where this writer, for one, owes much to the help and guidance of Mrs. Aline Morris and Mrs. Octavie Loria, and to the Library's wealth of published and unpublished papers. Cater-corner from the Library is the Museum itself, adjoining the Cathedral, with its own collection of documents and paintings, some of the latter appearing in this volume.

A short way down Royal Street is The Historic New Orleans Collection of the Kemper and Leila Williams Foundation, and I am indebted to its artist-curator Boyd Cruise for showing me through its several floors on the day it was opened to the public. On the Chalmette Battlefield itself, a few scant miles below, lies Jackson Barracks where my thanks extend to Mrs. Mary Oalman, custodian of files, for making available the historical records of the Adjutant General's Office.

Northwest of the *Vieux Carré* is the Louisiana Landmarks Society in Gallier Hall which provided excellent pamphlets and publications on the battle; and, close by, the New Orleans Public Library with its comprehensive Louisiana Division headed by Colin B. Hamer, Jr., who directed me to much invaluable material. Of great help, as well, was the Howard Tilton Library of Tulane University where Mrs. Connie Griffith, a knowledgeable guide and counselor, is director of the Special Collections Division. The *Bibliotheca Parsoniana,* or personal collection of E. A. Parsons in New Orleans, was likewise a source of valuable documents, though copies of many of its papers were obtained from other sources.

Further data was procured from the Genealogical Research Society of New Orleans, through the kindness of its director Charles L. Mackie, and, in Baton Rouge, from the State Archives and Records Commission, with the help of director A. Otis Hebert. Living descendants of those who participated in the defense of New Orleans in 1814–1815 were more difficult to locate but equally obliging and informative. Among this group, my thanks to Mrs. Rowena E. Mulhern of Rayville, Louisiana, for personal records of the de la Rondes, and for insight and information on the lives of other planters on whose fields the battle centered.

Eastern sources also yielded much material: The Enoch Pratt Free Library of Baltimore, Yale University and Sterling Memorial libraries, the Antiquarian

Society of Worcester, Massachusetts, the National Historical Society of Gettysburg, and the U. S. Naval Institute at Annapolis – the last for naval records of the battle. The National Archives in Washington and, of course, the manuscript division of the Library of Congress were and are an indispensable source of official government documents and papers of Andrew Jackson, President Madison, and Secretary Monroe, and other federal officials in the War of 1812.

Of great assistance throughout this work was the Ridgefield Library and Historical Association of Ridgefield, Connecticut, whose able staff obtained many hard-to-find books from libraries otherwise inaccessible. To Miss Phyllis Paccadolmi and Mrs. Aldo Girolmetti, in particular, my thanks for their patience and cooperation in this effort.

For much spadework and research help, my thanks to Don Rodriguez of New Orleans, especially for ferreting out contemporary local anecdotes and local records of the battle. Also to Mrs. Anne Blair of Baltimore for patiently reviewing 1814 and 1815 copies of *Nile's Register,* a rich source of letters and reports from New Orleans. And finally to Mrs. Joan St. George Saunders of London for tracking down documents and publications pertaining to the British side of the engagement – for it was England's battle, too, much as that nation was disinclined to dwell upon it.

With a bibliography appended to this volume, reference to retail stores may seem extraneous and inappropriate. But for those in search of out-of-the-way and sometimes local histories, two outlets deserve mention: Claitor's Bookstore, South Acadian Thruway, in Baton Rouge, and Bayou Books, in Gretna, Louisiana.

In keeping with this author's custom, or personal prejudice, there are no numbered references or footnotes in the text, due to a belief that the reader should not have to look elsewhere in the book for facts essential to the story.

A plea for indulgence. Much of this account is based on the reports of participants, on-the-field observers, and eyewitnesses. True of eyewitnesses everywhere, no two agree precisely. There are contradictions difficult to reconcile. A writer can only choose those circumstances and accounts which seem to fit the picture best, aware that others may not agree with those selections and interpretations.

Another matter, calling for no apology, is that of discrepancies in names and spelling. In a community that existed under ten flags and three nationalities, such discrepancies are common. De la Croix, for instance, may be found as Delacroix or de Lacroix; Plauché may be Anglicized to Plant; Hind may be singular or plural. Street names and places change with chameleon facility, as the city shifted from French to Spanish to American administration.

Similarly, titles and ranks of officers are capricious, as are the strengths of various military units. Terms like "regiment" and "battalion" do not conform to modern specifications (most were under strength, at that), while designations such as "sloop-of-war" do not necessarily define a sloop-rigged vessel, but rather any vessel under sail.

In numerous quotations appearing in the text I have, in the interests of clarity, taken such liberties as correcting misspellings and confusing punctuation. On the other hand I have allowed to stand certain questionable wordings where reported by accredited authorities. Adjutant-General Butler records Jackson as saying, of the British advance under withering fire, "Magnificent! But is it war?" Was Butler's memory accurate or (since his account was written later) was he inadvertently echoing the words of a French general during the charge of the Light Brigade at Balaclava? No matter. Perhaps great generals react and speak alike on comparable occasions. Let it stand.

I am much indebted to Mrs. Jane Lucas de Grummond, Professor of History at Louisiana State University, for her counsel and guidance throughout this work, and for her time and patience in checking the completed manuscript, a kindness which rescued the writer from many embarrassing slips. Thanks, too, for help and suggestions from Harnett T. Kane, an authority on Louisiana history and author of many books on New Orleans, who is, at this writing, engaged in a crusade to save the de la Ronde Oaks from the bulldozers of spurious progress.

Finally, much is owed by this writer to Thomas J. McCormack and Thomas L. Dunne of St. Martin's Press for indispensable direction and advice, as well as to Malcolm Reiss for ever considerate services too numerous to mention. If I have failed to mention others whose interest and encouragement contributed to this endeavor, I can only plead the dictatorial space limitations of these pages.

There is on the globe one single spot, the possessor of which is the natural enemy of the United States. It is New Orleans, through which the produce of three-eighths of our territory must pass to market.

Thomas Jefferson, 1803

I expect at this moment that most of the large sea-port towns of America are laid in ashes, that we are in possession of New Orleans, and have command of all the rivers of the Mississippi Valley and the lakes, and that the Americans are now little better than prisoners in their own country.

Lord Castlereagh, British Foreign Secretary, December, 1814.

Most people say that our American Republic was born on the Fourth day of July, 1776, in Philadelphia. This is not true. It was only begotten then. It was never confirmed until the 8th of January last.

Captain Henry Garland at New Orleans, February, 1815.

The Battle of New Orleans . . . wiped out all previous American defeats, ending the "Second War of Independence in a blaze of glory."

Samuel Eliot Morison in *The Oxford History of the American People.*

# Maps

*Maps designed by Theodore Miller*

# Prologue

Spring, 1812.

"Every hope from time, patience, and love of peace is exhausted, and war or abject submission are the only alternatives left to us."

So wrote Thomas Jefferson, architect of the Louisiana Purchase, on the eve of America's second war with England, which would later be referred to as the Second War for Independence.

Jefferson's two terms in the White House had reduced the country to a woeful state of unpreparedness, and James Madison's accession to the presidency in 1809 had done little to correct the situation. But even more serious was the reluctance of the young republic to fight again for the freedom and recognition it had forcefully declared in 1776. This was indeed "The War Nobody Wanted," during which the United States was more divided, more rocked by dissension, than it ever had been — or has been since.

For one thing, the roots of conflict lay not in American soil, but overseas where France and England had been at one another's throats since 1803. The United States had wanted no part of this war between "the strumpet governments of Europe." It wanted only to observe a course of strict neutrality, while maintaining its right of free trade on the high seas.

The two goals were incompatible. On trial throughout the first years of the European conflict was this concept of neutrality. Neither France nor England respected America's right to trade with the opposing power. Each resorted to search and seizure on the high seas. But Great Britain's "Orders in Council" provided also for the impressment of American seamen branded, rightly or wrongly, as deserters from the British navy.

*Free Trade and Sailors' Rights* was a handy slogan on which to mobilize the country. But the issues were actually various and cloudy, meaning different things to different sections of the nation and for different reasons.

In the West and South, war sentiment was strong, arising from regional interests unconnected with free trade and sailors' rights. The agricultural West looked with longing eyes on the fertile lands of Upper Canada where many Americans had already settled. As an excuse for invading and annexing Canada, westerners pointed to the threat from the Indian warrior Tecumseh and his hostile tribes which had, allegedly, been goaded by England to stir up trouble in that region.

Similarly the Southern states looked avidly to the Floridas — held by Britain's ally, Spain — as being a rightful, economic part of the United States. West Florida was a near and logical market for the immense produce of the Mississippi valley, and as such ripe for annexation. Again, Great Britain and her European ally, Spain, were accused of arousing the Indians to hostile action against their American landlords in the South.

But the territorial ambitions of the West and South meant little to New England, where overseas trade was the key not only to prosperity but to survival. And that trade was brought to a halt by the war. Here the anti-war Federalists, seeing peace at any price a bargain, were entrenched. Here opposition to the war would grow and reach a peak that bordered on disunion.

In short, there was no single cause of war with England. Only an interplay of causes, often contradictory. Nor was there any clear-cut unity of purpose. Division within the country was as great a threat as war itself. Dissension and protest were in fact distinguishing features, enervating factors, in perhaps the most unpopular war the United States would ever be embroiled in.

Along with these factors was one not always acknowledged: lack of communication in a world without steam or telegraph or cable. It hampered the settlement of irritating issues and hindered attempts to reach a peaceful understanding. Weeks before America declared war on Great Britain, England had taken steps to rescind its Orders in Council and remove a primary source of aggravation. Fifteen days after a treaty of peace had been signed in Belgium, one of the most bitter battles of the war was raging at New Orleans. Yet in each case the news arrived too late.

It was even unclear, at first, just who was the true enemy. While Britain's maritime policy hurt American trade and pride, Napoleon's measures to control the sea trade of the young republic were equally offensive. There were those in the United States who favored war with France, regarding England as the last hope of the free world, a bastion of defense against the spreading tyranny of Bonaparte. Only a senseless act of provocation, the attack in June 1807 by the British frigate *Leopard* on the U.S.S. *Chesapeake* — in which three American sailors were killed and four impressed — branded England as the greater malefactor.

Even so, while awaiting restitution for those killed and seized in the *Chesapeake* affair, Jefferson sought every alternative to war, every means of peaceful coercion to bring the belligerents into line. Total Embargo, imposed by Congress in 1807, restricting American ships and trade to American ports, did more harm at home than overseas, paralyzing the economy and furthering still more dissension and dissatisfaction. Replaced in Madison's administration by the Non-Intercourse Act, directed against France and England only, this new measure was equally ineffective.

Congress finally resorted to a curious and complex bit of not-so-subtle bribery. The Macon Act of 1810 — named for a Congressman who never wrote it, never favored or supported it — permitted American ships to trade with any and all countries. But should either France or England renounce its obnoxious maritime policies, an embargo would automatically be imposed upon the other, non-complying government.

Napoleon rose quickly to the bait. Here was a chance to drive a wedge between America and England. He let it be known that France would revoke its decrees against American shipping. Madison and his minister in London, James Monroe, invited England to do the same. Great Britain refused: Napoleon's word was not to be trusted; the

Emperor's gesture was merely a ruse to draw the United States into an unholy alliance against England. From here on, Anglo-American relations worsened to a point beyond repair.

War was now unavoidable but still, to a degree, unthinkable. Against the mightiest sea power on the globe, the United States had little or no navy. A bill to build thirty more ships was defeated in Congress by a vote of sixty-two to fifty-nine. What good would even a larger fleet be in a war with England? "Gun-boats are the only water defense which can be useful to us," Jefferson had earlier decreed. "They will protect us from the ruinous folly of a navy."

Likewise a standing army in times of peace was considered "inconsistent with the principles of a republican government." Though Congress voted a ten-fold expansion of the army, raising its number to 35,000, it was largely a paper increase. As late as April of 1812 only some 6500 Regulars were armed. (Even after war was declared on June 18, the number had risen to only eleven thousand.) A bill authorizing the enrollment of fifty thousand volunteers, patently a bit of wishful thinking, was allowed to die in Congress of indifference.

This unrealistic attitude did not avert the crisis. On June 4 the House approved Madison's call to war by a vote of seventy-nine to forty-nine. The Senate passed the declaration by the narrow margin of nineteen to thirteen.

Decision did not end dissension. Governor Caleb Strong of Massachusetts proclaimed a public fast to atone for declaring war "against the nation from which we are descended," while the state legislature urged all citizens to "Organize a *peace* party throughout your country, and let all other party distinctions vanish." Even Chief Justice Marshall, ordinarily an advocate of union, applauded "the great division between the friends of peace and the disciples of war," adding that "all who wish peace should unite for its attainment."

Not so among the representatives of West and South where the "War Hawks," a term coined at this time by the appeasement-minded Federalists, were strongly united by Henry Clay, the eloquent Speaker of the House. "What have we got to lose by peace?" Clay asked the nation. He answered the question himself in three words: "Character, commerce, honor!" Many of his fellow hawks would have added: real and recognized independence from the arrogant politics and policies of Europe.

The war was no more popular in England, where the London *Ex-*

*aminer* proclaimed: "If the Father of evil himself had planned this mischief he could not have contrived a rupture more hateful to humanity, or one more destitute of advantage to anybody, the Imperial Oppressor [Napoleon] excepted."

Nor was England, embroiled in the European conflict, any better prepared to fight a land war in America, in defense of Canada. Along the lengthy Canadian border from Montreal to the western corner of Lake Erie were scattered six thousand British Regulars. No regiments could be sent from Europe while Napoleon was on the rampage. From Canada's population of half a million, compared with seven million in the United States, there was no great hope for a stalwart volunteer militia. Heavily-populated Lower Canada might contribute, say, eleven thousand, while from Upper Canada, closer to the heart of the United States and therefore extensively settled by Americans, perhaps four thousand more might be recruited. At best, Great Britain could do little beyond fighting a defensive action along the border, at those points of land contiguous to the United States.

America had few generals of experience and merit, and no master strategy for the conduct of the war beyond the dictates of geography. Since Britain commanded the Great Lakes, United States forces were committed to three intervening land approaches if they hoped to invade Canada, the obvious initial goal: the Detroit peninsula, the Niagara between lakes Erie and Ontario, and the upper St. Lawrence River.

President Madison recommended an obvious opening thrust: up Lake Champlain to capture Montreal, thus severing the St. Lawrence waterway, the lifeline of the provinces. This would call for help from the well-organized New England state militias, as those closest to the target. But both Massachusetts and Connecticut refused to allow their militias to serve outside the state. In fact, throughout most of the war, the volunteer militias were emasculated by short-term enlistments and laws confining them to the defense of local borders.

The first year of the war in the Northwest was marked, for the Americans, by blundering incompetence and outright cowardice. Reluctant and ill-trained troops either failed to hold the ground they had gained or fled at the sight of British regulars. General William Hull's failure to strike effectively at Canada through Detroit, and his subsequent surrender of that city, were followed by the repulse of generals Stephen Van Rensselaer and "Apocalypse" Smith at Niagara, and the defeat of General Henry Dearborn at the foot of Lake Champlain.

The humiliation of these defeats was somewhat offset by surprising naval victories achieved in the Atlantic by the *U.S.S. Constitution* and Stephen Decatur's *United States*. The military importance of these triumphs was slight and the ships were thereafter confined to home ports by the strengthened enemy blockade. But they raised American morale and lessened objections to the war, at the same time shaking Britain's confidence in its vaunted maritime superiority.

The loss of Detroit aroused a militant spirit in the Western States, especially Kentucky, where thousands rallied to their new commander, General William Henry Harrison. Early in 1813 Harrison sent an advance guard under James Winchester to retake Detroit. Trapped by a formidable British unit at the River Raisin, Winchester reluctantly surrendered, and captured American wounded were massacred by Indian auxiliaries. "Remember the River Raisin" became a Yankee battle cry in subsequent engagements.

Another British atrocity to be remembered and recalled with fury took place some months later in Virginia while Rear Admiral Sir George Cockburn, "rough, overbearing, vain, choleric, and capricious," was marauding in the Delaware-Chesapeake area. English troops which overran the village of Hampton on the James engaged in arson, looting and (attributed to foreign auxiliaries) rape. Along with the River Raisin Massacre, the Rape of Hampton dispelled any apathetic attitude towards the enemy.

Things went somewhat better as the year wore on. Captain Oliver Perry's triumph on Lake Erie in September ("We have met the enemy and they are ours"), followed by Harrison's recapture of Detroit, sealed off the western Canadian border and virtually ended in a stalemate the war in the Northwest. Action swung further to the East where General James Wilkinson with six thousand troops so bungled an attempt to strike into Canada and capture Montreal that he paved the way for his subsequent court martial.

The first months of 1814 brought significant changes for both sides. With Napoleon's abdication and temporary peace in Europe, much of England's military might was free for reassignment. Some twenty thousand troops representing seventeen regiments, including many of Wellington's veterans, were sent to North America to punish the United States for its treacherous stab in the back while England was at war with tyranny in France.

American forces, too, had grown to close to twenty thousand men in arms. The troops had gained experience and confidence under younger and more able generals, notably Jacob Brown and Winfield Scott. Brilliant victory at Chippewa, gallant resistance at Lundy's Lane, and the rugged defense of Fort Erie demonstrated America's hardier fighting prowess, but led no closer to decision. War weariness among the people and a nearly bankrupt government in Washington, tended to offset any hard-won gains.

It was in this climate of checkmate that American and British commissioners sought to come to terms at Ghent, in peace talks that, at Russia's instigation, had been going on since January. England's initial terms, concerned with territorial boundaries, fishing rights and treatment of the Northwest Indians, had been severe. Most serious, and held in reserve like an ace up a gambler's sleeve, was a double clause to the effect that:

1. The Americans must not be allowed to incorporate the Floridas in their republic.
2. The cession of New Orleans is essential to insure to us the enjoyment of our privileges to navigate the Mississippi.

These were not idle demands, presented for the sake of argument and open to discussion. Possession of New Orleans and free navigation of the Mississippi were basic to British strategy, which now embraced a three-pronged offensive: invasion of the United States from Canada via Lake Champlain, punitive raids on America's East Coast cities to destroy the enemy's morale and, the *coup de grâce,* a piercing thrust through the soft underbelly of the continent at New Orleans.

Regardless of what happened elsewhere or what was decided in the talks at Ghent, New Orleans would be an invaluable hostage in the bargaining for peace. If England's terms were not met, she would retain possession of the city and thus control the Mississippi and its valley and the vast unopened territories to the West.

Up to this summer of 1814 Madison's government had given scant attention to New Orleans and Louisiana in the conduct of the war. All but forgotten was President Jefferson's turn-of-the-century warning:

There is on the globe one single spot, the possessor of which is the natural enemy of the United States. It is New Orleans, through which the produce of three-eighths of our territory must pass to market.

Jefferson was speaking, at the time, of Spain's cession of Louisiana to Napoleon, "from which point," he added, "we must marry ourselves to the British fleet and nation." But the Emperor himself had precluded this unwholesome marriage by selling Louisiana to the United States. France was too deeply involved in war with England to occupy the 827,000-square-mile territory. Furthermore, Napoleon believed its possession by the Americans "would strengthen forever the power of the United States and would give to England a maritime rival that will sooner or later humble her pride."

So far in 1814 England's pride had not been humbled although it had been somewhat chastened by American resistance. The projected invasion from Canada had bogged down with the Americans' signal victory under Captain Thomas MacDonough on Lake Champlain. Admiral Sir Alexander Cochrane's amphibious operation in the Chesapeake, though crowned with the burning of Washington, had been decisively repelled at Baltimore. Only the third phase of the planned offensive, the invasion of Louisiana, remained to be executed in atonement for these earlier defeats.

"From the moment that the British possess New Orleans," wrote Senator Timothy Pickering of Massachusetts, "the Union is severed," while peace commissioner Albert Gallatin, commenting on the new British offensive, warned the country that "the true and immediate object is New Orleans." Yet so far as preparations in this theater went, Madison and the War Department had done little more than appoint Major General Andrew Jackson commander of the 7th Military District, charged with defending the Gulf Coast and the Southern states.

The assignment was partially to pacify this independent, action-minded general ("all I ask is a chance to fight"). Nothing would happen in this quarter, beyond the British blockade of the Mississippi. Secretary of War John Armstrong cautioned Jackson not to believe "the report of a British naval force on our Southern Coast," and assured him that rumors of English measures to arouse and arm the Indians in Florida could be dismissed as "myths."

Now, in September, these myths were becoming an ugly reality. A formidable British army, backed by a mighty armada, was on the prowl and heading for the Gulf of Mexico. Its officers anticipated little resistance from the polyglot people of Louisiana. At New Orleans, for sure, this disappointing war would be concluded in a blaze of glory.

But what torch would light that blaze, and whose would be the glory, only history was likely to reveal.

# 1. The Siren City

"What a magnificent New France we have lost!" exclaimed Pierre Clément Laussat on delivering New Orleans and Louisiana, in behalf of France, to the United States.

President Jefferson, having spent fifteen million dollars in the greatest real estate venture in history, predicted: "The position of New Orleans destines it to be the greatest city the world has ever seen."

Jefferson, ahead of his time in human ecology, recommended that the city's growth be thinly spread for "beauty, pleasure, and convenience" — blocks of buildings alternating with green parks, for "under the cloudless sky of America . . . men cannot be piled on one another with impunity."

But the city heeded not. It remained a tight little crescent on the left bank of the Mississippi where the river briefly flowed from west to east. And its residents remained piled on one another in some ninety blocks of mostly two-story houses and narrow unpaved streets.

Into this compact area and its immediate environs were crowded some eighteen thousand people (Some said twenty thousand, some said thirty thousand, in those days of little census-taking, but all agreed that it was "at least as big as Washington."). It was dirty, noisy and unsanitary, and all but bursting at the seams.

This compression was not due solely to human perversity or European clannishness. The surrounding terrain was flat and open. But New Orleans was, in a sense, an "island city" — and was so referred to in early documents. It was flanked on all sides by water: the Mississippi on the south, Lake Borgne to the east, Lake Pontchartrain on the north, and to the west and southwest, the aqueous region of Barataria with its many hidden streams, or coulées, leading to Lake Barataria and the Gulf. The more solid terrain around the town was veined by innumerable bayous, or slow-flowing creeks, that were often little more than drainage ditches, leading from the swollen waters of the lower Mississippi to outlets on the lakes and on the Gulf.

Within these watery confines the town had grown and prospered under three flags — French, Spanish, French again, and now the Stars and Stripes of the United States. But its character and loyalties remained distinctly French, as were its origins. The city had been founded in 1718 by Jean Baptiste le Moyne, Sieur de Bienville, one of two brothers who had explored the territory nearly forty years after La Salle had descended the Mississippi to the Gulf. Bienville named his frontier town in honor of the French regent, the Duke of Orleans, and it was settled throughout succeeding years largely by emigrant adventurers enticed to America by John Law's Company of the West which, between 1717 and 1731, administered the territory for the King of France.

But New Orleans and the territory of Louisiana were ominously threatened by the outbreak of the Seven Years War in 1755. By 1760 England had all but squeezed France out of North America and gained free navigation of the Mississippi, a coveted right that Britain would not readily relinquish. Even before the Treaty of Paris ended the Franco-English war in 1763, the hard-pressed Louis XV ceded the territory to his ally, King Charles III of Spain.

The succeeding forty years were bitter ones, during which the Gallic temperament revolted against an erratic and arbitrary Spanish rule. New Orleans became a hotbed of conspiracy and underground resistance, developing a social climate of unrest that would endure well into the next century.

Came the glorious day when, in 1800, Louisiana was retroceded by Spain to France, which had never ceased to be, in spirit at least, the mother country. It was, however, three years before the Colonial Prefect, Pierre Clément Laussat, came up the river to pave the way for the new regime and share in the weeks of joyous celebration that attended his arrival.

Laussat had barely had time to catch his breath when word arrived that Napoleon had sold Louisiana to the United States. Incredible news! New Orleans felt again forsaken, cast off as an unwanted stepchild. On December 20, 1803, the disconsolate citizens gathered in the Place d'Armes, an untidy parade ground centered on the half-moon crescent of the river, as the French tricolor descended the staff to be folded tenderly for the second, final time. In its place were raised the unfamiliar Stars and Stripes, presaging what forbidding future God alone could tell.

But for a while the dreaded specter of social change was held at bay. The city remained predominantly French, though cosmopolitan in population. Architecturally, since its reconstruction under Spanish rule following the fire of 1788, it had acquired a more solid European look, becoming the fey, enchanting love child of miscegenation. From the three sides of the Place d'Armes the little metropolis had spread out, not like the spokes of a wheel, but in blocks of mathematical rectangles.

It was a city of gentle pastel colors, of graceful balconies embraced by iron lacework, of Spanish arches leading into cobbled courtyards and to secluded patios where blossomed bougainvillea, orchids and hibiscus. Vines and flowers were the theme and ornament of every home. There being no stone available, the houses were constructed of soft local brick, set within cypress frames and covered with Mississippi clay from the *batture*. They were flush with the streets, with of course no cellars in that watery terrain. The ground-floor apartments were devoted to shops, offices and stores, with living quarters on the floor above.

Most of the houses had flat roofs of cypress planks supported by strong beams and overlaid with compositions of tar, lime and oyster shells that in time became "like solid rock and never leak a drop." The same writer adds: "The tops of their houses are used as their backyards. The women wash, iron, sit to work and the men go from the top of one house to the top of another and visit their neighbors without having anything to do with the Streets below."

It was a sensible provision. For the straight but narrow streets were at times almost impassable — rivers of mud when the rains came, thick with powdery dust throughout the dry spells. The sidewalks, called banquettes, were little more than planks of cedar from abandoned flatboats. Beside them ran open gutters carrying the excessive rain-falls and the city's sewage to adjoining bayous and canals that led eventually to Lake Pontchartrain. At the street corners where the gutters crossed and joined, they formed what the French called *islets* — and little islands were precisely what they were.

The houses, even the city homes of wealthy planters, were not palatial. The exteriors were drab and stained with rain and fungus. But inside they were little gems, tastefully and richly furnished with European imports, Oriental rugs and drapes, lit by crystal chandeliers and Spanish candelabra. And back of each lay the secluded patio, fragrant with tropical shrubs and flowers. The balconies, too, were gay with potted flowers and entwined with ivy dripping in festoons to the streets below.

Many of the public buildings — the St. Louis Cathedral, the adjoining Presbytere, and the Cabildo which had formerly housed the Spanish City Council — had been donated by Don Andres Almonaster, an Andalusian of noble birth, who under the Spanish regime had been the city's leading benefactor. They occupied the north side of the Place d'Armes, presenting a striking facade from the river. Other notable buildings near the square were the convent and chapel of the Ursuline nuns, the Military Barracks housing twelve to fifteen hundred troops, and Fort St. Charles, the last in disrepair and of little significance as a military stronghold.

When Jefferson predicted New Orleans' glowing future as the great-est city in the world, he added: "There is no spot on the globe to which the produce of so great an extent of fertile country must necessarily come." It was of course the secret of New Orleans' present proud posi-tion. The city was wedded to the Mississippi which had nurtured its commerce for a century. Down from as far as Ohio, Illinois and Penn-sylvania came the produce of the North and East: coal, cattle, lumber, wheat and iron. Back up the river went the products of Louisiana, principally molasses, sugar, cotton and tobacco.

From the Gulf, 110 miles south, came ships from all over the world to give New Orleans its distinctive cosmopolitan flavor. They could approach the city, somewhat tediously due to curves and currents, by the Mississippi. Or, except for heavier merchant vessels, they could come by Lake Borgne and Lake Pontchartrain. Then, reconsigned to smaller craft, passengers and merchandise could proceed down the Bayou St. John and the Carondelet canal to the very heart of the French quarter.

The river even supplied the community with its water, carried in carts to the houses, stored in earthen jugs, and filtered before drinking. But in spite of precautions yellow fever, from contaminated water and poor sanitation, had plagued the city time and again. The river threatened in another way as well. Five feet above the level of the town, it hung above the city like a time bomb. Only the levees—fifty to a hundred yards thick—kept the river at bay. But sooner or later a crevasse, or break in the embankment, might develop, threatening the city and the sugar cane plantations to the south with paralyzing flood.

The river brought other woes as well. The city's location as a crossroads and a gateway to the West attracted an unwelcome horde of opportunists and adventurers of every calling. New Orleans became, as one young poet aptly termed it, the "Siren City," summoning the greedy, the ambitious and the underprivileged. The levee and the market swarmed with traders and merchants of every nationality and color, hawking wares as various as their personalities. Land speculators, con-men, gamblers, shady financiers and moneylenders, honest and dishonest lawyers, medical quacks and down-and-outers flocked to this seductive land of gullibility and easy living.

Easy living perhaps it was, although the Creoles took their diversions seriously and strove to maintain a surface gaiety throughout the first years of the war. Dancing was all-important. Hardly a night passed when the Conde Street ballroom was not crowded with New Orleans belles and blades. Many of these *soirées* were subscription affairs, to which the men contributed the money and the women were admitted free.

Simply getting to and from the ballroom was a small adventure. The muddy, ill-lighted streets were difficult for cabriolets and barouches. Elegantly coiffured women wearing coronets of pearls and diamonds, walked barefoot through the mud to spare their slippers, raising their white satin gowns to keep them clear of the pervading mire. Ahead marched several slaves to light the way with lanterns; behind walked slave girls carrying their mistresses' slippers.

The ballroom and the elegant and graceful dancers were, in the eyes of an overseas visitor, "far superior to anything witnessed in Europe."

The hall was lighted with 200 candles, and sixty young demoiselles, dressed in white, were the ornaments of the ball. They were simply but elegantly dressed, nearly all had white roses adorning their hair which was artistically curled and plaited with taste and dropped with grace in floating elastic spirals on a virginal forehead around an alabaster neck and upon rosy cheeks.

Yet even these elegant affairs were not immune to the prevailing tensions among rival nationalities and factions in the city. The Americans demanded Yankee jigs and reels and Yankee music; the Creoles insisted on their right to the fandango. Both were ready to defend their preferences with the sword. Only when wiser heads took over, with an alternating schedule of dances, was open conflict in the hall avoided.

Equally popular among New Orleans males were the famous Quadroon Balls (white ladies not admitted). Here the city's blue-bloods, dressed in tight pantaloons, snuff-colored coats and elaborately ruffled shirts and stocks, selected their partly-colored mistresses as at a slave mart. Here, too, duels were frequent, provoked by the slightest incident, and the fencing academies on Exchange Place did a thriving business.

In fact, dueling was almost a separate diversion of itself. Few had not crossed swords on the field of honor, known as "The Oaks," outside the city. Even Louisiana's Governor Claiborne had been forced to fight a relatively bloodless duel to defend his reputation, while his son-in-law was killed contesting an insult to the Claiborne name.

Two theaters likewise provided afternoon and evening entertainment. The fashionable Théâtre d'Orleans on Bourbon Street presented grand opera in addition to traditional French drama. To expose one's daughter in the amphitheater was the equivalent to her "coming out," a means of presenting her to society. The nearby Théâtre St. Philippe was less discriminating, often indiscreet and bawdy in its presentations. And here again was the ever-present conflict. The Ursuline nuns and many devout found the theater an insult to Catholicism. They complained to Claiborne that from time to time it had held them up to ridicule on the stage. Claiborne invoked the St. Philippe to observe a little more restraint.

Adjoining the theater was one of the many famous gambling houses in the quarter. Next to dancing and dueling, gambling was a popular obsession with the Creoles and had been for more than half a century. Bernard de Marigny, the city's social monitor and wealthy playboy, set something of a pace by wagering most of his father's fortune at the tables of Toussaint's, Newlett's and St. Cyr's on Chartres Street. He was reported to have lost thirty thousand dollars in a single night, and one of the streets in the Faubourg Marigny was named Rue de la Craps, after his favorite game of dice.

Each coffeehouse and café throughout the city had its separate clientele. The Café des Refugées, in the shadow of the Cathedral, catered chiefly to the West Indian exiles, many free colored from Santo Domingo. Maspero's Exchange on St. Louis Street was a favorite of the wealthy businessman and merchant. Tremoulet's and the *Vache qui Tété,* or "Suckling Calf," catered to the Creole aristocrats. The Hôtel de la Marine gathered most of the amiable drifters and expatriates from the waterfront and city, the proud and indigent. None of these retreats was popular with the Americans, who imbibed their coffee and whiskey at home. Besides wine, brandy and anisette, the popular Creole drink was the *petite gouave,* a deadly mixed syrup of potent alcoholic content.

Very much a part of the community — in fact, the aristocratic heart of it, though geographically detached — were the planters, whose fields extended like twin braids down both sides of the Mississippi where, just below New Orleans, the river turned abruptly from its west-east course to flow directly south. Coming originally from French Canada or France, many of noble ancestry, they had lived off their lands for from fifty to a hundred years. But their fortunes had soared when, in 1795, a distinguished compatriot, Étienne de Boré, had perfected a method of refining sugar. As rapidly as sugar supplanted the malodorous indigo as Louisiana's principal crop, the planters prospered, most of them retaining winter homes or *pieds-à-terre* within the city.

On the left or east bank of the Mississippi the level cane fields stretched from the outskirts of New Orleans almost to the Détour d'Anglaise, or English Turn, twelve miles or more below the city. They formed a broad inviting avenue, half a mile to a mile wide, bordered by dense cypress swamps on one side and the river on the other. A passable road along the levee connected the plantations with the city.

The plantation manors, or châteaux, were modest by European standards. Most were two stories tall, embraced on all four sides by double balconies supported by round Doric columns, early examples of Greek architecture in Louisiana. Batteries of tall French casements led, at floor level, from the balconies to the lofty-ceilinged rooms of the interiors. These were furnished with possessions brought or imported generally from France, including the marble mantles, the crystal chandeliers, the tapestries and friezes and the Aubusson carpets.

Most of the houses were smothered in trees, making their neatly whitewashed walls invisible from a distance. They faced the Mississippi at varying stretches of several hundred yards, and each had its frontal, formal garden hedged around with orange and lemon trees, with live oaks sometimes forming an avenue from house to river.

Out back were the customary red-brick sugar mill and storage houses and the mud huts for the slaves. The latter had their own vegetable gardens and chicken runs and were allowed to sell their produce where they could, to the owner or in New Orleans, as a step towards purchasing their freedom.

At the head of the ladder-like chain of plantations beginning just below New Orleans was the estate of the Macartys, a noble Irish family which had followed James II to France in flight from British persecution. As first mayor of New Orleans, Augustin Macarty had distinguished himself by ordering cargoes of imported ice destroyed because he feared that cold drinks "might make the citizens consumptive." The chilly freight was dumped into the Mississippi where blocks of slow-melting ice floated for days towards the Gulf.

From the second-floor balcony of the tall, square Macarty manor one could survey the whole pattern of planters' fields extending down the river in an orderly parade: Chalmette, Bienvenu, de la Ronde, Lacoste, Villeré, and Jumonville, names that in unforeseen ways would make their way into textbook histories to come — names closely linked to the Old Regime, the *Grande Époque* of the Sun King Louis XIV.

Directly south of the Macarty manor ran the Rodriguez Canal, once a millstream, now a weed-clogged ditch, transversing the upper end of the plateau. A military visitor to New Orleans some years earlier had observed that, should the city ever be assaulted by an enemy, the Rodriguez Canal would present a formidable position of defense.

Below Macarty's lay the plantation of the aging Ignace de Lino de Chalmette (who was inclined to spell his name "Chalmet"). It had been in the family since the earliest days of Colonial France. Next in order came Antoine Bienvenu's estate, one of the largest in diameter, but not so imposing or well-positioned as that of his neighbor, Pierre Denis de la Ronde, in dead center of the plantation belt.

Here the plain widened like the lower section of an hourglass, with de la Ronde's covering a good six hundred acres, reaching to the eastward curving cypress swamps. Shaded by vines and towering oaks which dripped with Spanish moss, the manor was built of solid masonry, cool as a tomb and just as permanent. Out of sentiment for the *Grand Monarque,* Louis XIV, under whom his great grandfather had served as *Chevalier à Cour,* Pierre had christened his chateau "Versailles." The name was not excessively pretentious. An admiring contemporary had remarked, "What Versailles is to France in unparagoned magnificence, Versailles on the bank of the Mississippi is to Louisiana."

Though an ancestral de la Ronde had fought with the English in the Revolutionary War, Pierre's loyalties were to his native France and, more ardently, to this corner of France he had created in the New World. As he confided only to close friends, he had great dreams for Versailles. Soon, when the war was over, he would build a city on this promised land, "Versailles-on-the-Levee," complete with its Rue St. Honoré and Champs Elysées, its own wharf to accommodate vessels from around the world, its parks and fountains.

Nor was that all. Twelve miles to the east, providing an outlet to the Gulf, would rise another city, Paris—Paris-on-Lake-Borgne. It would even have its own Seine. For the canal that bisected de la Ronde's estate and continued on to the bayous Mazant and Bienvenu, would be deepened and widened to form a navigable waterway connecting the two cities. Along the existing canal, de la Ronde's slaves were commencing to build a link by land, the *Chemin à Paris* or Paris Road. The twin cities would outshine New Orleans as centers of culture and gracious living.

It was a Periclean project, but, God willing, he would see it through. And because of it he would resist to the last drop of blood any enemy, of any race or nationality, who strove to take Versailles away from him or threatened its existence.

Below de la Ronde's was the plantation of Pierre Robin Lacoste, from whom de la Ronde had purchased portions of his land. Dryly witty in society, often ridiculously pompous, Lacoste, in his neighbors' eyes, was a bit peculiar. Lately, for example, as major in the volunteer militia he had been engaged in recruiting several corps of Negroes and mulattoes. A dangerous precedent, it was thought, encouraging Negroes, of whatever status, to bear arms. The threat of slave insurrections was a constant one among the planters.

Below Lacoste's was "Conseil," the plantation of Jacques Philippe Villeré, whose father had been killed in the 1768 revolution against Spanish domination in Louisiana. An ardent French patriot, educated at the University of Paris, Jacques, too, was a volunteer in the militia, outranking Colonel de la Ronde as Major General. He had two sons, Gabriel and Jules. The former, a militia major, had married de la Ronde's eldest daughter Eulalie.

Furthest down the ladder, as far as one could see from Macarty's balcony, was the estate of Charles Coulon Jumonville. Like the de la Rondes, the Jumonvilles stemmed from an old French-Quebec family with its roots in Bourbon France. Longer established in Louisiana than the de la Rondes, they had owned their plantation for close to a hundred years.

Not precisely a part of the plantation kingdom, but established just above it on the fringes of the city, was Bernard de Marigny, bearing a name as illustrious as de la Ronde. It was in fact a name older than New Orleans itself, an early de Marigny having accompanied Bienville in his turn-of-the-century explorations of the Mississippi Delta.

Bernard's father, Pierre Philippe de Marigny de Mandeville, had made an immense fortune in real estate, principally from the sale of land grants from the French and Spanish authorities. With it he built his country estate, named "Fontainebleau," as de la Ronde's was named Versailles, on the shores of Lake Pontchartrain, with another palatial house for city living between the Esplanade and the Champs Elysées in New Orleans.

Young Bernard, born in 1785, inherited this fortune when his father died in 1800. His cousin, young Charles Gayarré, with an urchin's envy, found him not only "one of the most brilliant and wealthy young men of the epoch," but "precociously wild and extravagant." Until he became of age, Bernard was raised by his kinsman, Lino de Chalmette, who had him tutored in England where he acquired the language and polished manners of the Anglo-Saxon nobility. Returning to New Orleans, Bernard renewed his efforts to dissipate his father's fortune and became, according to local chroniclers, "hero *par excellence* of New Orleans' social traditions."

De Marigny's daughters had married the sons of neighboring planters, thus creating a family monarchy over which Bernard held sway. Bernard himself had wedded Anne Mathilde Morales, daughter of Juan

Ventura Morales, Spanish Intendant at New Orleans before the American occupation. It had been love at first sight when the two met at a ball in Pensacola where Don Juan had finally retired. Bernard was challenged at the time by seven other suitors for Mathilde's hand. Explaining that he would gladly fight all seven, but only one by one, Bernard accepted the challenge. His first opponent fell with a thrust through the heart, and the other six promptly withdrew from the field of honor, leaving Bernard in possession of a wife.

Across the river, on the right or western bank, were other planters and plantations, but the mile-wide Mississippi hindered any casual intimacy between the two communities. Here the land lay somewhat as on the left bank: level cane fields were intersticed with ditches and canals between the river and the cypress swamps extending to the west. At the top of the chain of plantations stood the estate of Dr. William Flood, affectionately known as "Fat Doctor Flood," who had helped New Orleans combat its periodic plagues of yellow fever. His method involved liberal applications of cold water. Maunsel White, a military figure of Irish-French descent like the Macartys, had been one of his patients. White recalled that "bucket after bucket of Mississippi water was poured over me; the shock was terrible." It was a test of White's endurance, but it also brought the fever down.

At the foot of this plantation belt was the home of Manuel Andry, and directly across from de la Ronde's was the estate of Dusseau de la Croix, or Delacroix, founder and first president of the Louisiana Bank of which de la Ronde was a director. Occasionally de la Ronde rowed across the river to call on Delacroix, but in general he kept to his own associates on the left or east bank.

Most of the plantations were idle now, with the British blockade on the Gulf. Thousands of pounds of sugar were stocked in the storage houses, with no way of shipping them to market. The slaves were kept busy with make-work projects, such as clearing the canals of silt and debris.

On the left bank the canals, which bisected each plantation, were important not only for drainage and irrigation, but for the waterways they provided for the Spanish fishermen bringing their catches from Lake Borgne. These fishermen were a faceless lot, inhabiting a village of rough huts at the mouth of the Bayou Bienvenu. Little was known about their loyalties and national identities. But they were allowed to pass freely over the bayous and canals for the sake of the fresh fish and vegetables they had to offer. What they could not dispose of to the planters, they took up the road to New Orleans, leaving their pirogues by the levee since the canals were not open to the Mississippi.

Despite their compulsory leisure and their self-indulgences, the planters' life was not altogether hedonistic. Many of the established Creole aristocracy — "Creole" referring to the native born of French or Spanish parentage — were engaged in civil or miliary service. Not a few, like de la Ronde and Villeré, were officers in the militia, while Bernard de Marigny was active in organizing his compatriots in New Orleans to prepare for possible invasion. Bernard was, in fact, the acknowledged arbiter and leader of the French majority in that divided city.

In this respect, de Marigny rivaled the New Orleans lawyer Edward Livingston, self-appointed spokesman for the American community. The fifty-year-old Livingston was a shrewd, articulate attorney ("rapacious, unprincipled, and not to be trusted" in Creole eyes) and a former New York politician. He had left that city under the shadow of a financial scandal and in 1804 had come to New Orleans to recoup his fortune. He spoke French fluently and had married Louise Davezac, a French refugee from Haiti, thus establishing a somewhat unwelcome foothold in the French community.

When the Louisiana Territory became the Territory of Orleans under the United States, Livingston had been mentioned as its likely governor. In fact Andrew Jackson, who coveted that role himself, had supported Livingston, then a fellow Congressman in Washington, as a promising alternative. But the governorship had gone by appointment (after the Marquis de Lafayette had turned it down) to William Charles Cole Claiborne, a one-time lawyer and native of Virginia, in return for supporting Jefferson for President. When Louisiana became a state, Claiborne, somewhat stout and pompous at age thirty-eight, had been elected its governor over the militia General Villeré, a formidable adversary.

Claiborne's role was not an enviable one. He was caught in the middle of rival French-American factions and was not wholly acceptable to either. His greatest asset in the eyes of New Orleanians was his lovely wife Sophronie Bosque, a stunning Spanish Creole who had succeeded two earlier wives dispatched by yellow fever. New Orleans loved Sophronie, but they thought her husband graceless, obstinate and stupid: he did not speak French; he did not understand the Creole ways.

Claiborne was aware, and super-sensitively so, of the difficulties that he faced — as revealed in one of his many letters to President Madison early in his career as Governor:

> The credulity of these people is only equalled by their ignorance; and a vigorous magistrate, resting entirely for support on the good will of his fellow citizens, can at any time be exposed to immediate ruin by the machinations of a few base individuals.

Brooding further on the problems of his office, he concluded later:

> The population is composed of so heterogeneous a mass, such prejudices exist, and there are so many different interests to reconcile, that I fear no administration or form of government can give general satisfaction.

He was right to a large degree. He sat on a powder keg of conflict and dissension born of the heterogeneousness that he complained of. The French distrusted the sharp, rapacious Americans; the Americans slightly despised the effete and luxury-loving Creoles; the Spaniards were leery of both the French and the Americans, and in turn were regarded with suspicion. Hadn't the Spaniards once been the oppressive overlords? Weren't they now European allies of the British who were threatening Louisiana?

All down the line it went, group within group competing for position or, if not position, the retention of their inalienable rights and prerogatives. The Bourbon French were antagonistic towards their republican-minded cousins. The Catholic establishment was wary of the Protestant Americans and wondered what might happen to its venerable diocese if this new government continued. The Ursuline nuns again complained to Governor Claiborne that they had been ridiculed on the stage of the St. Philippe Théâtre. What was the Governor going to do about it?

Then there were the blacks or partly colored, some nine thousand of them, virtually half the population. Fifty percent of these were slaves, and so under tight control. The rest were *gens de couleur,* or free colored, many of them refugees from the bloody revolutions in

Cuba, Santo Domingo and Haiti. Envious and resentful of the white prerogatives, they were hard to place in the uneasy social pattern. Among them, too, were festering divisions. The mulattoes looked down on the all-black Africans, and even degrees of color established lines of separation.

Impossible to ignore, too, was the floating population that came down the river on flatboats and accumulated in a lawless horde along the waterfront. The boatmen were known as "Kaintucks" regardless of their origin, and the name Kentucky suffered from their reputation. When the flatboats were unloaded, unable to move upstream against the Mississippi current, they were sold for firewood or converted into floating brothels, gambling houses or saloons. Once paid for his cargo, the Kaintuck sought the pleasures of the city, which meant women, liquor and interminable brawling with the gendarmes.

It was partly from the Kaintucks that New Orleanians gained their early impressions of Americans, continuing to regard them as a source of so much recent misery. They even attributed a minor earthquake in the delta to the barbarians from the north. *Une telle chose ne se passe jamais sous les Espagnols ou Français!* But one thing the Americans had brought was war with England. At first that war had seemed a long way off, an affair of the United States and connected in no way with Louisiana, which had not become a state till 1812. The blundering battles on the Canadian border, the British raids on East Coast cities, had seemed too remote to think about.

Jefferson's Embargo and Madison's later measures to control trade with the European powers at first had little effect on the Crescent City. Its commerce was with the Eastern seaboard and with Spanish Florida. Though allied with England in the European war, Spain was still at peace with the United States; Florida and the Caribbean islands welcomed both American and British ships. But since May of 1813 England had extended its blockade from Long Island to the Mississippi Delta, virtually cutting off New Orleans at its roots.

As a result the business and commerce of the city had been stifled. Nothing moved. The Planters' Bank and the Bank of Louisiana had both suspended specie payments. Credit could be obtained only, if at all, by paying usurious interest rates. Noted the architect-engineer, Arsène Lacarrière Latour, a keen observer of the scene as evidenced by his *Memoirs,* "The people were anxious and depressed, all confidence had ceased, and with it almost every kind of business. Our situation seemed desperate."

While word had reached New Orleans that the British were assembling an armada in the Caribbean, aimed at invading Louisiana, it was not the danger of attack that most disturbed the New Orleanians. It was the disruption of their daily lives and occupations, the deprivations and inconveniences of wartime, that aggravated their discontent, and discontent was already a disease among so volatile a population. Where were the pleasures, the luxuries, of yesteryear?

Nowhere was stagnation more apparent than along the waterfront. In the warehouses and stacked on the docks and levee were some 150,000 bales of cotton and ten thousand hogsheads of sugar, which, with stocks of tobacco, whiskey, molasses, wines, and other produce, amounted to fifteen million dollars' worth of marketable wares. But the only route to Eastern markets, before the days of steamboats which could buck the Mississippi current, was via the Gulf, where two British warships lay in predatory waiting.

Perhaps no one felt the economic squeeze more keenly than the thirty-four-year-old promoter, Vincent Nolte, of German-Italian extraction. Calling himself either merchant or banker, Nolte had come to New Orleans from Germany in 1806 and again, for good, in 1812, finding the city "not only a nest of pirates, but a place of resort for every description of schemers and scamps, against whom nearly every other community was closed."

The remark was self-revealing. Though highly educated, Nolte himself was something of a scamp and schemer, out for what he could get by his wits and polished enough to worm his way into society. He had set himself up in New Orleans as a cotton merchant and with his own fleet of light-draft vessels traded extensively with the Spaniards in West Florida and even with the British enemy if they happened to be stationed there.

His latest mercantile adventure, in September 1814, had taken him to Pensacola. "Here," he wrote, "I sold my cotton, on the spot, at twenty-two cents per pound [acquired for half that cost in New Orleans], and in return purchased three packs of woolen blankets at five and a half to six dollars. With these I went through Mobile Bay and the small lakes back to New Orleans, where the blankets were worth from ten to eleven dollars. Everybody greeted this little venture of mine with the remark, 'Ah, you have been to visit your friends the English?'"

Nolte shrugged off such snide insinuations. He was as loyal as the next man, principally to himself. If some straight-laced Creoles looked upon him with suspicion, so what? He was merely, according to his own account, making the best of war's adversities, "relieving the joyless void of existence by an enterprising mercantile spirit."

There were others who carried on business as usual in these apprehensive months of 1814. Notable among them were the Baratarian pirates, who, war or no war, supplied the city with the luxuries that made life tolerable. From their fortified outpost on the island of Grande Terre sixty miles southwest of New Orleans and from numerous intermediate depots, they paddled their pirogues up the bayous to the city bringing English silver, china, leather and woolens, French wines and spirits, laces and perfumes, Spanish furnishings and jewelry—and above all, African slaves from the West Indies, smuggled from the islands or hijacked from Spanish slave ships.

The English blockade bothered them little. If necessary they could outsail or outshoot a British man-o'-war—sometimes even capture the vessel for the sake of its likely supply of arms and ammunition.

If New Orleanians sometimes questioned this illicit traffic, and not many did, self-interest prompted them to take a tolerant attitude. Governor Claiborne, however, took an increasingly jaundiced view of the freewheeling buccaneers, and in this he was supported by local revenue agents and authorities in Washington. Not only did the Baratarians challenge and belittle his authority, but with New Orleans threatened by invasion, it was no time to have the vulnerable southern approaches to the city occupied by a lawless, unpredictable band of renegades who might side with the enemy if lured by bribes or promises.

Unknown to the Governor, his wife Sophronie had met and been enchanted by the pirate leader Jean Laffite when the latter boldly visited New Orleans in disguise—disguised because revenue agents, summoned from Washington, were on his trail. Sophronie had known only that the handsome stranger was a wanted man, and in spite of her husband's position of authority she had wished him luck before they parted. Laffite had assured her that luck had generally been on his side.

Right now, however, he was not so sure.

# 2.  *Pirate and Paradox*

Until recently he had been a familiar figure in New Orleans, in the cafés and the gambling parlors, at the theater and the Quadroon Balls. His tall slender figure, his lean and handsome face, had turned the eyes of many a Creole demoiselle. It was rumored that he was wealthier even than de Marigny and de la Ronde; that his fortress-like mansion, though not as palatial as Versailles, was equally well furnished and provisioned; that his domain encompassed territory greater than all the riverside plantations put together.

He signed his name Jean Laffite (which history subsequently spelled Lafitte), and now, in September 1814, he was treading softly on streets which he had always traversed boldly and with pride. For there was a price on his head, and his brother Pierre was shackled by irons in the city jail.

In a city of colorful, capricious characters, where no one asked too many questions or probed too deeply into another's occupation, Jean Laffite was something of an enigma. One who tried to fathom his character concluded: "Patriot and pirate, he was—he is—Legend, Romance, Paradox, Mystery. His whole life, as Montaigne defined death, was *un grand peut-être*—a great Perhaps! He must have been a puzzle to himself."

Where had they come from, Jean Laffite and his brother Pierre? Jean spoke feelingly of France and of having witnessed and survived the Terror. Pierre talked boastfully of having served in the French Navy. Each registered his birthplace as Bordeaux. But the truth appeared to be that they had come from Haiti, to which the family had fled from Spain to escape the Inquisition.

There was a third and older brother with a number of aliases convenient to his trade. His name was Frédéric Alexandre, alias Frédéric Youx or Dominique You or simply "Captain" Dominique. Short and swarthy, with a hawk-like nose and flashing black eyes, his face was scarred with powder burns which gave him a sinister appearance that belied his rough good spirits and dependability. In his younger days he had been a skilled artillerist in the armies of Napoleon. Now, like many adventurous French Haitians, he was a privateer and a highly successful one, at that.

For privateering was a rich and fertile field. With the nations of Europe in conflict it was easy to obtain letters of marque from the warring countries to prey upon the vessels of their enemies. Those who did not bother with such licenses operated openly as pirates, though they preferred the name "corsairs." The French West Indies were their ports of call, the Caribbean and the Gulf were their convenient hunting grounds, and Spanish merchant vessels bearing African slaves or European luxuries were their remunerative targets.

Dominique set an example for his younger brothers, Pierre and Jean, that they could hardly help following. Both had had military training in Haiti and were excellent shots and swordsmen. After serving their apprenticeships with brother Dominique, they took to privateering on their own.

Sooner or later they visited New Orleans, for the Negro revolutions in Haiti were causing many of the French to emigrate to Louisiana. As early as 1803 Pierre Laffite sailed up the Mississippi with his privateer *La Soeur Cherie*. Armed foreign vessels were banned from the river, but Pierre got past the guns of Fort St. Philip by pleading that his ship had sprung a leak, was badly in need of repairs, and that his crew were suffering from lack of food. It was an emergency.

Once in the city, the ship was soon boarded by customs agents, and Pierre was forced to report that sixty-three of his crew had deserted. Yes, he admitted, all of them were Africans. There was no sign of a leaky hull and the ship was adequately provisioned. The authorities, including Governor Claiborne, suspected that the African "deserters" had been smuggled ashore and sold as slaves. But they had no proof, and Pierre was able to keep his profits from the sale and settle in New Orleans with a comfortable stake. He sent for his younger brother Jean, who joined him in the city.

They bought a modest home on Bourbon Street, not far from that of their cousin, Renato Beluché, a native of New Orleans and himself a successful privateer doing business with the smugglers in the southwest corner of the Mississippi Delta. Pierre set up business in a blacksmith shop on St. Philip Street, where skilled slaves fashioned lace-like grillwork to ornament New Orleans balconies. Jean opened a retail shop on Royal Street, well-stocked with European silver, fabrics, wines and other luxuries.

So quietly did the Laffites insinuate themselves into the pattern of New Orleans life that no one saw anything amiss. True, Pierre had a lusty capacity for drink and women and was believed to have a colored mistress, but no one quarreled with such tastes. He was unprepossessing in appearance, stout and of middle size, with dark eyes and brown hair crowding down his forehead, his face depicting sensuality and self-indulgence. He spoke English with a strong French accent and sought companionship among the more disreputable patrons of the Hôtel de la Marine in which he acquired a financial interest.

Jean was the opposite of his brother, tall and slender with dark penetrating eyes and black hair, his handsome face clean-shaven except for a trim beard marking his chin like an exclamation point. Dressed in conservative black, he was always impeccably groomed, courtly and courteous in manner. He was a skillful fencer, a graceful dancer, and spoke fluent English, Spanish and Italian in addition to his native French.

While Pierre stayed close to home on Bourbon Street, indulging in wine and women, Jean mixed freely in society, numbering among his friends such wealthy planters as Bernard de Marigny and Pierre de la Ronde, District Attorney John Randolph Grymes ("a monument of wit and learning"), and the lawyer Edward Livingston and Livingston's brother-in-law, Augustin Davezac. He was seen frequently with the banker Jean Blanque, the influential legislator Philip Louaillier, and freewheeling businessman Joseph Sauvinet, who was, in a sense not altogether clear, the Laffites' financial manager and adviser.

The brothers prospered in their first few years in New Orleans, and if many suspected that their two establishments were stocked with the contraband of smuggling and piracy, what was wrong with that? Smuggling had been a fact of New Orleans life for half a century. It was part of the city's economy. While some conscience-bound citizens decried this illicit operation, the general attitude of the appreciative Creoles was: *"Ces gens là font leurs affaires, pourquoi gâter leur métier?"* — those people are just attending to their business, so why interfere?

No one in New Orleans interfered, but times were changing. The Laffites had left Haiti at an opportune moment: the British were rapidly conquering the West Indies. Santa Lucia was the first to succumb, captured by a rising British officer, Edward Michael Pakenham, a favorite of the Duke of Wellington.

By the time that Guadeloupe had also fallen into British hands, the pirates and privateers were seeking new and safer havens. They found the perfect retreat in a land of "trembling meadows," twisting creeks and lakes and bayous sixty miles south of New Orleans. Someone had named the region Barataria, after Sancho Panza's legendary island in Cervantes' *Don Quixote*. The Bay of Barataria, debouching on the Gulf, was wide and shallow — too shallow for any warships that might try to interfere. It was protected at its mouth by the island of Grande Terre, six miles long and three miles wide — a sandy stretch of scrub oak, cabbage palms and orange trees, profuse with tropical vegetation.

Here for more than half a century a gypsy-like band of French and Spanish settlers had fished and trapped and engaged in smuggling, for this unmolested hideaway lay within easy reach of the New Orleans market. The Bayou Lafourche led to the Mississippi and the rich plantations, while the many lakes and lesser bayous extended in a clandestine network to the city.

It was a peaceful, pleasant community until the buccaneers arrived. These were a new and unfamiliar breed of men, ruthless, greedy and rapacious. They took possession of Grande Terre and installed their women in the thatched huts of the smugglers. If the latter resented the intrusion, there was little they could do about it. By 1810 the population of Grande Terre had doubled; there were some forty warehouses for stashing plunder, barracoons for captured slaves, arsenals, brothels and saloons. The peaceful, amiable life of smuggling was gone. This was blatant piracy, however much they liked to call it "privateering." No ship on the Gulf was safe; no nationality immune.

But as with every lawless community, internecine warfare was inevitable. Quarrels over the plunder, price-cutting in the market, fights over women, and just mayhem for the sake of mayhem, threatened the Baratarians with their own destruction. Possibly Jean Laffite, who was familiar with the territory and had dealt extensively with the smugglers, observed all this contention and took steps of his own to interfere. But the consensus is that the Baratarians themselves approached Laffite, possibly at the instigation of Jean's cousin Renato Beluché, and asked him to take over in the interests of peace and harmony.

Certainly Jean was a wise and obvious choice. He had proved himself a capable and disciplined executive in the handling of his own affairs. He was already straddling the fence between legitimate business and illicit smuggling. He had all the right connections in New Orleans, both among those in authority and those with money itching to be spent for slaves and other contraband. He also possessed his own brand of integrity, was persuasive and impartial, and was a man of natural authority.

Jean allowed himself to be drafted for the job of governor, king, dictator—call it what you will—of Barataria. His brother Pierre had suffered a stroke that left his face distorted and one eye out of line. He would remain in the city and handle affairs at that end with the aid of Joseph Sauvinet. Jean closed the shop on Royal Street and moved to Barataria, where he accomplished for that contentious, bellicose community what no one had been able to accomplish for the petulant, divided New Orleanians. He united the Baratarians into a solid, smoothly-run society, well organized and powerful.

One of his first acts was to obtain a letter of marque from the new republic of Cartagena, on the Caribbean coast of South America, thus giving his fleet of ships a certain legality in the eyes of questioning authorities. Since Grande Terre was a three-day trip by pirogue from New Orleans, he established a slave mart and trading post midway between them, on a shell-girt island and Indian burial ground known in New Orleans as "The Temple." On Grande Terre he built for himself a solid house of plaster-covered brick, with tightly-barred doors and windows, furnished and stocked with selected loot from Spanish merchant vessels.

Thus was born, in effect, the Free State of Barataria, with Jean Laffite its absolute authority. According to the merchant Vincent Nolte, who regarded the pirates as insidious competitors, "He [Laffite] called himself Emperor of Barataria and often published parodies of Napoleonic proclamations in the paper of his friend Leclerc." It is doubtful if Jean went in for such theatrics. He preferred to be known among his cohorts by the more modest name of *bos,* or "boss." But rule with an iron, Napoleonic hand he did.

Firmness was imperative. It was a rough and cutthroat crew that he commanded, already a thousand strong and augmented daily by fugitive pirates from the Caribbean, ex-convicts, army deserters, runaway slaves, and free Santo Domingans — the bloodiest of the lot. Dominique You had joined the band, along with Renato Beluché. Since they were both expert artillerists, their gunnery brought many prize ships into the Bay of Barataria. And among Jean's volatile lieutenants were the fiery Italian, Vincent Gambi, and his compatriot Louis Chighizola, dubbed "Nez Coupé" for having lost part of his nose in a saber duel.

Inevitably, among this twitchy, independent army, there were some who rebelled against Jean's dictatorial regime, which forbade, among other things, attacks on ships of the United States. One troublemaker was Vincent Gambi, who, during a council of war at Laffite's house, walked out in rebellion at one of the decisions. Later Gambi sent one of his lieutenants with an ultimatum: he and his band would take no further orders from Laffite.

Jean listened calmly to the emissary's challenge. Then he drew his pistol and shot the man dead.

"That put the fear of God into them," Dominique You observed with satisfaction.

Under Laffite's administration the Baratarians prospered — prospered too much, perhaps, for their own good. They were not only draining legitimate business from New Orleans, but depriving the government of immense amounts of revenue. Up to now, Claiborne had been only mildly disapproving, possibly tempered by Sophronie's sympathy for the "glamorous" privateers. It was an attitude shared by the majority of Creoles. The Governor complained to the United States Attorney General that even Louisianians of "exemplary integrity" condoned and supported the actions of the Baratarians; that when he denounced the smugglers as dishonest rogues, he met with the reply: "That is impossible, for my grandfather or my father or my husband was, under the Spanish Government, a great smuggler, and he was always esteemed an honest man." The Governor added that "it takes time to remove the influences and prejudices of former habits." He advised the Attorney General that he would pursue a policy of leniency and even conciliation towards the pirates, lest he arouse their active enmity.

But things were getting out of hand, particularly the smuggling and sale of slaves—a highly profitable operation for the Baratarians, but a traffic outlawed by the Federal Government since December of 1807. Slave auctions were openly advertised in the *Courrier de la Louisiane* and by notices posted in the city, giving the date and time of each transaction. As many as four hundred Negroes might be auctioned in a single day, at prices of from five hundred dollars to fifteen hundred dollars for a likely buck.

Meanwhile, in June of 1812 the United States Congress authorized the issuance of letters of marque to privateers who proposed to prey on British vessels. It was a significant commentary on the character of the Baratarians that only one of them took advantage of this legal opportunity, the others preferring Spanish targets although Spain was not at war with the United States. Renato Beluché, aboard his four-gun schooner *Spy* attacked and captured the British merchant vessel *Jane* and went through the red tape of trying to claim her as a prize.

Dominique You aboard his *Tigre,* without benefit of license, intercepted an armed British merchantman, relieved her of all negotiable merchandise and sailed joyously back to Barataria, ordering "Whiskey for all hands!" The whiskey had its effect. The *Tigre* was wrecked on a shoal, and its crew swam to shore, where they "regarded one another with lugubrious eyes."

"Don't look like that!" shouted Dominique. "Sapristi! I can get plenty of other ships where this one came from!"

It was no idle boast. Either to probe the pirates' strength at Grande Terre or to punish them for attacks on English ships, a British sloop of war, the *Sophia,* tried to force an entrance into Barataria Bay. She was severely mauled by Dominique's and Beluché's gunnery on the beaches of Grande Terre and barely escaped capture. Dominique boasted that he could have had her if he wanted. Word went back to the Admiralty in London: the Baratarians were a factor to be reckoned with in this war with the United States.

Claiborne was at his wit's end (a common position for the Governor) as to what to do about the pirates. As a local rather than a federal official he was hamstrung by the Legislature, which passed resolutions deploring the existence and the actions of the Baratarians, but refused to take punitive action. "There is little doubt," wrote Judge François-Xavier Martin, in New Orleans at that time, "that the ill-gotten money of Laffite played a part in the Legislature's disregard of Claiborne's request." As the military engineer Lacarrière Latour agreed, "New Orleans had sufficient troops for a well conducted expedition against the Baratarians but refused to take effective measures."

The federal government, however, was something else again, moved to wrath by the Treasury Department's loss of revenue. For all of eight months during 1812 Captain Andrew Hunter Holmes of the U.S. Army, heading a company of forty dragoons, roamed the "trembling prairies," hoping to ambush one of Laffite's flotillas carrying contraband to New Orleans.

An efficient pirate grapevine kept Laffite informed of Holmes's movements and location. Laffite's counter strategy was simple. He continued to send his convoys north, circumventing the enemy's camp by secret waterways. But to divert the attention of the enemy he dispatched an innocent pirogue as a decoy, to be captured by Holmes and found free of incriminating cargo — while the main convoy proceeded unmolested to New Orleans.

Inevitably, as this cat and mouse game continued, the Laffites slipped. In November of 1812 Jean and Pierre, the latter on an unlucky visit to the nest, along with twenty other pirates paddling their pirogues toward the city, fell into Holmes's trap. After a brief, fierce skirmish, outnumbered two to one, they were captured and taken to the city jail.

The wealthy Baratarians had no trouble posting bail. They were free, though awaiting trial, in twenty-four hours — in time to attend the birthday party of "General" Jean Humbert, former leader of the French expedition to liberate Ireland in 1798.

This was no trivial event. The doughty warrior, Humbert, was a man of appealing stature in the city, whose streets he paraded with military regularity. He never removed his uniform except, presumably, to go to bed. Each day at noon, in tricolor hat with regimental sword, he marched with drilled precision to the Hôtel de la Marine for game after game of dominoes, glass after glass of cognac, with anybody present.

At sundown, warmed by alcohol and memories, the general returned to the street where an army of urchins awaited his appearance. On command they fell in behind him and began their forward march, de-

lighted to serve as escorts to "le grand General de la République Fran-
çaise." In this glorious charade he would wave his sword at imaginary
enemies, lustily singing the "Marseillaise" or the "Chant du Depart"
and saluting the delighted citizens who crowded the balconies to watch
him pass.

Now, on November 25, 1812, his fifty-seventh birthday, the Place
d'Armes was crowded with Sunday revelers as Jean and Pierre crossed
over to the Hôtel de la Marine—Jean in his customary, fashionable
black, Pierre in his crumpled suit of gaudy green, stained with cordials
and tobacco—both brothers cavalierly tipping hats to their admirers.
What nerve! What courtly indifference to the charges being hurled
against them. *Ils sont épouvantables, ces gens là!*

But Humbert's birthday dinner marked a curious turn in Jean
Laffite's life. It was a lusty, bibulous repast, as one of the guests observed, "the bacchanalian song, the ribald jest, the pungent anecdote
adding zest to the revelry." But General Humbert sank deeper and
deeper in his cups. After one of the guests delivered a speech in praise
of the old soldier, Humbert struggled to his feet.

"Your words remind me of what I have become," he shouted
hoarsely. "Once I associated with the officers of the Emperor, even
with Napoleon himself. Here you find me among outlaws and pirates!"

Outlaws! Pirates! Who dared to apply such epithets to the Laffites?
Daggers were drawn and bedlam threatened. But Jean put his arm
around the general, who broke down, sobbing on his shoulder. Strife
was avoided, and by sober morning Humbert had forgotten what he'd
said. But Jean never forgot. To be called a pirate by Claiborne and the
hypocritical authorities was one thing; to be branded a pirate by a
General of the Grande République was another. Jean was seen no
more at the Hôtel de la Marine.

He was still free, for District Attorney John Randolph Grymes,
nursing puzzling reasons of his own, did not file formal charges till
the following April, in 1813. Then for eight months following, repeated
summonses were issued to bring the Laffites to trial. All returned with
the inscription, "Not to be found in New Orleans."

The Baratarians were, in 1813, at the height of their success, more
bold, more arrogant than ever. Charles Gayarré, an eyewitness to the
scene, observed that "their morals and general behavior declined in
proportion to their gain in wealth and power."

They indeed had wealth. The average Baratarian was receiving five hundred dollars a month as his share from the illicit traffic. This was spent on riotous sprees throughout the cafés of New Orleans, ending in frequent brawls with the City Guards. The New Orleanians began to look askance at this behavior. Even the once-shining image of Jean Laffite began to lose its luster, as his attitude became increasingly defiant and contemptuous.

Claiborne was driven to issuing another proclamation against the Baratarians, enjoining the citizens to have no further traffic with them. The proclamation closed with a notice that he posted in strategic places in the city:

> I, Governor of the State of Louisiana, offer a reward of *five hundred* dollars which will be paid out of the Treasury, to any person delivering John Laffite to the Sheriff in the Parish of New Orleans.
>
> > Given under my hand at New Orleans on the 24th day of November, 1813.
> > William C. C. Claiborne

Two days later, in identical locations as the first, appeared another notice of similar size and script:

> I, Bos of Barataria, offer a reward of five thousand dollars which will be paid out of my treasury, to any person delivering Governor Claiborne to me at the Island of Grande Terre.
>
> > Given under my hand at Grande Terre on the 26th day of November, 1813.
> > Jean Laffite

New Orleans laughed up its sleeve. That Jean Laffite! He had raised the ante tenfold and held the dim-witted Claiborne up to ridicule. Once again he was the bold and glamorous corsair—a modern Robin Hood. Walker Gilbert, a government surveyor who knew the region well and had noted the great amount of armament protecting Barataria, remarked, "I firmly believe that his Excellency the Governor runs a greater risk of being taken to Grande Terre and tried for his life than Laffite does of being punished for his crimes . . ."

But the joke soured when, late in January 1814, a band of revenue agents descended on Barataria to break up a publicized slave auction at The Temple. Their leader, J. B. Stout, was killed and two other agents fatally wounded. While the auction continued, with every black man sold, the rest of the agents were taken as captives to Grande Terre. Here Jean Laffite showed them his stores of looted treasure and invited them to help themselves. The prisoners were then released and returned to New Orleans with glowing tales of pirate generosity.

That was the last straw for Governor Claiborne. He appointed a Grand Jury to indict the Baratarians and order their arrest. Jean was safe at Grande Terre. But Pierre, though he first escaped detection "by hiding in a water barrel up to his neck," was finally seized in the cottage of his mistress, thrown in a cell in the Cabildo and shackled to its walls by heavy chains. He protested the chains: his delicate health could not withstand such treatment. But Judge Dominic Hall was adamant. The chains remained and application for bail was denied.

Word of the arrest reached Jean Laffite at Grande Terre. He promptly arranged a secret meeting with District Attorney Grymes at the cottage of his brother's mistress. What transpired is only suggested by an overheard remark by Grymes, "By God, I'll do it!" And later, "Livingston and I can get you out of hell, if necessary!" The next day Grymes resigned as District Attorney to join Edward Livingston in the defense of the Laffites. (By curious coincidence the Livingston family in New York had once financed the operations of the gentleman pirate, Captain William Kidd.)

New Orleans was astounded and another change of heart towards the Baratarians took place. If the ex-District attorney could resign his office to defend them, could there be anything so reprehensible about the pirates? Only the District Attorney who succeeded Grymes in office charged that his predecessor had been "seduced out of the path of honor by the blood-stained gold of pirates." Grymes promptly challenged him to a duel and crippled him for life.

The alleged fee of twenty thousand dollars each to Grymes and Livingston did not, however, secure Pierre's release. Nor was it much financial help to Livingston. Both were invited to Grande Terre to receive in person their generous retainers. Grymes made the trip alone, was lavishly entertained by Jean Laffite and started home with a sackful of gold doubloons. As he passed the riverside plantations it was mandatory that he stop at each for a friendly visit and a game of cards.

He lost the entire forty thousand dollars, but returned with glowing accounts of his entertainment and the behavior of Laffite.

"A fine fellow! Delicious food! Priceless linens and silver plate! And as for the wines and cordials — well!" And later: "What a misnomer to call the most polished gentleman in the world a pirate!"

No such encomiums were entertained by the authorities in New Orleans in early September 1814. The news, if it could be believed, looked grim. It also arrived tardily, making it difficult for anyone in New Orleans to keep track of rapidly changing events beyond their territory. In fact, communication or the lack of it was a prevailing factor in this theater of the war, at a time when steam and telegraph and cable were unknown.

It took thirty-odd days for news to reach America from Europe by even the fleetest vessels; nineteen days to travel from Washington to New Orleans by the fastest horses, two-thirds of the way through wilderness. Travel by boat down the Ohio and the Mississippi from, say, Pittsburgh could take weeks and even months. If by any chance some terms for peace were worked out by the American and British delegates conferring now in Ghent, it could take as long as eighty days for the news to reach New Orleans.

The most accessible city across the Appalachians from New Orleans was Baltimore, where *Nile's Register* was subscribed to and received by many New Orleanians. The *Courrier de la Louisiane,* a weekly paper in French and English, was given to reprinting certain items from the *Register,* such as the following, in turn reprinted from a London journal:

### AMERICA

Twenty-five thousand troops are forthwith to be transported to America; and already the public mind is prepared for the exertion of all our strength, in bringing that forward people to unconditional surrender.

No reference was made at this point to New Orleans as the target, but rumors of a British expeditionary force in the Caribbean were rife. In the event of an invasion of this quarter, the vast unprotected land of Barataria, with its many hidden waterways projecting to the city's gates, was an open invitation to an approaching enemy, much too vulnerable if controlled by an incalculable band of pirates.

Barataria and the Baratarians must be destroyed, if not by half-hearted revenue agents, then by the U. S. Regulars in the city, supported by Commodore Daniel Patterson's minuscule gunboat navy. Postponed so long, the attack could not have been projected at a worse time. With a British invasion likely—possible, at least—Governor Claiborne and his aides were harassed by the problem of priorities. How should the limited forces of the city be deployed? Who could be spared for military action elsewhere? What was the temper of the people towards the buccaneers of Barataria?

Anything he chose to do, the Governor believed, would be a gamble.

# 3.  Enemy on the Prowl

On the high seas in September 1814, bound for Jamaica aboard his flagship *Tonnant,* eighty guns, was British Vice-Admiral Sir Alexander Forrester Inglis Cochrane.

Cochrane, fifty-six years old, the son of an earl and considered "rather courtly and very much a gentleman," had been in command of North American naval operations since April 1. He had served under Sir George Rodney in the later years of the American Revolution and subsequently had participated in the conquest of French islands in the Caribbean, notably Martinique, where another able commander, Sir Edward Pakenham, had headed a successful landing force.

Throughout the previous winter Cochrane had been in London, concerned with planning a revitalized offensive in America. Punitive raids along the East Coast, principally around the Chesapeake, were to be followed, when more favorable autumn weather came, with the invasion of Louisiana. Cochrane's knowledge of the Caribbean and the Gulf of Mexico had highly recommended him for the assignment.

The amphibious campaign in the Chesapeake during most of August had not been altogether satisfactory, but victory in the last and crucial phase of the offensive, the capture of New Orleans, would erase all that. And Cochrane had left no stone unturned to pave the way and guarantee success. As early as April the Admiral had sent Captain Hugh Pigot of the frigate *Orpheus* to the mouth of the Apalachicola River in West Florida, to enlist the Creek Indians as British allies. The maneuver seemed sensible. The war had presented the Creeks with a once-in-a-lifetime opportunity to strike back at their American oppressors.

They had already done so, with self-destructive fury. Outraged by the Indian massacre of four hundred whites at Fort Mims, Andrew Jackson had led a punitive expedition against the Creeks, culminating in their crushing defeat at Horseshoe Bend on the Tallapoosa River, of which the Indian-hating Jackson had written, "the carnage was dreadful." Many of the outraged Creeks, having lost 23,000,000 acres of their hunting grounds by the treaty of peace which Jackson forced upon them, had retreated to West Florida, presumably still itching for revenge.

Arriving at Apalachicola in May, Pigot had reported to Cochrane that an estimated 2800 Creeks along with as many disaffected Choctaws were ready to side with the British. He reported further that they were familiar with firearms and easy to train, and that once affairs started rolling, at least one thousand Negroes, and probably many more, would rush to take up arms against the Americans. With this sizable force to count on, Cochrane decided he would need no more than three thousand British troops to conquer Louisiana, "a piece of folly so childish," observed English historian John Fortescue, "that it ought to have warned British Ministers against listening to any of his projects. Listen they did, however. . . ."

Acting on Pigot's advice, Cochrane decided that his next step would be the capture of Mobile. It was the only American-held outpost between New Orleans and Pensacola—the latter already a haven for British expeditionary forces, although held by supposedly neutral Spain. From Mobile the troops would move overland to Baton Rouge, occupy that city and cut off New Orleans from above.

It was a sure-fire plan to cripple the Americans. He wrote to the Minister of War, Earl Henry Bathurst, "I have it much at heart to give them a complete drubbing before Peace is made, when I trust their Northern limits will be circumscribed and the Command of the Mississippi wrested from them."

In late August, to implement this preliminary conquest, Cochrane dispatched a four-ship squadron to the Gulf, led by the youthful Captain Sir William H. Percy aboard the twenty-eight gun *Hermes*. He was accompanied by Colonel Edward Nicholls with a small force of three hundred marines. They were to pick up the promised Creeks and Choctaws at the Apalachicola River and take them to Pensacola, where they would be trained for the attack on Fort Bowyer guarding Mobile Bay. Once Fort Bowyer had been reduced, the capture of Mobile, thirty miles up the bay, was a foregone conclusion.

Although Percy and Nicholls had brought three hundred barrels of ammunition and 2500 muskets (one report mentioned twenty thousand!) for the Indians to be recruited, only six hundred Creeks and Choctaws were seen fit to take to Pensacola. And these were a grotesque and ludicrous bunch at that, as they paraded the streets of that venerable city, dressed in the gaudy scarlet jackets of the British army, but without the customary pants, for which they substituted their familiar loincloths. The marines, who were to be the solid core of this unprofessional army, regarded them lugubriously. They had received their orders from Colonel Nicholls:

As to the Indians, you are to exhibit to them the most exact discipline, being a pattern to those children of nature. You will have to teach and instruct them; in doing which you will manifest the utmost patience . . . and never give them just cause of offence. Sobriety, above all things, should be your greatest care — a single instance of drunkenness may be our ruin. . . .

While these exercises were continuing at Pensacola, Admiral Cochrane had one more ace up his sleeve. Whether or not it was impressed upon him by an incident preceding his arrival at Jamaica is uncertain. But it surely may have been.

As units of the fleet passed Haiti they had been intercepted by a privateer, about which Captain John Henry Cooke aboard the transport *Helen* noted:

The decks of this vessel were crowded with a group of piratical independent-looking fellows, of all sorts of complexions. While carelessly lounging in every possible posture, some leaned over the gunwale, whilst others stood erect with arms folded or akimbo. These men wore red and striped shirts; many of their sleeves tucked above the elbows of their brawny arms;

their heads cased in various colored handkerchiefs or hairy caps, and other
outlandish gear. . . .

At first they hailed us in French through a hoarse speaking trumpet, a
language we pretended not to understand; they then questioned us in
English. But finding that we were only a transport, they took no further
notice, and ploughed through the water to reconnoitre the body of the
convoy.

The pirates singled out as a likely target the small war vessel
*Volcano,* aboard which Lieutenant George Gleig was a witness to the
action. After an exchange of shots with the privateer, the *Volcano*
endeavored to sheer away. "But such was the celerity [of the pirate
ship]," wrote Gleig, "she was alongside in less time than can be imagined; and actually dashing her bow against the other, attempted to
board. Captain Price, however, was ready to receive them. The defenders were at their posts in an instant, and the enemy discovering,
when it was too late, the mistake into which he had fallen, left about
twenty of his men upon the *Volcano*'s bowsprit, all of whom were
thrown into the sea; and filling his sails, sheered off with the same
speed with which he had borne down."

While the pirates had been repulsed, they had provided food for
thought. The attack had delayed the expedition and served as a reminder that the Gulf was infested with privateers based on Barataria
below New Orleans. The territory they controlled, with innumerable
secret waterways leading to the city, would be invaluable to the
British invasion plans if the pirates could be enlisted as guides and
fighting allies.

Cochrane and Percy agreed to detach from the fleet at Pensacola,
Captain Nicholas Lockyer of the sloop of war *Sophia.* He would sail
to the island of Grande Terre at the mouth of Barataria Bay and contact one Jean Laffite, the rumored leader of the pirates. Lockyer would
have with him letters from unimpeachable British sources promising
Laffite rewards that he would find difficult to resist, if he pledged his
men to the support of the invasion. Having gained the support of the
Baratarians, Lockyer was to return at once to Pensacola, to join in the
subjugation of Fort Bowyer.

On the morning of September 3, 1814, Jean Laffite relaxed on the
balcony of his manor on Grande Terre and studied the waters of the
Gulf through his companionable telescope. Beside him was a letter

from his cousin Renato Beluché, who was privateering in the Caribbean. It was dated from Havana, August 8, 1814, and informed Laffite of a British naval expedition headed for the Gulf.

They touched here for aid in gunboats, small vessels, etc. and for leave to land at Pensacola, all of which were refused by the captain-general. However, I learn that they are determined to land at Pensacola with or without leave, where they will embark their collection of artillery. The colonel was conveyed with his troops in two sloops of war, the *Hermes,* commanded by the hon. W. H. Percy, and the *Caron,* commanded by the hon. P. Spencer, who, with such vessels as may be on the station, will cooperate with the land forces . . .

The brig *Orpheus,* some time past, landed arms and some officers at Apalachicola to arrange with the Creek nation for future operations against Mobile, New Orleans and that district of the country . . .

The whole nation are ready to join the British troops under Colonel Nicholls, who will immediately on his arrival issue his proclamation, declaring all slaves who will join their standard free and liberated forever from their masters. He will also issue another to the Indians, promising all their lands taken from them by the United States . . . Having thus prepared the minds of the negroes and Indians, he will on arrival of two or three black regiments from Nassau, etc. of fine troops, calculated for that climate, push for New Orleans — first having secured and fortified Mobile point, and taken Mobile, as well as placed a force at every point on the lakes . . . as well as Plaquemines in order to cut off all trade of the Mississippi. The force with him is small, but he will soon be reinforced from Bermuda, etc. — the flying artillery appears well calculated for his operations in that country.

So the British were on their way. It seemed of little concern to Laffite. His tough legionnaires, variously estimated at between two thousand and five thousand, his heavily armed fleet, plus the batteries on the beach, had routed English ships before. But what if the British came overland from Mobile and attacked New Orleans from the east? What if they took possession of the city and the river? That would be rough on business.

Idly he turned back to his telescope, scanning the Gulf where the wild ducks had already started their flights in *V*-formations to the south. As if in confirmation of Renato's letter, a sloop-of-war flying the Union Jack appeared in focus. He could barely make out her name, *Sophia.* They had driven her away before. What was she doing back?

Her actions were peculiar. A Baratarian schooner rested in the channel. The *Sophia* opened fire on her, driving her ashore. Was this a prelude to attack or just a warning show of force? Equally puzzling: a white flag rose on the *Sophia*'s mast, signaling a peaceful mission!

Jean descended to the beach where an aroused horde of pirates had assembled, angry at the firing on their schooner. Jean commandeered a pirogue to take him to the British vessel. As stout hands rowed him out to the *Sophia,* the British ship lowered a gig and proceeded towards the shore to meet him. In it were two uniformed officers later identified as Captain Nicholas Lockyer of His Majesty's Navy and Captain McWilliams of the Army.

As the two vessels approached, one of the officers shouted, "We are looking for Jean Laffite."

"Follow me," said Jean in French. "I'll take you to him."

As the parties stepped ashore, Jean told the officers, "I am Jean Laffite."

He had nothing to fear from the admission. Around him were grouped two hundred menacing pirates, stirred to wrath by the sight of British uniforms. There were cries of "Hang them! . . . Shoot the British spies! . . . Throw them in the brig!" Jean silenced the mob and escorted his visitors to the castle, slamming the iron gate behind them.

After an exchange of pleasantries in French through an interpreter (Laffite spoke English but preferred this secondhand approach) and after several rounds of excellent hijacked Burgundy, McWilliams got to the point. He placed before his host a packet of documents and letters from his superiors, which he said spoke for themselves. Would Laffite please read them?

The first was a public proclamation, already being circulated by British agents in New Orleans, calling on Louisianians to cast off the yoke of Yankee imperialism and join their British liberators in the coming fight for freedom. It was signed by Edward Nicholls, the colonel mentioned in Renato's letter. The second, also signed by Nicholls, was addressed "To Monsieur Laffite, Commandant at Barataria." It was headmarked "Pensacola."

Sir:

I have arrived in the Floridas for the purpose of annoying the only enemy Great Britain has in the world, as France and England are now friends. I call on you with your brave followers to enter into the service of Great

Britain in which you shall have the rank of Captain, lands will be
you all in proportion to your respective ranks on a peace taking pl
invite you on the following terms.

Your property shall be guaranteed to you, your persons protected — in return for which I ask you to cease all hostility against Spain or the allies of
Great Britain.

Your ships and vessels to be placed under the orders of the Commanding
officer on this station until the Commander-in-chief's pleasure is known but
I guarantee their fair value at all events . . .

We have a powerful reinforcement on its way here and I hope to cut out
some other work for the Americans than oppressing the inhabitants of
Louisiana.

Laffite had a disconcerting habit of closing one eye when in con-
ference, something between a sarcastic wink and a signal of possible
sympathy. He closed one eye at McWilliams and waited. McWilliams
enlarged on the terms in Nicholls' letter. In addition to a captaincy in
the navy, Laffite would receive thirty thousand dollars in cash. Since
it was known that his brother was in jail, how could he reject this
opportunity for his release? The Americans were already threatening
Barataria with invasion. Laffite's future, along with the many rewards propounded, lay plainly with the British.

A third document was supposed, perhaps, to be the clincher. It was a
letter signed by Captain the Honorable William Henry Percy and proposed that, should the Laffites refuse to come over to the British side
they should be enjoined to remain completely neutral. If this, too, were
rejected, then the Baratarians, their ships and all their possessions,
would be subject to total destruction by an overwhelming British force.

Ignoring that threat — Laffite was not intimidated by threats — Jean
appeared to be impressed. "Your plan is nearly perfect," he remarked.
But, he reminded the English gentlemen, it was plain that his men
resented this intrusion by the British. He would have to appease and
reason with them. He asked to be excused, to do so.

When he left the room, the mob outside pressed close against the
window bars, shouting obscenities at the "spies" and threatening them
with lynching. Lockyer tried the door. It was barred. They were
prisoners. They remained imprisoned throughout the sultry night.

In the morning Laffite blithely reappeared. He apologized for the
menacing attitude of his men. They were a rough lot and needed
handling. Again he asked for time to bring them into line.

Lockyer had no alternative but to agree, disappointed for the moment but convinced that time would bring the Baratarians to his side. He and McWilliams returned to the *Sophia* to await Laffite's decision.

What went on in Laffite's mind during the succeeding hours is impossible to figure. He had been outlawed by his adopted country. An American expedition to destroy his stronghold was, he knew, in preparation. He was squarely in the middle of opposing forces closing in.

On the other hand, what was a captaincy in the British Navy compared to his absolute command of Barataria? What was the offer of thirty thousand dollars compared to the half a million dollars' worth of treasure on Grande Terre? He had no love for the Americans, but no love for the British either. He was a corsair at heart, seeking no master, and should the British dominate the Mississippi and the Gulf, the days of easy privateering would be ended. As for his brother Pierre, Jean would effect his release in one way or another.

In a sense he held all the cards and he knew he had the British officers off balance. Just as their firing on the innocent schooner had been an act of intimidation, a reminder of British fire power, so his angry mob of Baratarians, for which he was grateful and whose performance he had no doubt instigated, had impressed the British with the martial independence of the Baratarians. It had been a well-planned drama.

The following day he dispatched a letter to Jean Blanque, his influential friend, enclosing a letter to be delivered to the Governor. His letter to Blanque read in part: "Though proscribed by my adopted country, I will never let slip any occasion of serving her or of proving that she has never ceased to be dear to me. Of this you will here see a convincing proof." He enclosed the documents submitted to him by Lockyer and McWilliams, adding: "You will see from their contents the advantages I might have derived from that kind of association."

> In short, sir, I make you the depository of the secret on which perhaps depends the tranquility of our country; please to make such use of it as your judgment may direct. I might expatiate on this proof of patriotism but I let the fact speak for itself.
>
> I presume, however, to hope that such proceedings may ameliorate the situation of my unhappy brother, with which end in view I recommend him particularly to your influence.

He closed with flattering reference to Blanque's good judgment and sense of justice, just as his enclosed letter to Claiborne referred to the personal admiration which prompted him to "address you on an affair on which may depend the safety of this country."

I offer to restore to this state several citizens who perhaps in your eyes have lost that sacred title. I offer you them, however, as you would wish to find them, ready to exert their utmost efforts in defense of the country. This point of Louisiana, which I occupy, is of great importance in the present crisis. I tender my services to defend it; and the only reward I ask is that a stop be put to the proscription against me and my adherents, by an act of pardon for all previous delinquencies. I am the stray sheep, wishing to return to the sheepfold.

There was more; but "the stray sheep, wishing to return to the sheepfold" was a moving appeal to Claiborne's leniency.

After dispatching these letters by pirogue to the city, Laffite sent a third note to Lockyer on the *Sophia*. In it he requested a fortnight's time to put his affairs in order and overcome the opposition of certain of his men. He closed with the flattering and reassuring sentence: "You have inspired me with more confidence than the admiral, your superior officer, could have done himself; with you alone I wish to deal and from you also I will claim, in due time, the reward for the service which I may render to you."

No more artful statement could have been invented to mislead the British officers into believing that their proposition would bear fruit. Lockyer's orders from Percy, endeavoring to organize an anti-American army of Creeks at Pensacola, had been to rejoin him there "with the utmost dispatch." He was tempted, however, to remain anchored off Grande Terre to await confirmation of his agreement with the Baratarians.

Within twelve hours Blanque had received the letters from Laffite, which he promptly delivered to the Governor. Consternation resumed its customary place in Claiborne's mind. He promptly called a meeting of his more trusted advisers: Commodore Patterson of the Navy, Colonel Ross of the U.S. Regulars, Pierre F. Dubourg, Collector of U.S. Customs, and Major General Jacques Villeré of the militia. What action did they recommend? Ross and Patterson branded the British documents as forgeries and advised ignoring them. Villeré believed they were genuine, and recommended opening negotiations with the Baratarians and enlisting their aid in the defense of the city. Barataria was vulnerable territory, an obvious avenue of approach for an amphibious attack on New Orleans; no one knew it better, or could better defend it, than the tough and well-armed pirates.

To Patterson the Baratarians were a challenge to his authority in Louisiana. He was itching to wipe them out. So was the Navy Department in Washington, which had sent to New Orleans for that purpose the fourteen-gun schooner *Carolina* (if the Baratarians had done nothing else for the defense of New Orleans, they had prompted this formidable addition to the Commodore's insufficient navy). Patterson and Ross were already planning an expedition against Barataria, not reluctant to admit that the rich loot they might acquire from the pirate stronghold was a potent motive.

No answer was sent to Laffite's plea for clemency and alliance with the Americans. And it did not help the pirates' cause when, on September 9, the following notice appeared in the *Courrier de la Louisiane:*

100 Dollars Reward

Will be paid for the apprehension of Pierre Laffite who broke and escaped last night from the parish prison. Said Pierre Laffite is five feet ten inches tall, of robust stature, light complexion, and somewhat cross-eyed. Further description is considered unnecessary, as he is very well known in the city.

J. H. Holland
Keeper of the Prison

So Pierre had broken his shackles and the stout bars of his cell. How, remained a mystery — though it was rumored that pirate money had effected his release and jailer Holland's offer of a reward was simply a cover for his guilt.

Though Claiborne acquiesced to the punitive expedition against Grande Terre, he was of two minds about it. Laffite might already have rendered a valuable service. The British documents, if genuine, were the most explicit warning to date of British intentions. He promptly sent copies to Jackson as representing important military information. He added a postscript appraising the situation.

"There is in this city a much greater *Spirit of Disaffection* than I had anticipated, and among the faithful Louisianians there is a *Despondency* which palsies all my preparations." In view of this, he added: "Laffite and his associates might probably be made useful to us." Jackson's reply was emphatic. Have nothing to do with the "hellish banditti." The General saw the pirates as potential enemies rather than potential allies. "Let me beg you, immediately, to cause them to be arrested and detained . . . Unless some precautions of this nature are used, you rest in a fatal security; you will have to lament your country ravaged, and your city reduced to ashes by these incendiaries."

Nicholas Lockyer, despairing of a satisfactory commitment from the Baratarians after waiting out the prescribed fortnight, had barely sailed away on the *Sophia* to rejoin his commander at Pensacola, when Patterson's expedition descended the Mississippi with seventy troops in barges, the schooner *Carolina,* and six gunboats commanded by Captain Thomas Catesby Jones. They arrived off Grande Terre on the misty morning of September 16.

Laffite had anticipated an attack—either by Patterson's men or by a reinforced detachment of the British seeking revenge for the rejection of their terms. He had transferred most of the arms and ammunition along with the more valuable merchandise, including smuggled Negroes, to a wilderness island at some distance from Grande Terre. He and Pierre, along with many of the pirates, had retreated into hiding, leaving Dominique in charge.

Expecting the British, Dominique was astonished to see the American flag at the masthead of the *Carolina.* He was reluctant to fire on Americans, knowing that Laffite still hoped for amnesty. Accordingly he put up no resistance and a good five hundred of the pirates disappeared.

Patterson captured eighty men, including Dominique and Vincent Gambi, six schooners and eight other vessels and quantities of loot, destroying the huts, the sheds, the barracoons. There were no casualties. Patterson's squadron returned to New Orleans, where the pirates were jailed and the commodore filed a claim for prize money represented by the merchandise and vessels he had taken.

How wise a move the raid had been became a subject of dispute. Two thoughtful commentators, Charles Gayarré and Judge Alexander Walker, branded the action as unwarranted, unwise, and "truly ungrateful" in view of the services the Baratarians had offered. Both believed that the privateers were potential, valuable allies of the United States. In any event, Pierre and Jean remained in hiding, conducting secret meetings from time to time with Grymes and Livingston, who reassured them that time was on their side.

Time, however, was fast running out — as Governor Claiborne, an accurate barometer of the stormy climate of New Orleans, was too well aware.

# 4. *"Dark and Heavy Clouds Hang Over Us"*

"I am not at the head of a United and Willing people" ... "Our country is filled with spies and traitors ..."

"The natives of Louisiana are a virtuous, a gallant People" ... "I calculate with certainty on the great mass of the population."

"The troops now in Louisiana are inadequate to our defense in case of attack."

"We are well disposed in case of attack to make a good defense."

"It is not believed that the British are in Force anywhere in our vicinity."

"It seems certain that the British will invade this quarter of the continent."

He was like a man revolving in a squirrel cage, was W. C. Claiborne, during the weeks and months when New Orleans rested diffidently in the growing shadow of catastrophe. Truly dedicated to the welfare of his people, the Governor vacillated with every change of wind on how to act, what stand to take — dispatching one contradictory message after another to Jackson, to Secretary of State Monroe, to officials in Washington and to Louisiana officers and legislators.

51

As Governor he was also titular commander of the state militia, but he found its mobilization "a herculean task." Conforming in December 1813 to President Madison's requisition for U.S. troops from the states' militias, Claiborne had sent out a call for two divisions — the first to be recruited from the residents of New Orleans and environs, the second to come from Baton Rouge and the upriver western parishes.

From the latter, outlying territories, increasingly settled by Americans, there was a heartening response. The Second Division quickly rallied to the command of General Philemon Thomas of Baton Rouge. But in New Orleans itself there was outright defiance. Newspapers assured the population that there was "no law to authorize, and no necessity to justify the requisition," and Claiborne was denounced as "the tyrant of the day." The Legislature did nothing to allay this spirit of rebellion, declaring the requisition "unnecessary, illegal, and oppressive."

The New Orleanians themselves were not averse to fighting for their city, but only *if:* if an invasion actually occurred, if they were commanded by officers of their own election, and if they were not ordered to serve outside the city. In short, as Claiborne complained to General Thomas Flournoy, in charge of militia for the 7th Military District, they would fight for themselves, for their own community, but not for the United States and not under American commanders.

In late February 1814, four hundred militiamen of the Second Division marched into the city and were quartered in the Magazine Barracks just across the river. Claiborne thought their good example augured well for another appeal to the local citizens. Major General Villeré succeeded in forming a New Orleans company or two, but for the most part the resistance was the same. The Creoles would mobilize when and if the danger became imminent. Wedded to their families, their jobs, their many idle-time amusements, they were not interested in playing at being soldiers in the face of a chimerical or nonexistent threat. Eat, drink and be merry, for tomorrow will be just as gay and free of worry as today.

Word of their noncompliance reached the Second Division, already disdainful of the "effete and pleasure-loving Creoles." Its officers consulted with the Governor and offered to enforce obedience to his order. Just let the Second Division on the streets, with rifles and bayonets, and they'd see that the "frogs" fell in line. When this suggestion

reached the ears of the Creoles, they were ready to march at once —
against the "barbarian" Americans.

Wisely, Claiborne rejected any such enforcement of the draft, which
would have meant civil war within the city. That night, forty of the
Second Division deserted in manifest disgust. Why should they fight to
defend New Orleans when the citizens themselves refused to? Claiborne discharged the rest and sent them back to Baton Rouge.

Though the French and Spanish Creoles were at this point uninspired
to bear arms for the United States, they were easily engaged in
quarrels and conspiracies among themselves. In March the irrepres-
sible General Humbert, wearying of his dominoes and brandy at the
Hôtel de la Marine, was itching for action, any kind of action. Since
there were no British around as yet, he headed a band of French
guerrillas intent on invading Texas and overthrowing Spanish domination in that territory. Claiborne intervened with a strongly-worded
proclamation warning of dire penalties that such action would incur.
For once his words were heeded and the expedition was canceled.

At the same time, the Spanish colony in New Orleans, conscious of
its country's alliance with Great Britain, was rumored as favoring a
British invasion that might return Louisiana to the Spanish Crown.
Among others, suspicion focused on Alexandre Declouet, Senior
Colonel in the phantom militia, on the basis of his belonging to "an
ancient Creole family much patronized by the Spanish government."

De Marigny considered Declouet a man "of limited intellect, and not
qualified to fill the position he occupied," but regarded the rumors
of conspiracy "a bit of foolishness." Claiborne himself refused pre-
maturely to condemn Declouet, a good friend of Magloire Guichard in
the Legislature. But he increasingly wondered who could be counted
on as loyal, in the militia, in the Legislature, in the city. As he wrote
to Jackson, "I think with you that our country is filled with spies and
traitors."

Even the French, supposedly a tightly integrated clan, were not
above turning on their own. When the generally popular French consul,
the Chevalier Louis de Tousard, spoke out for Claiborne and urged all
able-bodied Creoles to respond to the militia call, his home was stoned,
and the seal of the Bourbons was torn from its doorway and confiscated — after which a guard was posted at the building.

On July 4, 1814, a seemingly favorable date for patriotic exhortations, Secretary of War John Armstrong proclaimed new quotas for the states' militias, calling for 2,500 men from Tennessee, five hundred from Kentucky and one thousand from Louisiana. Claiborne again relayed the call to officers throughout the state. The response was sluggish, but there was some indication that, if he kept at it long enough, sooner or later a militia would be formed. But he continued to note that there were many citizens "much devoted to the interests of Spain, and their partiality for the English is not less observable than their dislike for the American Government."

The recalcitrance of the population did not take him by surprise. He was disillusioned in the New Orleanians, just as they were disenchanted with the Governor. On August 24 he wrote to Jackson, "I have a difficult people to manage; Native Americans, Native Louisianians, Frenchmen, Spanish, with some English." He complained that *"that ardent zeal* which the crisis demands" was lacking, and unless the city could be garrisoned by "a Respectable Body of Regular Troops," its resistance to an enemy would be feeble. Though jealous of his own supreme position in Louisiana, the Governor longed for Jackson's presence and support. He himself, though he might not admit it, lacked the iron hand to press this diverse population into a united front.

It would take some evidence of clear and present danger to awake New Orleans to its peril. But that evidence was accumulating. In fact, British intentions to attack the soft underbelly of America through the Crescent City were perhaps the worst-kept secret in military history. The Washington Government had been forewarned of it by spies in Cuba and correspondents in Bermuda and Jamaica. Jackson's aides had intercepted a letter from a Pensacola resident to a friend in Mobile which read in part: "Great events are in embryo . . . I tremble for what you already have at stake in case of resistance . . . before one month it will be your inevitable fate to change masters again."

Another anonymous letter from Havana to a recipient in New Orleans described in detail the British expedition for the conquest of Louisiana, with its plan to free and arm the slaves, enlist the Indians, and ravage the Mississippi Valley. "When I have stated these facts, it will become your duty, and the duty of every citizen in the state, to rise in mass and defeat this most damnable plan of burning and carnage, the most horrible and atrocious ever before projected by a civilized nation. You have not a moment to lose; because if they get a footing, it will be very difficult to get clear of them. I . . . insist upon you again to save the state and the property of the planters at this awful crisis."

With no precautionary thought for the military value of surprise, English newspapers openly boasted of the forthcoming invasion, and the *Courrier de la Louisiane* reprinted these pronouncements for its readers.

The fact that New Orleans, with its diverse multiracial population, was an ideal target for psychological warfare, helped to bring it further warning of the enemy's intentions. During the first week of September rumors circulated regarding the British overtures to Jean Laffite and the Baratarians. These were confirmed when a boldly printed manifesto—a copy of which Laffite had earlier received from the British Colonel Nicholls and had forwarded to Claiborne—appeared on the streets and in the taverns of the city, circulated by anonymous agents. At Maspero's Exchange and Tremoulet's, the Hôtel de la Marine, the Café des Refugées, the patrons read:

Natives of Louisiana! On you the first call is made to assist in liberating from a faithless, imbecile government, your paternal soil: Spaniards, Frenchmen, Italians, and British . . . you also I call to aid me in this just cause. The American usurpation of this country must be abolished, and the lawful owners of the soil put in possession. I am at the head of a large body of Indians, well-armed, disciplined, and commanded by British officers—a good train of artillery with every requisite, seconded by the powerful aid of a numerous British and Spanish squadron of ships and vessels of war. Be not alarmed . . . . at our approach; the same good faith and disinterestedness which has distinguished the conduct of Britons in Europe, accompanies us here . . . a flag over any door, whether Spanish, French, or British, will be certain protection . . .

The proclamation went on to address the citizens of the upriver state of Kentucky (curiously, it omitted any appeal to Tennessee or the Mississippi Territory), assuring them of the free navigation of the Mississippi and freedom from the "grievous imposition" they had suffered from the government in Washington. It was signed by "Lieutenant-Colonel Edward Nicholls, commanding his Britannic Majesty's forces in the Floridas."

An astute psychologist would have found much wrong with this appeal to different factions in Louisiana and adjacent areas. For one thing, it did not take account of the jealousies and suspicions which divided them. Its reference to both French and Spanish, not to mention English, as "lawful owners of the soil" raised the question as to which, specifically, the term referred to. Did the British intend to restore Louisiana to the French? To the Spanish? To the English? The very question raised distrust and division in the city, already psychologically partitioned.

But one thing the British manifesto did accomplish. At long last, New Orleans and Louisiana awoke to the fact that, though far from united, they were indeed endangered.

As a result of this awakening, enlistment in the state militia showed a marked increase. In addition, the Orleans Battalion of Volunteers — which Vincent Nolte regarded as "the only perfectly armed, well equipped, and really disciplined corps" in the city — strengthened and increased its ranks. The original unit was one of long standing: the Carabiniers d'Orleans, an elite group of young men from the city's finest families, commanded by Major Jean Plauché.

Now four more companies of volunteers were organized, many of whose officers were veterans of Napoleon's armies. There were the Dragoons under the cocky little Captain Henri St. Gême, an emigrant from Haiti, whose five-foot stature was extended by a foot-high plume protruding from his cap. There were the Francs under Captain Jean Hudri, and the Chasseurs under Captain Auguste Guibert, and finally the Louisiana Blues, a company of Irish-Americans under Captain Maunsel White, whom Bernard de Marigny considered "the Ajax of the army; in spite of his tall stature, increased by a high plume, he never bowed his head to bullets . . ."

It was not a large battalion, less than four hundred at this time, though enlistments increased its numbers to 550 or six hundred men as the situation grew more critical. Its aristocratic background and showy appearance appealed strongly to the Creoles' fondness for theatricals. As time went on, Plauché was elevated to commander-in-chief of the battalion, and his place as captain of the Carabiniers was taken by Pierre Roche, a Napoleonic veteran and now a French book-seller in New Orleans.

Each company had its own distinctive and imaginative uniform, with emphasis on color, contrast, and extravagant embellisment — blue jackets faced with buff, red jackets faced with blue or gold, epaulettes on the right shoulders, the left shoulders, beige trousers, white trousers, shining boots, polished black hats with towering plumes and glittering ornaments. Precision drilling was their specialty, a proud performance, and the Place d'Armes echoed daily with their smartly-stepping military band.

Other volunteer units were born of the same sense of impending crisis. Thomas Beale, an elderly American reputed to be a peerless marksman, organized a company of Orleans Riflemen, composed principally of business and professional men. A young Natchez planter, Major Thomas Hind, headed a detachment of hard-riding Mississippi Dragoons, already serving with Andrew Jackson near Mobile. The Free Men of Color, more than ever anxious to assert their identity, were organized into two companies under the command of Michel Fortier, a prosperous Louisiana planter.

In addition to the militia and the volunteers, there were, of course, the U.S. Regulars stationed in the Military Barracks under the command of Colonel George T. Ross. These were the 44th Infantry under Captain Isaac L. Baker, and the 7th Infantry under Major Henry Peire. Portions of both were serving now with Jackson near Mobile. The two regiments were understrength, numbering seven hundred in all. Ross was reluctant to seek additional recruits among the French and Spanish population, regarding them as unstable and apt to desert.

As for the state militia, the Governor was equivocal. While he wrote to Jackson that "much confidence may be reposed" upon them, he was already relying more and more on aid from the nearby states of Kentucky and Tennessee, the latter in Jackson's military district. While noting that opposition to the Louisiana militia was declining, "there is not displayed," he rued, "that enthusiastic ardor which is to be found in the Western States." To Governor Willie Blount of Tennessee he wrote, "We shall, in any event, be made secure by those brave and determined men who are hastening from Tennessee and Kentucky. I await their arrival with much anxiety."

It there was one man who had little doubt about British intentions to strike at New Orleans, and less doubt about the need and means of meeting that attack, it was Commodore Daniel Todd Patterson, head of the naval base across the river, who had masterminded the attack against the Baratarians. Though only twenty-nine years of age Patter-

son had behind him fifteen years of rugged training in the navy. Among
other posts, he had served under Bainbridge against the Barbary pirates
and had later been schooled in naval tactics while serving with the
young commander, David Porter.

Serving his second term at the New Orleans station where he had
first assumed command in 1803, Patterson had thoroughly acquainted
himself with the strange topography of the Mississippi Delta. He knew
more about its lakes and bayous and possible water approaches than
anyone, except possibly the pirate leader, Jean Laffite. In the combined opinions of three naval authorities, "Patterson's prescience, his
strategic foresight, his moral courage, decision and spirited leadership"
were a vital factor in the ultimate fate of Louisiana and New Orleans.

The forces under Patterson's command were small. They hardly
seemed capable of offering any strong resistance to invasion, except for
the fact that the waters surrounding New Orleans were shallow, tricky,
and admitted no heavy warships of an enemy. The Mississippi River
was effectively guarded by Fort St. Philip well below the English Turn.
Patterson's fleet, typifying Jefferson's concept of a "Gunboat Navy,"
included six armed sloops mounting up to five guns each; the fourteen-
gun schooner *Carolina,* sent from the east for his attack upon the
Baratarians; and several small sloops of war. He had an adequate
arsenal of naval ordnance, but no additional ships on which to place his
guns. Riding beside the levee was the merchant vessel *Louisiana,*
which he could use if he could find the personnel to man her.

The river front teemed with idle sailors of all tongues and nationalities, with Kentucky boatmen and unemployed roustabouts, all stranded
by the blockade of the Gulf. But Patterson could not induce them to
enlist. The stagnation of New Orleans was a pleasant excuse for idleness. Women and liquor were cheap. There was a euphoric sense of
"do as you please" in the Crescent City. Anyone who tried to rock the
boat should be avoided.

So the *Louisiana* remained inactive beside the levee, although Patterson kept his eye on her. Like Jackson, he felt that the enemy might
come by way of Pensacola and Mobile, but New Orleans was the
ultimate and certain goal. When Jackson requested his aid in defending
Mobile — some gunboats at the least — Patterson demurred. He couldn't
spare them. He himself had written off Mobile. Exposed and ill-
defended, it would fall. And when it did, as he wrote the General:

The numerous avenues to this truly important City, the greatest depot of the Western Country, will then be left open to the enemy, who will in that event, be able without difficulty to introduce in the Country any number of troops they wish, without opposition, and obtain possession of it . . . and it appears to my mind that this is the most important place to defend, and more capable of being defended by a small force.

Patterson would keep his gunboats and the *Carolina* close to home. He had his own plans for defense, making the most of his limited resources. The gunboats would be stationed on Lake Borgne, where their shallow draft and maneuverability would make them effective against any naval force that tried to penetrate the lakes. "Should the Gun Boats be withdrawn," he warned, "or cut off from the neighborhood of this City, the enemy will have it in their power to commit depradations on the coast with impunity from their small cruisers."

Attached to a short fuse, Jackson was miffed by Patterson's refusal to send the gunboats to Mobile. He thought briefly of pulling wires in Washington to bring the navy under his command. But later he thought better of it and wrote the Commodore that he understood the latter's situation and would respect the division of authority. Possibly he was mollified by Patterson's straightforwardness and understandable frustration. "I have only to regret," the Commodore wrote, "that my Force is not as large as I could wish, or such as to afford that aid which you may require." At the moment, Patterson advised the General, he was off to Barataria to wipe out the buccaneers of Jean Laffite.

While Patterson was engaged, in early September, with clearing Barataria of the pirates, and while Colonel Nicholls's proclamation was still tauntingly fresh in everybody's mind, a group of distinguished citizens met at Tremoulet's coffeehouse on September 15. They had been summoned there by Edward Livingston to form a Committee of Public Safety. The list of members read like a roster of New Orleans aristocracy. With Livingston as chairman, the others were Pierre Foucher, Dusseau Delacroix, Benjamin Morgan, George M. Ogden, Dominique Bouligny, Jean Noel Destrehan, Jean Blanque and Augustin Macarty. The three Americans—Livingston, Morgan and Ogden— gave the predominantly Creole committee a bipartisan flavor.

"We owe ourselves," Livingston told the group, "to disavow the calumnious insinuations of the English that there is disaffection among

Louisiana citizens. We owe ourselves to show the rest of the United States that we are not unworthy of a place among them."

While Livingston could hardly have expected an immediate change of heart among New Orleanians indifferent to the threat of war and hostile to Americans, he had picked his committee from those sympathetic to his views, and he knew the value of appealing to Creole pride and their resentment of "calumnious insinuations."

Among other things the committee would investigate the state of the city's defenses, and cooperate with the constituted civil and military authorities in moves to strengthen them against invasion. It would mobilize the civilian population and from those disabled or too old to fight would form a veterans' corps and volunteer fire brigade to police the city and protect private property.

Most importantly the committee strove to combat any sentiment that favored surrendering the city to the British. Capitulation would not bring peace but only pave the way for future war, since the possession and free navigation of the Mississippi were as essential to the West "as the blood is to the pulsation of the heart." On this subject it issued a proclamation to all citizens warning them of the dangers of surrender:

> A war ruinous to you would be the consequence. The enemy, to whom you would have had the weakness to yield, would subject you to a military despotism, of all others the most dreadful; your estates, your slaves, your persons would be put in requisition, and you would be forced at the point of the bayonet to fight against those very men whom you have voluntarily chosen for fellow citizens and brethren. Beloved countrymen, listen to the men honoured by your confidence, and who will endeavor to merit it; listen to the voice of honour, of duty, and of nature! Unite! Form but one body, one soul, and defend to the last extremity your sovereignty, your property – defend your own lives, and the dearer existence of your wives and children.

A few days after the Committee of Public Safety was formed, the Legislature, never partial to Livingston, appointed what was essentially a rival Committee of Defense. Though it consisted of only three men, those three were influential spokesmen for the French community. Joseph de Rofignac was its president, the other two being Philip Louaillier, outspoken member of the Legislature, and Bernard de Marigny, vigorous champion of the Creole cause.

It was inevitable that these competing bodies clashed. They disrupted one another's authority, wrangled over legislative measures, made an issue of each resolution for their common safety. Through mutual distrust, they hampered each other's usefulness and checkmated valuable proposals for united action.

However, the Committee of Safety could draw some measure of support from the pusillanimous Legislature which had sired it. Within reason, and with Livingston's persuasiveness, it could call on public funds to implement its resolutions. Its first action was to vote the necessary moneys for a ceremonial sword to be awarded Major William Lawrence for his gallant defense of Fort Bowyer in Mobile Bay during attack by a vanguard of the British expeditionary forces en route to Louisiana.

Edward Livingston himself took more positive steps. Perhaps from innocent zeal, he sought to recommend his services to the absent commander, General Jackson, usurping a role which Claiborne felt was his. Three days after his Committee of Safety had been formed, he sent the General detailed suggestions for the defense of New Orleans, noting that "This Country is strong by Nature, but extremely weak from the nature of its population. From the La Fourche downwards on both sides of the river, that population consists (with inconsiderable exceptions) of Sugar Planters on whose large Estates there are on an average 25 slaves to one White Inhabitant. The maintenance of domestic tranquility in this part of the state obviously forbids a call on any of the White Inhabitants to the defense of the frontier. . . ."

Livingston expressed little regard for, in fact barely mentioned, the local militia, the Regulars stationed in New Orleans or the Creole volunteers. But he astutely recognized the vulnerability and ambivalence of the planters, with large estates and personal interests to defend. To what extent would they put the protection of their property ahead of the protection of the state?

In detail Livingston listed the troops that would be required to safeguard this vulnerable territory, insisting that "the only hope of preserving this place in case of a serious attack lies in an efficient force to be furnished by you." This "comparatively small force" would consist of two thousand men on the left bank of the Mississippi between the city and the English Turn, to guard the river and the Chef Menteur and the plantations; 1500 on the right bank between the city and the Bayou

Lafourche; and a thousand at The Temple to guard Barataria—4500 men in all. In a subsequent letter, Livingston upped the number to five thousand.

Jackson forwarded Livingston's letter to Monroe, with the notation: "The Citizens of New Orleans have addressed me, calling for additional defense. My whole force would not satisfy the demands they make." To repeated demands for his presence in New Orleans, from Claiborne and Livingston especially, his replies from Pensacola and Mobile were all the same: "I shall leave when this quarter of the South is safe." Meanwhile, as his surrogate, he placed Lieutenant-Colonel William MacRea of the U.S. Army in command of all the troops and defense of the city, until he himself should get there.

He had, of course, thanked Livingston for his communication of September 18. Now he received a second letter from that eager citizen, offering his services as aide-de-camp. It was accompanied by a bottle of vintage claret obtained from Jean Laffite. Jackson thanked him for the "Barataria Claret," but told Livingston that military procedure allowed him only two aides-de-camp, and both those positions were filled. However, he would hope to make future use of Livingston's obvious knowledge and abilities.

On September 21 Jackson issued, by way of a messenger to Claiborne, his proclamation to the citizenry in answer to that circulated by the British. Warning the people that "the base, the perfidious English have attempted to invade your country," it continued:

Louisianians! The proud Briton, the natural and sworn enemies of all Frenchmen, has called upon you, by proclamation, to aid him in his tyranny, and to prostrate the holy temple of our liberty. Can Louisianians, can Frenchmen, can Americans, ever stoop to be the slaves or allies of Britain? The proud, vain-glorious boaster colonel Nicholls, when he addressed you ... had forgotten that you were the votaries of freedom, or he would never have pledged the honour of a British officer for the faithful  performance of his promise, to lure you from your fidelity to the government of your choice. I ask you, Louisianians, can we place any confidence in the honour of men who have courted an alliance with pirates and robbers? Have not these noble British . . . done this? Have they not made offers to the pirates of Barataria to join them and their holy cause? And have they not dared to insult you by calling on you to associate, as brethren with them, and this hellish banditti?

Jackson himself would soon be urged to effect an alliance with the "hellish banditti," and public sentiment favoring this policy detracted from his message, which many Creoles considered condescending. They did not accept the implication that they could be "slaves" of anybody, particularly when this reference was followed by the premonitory admonition, "The individual who refuses to defend his rights, when called upon by his government, deserves to be a slave, and must be punished as an enemy of his country, and a friend to her foe."

This absent commander, this little-known general, it was felt, scolded too much, threatened too much and was too much of an alarmist.

Claiborne, however, tried to inject a note of harmony and optimism. He wrote to Jackson on October 24, "Your address to the Louisianians is well received . . . You have inspired them with Confidence, and I am in the proud belief that, in any event, they will prove faithful to the United States."

Did the phrase "in any event" mean "in spite of everything"? For Claiborne was still haunted by the specters of disaster. In the same letter he informed Jackson that he was withholding the latter's laudatory proclamation to the Men of Color, because he feared it might arouse further distrust between the white and black sections of the population. The following day he wrote to James Monroe requesting sabers and pistols for the mounted militia, "for in the event of an insurrection among our slaves, Cavalry are the troops which can act with greatest advantage."

There were traitors around every corner, the Governor was certain, spies behind every tree. Late that October he sent to General Jackson a copy of an intercepted letter from one Colonel Colliel to Juan Ventura Morales, Bernard de Marigny's father-in-law now living in Pensacola. It outlined the "weakly prepared defenses" of the city. Was this treason or simply an innocent leakage of information? "Colliel," pleaded Claiborne, "is an old man and the father-in-law of Mr. Delacroix, one of our wealthiest Sugar Planters, a director of the bank, and a member of the Committee of Safety." Jackson was unimpressed with Colliel's references. He wrote to Claiborne to throw the rascal out. The Governor shipped the Colonel back to Pensacola.

As October gave way to November, and the militia drilled in the Place d'Armes while the uniformed volunteers paraded through the streets to give the city a somewhat festive military air, Claiborne bombarded Jackson with innumerable importunate letters. On November 4 he wrote the General, "The requisition of a Thousand Militia Infantry will very soon I trust be completed." This, with the regular infantry and the volunteers, would, he promised, give Jackson an auxiliary force of two thousand men.

Later the Governor reduced this figure to 1,200. He had been optimistic about the militia and was obliged to report, "There are many defaulters among the drafted men, some from long and continued indisposition, but most I fear from a bare and wilful neglect of duty . . ." The second Division of militia had been reassembled and ordered to return from Baton Rouge, but, Claiborne noted, "there have been frequent desertions."

One of the problems of the militia was its short term of enlistment — now only three months, which Andrew Jackson had been anxious to extend to six. In the upper territories, militiamen had been known to simply pack up and leave when their three months were up, without so much as a farewell to their officers. They had even composed a popular ditty to march to on such occasions.

> . . . home we go,
> Or be found in gore,
> And never come here no more . . .

Increasingly, Claiborne appealed by overland post for Jackson's counsel. That counsel offered little comfort. It was to grant the militia no special dispensations, as to length of enlistment or service outside New Orleans and Louisiana.

The Governor kept Jackson informed of how he deployed the various military units — to garrison the forts above and below the city, to guard the bayous, plains, and highways over which an enemy might approach. But he needed men, many more men for a secure defense and hoped that by some miracle the General would supply them.

In spite of Jackson's rueful comment to his relatives in Nashville that "Dark and Heavy clouds hang over us," all was not dark. He received good news from Washington — a rare occurrence. After the inglorious burning of the Capitol in August, John Armstrong had been fired as Secretary of War. Jackson had had little use for Armstrong, blaming him for "the imbecility of our military preparations . . . as well as the general apathy which has pervaded the greater section of the Union . . ."

Now James Monroe, still Secretary of State, was assuming Armstrong's duties *ad interim*. Though strapped by the circumstances of a bankrupt government, Monroe was at least concerned about the fate of New Orleans. He wrote Jackson that he was transmitting a hundred thousand dollars to Governor Blount of Tennessee, for the General to draw on for campaign expenses. Further, he authorized Jackson to call on the states of Kentucky, Tennessee and Georgia, for whatever troops (within rational limits) he might need.

Accordingly, Jackson was able to give Claiborne some encouraging assurance:

> Being desirous to place New Orleans and its vicinity in a state of perfect security, I have ordered a force of Five Thousand five hundred men from Tennessee and Kentucky to proceed by forced marches direct to your city. . . . Independent of this I have notified Governor Holmes to hold the whole Militia of the [Mississippi] Territory in readiness to march at a moment's warning . . . .

On November 10 the Governor convoked a special session of the Legislature. He did so somewhat tremulously. He and the Legislature were barely on speaking terms, and he remembered with bitterness their earlier opposition to the drafting of militia. But measures were needed and money was needed to prosecute the war. As a means of arousing their support he read them a letter received by him from General Jackson:

> Recent information from the most correct sources has been received of an expedition of twelve or fifteen thousand men, sailing from Ireland early in September last, intended to attempt the conquest of Louisiana. You will therefore see the necessity of preparing for service, at an hour's notice, the whole body of Louisiana militia. I rely on your patriotism and activity, and hope not to be disappointed.

The Legislature itself was a battleground of conflicting opinions, its efforts devoted, up to now, to fence-straddling and compromise. Its torpor and indecision aroused even Philip Louaillier to a diatribe directed at his fellow members: "Are we always to witness the several departments entrusted with our defense languishing in a state of inactivity, hardly to be excused even in the most peaceful times? No other evidence of patriotism is to be found than a disposition to avoid every expense, every fatigue. Nothing as yet has been performed. It is the duty of the Legislature to give the necessary impulse."

They were brave words, but the civil climate of New Orleans was not ready for them. As Benson Lossing wrote of the Legislature itself, "the members were divided into several factions, and there was neither union, nor harmony, nor confidence to be found. The people, alarmed and distrustful, complained of the Legislature; that body, in turn, complained of the Governor; and Claiborne complained of both the Legislature and the people."

Claiborne did complain to Jackson a week later, reporting that "the Legislature have not as yet done anything to damp the public ardor. But I hope this body will be justly impressed with the dangers to which we are exposed, and will warmly second all my efforts. But I fear, I much fear, they will not act with the promptitude and the energy which the crisis demands."

This time the Governor's charges were a little premature. Three days later the Legislature voted a loan of twenty thousand dollars, plus the allocation of seventeen thousand dollars from the treasury, to General Jackson "for the procuring of workmen and materials for such fortifications as he should see fit to erect." It later tacked a further eleven thousand dollars on to that amount. Claiborne's approval of this measure was qualified. Why hadn't the money been assigned to him, as head of the militia, instead of to Andrew Jackson? He began to have twinges of doubt about relations between the General and himself.

Late in November, a month after Jackson had requested it, Claiborne got up sufficient nerve to publish the General's proclamation to the free blacks of Louisiana, welcoming those who wished to enroll in the militia or as volunteers. As he reported to Jackson, he was fearful of the consequences:

> Your address, sir, to the Chosen Men of color will be printed on this day; I will use my best efforts to promote your wishes, but I do not know with what success. I have already apprised [you] of the distrust which exists here against this Class of people. I believe it ill found but its existence may, and I fear has in some degree, indisposed [sic] them towards us.

The Governor felt he had enough to cope with, without this added problem of the colored population of New Orleans. But it was like a dark cloud hovering above the city. It would not go away. It was part of the stormy climate of the community, just as it had been for many turbulent decades a vital part of Louisiana's history.

# 5. *Black Power: An Eagle on Their Caps*

Andrew Jackson hailed them as "brave fellow citizens" and "sons of Freedom." The more cautious Governor Claiborne referred to them as men of "sustained good character, . . . valor and fidelity." To Pierre de la Ronde their proud position was a threat to the docile subserviency of his slaves. But that which spoke most eloquently of their new role in Louisiana and America was the rat-a-tat-tat of the young Negro drummer Jordan B. Noble in the Place d'Armes — announcing that for the first time in history colored troops, with their own regimental colors, and their own rights as members of the white society, were drilling for the defense of the United States.

It was, that autumn of 1814, a moment of truth for the Negro in the new republic — culminating a long and turbulant history of the black man in Louisiana, a history distinct and different from those in other parts of North America. While the term "Black Power" was not yet familiar, its reality was acknowledged here before it was recognized, in any terms other than negative or derogatory, elsewhere in the Union.

From the time he first assumed office as Territorial Governor in 1803, the role of the blacks in Louisiana had presented Claiborne with incessant quandaries. Their numbers alone indicated the size of the problem. Over half the population was of Negro ancestry, almost

69

evenly divided between free colored and slaves. Of these two classes it was hard to say which presented the more difficulties. On the plantations such as de la Ronde's, slaves outnumbered whites by thirty or fifty to one, and there was constant fear of insurrection. The free colored, on the other hand, raised the question of what equal, or near equal, rights might lead to. To what extent should they be granted privileges and prerogatives before the balance of power shifted in their favor?

The situation had its roots deep in New Orleans' history which, as in the relation which Paris bore to France, was essentially Louisiana's history. Negroes began arriving in Louisiana when the Compagnie des Indes, successor to John Law's Company of the West, administered the Territory for a quarter century after 1717. The company imported two thousand slaves from French Africa along with four thousand whites to settle the new territory. The slaves would be used to cultivate the fields and work the nonexistent gold and silver mines which were touted to prospective European immigrants.

The ratio of two whites to one black did not remain constant. A lack of wives depressed the birth rate among whites, while the Negroes, encouraged to breed, increased substantially. As early as 1724, the Black Code, modeled after the *Code Noir* of Saint Domingue, was instituted under the then governor Étienne Périer. In addition to prescribing guidelines for the treatment of the Negroes, the Code included the first civil rights proclamation in North American history:

> We grant to manumitted slaves the same rights, privileges, and immunities which are enjoyed by freeborn persons. It is our pleasure that their merit in having acquired their freedom shall produce in their favor, not only with regard to their persons, but also to their property, the same effects which our other subjects derive from the happy circumstances of their having been born free.

As the clause suggests, it was possible under the Code for a slave to obtain his freedom. This might be granted out of humane considerations or often in recognition of unique skills. Some became fencing instructors, silversmiths, cabinet makers, musicians and even dancing masters. Or freedom might be purchased with money supplied by a relative or earned by extra work on the plantations — selling eggs, chickens and garden produce, for example, to plantation owners.

Again, freedom might be obtained by special services to the community, although such services might be obnoxious. One slave, at the moment of being granted liberty, was assigned to the post of public executioner. Before being conducted to the gallows, he severed his right arm with an ax to escape an assignment repellent to his dignity and feelings.

Though miscegenation was frowned upon, in fact forbidden by the Black Code, it was impossible to control in a society so lacking in eligible females. Under both the early French and Spanish administrations, mixed unions gave birth to a whole new intermediate race, the *gens de couleur,* or free colored. Any progeny of mixed blood, regardless of circumstances, was pronounced "born free" — and as miscegenation increased under the Spanish occupancy, from 1763 on, so did the number of free colored rapidly increase. These went into businesses and vocations of their own, often gained substantial wealth, owning their own plantations, property and slaves. To the resentment of other citizens, the light colored often called themselves "Creoles" — not quite, however, bridging the social gap between themselves and the native-born French and Spanish.

Perhaps the most significant step a slave might take to gain his freedom or a free man of color might take to raise his status, was service in the colonial or territorial militia. From the very beginning, with manpower scarce, the Negroes were a significant factor in the security and defense of New Orleans and the Louisiana Territory. They made good soldiers. For one thing, they were tougher, more inured to hardship than the French and Spanish. Often they fought more fiercely — they were fighting not only for their lives but for recognition, a strong motive.

As early as 1729 Governor Périer first called for Negro aid in the defense — in this case, the salvation — of Louisiana. A massive uprising of Natchez Indians threatened to exterminate the scattered French settlements in the Mississippi valley. Périer conscripted a force of slaves among New Orleans owners and, with some regular militia, launched a counterattack in which the Negroes, according to the Governor, "did deeds of surprising valor." In fact, Périer wrote, he could have used more of them "instead of the French soldiers who were so ineffective."

Some of the slaves, like one François Ticou, were granted their freedom in return for bravery. But a proposal resulting from this campaign, that of forming a permanent corps of black militia "ready to march at a moment's notice," came to grief at a subsequent unfortunate event. The following year the first slave conspiracy in Louisiana was aborted.

The protagonist of the plot was a Bambara Negro named Samba, who had organized an unsuccessful mutiny on the slave ship that carried him to America. Despite this, after landing in Louisiana, he professed to having become a Christian, learned to speak French and was made a trusted commander of the Africans brought to New Orleans by the Company of the Indies.

Samba conspired with eight of his black compatriots to incite the slaves of New Orleans to a wholesale massacre of their masters, planning then, with captured weapons, to take over the city and the territory and establish a sort of "Bambara Republic" in North America, a Promised Land for Africans of whatever origin.

The plot was revealed by an informer, and Samba and his co-conspirators were put to death. But the alarming incident would haunt the French community for generations. The possibilities of future slave conspiracies would, according to one historian, "affect the development of the Negro troops throughout the entire course of their history."

The effect was not immediate, however. In 1733 Périer was succeeded as governor by Jean Baptiste le Moyne, Sieur de Bienville, founder of New Orleans back in 1718. When, three years after his taking office, the Indians took to the warpath once again, Bienville assured the colonial minister that "for want of soldiers I shall send out militia and even Negroes" to subdue the renegades. He did so, and in this counteroffensive a Negro captain of militia, Charles Simon, helped to erase the stigma of Bambara Samba by a foolhardy but courageous feat. Racing up a hill on which the enemy was entrenched, "though the Indians sallied out and balls were raining around him," Simon reached a corral where the Indian horses were held in waiting, seized the best among the mares and rode back to his camp without a scratch.

It was sheer exhibitionism designed, according to one commentator, "to gain esteem for black soldiers in the eyes of the French." This it did, and more. In subsequent missions Simon's company operated as a free, autonomous, all-Negro unit.

Altogether, under the French regime, the Negro made significant strides toward recognition and equality. Scores had gained their freedom, albeit at the risk of life on the battlefield. They had been used in

combat of necessity, but had earned the confidence of native whites.
"And crowning all this," writes one historian, "was the simple fact that
Negroes helped save Louisiana from destruction by the Indians, the
colony's first formidable enemies."

In 1763 the white banner of the Bourbons with its golden fleur-de-lis,
which had flown over the Place d'Armes for almost half a century, was
replaced by the red and yellow flag of Spain. The Black Code was
passed on, unamended, to the new regime. The free colored, as a class
midway between white and slave, became more numerous, and Negro
service in the militia reached new heights. Perhaps the often bronze
complexion of the Spaniards helped obscure the color line.

Significantly, Louisiana Negroes played a substantial role in the
American Revolutionary War, albeit under a Spanish commander,
when Spain joined France as allies of the new United States. (The U S.
Congress itself opposed the use of Negro troops, reflecting the outspoken attitude: "Is it consistent with the Sons of Freedom to trust
their defense to slaves?") In 1779 the dashing young Governor and
colonel, Bernardo Galvez, led a half-white, half-black army in a successful campaign to drive the English from Louisiana and the Mississippi valley.

In praising his army for its performance, Galvez noted: "No less
deserving of eulogy are the companies of Negroes and free Mulattoes
who . . . conducted themselves with as much valor and generosity as
the whites." Later that year, with more slaves and free colored added
to his force, Galvez took possession of Mobile and Pensacola, during
which six names earned immortality in Negro history: Lieutenants
and sublieutenants Bautista Hagon, Felipe Reuben, Francisco Dorville, Noel Carriere, Bacus Nichols and Luis la Nuit. All were cited for
bravery and rewarded with medals of honor from His Majesty, the
King of Spain.

Writes Professor Roland C. McConnell, a student of the Negro's
role in Louisiana's history:

The organization and use of the colored militia by Galvez in the American
Revolution was another step in the development of Negro soldiers in Louisiana. Not only had these troops performed creditably against the British,
their first experience against trained European soldiers, but they . . . contributed to America's winning of independence by helping to close the gate-

ways to the American West and South through which the British planned to strike at the western flank of the colonies. In so doing they engaged British troops which might have been used elsewhere.

Serving then as a captain in Galvez's ranks had been a white New Orleanian named Michel Fortier, of an ancient and distinguished family of planters. Fortier observed the resourcefulness and courage of the Negroes, never forgot it, and years later helped to bridge the acceptance gap between French and American attitudes towards the black man.

While colored regiments were sometimes commanded by white officers with black subordinates, they were often commanded by blacks of their own choice. Military discipline and pay were applied without discrimination between either race. Yet among the black militia there was discrimination based on color and insisted on by blacks themselves. *Pardos,* or light-colored, preferred their own segregated units, while *Morenos,* or dark-colored, chose to serve with troops of a corresponding shade of black.

In the early days of the Spanish regime the colored troops proved invaluable in the so-called "Cimarron War." *Cimarróns,* or runaway slaves, had grown in numbers and established fortified hideouts in the swamps and wilderness. From these they conducted lightning-like raids on the white communities. One such clandestine group headed by Juan Malo, "Second Knight of the Ax," so terrified New Orieans that even the slaves and the free men of color were alarmed. Francisco Luis Hector, Baron de Carondelet, upon becoming Governor in 1791, decided that the most effective weapon against the Cimarrons was the colored militia, who could operate in "places too impenetrable for regular troops." He was right; the Cimarron threat had all but vanished by 1795.

It was replaced, however, by danger from another quarter. The effects of the French Revolution had reached Haiti and almost simultaneously repercussions were experienced in Louisiana (often considered at that time "a Caribbean country"). Many French Creoles had refused to accept the cession of their country to the Spanish Bourbons. New Orleans became more than ever a city of conspiracies, of plots and counterplots and occasional outright revolt against the Spanish government. Baron de Carondelet had every reason to wonder which way the militia's loyalty would go. As a whole, however, although a number of colored officers were brought to trial (and acquitted), including the Indian baiter Charles Simon and the bemedaled Francisco Dorville, the colored troops remained loyal to the government.

Considering the many changes in administration, and the disaffection that was part of the New Orleans temperament, this loyalty would seem remarkable. By the Treaty of San Ildefonso in 1800, Louisiana was ceded to Napoleon, although the French did not officially take possession until three years later. During the interval the Marquis de Casa Calvo was sent to Louisiana to persuade the colored officers to shift their allegiance and services to the Spanish Governments in North America, and march their troops into adjacent Spanish territories. Some later claimed they were thrown into prison to force them to agree, but apparently none yielded; even to severe coercion.

Such was the status of the free colored when, in 1803, Pierre Clément Laussat took possession of Louisiana in behalf of France and twenty days later officiated at its transfer to the United States. As the Stars and Stripes were raised above the Place d'Armes, the country inherited "an organized and disciplined colored militia which, in the service of Spain, had earned a bright military reputation for defending Louisiana from both internal and external foes." What use would the new administration make of this unfamiliar legacy?

There was a clue in the fact that Claiborne requested the white militia to stand guard in the Place d'Armes during the ceremonies, to put down any demonstration by the colored troops protesting Louisiana's transference to the United States.

Almost immediately upon taking office Governor Claiborne was engaged in his favorite exercise of wallowing in problems, some real and some imaginary. One of the less imaginary was what to do about the Negro population of New Orleans and Louisiana, which had risen to a status not acceptable to the rest of the United States. Before a week was up he had written to Secretary of State James Madison:

> . . . my principal difficulty arises from two large companies of people of Colour, who are attached to the service, and were esteemed a very serviceable corps under the Spanish government. Of this particular Corps I have reflected with much anxiety. To recommission them might be considered as

an outrage on the feelings of a part of the Union and as opposed to those
principles of policy which the safety of the Southern States had necessarily
established. On the other hand, not to recommission them would disgust
them, and might be productive of future mischief. To disband them would be
to raise an armed enemy in the very heart of the Country, and to disarm them
would savour too strongly of that desperate system of Government which
seldom succeeds.

Claiborne asked for instructions from the State Department. There
were good reasons for his anxiety. New Orleans was short of troops,
and trouble with Spain over the disputed borders of Louisiana—in fact,
over Napoleon's right to sell the territory in the first place—was becoming ominous. It was uncertain how the colored population, accustomed to the liberal laws of Spain, would react to restrictions imposed by the United States. The colored militia represented a much-
needed military force, *if* it proved loyal and *if* the community would
accept it.

Slaves of course were another matter. The planters regarded them as
essential to the economy and resented a Territorial act that prohibited
their further importation. As one writer observed of the years immediately following Louisiana's annexation to the Union, "Settlers were
hurrying in from the North and East. The fertile soil cried out for cultivation. No one could do the work like the Negroes. Black men soon
brought from $800 to $1000 each in New Orleans, with planters
frantically bidding against one another for them. Probably never before
or since has there been so urgent a demand for labor."

Slaves were easily smuggled into the city, some from West Florida
and Cuba, more from Barataria where the pirates collected them from
hijacked slave ships in the Gulf. Public sentiment being what it was,
there was little Claiborne could do about it. As he wrote to President
Jefferson:

The Searcher of all hearts knows how little I desire to see another of that
wretched race set his foot on the shores of America, and how I detest the
rapacity that would transport them to us. But, on this point, the people
here are united as one man. There seems to be but one sentiment throughout
the province. They must import more slaves, or the country is ruined forever.

It should be said in behalf of Claiborne that, for a Virginian raised in the Southern tradition, he appeared extraordinarily open-minded about the black half of the population — more tolerant in some ways than he was toward the Creoles, whom he mistrusted from the beginning and regarded as somewhat wayward children. In that respect his attitude was similar to that of Andrew Jackson. Jackson, a slave holder himself in Tennessee and geographically another southerner by birth, was generally sympathetic and appreciative of the black man's position in that temporal society. This was in marked contrast to his attitude towards the Indians, whom he generally mistrusted, avowedly subscribing to the maxim "the only good Indian is a dead Indian."

Madison's belated reply to Claiborne's query as to what to do about the black militia was typical of the Secretary's arch evasiveness. Not he, but his secretary advised: "The peculiar circumstances attending the mulatto corps will require much delicacy of management." Claiborne was thus left with his own dilemma, one aggravated by the fact that Louisiana was flanked on east and west by Spanish-held territories, and the Spaniards continued their appeal to the colored militia to defect to Spain.

There was the fact, too, that a good one-fourth of New Orlean's population was composed of the free colored, a segment that could not be offended with impunity. They included those engaged in handicraft, businessmen, and even cotton planters owning substantial properties around the city. As Professor McConnell noted:

> They were a closely knit, proud class of people, many of whose members could trace their ancestry through two and three generations of freedom. They were never forgetful of the fact that they had come under the jurisdiction of the young American Republic as free men, nor were they unmindful of their Creole heritage. They were especially proud of their militia whose roots were planted deep in the past of Louisiana, whose record had been commendable, and to which every-able bodied man of their group belonged.

Among the black community, considerable prestige was attached to membership in the militia. Many free colored so enrolled were leaders in other fields as well. Ranking officers enjoyed significant status, and their marriages in the Cathedral were events of social interest. They frequented the same taverns as the whites, and outside the home there was little segregation. Above all they wore, as military insignia, an eagle on their caps — proclaiming their membership in a free society where all men were created equal.

Among the Creole community, including its members in the Legislature, there was considerable apprehension over the colored militia, whose armed presence might inspire or abet an insurrection of the slaves. But Claiborne was not without supporters. Benjamin Morgan, an American prominent in both business and politics, wrote to influential friends in Washington that the free colored were a numerous and respectable class in New Orleans, had enjoyed liberal rights under the Spanish regime "and could certainly become an asset to a new country." He believed that they should enjoy full rights of citizenship, instead of being allowed to become "formidable abettors of slaves."

While Claiborne awaited positive advice from Washington, the free colored took the initiative and spoke up for themselves by drafting a memorial to the U.S. Congress — half an oath of loyalty, half a reminder of the civil rights that had been promised to them and their expectation that these rights would be observed. It was signed by fifty-five prominent members of the black militia, and it read in part:

> We are Natives of this Province and our dearest Interests are connected with its welfare. We therefore feel a lively Joy that the Sovereignty of the Country is at length united with that of the American Republic. We are duly sensible that our personal and political freedom is thereby assured to us forever, and we are also impressed with the fullest confidence in the Justice and Liberality of the Government toward every Class of Citizens which they have here taken under their protection.

It was the first time in United States history that an organized group of Negroes had petitioned for full citizenship and equal rights and had thereby challenged the Washington government and the American people to implement those principles of freedom which they so readily expressed, principles for which the free colored of Louisiana had fought in the Revolution, though under the flag of Spanish allies. Freedom was part of the American Dream, although, as one historian noted, "the dream was just unfolding and must from the beginning face the harsh realities of capitalistic slavery."

No New Orleans printer would accept the document for distribution, and it never reached the Congress. But it did come to the attention of Claiborne and he approved it. He assured the Negroes that "under the protection of the United States, their liberty, property, and religion were safe" and that "their confidence in the American Government would increase as they became acquainted with the principles, wisdom, and virtue with which it was administered."

It was hardly a positive answer, but the Governor was under pressure from both sides. A portion of the citizens called for strengthening the militia; the rest, by far a majority, wanted it diminished or disbanded altogether. Claiborne took cautious steps toward bolstering the colored troops. He recognized an ally in Michel Fortier, who had witnessed the performance of the colored units serving under Colonel Galvez in the Revolution. Fortier, now forty-three and a prosperous and distinguished planter, would, Claiborne thought, lend status to the black militia in the eyes of New Orleanians. In 1804 the Governor made him senior major in command of the Negro units.

At first the colored troops resented Fortier; they would have preferred an officer from within the group. But, willing to compromise, they went along with the appointment. As a token of esteem Claiborne presented the battalion with a red and white striped flag of silk, their own regimental colors, a gesture which afforded them considerable pride.

The flag became a matter of contention. The Louisiana *Gazette* declared that the ensign was too large, eclipsing the colors of the all-white companies, and complained, too, that many Negro officers outranked those in the white militia. The issue became so heated that Claiborne informed Secretary of War John Armstrong that he was obliged to post guards around the Place d'Armes while the Negro troops were drilling, to control the "mob" that was angered by the spectacle.

Meanwhile events conspired to cast further doubt upon the black militia. The revolution in Haiti had spread its spirit of unrest to Louisiana. With tension between the races rising in New Orleans, Claiborne disbanded the colored militia by the simple means of omitting it from all orders to the state militia after October 1804. It was an unwise move. The omission further embittered the neglected corps, and in January 1806 a conspiracy was unveiled that would have sent free colored troops to join former Spanish Governor Casa Calvo in an attack on the United States.

It was Francisco Dorville, Galvez's medal-winning officer, who was accused of leading the conspiracy. Dorville, now a captain, sported a Spanish cockade and referred to himself as *"commandante de mulatos de la Dominación Española"* — mulatto commander under Spanish domination (as if Spanish domination still existed). According to a colored informer named Stephen, it was at Dorville's house that the conspirators met regularly, "all with guns and powder and other military arms." They awaited only word from Casa Calvo to rise up and take the city.

The conspiracy proved to be no more than a vanity-flattering charade. As a precaution, Claiborne ordered a militia company to stand guard every night. Other than this he did not seek to accuse or punish the "conspirators" who appeared to be simply talking to themselves, without support of the black community. If anything, this false alarm, the Governor believed, further underscored the need to bring the black man back into the regular militia.

Letting the matter simmer down and cool for a year, Claiborne again appealed, in 1807, for reinstatement of the black militia, supported in this by Michel Fortier. He was promptly challenged by the Louisiana *Gazette,* which quoted the words of Daniel Clark, an American politician, businessman and social figure in New Orleans. Clark charged that Claiborne had woefully ignored the white militia while touting his preference for colored troops.

The generally mild-mannered Claiborne demanded a retraction of the charge. Clark only repeated the accusation more forcefully. With surprising mettle the Governor challenged his fellow citizen to a duel with pistols. On June 12 they met beneath The Oaks, and Claiborne was wounded in the shoulder. He had, however, sustained his honor and gained a certain reputation as a man of firm adherence to his principles. But the cause of the black militia languished.

In 1809, with Napoleon's legions well-entrenched in Spain and Portugal, hostilities spread to the French-held islands of the Caribbean. French and free colored refugees from Santo Domingo poured into Louisiana. In three months, May to August, fifty ships brought 6,060 immigrants to New Orleans. Of these, less than two thousand were white. The remaining four thousand or more were almost equally divided between free colored and slaves. In three months, the balance of population in the city was heavily weighted in favor of the blacks.

Claiborne could not deny asylum to the refugees. But he wrote to Maurice Rogers, United States Consul in Cuba, to try to restrict the emigration of free colored to Louisiana. "We have already a much greater proportion of that population than comports with the general interest." He also tried to persuade the colored immigrants to leave the Territory for greener pastures better able to support them. All measures forcing them to do so failed.

In January of 1811 an insurrection of slaves—what New Orleans had dreaded—took place on Manuel Andry's plantation, then forty miles above the city. After wounding Andry and murdering his son, the slaves moved down towards the city, sacking and burning the plantations which they passed, seizing arms and gathering recruits among the slaves. A lone planter, Pierre Trepagnier, stood them off, defying the mob from his balcony with a single fowling piece. The black army, five hundred strong, bypassed Trepagnier's and continued on towards New Orleans.

In the city "the confusion was beyond description." Claiborne sent General Wade Hampton with a handful of Regulars and two small companies of volunteers to intercept the Negro column. When the free men of color forgivingly offered their services, Claiborne placed them under the command of Major Peter F. Dubourg, white, and sent them off, reporting later that they performed their mission "with great exactitude and propriety." Sixty-six slaves were killed in the ensuing battle, some escaped into the swamps, and the rest were captured and hung from trees along the river as a grisly example and deterrent.

As a curious footnote to this event, the intrepid Trepagnier, who had successfully defied the slaves, disappeared shortly after the incident and was never seen by anyone again.

Strangely enough, the slave insurrection promoted a reactivation of the black militia. For one thing, none of the free colored had done more than deplore the insurrection. And the conduct of those who had rallied to the call for volunteers now recommended them to serious consideration. With the declaration of war against Great Britain on June 12, 1812, nine weeks after Louisiana became a state, the need for troops for the city's defense became critical. A militia bill passed by the Legislature in August called for 2200 volunteers. More particularly it authorized the Governor to enroll "Certain Free People of Color," with the only provision that their officers be white and that they themselves be holders of a small amount of property. Presumably and perhaps rightfully, property owners would be bound to loyalty by respect for their possessions.

Immediately Claiborne set about organizing four colored companies of sixty-four men each, a number prescribed by the Legislature. It was to be known as the Battalion of Free Men of Color and would be commanded by Major Fortier, who, incidentally, paid for their equipment. Second in command was de la Ronde's neighbor, Pierre Lacoste. Claiborne, presumably with Fortier's approval, ignored the Legislature's call for all-white officers and commissioned three blacks as second lieutenants — Isadore Honoré, Jean Louis Dolliole, and Étienne Saulet. It was the first example of colored officers being commissioned in the militia of any state of the Union.

To some extent, New Orleans was simply reverting to conditions that existed under Spanish domination, when colored troops were led by colored officers of the line. But this was now the United States, and more specifically the South, and in that respect the situation was unique. It would not be duplicated elsewhere in the country for many years, and not in the South for generations.

So long as General James Wilkinson remained in command of the 7th Military District, the colored militia was never usefully employed. The Negroes drilled regularly in the Place d'Armes, and no angry mobs assembled to deride them. But in May of 1814 Andrew Jackson assumed command of the District, and their future looked distinctly brighter. Fortier, Lacoste and the other officers of the battalion urged the enlistment of all free men of color in New Orleans and vicinity, the eligible number being estimated at eight hundred. Claiborne submitted the proposal to Jackson, but limited the number to four hundred, a figure which the General hastened to approve.

In the interminable correspondence that now passed between the General and the Governor, between New Orleans and Mobile, Jackson warned Claiborne that "inciting the black population to insurrection and massacre" would be an objective of the British in their expedition to Louisiana. The same warning was given in the unsigned letter to Jean Laffite, presumably written by Beluché. The writer advised that Colonel Nicholls, upon his arrival off the coast, would issue a proclamation "declaring all slaves who will join their [the British] standard free and liberated forever from their masters."

It would seem that the English were well aware of New Orleans' constant fear of a slave rebellion—fear, in fact, of the blacks per se. This was expressed in a report from British naval Captain Sir James Lucas Yeo on the defenses of Louisiana which Admiral Cochrane and General Keane had all but memorized. Yeo noted:

It is not for me to judge of its Political Expediency, but from the information I have been able to obtain and the little local knowledge I have acquired, I am persuaded there is nothing that would cause more alarm and consternation than the bare apprehension of our Black Troops being employed against them.

It was, of course, a measure already projected. Two West India regiments had been assembled in Jamaica to join in the invasion of Louisiana.

In late September Jackson sent from Mobile to Governor Claiborne a confirmation of his wish to make full use of the colored militia. Noting the need for soldiers to defend New Orleans, he continued:

The free men of color in your city are inured to the southern climate and would make excellent soldiers. They will not remain quiet spectators of the contest. They must be either for or against us. Distrust them, and you make them your enemies. Place confidence in them, and you engage them by every dear and honorable tie to the interest of the country by extending to them equal rights and privileges with white men. I enclose you a copy of my address to them for publication, and wish an experiment be made for raising a Regiment of them. They will be officered by white men except the non-comissioned officers and be placed upon the same footing with other volunteers for the war. Should you succeed in raising a Regiment, Battalion or company advise me and I will send one of my aides to organize and pay them their Bounty under the act of Congress placing them on an equality with soldiers procured by enlistment. No objection can be raised by the citizens of New Orleans on account of their engagement as they will be removed from amongst them if fears of their fidelity are entertained. I also enclose you for publication an address to the citizens of Louisiana [on this subject] . . .

Jackson's proclamation to the Free Men of Color, whom he addressed as "Sons of Freedom," opened with the statement: "Through a mistaken policy you have heretofore been deprived of a participation in the glorious struggle for national rights in which our country is now engaged. This no longer shall exist." He referred to their "intelligent minds" and "love of honor," and added: "In the sincerity of a soldier, and the language of truth, I address you."

> To every noble-hearted freeman of color, volunteering to serve during the present contest with Great Britain, and no longer, there will be paid the same bounty in money and lands now received by the white soldiers of the United States, viz. one hundred and twenty-four dollars in money, and one hundred sixty acres of land. The non-commissioned officers and privates will also be entitled to the same monthly pay and daily rations, and clothes furnished to any American soldier.

With a rare understanding of existing Negro-white relations, he added:

> Due regard will be paid to the feelings of freemen and soldiers. You will not, by being associated with white men . . . be exposed to improper comparisons, or unjust sarcasm. As a distinct, independent battalion or regiment pursuing the path of glory, you will, undivided, receive the applause and gratitude of your countrymen.

Jackson's demand for respect and equal treatment for the colored troops was no idle promise. When Assistant Paymaster Allen of the 7th Military District balked at handing over cash to colored soldiers, the General lashed out at him:

> Be pleased to keep to yourself your Opinions upon the policy of making payments to particular corps.
> It is enough for you to receive my order for the payment of troops . . . without enquiring whether the troops are white, Black or Tea.

Claiborne withheld publication of Jackson's proclamation to the free colored on the ground that, as he wrote to the General, "many excellent citizens will disapprove the policy you wish to observe toward the free people of color." But he let the General have no doubt: he himself had not lost confidence in the colored population and agreed with Jackson that it was better to have them with you than against you.

"But," noted the Governor, "this mode of reasoning makes no impression upon some respectable citizens here. They think that, in putting arms in the hands of men of color, we only add to the force of the enemy, and that nothing short of placing them in every respect upon a footing of equality with white citizens (which our Constitution forbids) could conciliate their affections."

Still harrassed by uncertainty, Claiborne consulted with de Marigny's Committee of Defense, generally excluding from his plans any consultation with Livingston's rival Committee of Public Safety. What did the members think of Jackson's proposal for a regiment of colored troops?

Somewhat surprisingly they endorsed it, "provided there would be a guarantee against retention of the regiment when the war was over." For, as Claiborne expressed it to Jackson, "if at the close of the war, the individuals were to settle in Louisiana with the knowledge of the use of arms, and that pride of destination which a soldier's pursuits so naturally inspire, they would prove dangerous."

In other words, as Marcus Christian, a student of the Negro's role in the Battle of New Orleans, noted:

> Since the more cautious whites did not relish the idea of a large group of armed Negroes in their midst, here was the opportunity to bring them into the city somewhat as mercenaries, and then, after victory is won, pay them off and let them shoulder their rifles and march away to . . . any place far removed from New Orleans.

It was a full month before Claiborne mustered enough nerve to publish Jackson's proclamation to the free colored, although he assured the General "I continue to think that, in the hour of trial, they will prove a meritorious corps." Before releasing the proclamation he started implementing it by commissioning a free man of color, Ferdinand Listeau, to the rank of captain and sending him with a detachment of forty-five black troops to garrison Fort St. Philip guarding the Mississippi River.

When the proclamation was finally published on October 24, there was the anticipated wave of protest. According to Charles Gayarré, Louisianians considered it "exceedingly objectionable, on the ground of it putting colored men too much on a footing with the whites. . . . It was still more strenuously denied that they could, whether 'natives' or 'adopted children,' be properly designated as 'Americans' . . . Even those who were best disposed toward that peculiar class of the population objected to their being raised to the dignity of being denominated 'fellow-citizens' and the 'countrymen' of the white race."

Even in a community of a dozen or more minorities, prejudice, perhaps under the American influence, was focused on the black man. It sprang largely from economic fear—fear that the blacks might not always submit to slavery, might indeed throw off the yoke by force. What would happen to the planters then? Or to New Orleans? To Claiborne's credit, however, and that of the Legislature, the mobilization of colored troops proceeded. Jean Baptiste Savary, a Santo Domingan and former officer of the French Republic, proposed raising another black battalion from among his fellow refugees. Claiborne held him off till Jackson should arrive—an event which both the Governor and Edward Livingston had been promoting by persistent, importunate letters to the General.

# 6.  *Beauty and Booty*

On the west end of the island of Jamaica in the Caribbean, bracketed by jutting points of land eight miles apart, lies crescent-shaped Negril Bay, ordinarily an uninhabited and tranquil paradise.

But in late November 1814 it was anything but uninhabited and tranquil. The beaches between the languid surf and the inland border of royal palms and stunted cedar were crowded with tents, shacks, booths, and piles of lumber. Among them lounged and strolled or strutted some six thousand troops, red-coated, green-coated, some with bright tartans — the vanguard of a mighty army yet to be completed. On the fringes of this vast encampment, brightly-bedecked natives peddled the produce of the island, peddled the women themselves to any who would have them.

Quartermaster William Surtees, who had witnessed many such British bivouacs on many foreign shores, found the place "generally like a fair; for the inhabitants had assembled in great numbers, bringing with them livestock and poultry and vegetables &c. for sale, all of which were greedily bought up at prices high enough, I warrant you."

The waters of the bay were jammed as they had never been before or would be again, "seventy or eighty sail of vessels . . . so closely wedged together that to walk across the decks from one to the other

87

seemed, when at a little distance, to be far from impracticable." Some fifty of these vessels were wooden-walled British warships of all rigs and sizes, flying the Union Jack along with regimental colors and the burgees of commanders — the mightiest armada ever assembled in this part of the world.

Consider the ships themselves, pride of the indomitable British Navy. Standing out to sea like a mother hen, the flagship *Tonnant,* eighty guns, with Vice-Admiral Sir Alexander Cochrane in command. Riding deferentially closer to shore, the *Royal Oak,* seventy-four guns, under Rear-Admiral Pulteney Malcolm. Then the *Norge, Bedford, Ramilies* and *Asia,* each with seventy-four guns; the *Dictator, Diomede* and *Gorgon,* spouting from forty-four to fifty-six guns each; the *Alceste, Hydra, Weaver, Traave* and *Belle Poule,* each with thirty-eight guns. There were more, many more — brigs, schooners, frigates, barques and barquentines. Nelson had nothing like this against the French and Spanish at Trafalgar. Sir Francis Drake, much earlier, would have been lost commanding such a fleet, one which heavily outweighed Spain's "Invincible" Armada.

They had been arriving since November 15, building up almost day by day, in seemingly limitless numbers of ships and men. They had swept into the harbor with successive waves of veteran troops from many foreign battlefields — some from the Chesapeake, some from the Spanish Peninsula, some from France and some direct from England. Many had suffered casualties against Napoleon's legions; others were relatively fresh; all were professionals steeped in the art of gentlemanly warfare.

Among the first to arrive were the regiments which had fought along the Chesapeake and the Potomac, who had put the torch to Washington and been repulsed at Baltimore. These were the 4th regiment of infantry, or King's Own, which had fought for five years under Wellington; the 21st regiment of Royal Fusiliers, which had served in Egypt; the 44th East Essex Regiment under Colonel Brooke, who had succeeded General Ross, who fell at Baltimore; and the 85th Light Infantry, which had been active in the siege of Bayonne.

Later arrivals were the 95th Rifle Corps, distinguished from the redcoated regiments by their smart green jackets, and two squadrons of the 14th Duchess of York Light Dragoons. Proudest of all were the ancient 93rd regiment of Highlanders under their gallant commander

Lieutenant-Colonel Robert Dale. Their military record had been re-
stricted, but their reputation for discipline and upright conduct was
haughtily beyond reproach. More than all others, they looked the part
of the contemporary warrior, all over six feet tall, richly uniformed in
bright tartan trousers and flat-topped, tasseled hats of red and yellow.

There were also two somewhat bewildered colored regiments, the
1st and 5th West India, who mixed little with their brethren in arms.
And there were the usual army auxiliaries of artillerists, sappers,
miners, rocket brigades and engineers. Many of the officers had brought
their wives. There was also a small army of civilian personnel equipped
to take over the administration of Louisiana. They were headed by an
attorney general, an admiralty judge, a Superintendent of Indian Affairs
from Canada, and a secretary for the colony who awaited the arrival of
an as-yet unidentified Governor.

Until the latter appeared, the Honorable Mr. Elwood from Trinidad
would be Lieutenant Governor. The ambitious Collector of Barbados
would assume control of the territory's finances. He had with him five
fashionable, marriageable daughters, who chattered gleefully of the
balls and cotillions they would lead at New Orleans and of the eligible
husbands whom they hoped to find there.

On the bay, small rowboats passed to and from the ships and to and
from shore, bearing brilliantly uniformed captains and lieutenants on
social visits to their fellow officers. Similarly, throughout the bivouac
on the beach the soldiers circulated sociably, greeting old friends and
making new ones on the basis of compared experiences.

Except for the senior officers most of them were young, although already veterans. Quartermaster William Surtees of the 95th Rifles, now
thirty-four, had been in the army since fourteen years of age and had
served under Wellington in Spain and France. He was keeping a diary
and noted now that as food and water were carried from shore to the
vessels in the harbor, his boat was forced to pass close to a British
prison ship. Captive Americans aboard the ship were apt to taunt them
with such comments as, "So you've come to attack our country, have
you? Well, get yourselves measured for your coffins, boys." Surtees
found such sentiments "insolently coarse."

Segeant Jack Cooper of the Royal Fusiliers was the typical camp
complainer. He griped principally about his seven-year enlistment. His
term had been almost completed when he found himself on the high

seas bound for America, with no turning back. In contrast, Lieutenant George Robert Gleig and Captain Charles Grey of the 85th, both barely twenty, shared a common dedication to the military life. Both had been in on the siege of Bayonne and later participated in the siege of Washington and Baltimore.

Gleig, who kept a meticulous account of his campaigns in the form of letters, regaled his comrades with tales of the burning of Washington. How they had dined in the White House on a still-warm meal which President Madison and his wife Dolly had left on the table as they fled the city. Of the burning of the Capitol, justifiable to Gleig as a punitive act of war, he reported, "I do not recollect to have witnessed, at any period of my life, a scene more striking or more sublime."

But one unforgettable memory haunted the Lieutenant's mind. It was during the advance on Baltimore, harassed by enemy snipers, when a riderless horse charged past him with its saddle stained with blood. He braced himself for the worst, and advancing at double-time came upon General Robert Ross, commander of the army, lying in the agonies of death. Ross had been shot in the back by a sniper and had fallen into the arms of his aide, Duncan MacDougall, who was destined to replay that role with a different cast on a different battle-field months later.

While Ross's command was temporarily assumed by Lieutenant-Colonel Francis Brooke, the General's death had a significant effect on the expedition now assembled for the conquest of Louisiana. Admiral Cochrane for the navy, and Ross commanding the army, had shared joint responsibility for this American campaign. Ross had specific orders to concur with Cochrane only as guided by his own good judgment. With Ross gone, the mantle of commander-in-chief fell by circumstance on Major General John Keane, ten years Ross's junior and improperly groomed for such responsibility.

Keane was in the dubiously enviable position of an understudy suddenly called upon to fill the star's role. Son of a baronet in Parliament, he had become a captain in the army at the age of thirteen, on the basis of family influence. In a day when promotions could be purchased, he had risen steadily in the military hierarchy, serving as staff officer and acquiring little battlefield experience. He had been a brigadier general in Wellington's army for a year, but was accustomed to obeying orders and not giving them.

He was aware that this accidental promotion might not last; aware, in fact, that his successor had already been chosen in London and was on his way, although still unknown by name to the bulk of the army at Negril Bay. And he was painfully conscious of being at present no more than a stooge to Cochrane, at least in the eyes of the Admiral himself. In his possession was a document that rankled sorely. It was a letter from Lord Bathurst, British Minister of War, advising him that he was to be guided "by the counsel and opinion of Vice-Admiral Sir Alexander Cochrane, to whose views it is the desire of his Majesty's Government that you should pay every deference."

Keane found himself constantly paying deference to Cochrane, secretly hoping that as things developed he might play a significant part in the conquest of New Orleans before his successor arrived. He had good officers to count on. Colonel William Thornton of the 85th, who had been badly wounded at Bladensburg but had since recovered, was a man of outstanding initiative and daring. Major Robert Rennie, the most war-scarred of all the officers, was an instinctive battle-lover, one who performed best under the stimuli of risk and action. Both were dependable, quick-thinking leaders. Colonel Thomas Mullins of the 44th was something else again. Stubborn and proud of his aristocratic breeding, his ego bolstered by an ambitious wife who accompanied the expedition, he operated strictly by the book and was hardly popular with his troops.

Most of the others were veterans of distinguished record. Colonel Francis Brooke of the King's Own had proved an able subordinate under the fallen General Ross. Colonel Robert Dale of the Highlanders, Major Samuel Mitchell of the 95th, and Lieutenant C. W. Whitby of the 1st West India, were all of experienced dependability. Keane felt he had little to worry about in his subordinates, if only he could keep control of the doughty Admiral who had become the *de facto* leader of the expedition.

Now somewhat belligerent and edgy, due to unforeseen setbacks in the Chesapeake, Cochrane was impatient to be on his way to New Orleans where, it was estimated, some fifteen million dollars' worth of merchandise in storage promised his sailors the prize money that they had not gained in previous campaigns. Plunder was part of the navy man's incentive and was readily acknowledged as a realistic motive. In fact, the phrase "beauty and booty"—the first referring to the

seductive females of New Orleans — was an oft-repeated watchword of
the expedition, though lacking the Admiralty's official sanction.

But there were, of course, far more significant objectives. Cochrane's
revised instructions from the Admiralty, following his reverses in the
Chesapeake, defined the dual purpose of the expedition:

> First, to obtain command of the embouchure of the Mississippi, so as to
> deprive the back settlements of America of their communication with the
> sea; and, secondly, to occupy some important and valuable possession, by
> the restoration of which the conditions of peace might be improved, or which
> we might be entitled to exact the cession of, as the price of peace.

Once New Orleans and/or Baton Rouge was captured the army
would be in a position to close in with the ten thousand British troops
poised now in Canada, to isolate the entire North American continent
west of the great river. Whatever was agreed upon by the peace commissioners in Ghent, Great Britain would never let that territory go —
unless for immense concessions that would include free navigation of
the Mississippi.

Cochrane was in possession, too, of a rather remarkable document
written by Captain James Lucas Yeo of the English naval forces on the
Great Lakes — remarkable for its prescience and accuracy. Where Yeo
got his information from remains a mystery, since he had not seen
service in Louisiana or the South. One can only assume that the commander was part of some secret British information network, gathering
data from all theaters of the war. His report read in part:

> The City of New Orleans is not Fortified, nor furnished with means either
> for Hostile or Defensive operations.
> Almost the whole of their Troops (consisting of undisciplined Militia)
> have been sent to Mobile for the purpose of seizing on Pensacola and every
> other part of the Spanish Possessions in West Florida.

Advising that the ascent of the Mississippi would be plausible,
"with only two small forts to oppose you" (his only erroneous assumption), Yeo rightfully estimated the limited naval defenses of the city and
predicted its easy destruction by bombardment. As to resistance from
the native population, "At New Orleans there is nothing but Faction
and discontent and the American Party is by far the weakest."

He then made a provocative observation on the presence of the West India regiments that would presumably take part in the invasion:

> The Population of the slaves in the Southern Provinces of America is so great, that the People of Landed Property would be panic-struck at the sight of a Black Regiment on their Coast, and nothing would more effectually tend to make the War with this country unpopular, than the knowledge of such a measure being in contemplation.

In spite of Yeo's encouraging report on the defenselessness of New Orleans, Cochrane was aware of formidable difficulties. He discounted the "plausible" ascent of the Mississippi. Its mouth was too far from the city; he was too impatient for such a tedious approach. On the other hand, the many alternative waterway approaches to the city were tricky and shallow. They would not admit the heavier men-of-war and transports of his fleet.

He would need light-draft vessels to transport the troops ashore and establish a beachhead, and had wanted to purchase such craft, like the Dutch schuyts available in Holland, before leaving Europe. But the Admiralty had suggested that he would save money by purchasing or having barges built by native workmen in Jamaica.

He hadn't saved money; the natives had charged him outrageously for labor and material. On top of that, an operation intended to be kept secret had become well known thoughout the islands, and news of his preparations had been doubtless circulated in America. In fact, Artillery Captain Benson Hill insisted in writing that these negotiations to hire and build small landing craft were the reason why "many persons who ought to have remained in ignorance were aware that New Orleans was the intended scene of action."

However, Cochrane had the barges, some forty of them, ready to be loaded on the transports — along with a number of trim little sloops and schooners, fifteen or twenty tons each, designed to penetrate the shallow lakes and bayous of the Louisiana coast, where the larger vessels could not trespass.

Two likely points of penetration had been contemplated: Mobile Bay, 130 miles east of New Orleans, and Barataria. The existence of secret waterways in Barataria was well known to British naval officers who had earlier, and unsuccessfully, sought to drive the pirates from their lair. These water approaches would be useful, but only with the buccaneers' cooperation. Nicholas Lockyer had returned to Pensacola without any firm commitment from the pirate leader, Jean Laffite, although still hoping to obtain it.

Captain Percy, lurking off Pensacola with his four-ship squadron, could not wait. On September 12, following Cochrane's general orders, he made immediate preparations to assault Fort Bowyer guarding Mobile Bay — boasting that, once all was in readiness, that flimsy structure would fall "in twenty minutes." As the vessels assembled off Mobile Point, Colonel Edward Nicholls began landing his 730 Indians and marines, along with two pieces of artillery, on the narrow sandy neck behind the fort. Against an effective force of 1330 men and ninety-two guns on ship and shore, Fort Bowyer's defenders seemed hopelessly outnumbered and outgunned.

The British had lost the advantage of surprise. As the troops at Negril Bay complained, there had been too much leakage of information about their plans. Andrew Jackson, with temporary headquarters at Mobile during the late summer, was fully aware of what was going on at Pensacola. In pressing for military aid from Tennessee he wrote to Governor Willie Blount that ten thousand British troops were momentarily expected at Pensacola, that these were the vanguard of 25,000 of "Lord Wellington's army," and that "the Emperor of Russia has offered 50,000 of his Choicest troops to his Britannic Majesty for the Conquest of Louisiana." On what basis he brought Russia into this threatened invasion is unclear. But the mere fact that the Czar had formerly offered to mediate a war which Jackson clearly wanted, may have caused him to regard that nation as an enemy.

Following his time-tested formula of "what would I do if I were the enemy?" Jackson reasoned that any invasion of Louisiana would come by way of Mobile, proceeding overland to New Orleans or Baton Rouge. For the moment he would forget about Pensacola and concentrate on strengthening Mobile.

He sent out urgent calls for militia from Tennessee, the Mississippi Territory, and Kentucky — although the latter state was not within his military jurisdiction. He counted particularly on Brigadier General Coffee's Tennesseans, who had spearheaded his conquest of the Creeks. He expected no help from Madison's government, which had been virtually *in absentia* since the burning of the Capitol. Nor did he look for aid from the Louisiana militia. They were needed in New Orleans, and there was doubt if they would agree to serve outside the state.

It would take weeks for any militia to arrive, and there was little that Jackson could do. But he took what steps he could. He ordered that the previously abandoned Fort Bowyer should be reactivated and sent Major William Lawrence with 130 Regulars to garrison it. It was not much of a force, but it was all that he could spare. Lawrence and his Regulars worked like Trojans strengthening the ramparts of the fort and in the brief time available were able to put twelve of its twenty guns in commission. The major then pledged his small detachment to hold the fortress at all reasonable costs.

On midnight of September 13, Jackson, with engineer Howell Tatum, sailed down the bay from Mobile to see how things were going. He was intercepted by the American schooner *Shark*. Its skipper had a message for the General, namely that "a number of British Armed Ships lay off the bar, and from their maneuvering, etc., showed a design of attacking the fort, or passing it for Mobile." Had Jackson continued he would have found himself in the enemy's midst and become the prize captive of the war. He ordered his vessel to swing back to Mobile. But a strong north wind, plus the poor sailing qualities of the schooner, made the going slow. Pushing into the mouth of a creek, the General commandeered a pirogue and was rowed the rest of the way to Mobile, arriving the following evening.

On September 15, after some preliminary shelling from the ships, the two-pronged attack on Fort Bowyer from land and sea began in earnest. Along the tongue of land leading to the fort an extraordinary throng advanced—six hundred Creeks and Choctaws in red British jackets and assorted hats, clumsily bearing unfamiliar muskets, with swords dangling between their naked legs, and tripping them up as they straggled across the sand. Flanking them, like herding sheepdogs, were two units of marines. Lawrence let them approach to within close range, then unleashed a barrage that sent them howling to the rear.

On the seaward side of the fort the four warships mounting ninety guns and manned by six hundred sailors and marines approached within close range and turned on everything they had in a thunderous barrage

of ball and grapeshot. Simultaneously, the marines and Indians let go
with their artillery. Pinned between these cannonades, Lawrence returned the fire from both sides, and in minutes the fort, the ships, the
men on land were enveloped in a cloud of smoke.

The flag of Percy's ship *Hermes* was blown away, and Lawrence
gallantly withheld his fire until the British could raise it to the mast
again. Then he turned all his guns upon the *Hermes,* cutting her cable
and sending her aground beneath the fort. Percy set fire to the stranded
ship and transferred his crew and wounded to the *Sophia,* leaving the
*Hermes* to total destruction when its magazine exploded.

Marine Colonel Edward Nicholls, who had recruited and trained the
Creeks and Choctaws at Pensacola, had lost an eye in the bombardment. Now with his remaining eye he saw the Indians pinned down
behind the fort. He ordered the land forces to withdraw and retreat by
land to Pensacola, where the damaged fleet would join them. The
British had suffered 162 men killed and seventy-two wounded. Lawrence had lost just eight men, four killed and four wounded.

Fort Bowyer was a humiliating defeat for the British and one for
which Captain Percy would later face a naval court of inquiry for
having lost one of His Majesty's ships. He was exonerated, however,
on the grounds of having taken a "calculated risk" (risk?—with the
initial odds so greatly in his favor?) to capture and hold a key position
on the Gulf. Now that Mobile was secure to the Americans, Percy's
fleet fell back on Pensacola, sixty miles east of Mobile—the only
remaining friendly beachhead for the invasion of Louisiana.

Jackson now set his sights on immobilizing Pensacola. He had no
authority to invade West Florida, but he had long regarded such a step
as necessary to the safety of his Southern District. Spain, he felt, was a
potential if not *de facto* ally of Great Britian and was harboring and
abetting British troops and hostile Indians quartered by permission on
Spanish soil.

As early as June he had written to Secretary Armstrong from Tennessee requesting permission to take action, and had received no reply.
He had written again in August, demanding to know "How long will
the Government tamely submit to open insult from Spain? Temporizing
will not do." Still no reply.

When Monroe succeeded Armstrong as Secretary of War, Jackson
tried again. "Will not the government order Pensacola Seized, and

garrisoned by our troops?" All he proposed to do was "keep the Spaniards in their shell." Again, no direct answer.

Jackson had had previous instructions not to aggravate the Spaniards and drive them over to the English side by rash offensives. But he decided to take matters into his own hands and to regard the Government's silence as tacit consent. First, however, he settled for a vitriolic campaign by letter, accusing Don Matteo Gonzalaz Manrique, Commandant of Pensacola, of sheltering hostile British troops and inciting the Indians to acts of aggression against the United States. The Commandant replied that he was simply offering a sort of diplomatic immunity to the homeless Creeks and harborless British, and what was the United States doing about the Baratarian pirates who preyed with immunity on Spanish vessels?

The tact and diplomacy which Jackson had been advised to use became a little sharp-edged. As to the renegade Indians "for whom your Christian bowels seem to sympathize and bleed so freely," the General promised "An Eye for an Eye, Tooth for tooth, and Scalp for scalp." The Spanish Commandant had "thrown down the gauntlet, and I will pick it up." He concluded: "Your excellency will be pleased in future not to view me as a diplomatic character, unless proclaimed by the mouths of my cannon."

Gonzalaz continued to protest his innocence (which Jackson regarded as further "contortions of the bowels"), until the General himself appeared near Pensacola the first week of November. By this time the reinforcements he had sent for had arrived. General Coffee joined him with two thousand mounted Tennesseans. These, with seven hundred Regulars and a detachment of Mississippi Dragoons under the gallant Major Thomas Hind, gave Jackson the core of a solid army of three thousand troops. They arrived at the gates of Pensacola on November 6, and Jackson sent Major Henry D. Peire of the 44th Regulars with a flag of truce to Governor Gonzalaz. Peire carried an ultimatum from his general, demanding that the town's two principal forts — St. Michael, garrisoned by Spaniards, and Barrancas, manned by British troops — be peacefully surrendered.

The flag was insolently fired on by the guns of Fort St. Michael, and Jackson sent his troops storming into town. They captured its only battery at bayonet point and overwhelmed the city, street by street. In the midst of this relatively bloodless action, an officer reported to

Jackson that Gonzalaz himself had stumbled out of his home, bearing a white flag and requesting that the General meet him at his house to discuss the terms of surrender.

Jackson hurried to the Commandant's home, to meet Gonzalaz face to face, whereupon the Spanish Governor excused himself for a moment. The instant he had left the premises, ships in the harbor opened fire on the house, missing the roof by inches. It had been a trap! Jackson had barely escaped such a pitfall at Mobile and had walked submissively into this one. "I was then Justified," Jackson reported to Monroe, "to have carried destruction every where."

But he did not yield to that temptation. Taking shelter, he ordered a detachment of militia to round up Gonzalaz and bring him back. Tell him, said Jackson, that "here we shall live or die together!" Gonzalaz returned, with fulsome apologies, and the firing from the harbor ceased.

With no real choice, Gonzalaz consented to yield the city. Fort St. Michael held out briefly, then surrendered, while the British at Fort Barrancas, six miles to the west, blew the place up on orders from their Captain Woodbine and retreated to the safety of Percy's vessels waiting just off shore.

The fall of Pensacola, on top of the British defeat at Mobile, clarified certain points that badly needed such clarification. The Spanish could no longer count on the British, who had abandoned them just at the moment when they had begun to hope for the return of Louisiana to the Spanish Crown. The British could no longer count on their Spanish allies, who appeared incapable of putting up any effective resistance. The Indians could count on neither, having seen both defeated.

While it was no distinguished victory for Jackson's little-contested army, it temporarily removed the threat of an invasion via Pensacola or Mobile. Only a direct attack on New Orleans, the primary target, remained open to the British. The General had received repeated pleas from Governor Claiborne and Edward Livingston, urging his presence in the city—"to overawe disaffection" and bring to heel the reluctant militia, not to mention the refractory New Orleanians. With proper precautions, he was free to go.

Pensacola, he felt, was safe for now. Both major forts were garrisoned by U.S. troops. The umbrageous Spanish governor had done an about-face and seemed diplomatically amenable to the American occupation. He had signed his last letter to Jackson, "your most faithful and

grateful servant, who kisses your hand." Leaving two regiments of
Regulars and some militia to guard Mobile and placing the region under
the command of Brigadier General James Winchester, Jackson left for
New Orleans on November 21. He would go overland on horseback,
to reconnoiter the approaches to the city and the opportunities for
their defense.

When news of the action at Pensacola and Mobile reached Negril
Bay, Cochrane and Keane revised their plans. There would be no
overland expedition from these points to Baton Rouge. Barataria, too,
was out as an invasion route to New Orleans: the pirates' delay in responding to their offer was too plainly a sign of their reluctance. The
army would have to proceed directly to New Orleans via Lake Borgne
on its eastern flank.

Neither Cochrane nor Keane nor any of the expeditionary force at
Negril Bay appeared disheartened by this enforced decision. All was
confidence and gaiety aboard the ships and in the tented bivouac as
preparations were made for their departure. The Collector of Barbados
watched with approval as his five marriageable daughters flirted with
the bachelor subalterns, while Lady Mullins continued to reign over
the social activities of officers' wives. It was like a vast carnival preparing to hit the road for more promising and profitable grounds.

On November 25 the fleet was ready for departure. The flat-bottomed
landing boats obtained in Jamaica were hoisted to the decks, where
they each would be fitted with a carronade. The eight regiments
mounted the gangways to the transports. Altogether, Cochrane and
Keane had eight thousand troops, while the fleet itself counted ten
thousand sailors and 1500 marines, plus the artillerists and engineers—
a total force of twenty thousand.

Still at sea and yet to join them in Louisiana, was a third wave of the
expedition under Major General John Lambert. It would supply three
more regiments—the 7th, 40th and 43rd—totaling 2700 additional
troops. Behind Lambert's fleet, racing towards America from England,
was the frigate *Statira* bearing the new commander-in-chief of the expedition, replacing the fallen General Ross and the surrogate leader,
General Keane. There was not time to wait for Lambert or the *Statira*.
These reinforcements and the new commander would join the fleet in
Louisiana.

The *Tonnant,* bearing Keane and Cochrane, pulled out first to reconnoiter the point of rendezvous—somewhere in the Mississippi Sound below Lake Borgne. From there they would play it by sight and ear, deciding on a final beachhead. On the following day the fleet followed its Admiral out of Negril Bay, stretching out over several miles. George Gleig aboard the *Fox* observed:

> It is impossible to conceive of a finer sea-view than this general stir presented. Our fleet amounted now to upwards of fifty sail, many of them vessels of war, which shaking loose their topsails, and lifting their anchors at the same moment, gave to Negril Bay an appearance of bustle such as it has seldom been able to show. In half an hour all canvas was set, and the ships moved slowly and proudly from their anchorage, till having cleared the headlands, and caught the fair breeze which blew without, they bounded over the water with the speed of eagles, and long before dark, the coast of Jamaica had disappeared.

Alexander Walker, writing some years after the event but often on the basis of eyewitness accounts, describes the temper and tendons of the expedition:

> Never did a fleet and army proceed towards their destination with higher hopes and in better spirits than the British expedition for New Orleans. So confident were they of success that a full set of civil officers to conduct the government of the Territory accompanied the army. There was also a government editor and printing press to expound the policy and publish the orders and proceedings of the new government. There were many merchant ships in the squadron, which had been chartered expressly to bear away the rich spoil that was expected to reward their capture and occupation of the city. It was indeed regarded an expedition to occupy, rather than invade a defenceless country, as a pleasure party and speculative adventure more than a warlike enterprise. Hence the festivity and high hearted jollity which enlivened the crowded decks of the British war vessels and transports, as they moved majestically over the calm water of the Gulf.

But neither the waters nor the voyage were altogether calm. Mishaps and misfortunes plagued the fleet. Two ships collided, one cutting the other in half. The hurricane season lived up to its promise of heavy rains, high seas and adverse winds. Many of the troops and sailors were poisoned by contaminated pork brought aboard at Negril Bay. The wife of an officer died of shipboard fever.

On December 10, in sight of the American coast between Mobile and Pensacola, the fleet made contact with Captain Percy's squadron, to which they looked for the promised Indian reinforcements. Colonel Nicholls brought some samples of these promised warriors aboard the transports, to introduce them to the troops. Quartermaster Surtees, for one, was not impressed:

> They were the most grotesque-looking figures; most of them were dressed in some old red coats, which they had got hold of by some means, with cocked hats of the old fashion. . . . They had tremendous large rings, &c. hung in their ears, the laps of which were stretched nearly to their shoulders; some of them also wore rings in their noses; and some of them were without any sort of lower garments, having nothing but a sort of cloth tied around their waist, which passed through their legs and fastened before. These people it was intended should bring their warriors to New Orleans; but, owing to some cause with which I am not acquainted, none but these three or four chiefs ever came near us.

No one was disappointed in the poor showing of the Indians. The expedition did not need them. The Baratarians would have been an asset had they opened their territory to the invading British troops, but they, too, had been discounted. Surely the French Creoles, along with the Spanish element of the population, could be counted on to aid a movement that might free them from American domination. And surely hordes of Negro slaves would seize this opportunity to rebel against their masters and undermine the American defenses from within.

Blithely the fleet sailed on to Mississippi Sound. They were two weeks behind schedule, but that hardly seemed to matter. Nothing could stop them now. They had an invincible force of ships and men. There were no reports of a defending army in their path. Ahead lay Beauty and Booty waiting only to be claimed. "A handsome, powerful, graceful athlete was this," according to George Gleig, "about to go acourting in New Orleans."

En route to that city, Andrew Jackson wrote to his devoted wife Rachel that he hoped she might be able to meet him there, adding that "the darkest hour of all the night is just before the day."

# 7. *"Vive Jackson!"*

Winter mornings are proverbially wet and chilly in New Orleans. The mist which during the night broods over swamp and river turns to frost by daylight. But the dampness remains and so does much of the fog to cloak the city in a dismal shroud.

Two homes, however, on this first day of December, had been brightly lit since early dawn, with hearthstone fires and shining candelabra helping to dispel the gloom. In Bernard de Marigny's manor on the Esplanade, all was in readiness for such a breakfast as only his Parisian chef could orchestrate. Family silver sparkled on the damask tablecloth. "The salon in my house was spacious," Bernard had finished writing in his journal, "and no detail neglected so that the reception might be worthy of the guest."

But no guest arrived, even though carriages waited outside to bring the visitor to town when summoned. As Bernard thumbed his glass of port and lit another cigar, he wondered first about this tiresome delay, then about what appeared to be a calculated snub. He was not overly sensitive, but never before had a de Marigny's invitation been ignored.

"My name," he wrote in his journal, "was not unknown to him. He had very recently been the guest of my father-in-law, M. Morales [Juan Ventura Morales, former Spanish Intendant at New Orleans], who made known to me the desire of the General to stay with me, and it would have been infinitely agreeable to receive him. . . ."

De Marigny was not a petty man, but this was no petty slight that had been handed him. The seeds of a lasting resentment had been sown.

Twelve miles to the north on the Bayou St. John, similar preparations had been under way since dawn. As at de Marigny's, the Spanish-style mansion of John Kilty Smith glowed with firelight and polished candelabra. Smith, a wealthy and retired bachelor, had engaged the services of an aristocratic Creole neighbor to supervise the preparations of a breakfast "in that style of cookery for which the Creoles are renowned."

Again in a somewhat different way, the only disappointment was the guest himself—not only his uncouth appearance but his brusque disdain of food. For Andrew Jackson, though he had lived on acorns in the field when fighting Indians, had a queasy stomach. Barely looking at the banquet spread before him, he asked for a bowl of hominy and ate it almost wordlessly.

Said the Creole hostess later to her neighbor, "Ah, Mr. Smith! You ask me to receive a great general. I make your house *comme il faut* and prepare a splendid *déjeuner*—all for an ugly old Kaintuck flat-boatman."

Her disdain was not unwarranted. For Andrew Jackson's first appearance in New Orleans was not one to arouse enthusiasm or inspire confidence. He was tired, dirty, and drenched to the skin. He could have come tidily by water from Mobile. But he had traveled circuitously some 350 miles for eleven days through the wilderness "to have a view at the points at which the enemy might make a landing." He suffered from dysentery; his damaged arm and shoulder twinged from the un-extracted bullet of a duel; he had little breath to spare for pleasantries.

Even Smith shared some of his hostess's dismay as he observed "A tall, guant man, very erect. . . with a countenance furrowed by care and anxiety. His dress was simple and nearly threadbare. A small leather cap protected his head, and a short blue Spanish cloak his body, whilst his high dragoon boots [were] long innocent of polish. . . . His complexion was shallow and unhealthy; his hair iron grey, and his body thin and emaciated like that of one who had just recovered from a lingering sickness."

But Smith noted, as so many others had and would, that a "fierce glare" infused the General's "bright and hawk-like eyes."

Accompanying the General were others of a more conventional military presence: his adjutant-general, Colonel Robert Butler, and his handsome military secretary, Captain John Reid. The trio had been joined at Fort St. John, before proceeding to the Smith estate, by Major Hughes of the 7th Infantry and Major Chotard of the Louisiana militia.

At ten o'clock the party rode into the city, where the cannon of Fort St. Charles thundered a greeting and summoned the citizens to the streets for a view of this backwoods curiosity who had come to save them. Edward Livingston had organized a welcoming committee consisting of himself, Governor Claiborne, Mayor Nicholas Girod and Commodore Patterson. Claiborne introduced the General in a drizzling rain, observing that, "The sun is never shining more brilliantly than when you are among us."

Among the spectators in the street, his high coat collar turned up to conceal his identity, was Bernard de Marigny. He had finally ridden at noon to Fort St. Charles to inquire what had happened to his guest and had been told perfunctorily that "there had been a change of plans." No more.

Perhaps his bitterness arose from more than the affront to his proffered hospitality. For he complained in his memoirs that those who waited on the General appeared to be self-seeking opportunists, currying his favor, hoping for privileged appointments. He then naively noted: "I was then twenty-nine years old, and one can easily appreciate the fact that had the General come to my house and offered me a position as Chief of Staff I should have accepted his offer."

When it came time for Jackson to address the crowd, it was Edward Livingston, awkward in stance and appearance but vibrant of voice, who translated his address in French. The General was, as he had said himself, "a fighter, not a writer." But while the voice and eloquence were Livingston's, the words were distinctly Andrew Jackson's. And the gist of his message was that he had come to New Orleans with a single purpose, to "drive their enemies into the sea, or perish in the effort."

The effect, wrote Alexander Walker, was "electric. . . . Countenances cleared up. Bright and hopeful were the words and looks of all who . . . caught the heroic glance of the hawk-eyed General." New Orleanians of one accord responded with the cry of "*Vive* Jackson."

Young Charles Gayarré was in the enthusiastic crowd, noting of

Jackson that "His lip and eye denoted a man of unyielding temper, and his hair, slightly silvered, stood erect like quills round his wrinkled brow, as if they scorned to bend." With considerable insight Gayarré reflected later that Jackson was precisely right, in character, for the time and the occasion. If Jackson was not a genius, Gayarré observed, "his rock-hewn will took the place of genius."

Actually, the crowd which now saluted him knew very little about this forty-seven-year-old stranger who had come to save them from destruction. Communication between the city and the rest of the United States was tardy, sketchy and inaccurate. They had heard his name mentioned as a Senator from Tennessee. They had learned, of course, that he had routed the Creeks and appropriated much of their territory and had captured Mobile and Pensacola.

Beyond that, he was a foreigner from up north where he was noted for his dueling and brawling and his intransigence as a circuit-riding lawyer. It was rumored that he had married a backwoods woman named Rachel Donelson before her divorce from an earlier husband had been granted, and had fought in the streets to defend her name. In a pistol battle with the Benton brothers, Thomas Hart and Jesse, he had almost lost his life, and he still carried a bullet in his shoulder.

They must have sensed that above all he was a fighter, a man who regarded anyone who crossed him as an enemy. But perhaps not known was his ingrained hatred of the British. During the Revolutionary War when he was fourteen, a British officer—one of those heading the invasion of the Carolinas—had demanded that the red-haired youngster shine his boots. The youth had refused. The officer had whipped his saber across Andy's cheek, leaving a scar that he would carry to his grave. Some day, he vowed, that scar would be avenged.

With the welcoming ceremonies over, the General wasted no time in getting down to business. He and his aides rode to the three-story building at 106 Royal Street which had been reserved for his headquarters. With him in his second-floor chambers were Patterson, Livingston, Ross and Claiborne who, each in turn, reviewed the steps taken for the town's defense. Much more remained to be done, but Jackson's immediate problem was to familiarize himself with the terrain. In this he was greatly assisted by Arsène Lacarrière Latour, chief engineer for the 7th Military District.

In 1802 when he arrived in New Orleans from his native France, Latour was engaged in surveying and mapping the city and its environs for Napoleon's projected occupation of the territory. His charts were later turned over to James Wilkinson, then military commander of the district, and also—for reasons unknown—to the Spanish authorities in West Florida, by which they fell subsequently into British hands. A man of many parts—engineer, architect, cartographer and builder—he had constructed numerous notable buildings in the city. He had been recommended to Jackson by Edward Livingston as "a man of perfect honor and integrity, speaks both French and English fluently."

Given the courtesy title of "Major," Latour's role in subsequent events was an important one. In addition to submitting his portfolio of detailed maps, he was Jackson's close adviser on the location and construction of fortifications, and served, too, as occasional scout in the territory that he knew so well. On top of it all, he served the cause of history by keeping a day-by-day account of these critical days in New Orleans, based on his own and other eyewitness observations.

This is not to slight the services of another engineer on Jackson's staff, Major Howell Tatum, who was, at the moment, checking the fortifications beyond the city limits. Tatum, as well, kept a daily journal of this period in Louisiana's history, less accurate than Latour's, but with the immediacy of one forever on the run between engagements.

Now with Latour's maps spread open on the table, Latour and Livingston, with Patterson's corroboration, reviewed six likely approaches to New Orleans which the enemy might take. Because of the nature of the terrain, all were, of necessity, by way of water, at least in the initial stages.

They were, to the west, the Bayou Lafourche leading north from the Gulf to the Mississippi River forty miles above New Orleans, and Lake Barataria with its contiguous lakes and bayous leading more directly to the city. But this was difficult territory over which to lead an army without the now-fugitive Baratarians to serve as guides.

The Mississippi River was, of course, another potential route, though its many convolutions plus the opposing current and the sometimes adverse winds would make it difficult for sailing vessels (Tatum wrote it off as "impossible"). No one, at this point, recommended trying to fortify its several distant mouths. But Fort St. Philip, fifty miles below the city, should be strengthened, as well as the batteries on both sides of the English Turn.

To the east was the Bayou Terre aux Boeufs leading to the Mississippi just below the English Turn, a possible point of landing, but still fairly distant from the city. Then there was Lake Borgne, leading north to the Gentilly Plain and Chef Menteur, and west via many bayous and canals to the plantation fields along the river.

Finally, an enemy might pass from Lake Borgne through the passes of the Rigolets into Lake Pontchartrain, and thence descend on the city from the north, by way of the Bayou St. John and the Carondelet canal. At The Rigolets, the Fort de Petites Coquilles, as yet unfinished, offered some protection, with Fort St. John at the mouth of the Bayou St. John providing a formidable shield.

As a somewhat contradictory aside, perhaps refuting the value of his colleague's maps, Tatum inserted the following observation in his journal:

> It will be sufficient here to note, that no correct information could be obtained respecting the Topography of any part of this country, even from the best informed persons of the Country or City. It appeared that scarcely any person had made enquiry further than the limits of his own possessions, and many had failed to acquire even that knowledge, or if they possessed it, did not choose to reveal it, lest it lead to the discovery of waterways used for smuggling.

Jackson himself seems to have shared this view, complaining of "the total ingnorance I have found among all descriptions of persons" regarding the topography of New Orleans. In any event, he planned to reconnoiter the terrain in person in the days that hopefully remained before the enemy made his move.

Before the meeting ended, Jackson made several additions to his staff from among the many eager volunteers. Livingston easily promoted himself to the role of aide-de-camp and did the same for his brother-in-law Augustin Davezac and his legal partner John R. Grymes. Also added to Jackson's staff were Abner L. Duncan, the Creole baiter, and United States Marshal Pierre le Breton Duplessis.

There were others the General had his eye on. Though Pierre de la Ronde was sometimes listed as an aide-de-camp (by historian Henry Castellanos, for one), it seemed doubtful that he was ever so appointed. But he proffered his services as one who knew the plantation territory well, and Jackson would make good use of him. Eager to join the group, and becoming in fact a member without portfolio, was the redoubtable General Humbert, who seemed always to be standing by, always ready to undertake anything that promised action and excitement.

Colonel Arthur P. Hayne, Inspector General and a demon for detail, took much trivial routine from Jackson's shoulders. He was, at the moment and at Jackson's request, reconnoitering the Mississippi Delta with a view to its defense—and would shortly return with the opinion that "a *Fortification* in *Siberia* would be of as much service in defending the Mississippi" as the insufficient batteries then covering the several passes at its mouth. His conclusions as to the need for batteries further up the river would concur with Jackson's.

Governor Claiborne, feeling increasingly slighted by Jackson's appointments and noting the deference the General paid to Edward Livingston, took a dim view of this semi-military clique. He himself had personally urged the General to hasten to the city, in view of the danger to New Orleans. But he now complained that "Those who immediately surrounded Jackson on his arrival, with a view to enhance his reliance on them, availed themselves of every opportunity to increase his sense of danger."

Perhaps it was all a matter of one's point of view. Judge François-Xavier Martin, a Claiborne appointee, had written a month earlier: "The Governor, who was not unwilling to increase his own merit by magnifying the obstacles he had to surmount, stated in his correspondence with Jackson every opposition he met with, and did not fail to represent everyone who did not think as he did, as inimical to the country."

That evening, after an arduous twelve-hour day, Jackson was presented to New Orleans society at the home of Edward Livingston— who else? Having heard rumors of the General since his arrival in the city, Madame Livingston harbored a feminine reluctance to entertain "that wild Indian fighter." But her husband assured her, "He will capture *you* at first sight." And indeed the transformation was remarkable when Jackson, shaved, powdered and spruced up, arrived in full-dress uniform, "a blue frock-coat with buff facings, white waistcoat and close fitting breeches," with (finally) highly polished boots.

"I had to confess," noted Livingston, "that the new uniform made almost another man of him. He had two sets of manners: One for headquarters, the other for the drawing-room."

There was food for thought in this when the following day the General, at his own request, reviewed the New Orleans volunteers in the Place d'Armes. Four-fifths of them were Creoles. It was not a ratio that would endure, but it was one he had to work with at the start. Knowing no French, having little knowledge of the Creole character and background, he would have to use diplomacy and tact. Surprisingly, in view of his low boiling point, he did.

Five companies passed on parade that Friday, representing the Battalion of Orleans Volunteers under the command of Major Jean Baptiste Plauché. It consisted, according to Vincent Nolte, of "about 550 men, and counting among its officers men who had fought beneath the eye of Napoleon. . . ."

Fortunately, perhaps, the Place d'Armes was then no larger than it is today, which made it seem overwhelmed with marching troops and enthusiastic citizens. Flags and handkerchiefs waved from the windows, urchins perched on the roofs and trees, the drum rolls of Jordan Noble and the blaring notes of the Battalion band echoed against the walls of the Cathedral.

First came the Carabiniers d'Orleans captained by Pierre Roche, one of the Napoleonic veterans Nolte had referred to. Then followed "the glittering, shimmering, blue-and-silver" Dragons à Pied, or Dragoons, commanded by Henri de St. Gême. St. Gême, in civilian life, was rumored as fencing merchandise for the Baratarian pirates, a highly forgivable offense.

Next came the Francs under Captain Jean Hudri, the Chasseurs captained by Auguste Guibert, and finally the only American company in the battalion, the Louisiana Blues commanded by de la Ronde's son-in-law, Maunsell White.

In spite of their pitifully small numbers (Nolte's figure of 550 was an optimistic one; other estimates were as low as 385), Jackson allowed his normally enigmatic face to register approval. He smiled, saluted and later complimented the individual officers on the performance of their troops. What he thought of the meagerness of this force, he kept to himself. The audience seemed enthusiastic, and he would not dampen their spirit.

But much of that audience enthusiasm was for Andrew Jackson, that once-mythical figure about whom doubts were now dispelled. His authoritative presence, his bold assurance, infected the people with a spirit of self-confidence they badly needed. More than that, he began almost mystically to unite them. The jealousies and suspicions, the cantankerous disputes, began to wain before a common leader and a common purpose. Lethargy was replaced by zeal, diffidence by patriotism and a willingness to sacrifice—all this the more remarkable because of the division that had hitherto existed.

Even the Legislature buckled down to business. Besides allocating Jackson money to build fortifications where and as he might see fit, the Legislature called upon the planters to supply slave labor for these projects. The women of the town were organized to make bandages and clothing, and supply "comforts" for the troops—those expected and those present in the city. Livingston's Committee of Public Safety was drilled in its assignments in the event of an attack. Many local officials and members of the Legislature—among them Judge François-Xavier Martin, later to become an eminent historian of New Orleans and Louisiana—joined the veteran guard designed to police the streets.

From the beginning, the major problem was obtaining troops and arms and ammunition. The desultory militia and the two regiments of U.S. Regulars under Colonel Ross, along with the small Battalion of Orleans Volunteers, were only a beginning. Bernard de Marigny was well aware of this. He was sufficiently inspired by patriotic zeal to humble his natural pride and call on Andrew Jackson with his three-man Committee of Defense.

The meeting between de Marigny and Jackson was described as "cool." But Bernard's appeal was ardent: pardon and free the Baratarian pirates and enlist them in the army.

Edward Livingston, of course, as chairman of the rival Committee of Public Safety, was not among the petitioners. As their legal representative he was sympathetic to the Baratarians. As something of a Jackson protégé, his presence might have made a difference. But de Marigny was shrewd enough to bring along Augustin Davezac, the lawyer's brother-in-law, to give the commission a bipartisan appearance. They pleaded at length for the Baratarians' acquittal and acceptance, but, reported de Marigny, "The General was unrelenting. He told us these men were being pursued by United States Civil Officers, that many were in prison . . . that he did not wish, could do nothing about the matter. The Committee withdrew, very much grieved at such determination."

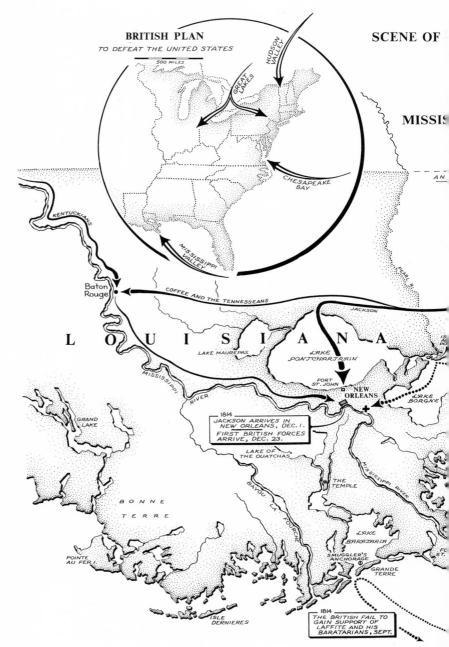

BRITISH PLAN
TO DEFEAT THE UNITED STATES

SCENE OF

MISSIS

HUDSON VALLEY

GREAT LAKES

500 MILES

CHESAPEAKE BAY

AN

KENTUCKIANS

MISSISSIPPI VALLEY

PEARL

Baton Rouge

COFFEE AND THE TENNESSEANS

JACKSON

L O U I S I A N A

LAKE MAUREPAS

LAKE PONTCHARTRAIN

MISSISSIPPI RIVER

FORT ST. JOHN

NEW ORLEANS

LAKE BORGNE

GRAND LAKE

1814
JACKSON ARRIVES IN
NEW ORLEANS, DEC. I.
FIRST BRITISH FORCES
ARRIVE, DEC. 23.

LAKE OF
THE OUATCHAS

BAYOU LA FOURCHE

THE TEMPLE

MISSISSIPPI RIVER

BONNE
TERRE

LAKE
BARATARIA

SMUGGLER'S
ANCHORAGE

GRANDE
TERRE

POINTE
AU FER I.

ISLE
DERNIERES

1814
THE BRITISH FAIL TO
GAIN SUPPORT OF
LAFFITE AND HIS
BARATARIANS, SEPT.

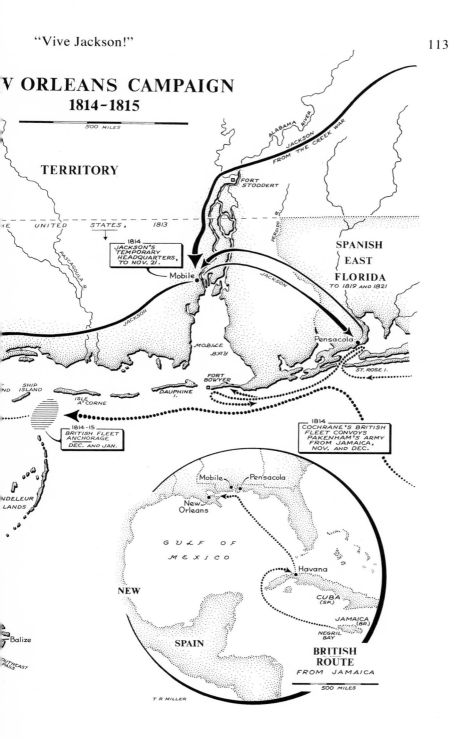

# ⅴ ORLEANS CAMPAIGN
## 1814–1815

500 MILES

TERRITORY

ALABAMA RIVER

JACKSON FROM THE CREEK WAR

FORT STODDERT

ᴴᴱ UNITED STATES, 1813

PERDIDO R.

SPANISH EAST FLORIDA
TO 1819 AND 1821

PASCAGOULA R.

1814
JACKSON'S TEMPORARY HEADQUARTERS, TO NOV. 21.

Mobile

JACKSON

JACKSON

MOBILE BAY

Pensacola

ST. ROSE I.

SHIP ISLAND

FORT BOWYER

ᴺᴰ ISLAND

ISLE A' CORNE

DAUPHINE I.

1814–15
BRITISH FLEET ANCHORAGE DEC. AND JAN.

1814
COCHRANE'S BRITISH FLEET CONVOYS PAKENHAM'S ARMY FROM JAMAICA, NOV. AND DEC.

ᴺᴰᴱᴸᴱᵁᴿ LANDS

Mobile   Pen'sacola

New Orleans

GULF OF MEXICO

Havana

CUBA (SP.)

NEW

JAMAICA (BR.)

NEGRIL BAY

Balize

SPAIN

BRITISH ROUTE
FROM JAMAICA

ᴼᵁᵀᴴᴱᴬˢᵀ PASS

T R MILLER

500 MILES

That first week in December was a period of feverish activity. His aides complained that Jackson never slept. The General was keenly aware of the vulnerability of the city: obvious points of danger could be fortified, but there were too many secret waterways to cover, especially the many creeks and bayous leading from Lake Borgne to the plantations just below the town.

Jackson's first act was to order that all these waterways be blocked or filled in. Trees should be felled to obstruct the smaller creeks, called coulées, winding through the marshes, while the canals on the plantations—though serving a useful purpose in normal times—should be drained or filled, to make them impassable to landing craft. To Colonel de la Ronde, particularly, and to Major General Jacques Villeré, he assigned the responsibility for this important effort.

As to Lake Borgne and Lake Pontchartrain, both forming likely avenues of attack, Patterson assured Jackson that his gunboats were patrolling the former, fully alerted to the danger. Admittedly these little ships could not withstand a major enemy naval force, but they would serve as "the eyes and ears" of Jackson's army and could fight a delaying action if the enemy should penetrate the lakes. Jackson was sufficiently confident to write Monroe, "The gunboats on the Lakes will prevent the British from approaching in that quarter."

In spite of Colonel Hayne's exhaustive report on the defenses of the Mississippi, and Tatum's assurance that the river was an "impossible" invasion route, Jackson decided to see for himself. In fact, he meant to cover the entire area of New Orleans, by foot, on horseback or by boat, to view the existing defenses and the need for further effort. On December 4 he left with Commodore Patterson and majors Tatum and Latour, to reconnoiter the Mississippi as far as Fort St. Philip.

The trio found Fort St. Philip, which Jackson regarded as "the key to the defense of the River Mississippi," in promising repair, although the general ordered all wooden construction dismantled and destroyed for fear of fire. He also demanded that two batteries be constructed on opposite banks of the river, to provide a cross fire at this point. On the return trip, a small fortification with additional batteries were ordered for the English Turn, and a nest of cannon to guard the head of the Bayou Terre aux Boeufs.

During the Commander's absence, Claiborne brooded on his situation. It was humiliating; nobody told him anything, asked his advice or looked to him for important missions. He was not self-seeking, he told himself, only patriotic. He began to see himself as the rightful leader of his people in this time of crisis — even conceivably, fate willing, Andrew Jackson's logical successor.

Like many others, he was genuinely concerned about the General's health — and conscious of its implications. He drafted an obliquely-worded letter to Secretary Monroe, acknowledging at the start his great respect for Andrew Jackson. "But in the event of General Jackson's Death, or absence from the District, it is not impossible but some contest may arise as to the right of Command. . . ."

He then went on to do a little spadework in anticipation of this contest:

> I should be unwilling to acknowledge any other officer of the Regular army or of the Militia, on duty in this station, as my military superior. . . . Diffident as I am of my Military Talents . . . I solicit that General Jackson may be instructed to consider me as second in Command. . . . Be good enough I pray you, Sir, to bear this message of mine to the President and to inform me how far he may be disposed to grant it. . . . I am unwilling to remain an inactive spectator of the Struggle.

Nothing came of Claiborne's appeal, and to his credit he continued to submit faithfully to Jackson's orders, though with growing, smoldering resentment.

Jackson's return to the city from his down-river expedition coincided with an unforeseen event: the arrival of the new side-wheeler *Enterprise,* skippered by young Henry Miller Shreve. It was not the first such revolutionary craft to visit the Crescent City, thanks to the Fulton-Livingston (Robert Livingston, brother of Edward) monopoly of steamboat traffic on the river. In 1812 the *New Orleans,* built by Nicholas Roosevelt of the family of future presidents, had astounded and delighted New Orleanians. It was an omen of the future of their city!

Shreve, an experienced and independent skipper, was attempting to break the Fulton-Livingston monopoly by this unauthorized visit, and Edward Livingston moved to have the vessel seized. Jackson intervened. He saw in the *Enterprise,* free of dependence on wind and current, a valuable tool. He sent Shreve back up the river to search for the dilatory flatboats bringing arms and ammunition to the city, then used the ship for evacuating women and children from the danger zone. Later the *Enterprise* would be useful in bringing troops and ammunition and provisions from New Orleans to whatever battlefield fate might prescribe.

Mailed at this time to Jackson, and on its way from Secretary of State and War Monroe, was a letter that may have expressed the beliefs of the Washington government at this moment or may have been simply a bit of federal whistling in the dark.

> Sir: Intelligence was received yesterday from Cuba on the 9. ultimo, that the British force from this bay, under Admiral Cochrane, had united at Jamaica with other troops, and had sailed . . . to make an attack on New Orleans. It is hoped that you will have long since taken a suitable position on the river to afford complete protection to that City. . . . Your presence at such a point . . . with the main body of your troops will be of vital importance. It will inspire the Inhabitants with confidence, and animate them to vigorous exertions. It will enable you to direct your whole force to the proper points and to make the necessary preparations to meet the enemy. . . and to overwhelm him wherever he presents himself. All the boasted preparations which the British government has been making thro' the years, with veteran troops from France and Spain, after having been gloriously foiled in attacks on other parts of our Union, is about to terminate in a final blow against New Orleans. It will, I hope, close there its inglorious career, in such a repulse as will reflect new honor on the American arms. . . .

Perhaps it was just as well that the mail took six to eight weeks to reach New Orleans from the eastern seaboard. The blithe assumptions of a government that had done little or nothing to make its predictions come about, would certainly have struck the General as ironic. Troops to "overwhelm" the enemy! Jackson circled the word "troops" and wrote in the margin, "at this date I could not have wielded more than 2500. . ." On the bottom of the page he noted that "this was the first letter I received from the Dept. since the 19th of october 1814." With these scratchy comments he sent it back to Monroe on the day that he received it—February 18, 1815. By that time, he had little more to do.

In his first ten days in the vicinity Jackson and his aides, sometimes with Patterson and sometimes with Ross, had covered the terrain south, west and north of New Orleans. To the east, from the Carondelet canal to the Chef Menteur, stretched the Plain of Gentilly, sentimentally named by the exiled French for a commune in the Department of the Seine. With a penchant for fixations, Jackson now made up his mind that here the British would probably attack. It presented solid, level ground not too far from the city—a peninsula with a lengthy shoreline on which to effect a landing. There were marshes on both sides and the plain itself was narrow, disadvantageous to an enemy. But once the General entertained a hunch he was reluctant to let go of it.

On December 14 he rode out along the Chef Menteur Road to reconnoiter. With him was Major Latour. Halfway to the point a courier from Patterson galloped up to report that sails, apparently headed for the Bayou Terre aux Boeufs, had been sighted on Lake Borgne by Colonel de la Ronde. Some firing on the lake had also been reported. Jackson dispatched Latour to ride south and investigate. It could be another of the false reports generated by an anxious, nervous city.

He himself continued on along the Bayou Sauvage to its mouth on the marshy waterfront, a mile from where Chef Menteur points an accusing finger at Lake Borgne. He had a long shoreline to guard, six hundred miles of it from Mobile Bay to the Sabine River, with little more than two thousand inexperienced troops and a flotilla of five gunboats and two small auxiliaries on Lake Borgne.

Lake Borgne had always been a point to watch, its mouth wide open to the Gulf of Mexico. Just the day before, Jackson had received a report from Lieutenant Catesby Jones's gunboat navy that enemy vessels had made their appearance near the mouth. He had written to Coffee at Sandy Hook near Baton Rouge, "I expect this is a feint, to draw my attention to that point when they mean to strike at another. However, I will look for them there, and provide for their reception elsewhere."

Coffee had meanwhile written Jackson and their letters crossed. The Tennessean reported that his troops were honed for action "and will be always ready to receive your orders, and march when called for at the shortest notice. . . ." Acknowledging Jackson's communication he closed with the heartening note:

I am glad to learn you feel secure from an enemy [coming] by way of the Mississippi, as I cannot believe they can ever land at Orleans through the Lake. Should they attempt such a landing . . . in the swamps, we could ask no better Christmas frolic than to cut them off from their Craft, and never let them again embark. I cannot believe they will land at all. . . .

They were reassuring thoughts to entertain, here, alone, on the desolate Chef Menteur. But still the General felt uneasy. Where would the British strike, and when? Though not by nature a religious man, he had reason to thank God for Coffee's readiness and to pray for whatever help and guidance he could get.

# 8.   *"Clear the Lakes!"*

Lake Borgne. A name to remember. "Half-blind Lake" it meant in French. In winter, especially, the name applied. Its vitreous slate-gray surface, barely noticing the worn December sun, stared vacantly skyward like a sightless eye.

But that first week of December 1814, it was not altogether sightless. Like falcons scouting for their prey, three of Patterson's black-hulled gunboats, the Commodore's "eyes," patrolled Lake Borgne with glasses focused on the Gulf, where two more armed sloops probed for signs of the approaching foe.

Coming he was, that much was certain. When Patterson returned from his downriver reconnaissance with General Jackson, he was handed a letter by a friendly Choctaw scout. It was from Pensacola, dated December 5, and unsigned. The person who had sent it, the Indian said, was "dark complexioned, had a long mustache, and spoke like a Frenchman." Beyond that, his identity remained a mystery. The letter read:

Sir—
I feel it a duty to apprise you of a very large force of the enemy off this port, and it is generally understood New Orleans is the object of attack. It amounts

119

at present to about eighty vessels, and more are momentarily looked for, to form a junction, when an immediate commencement of their operations will take place. I am not able to learn how, when, or where the attack will be made; but I heard that they have vessels of all descriptions, and a large body of troops. Admiral Cochrane commands, and his ship, the *Tonnant,* lies at this moment just outside the bar; and probably no means will be left untried to obtain their object. The admiral arrived only yesterday noon.

The report came as no surprise to Patterson. Once the British had lost Mobile as a springboard for invasion, and the Baratarians had denied to them the western Mississippi delta, there was no approach open save lakes Borgne and Pontchartrain — connected by "passes," or channels, called "The Rigolets" — and the bayous flowing into them. He had prepared his naval strategy with this in mind. As he advised General Jackson,

> My idea is to station my vessels at different points of the Lake [Borgne] to the eastward of this, and if attacked by too superior a force, to retreat to the fort at The Rigolets, then make a stand and aid the Battery in the defense of that important Pass. For should this part of the country be invaded, it strikes me it will be by that route as no enemy will I think be so unwise as to attempt it by way of the River, where their shipping can be destroyed by fire vessels. . . .

The Mississippi, he believed, was safe for now. Warships would have a hard time passing Fort St. Philip and its double batteries; a hard time, too, bucking the current and the many convolutions of the river, in vessels dependent on quixotic winds. If they should, by chance, get within ten miles of New Orleans, he had the *Carolina* well positioned to rake the river with its heavy naval guns. And one of his gunboats patrolled the river in the vicinity of Fort St. Philip.

But the lakes were something else again. If the enemy tried to put troops ashore on Lake Borgne, they could only do so by means of light-draft landing boats. In that event Patterson's tiny gunboat navy would be useful.

He had sent the five gunboats to Lake Borgne on December 5, along with the tenders *Sea Horse* and *Alligator.* The flotilla was under the command of Lieutenant Thomas Ap Catesby ("Tac") Jones. Jones, a young, sharp, capable officer had never served on any other craft during his short term in the navy, and gunboats he knew as a drake knows his ducklings. His orders from Patterson were "Proceed to Pass Christiana for reconnaissance. If the enemy force tries to cut off the gunboats, retreat to The Rigolets. There, with the protection and help of Fort Petites Coquilles, sink the enemy or be sunk."

It was a tall order. For one thing, Fort Petites Coquilles was no great shakes as a protective bastion. It had never been completed; it was weakly garrisoned and weakly gunned. Regardless of that, however, pitting seven small boats against the might of the British Navy was like expecting a handful of minnows to block the passage of a whale. Patterson did not deceive himself or his colleagues as to the potentials of this small flotilla. In a later order to Jones he directed him "to take such position as would enable you, if the enemy should make its way into Lake Borgne, to cut off their barges and prevent the landing of their troops."

Even that, Patterson reasoned, might be difficult. What sort of landing vessels did the British have? Would they be armed? What kind of escort vessels would protect them?

Patterson believed and hoped that the gunboats could fight an effective delaying action and thereby give Jackson's forces time to prepare their defenses against an assault by land. A land attack would probably come via the plantation fields below the city, the Plain of Gentilly to the east, or possibly by way of Lake Pontchartrain lying north of New Orleans and connected into it by the Bayou St. John and the Carondelet canal.

Tac Jones's flagship was a little sloop of eighty tons. No name. The gunboats were not graced with names, but simply numbered. The four other gunboats in his squadron were commanded respectively by sailing-masters John Ferris and George Ulrick, and lieutenants Isaac McKeever and Robert Spedden, all young and somewhat inexperienced, but spunky. The flotilla numbered twenty-three guns in all, four or five to a ship, and 204 enlisted men well-armed with knives, swords, dirks and muskets.

On December 9 the flotilla was stationed, as directed, just inside the Pass Christiana, at the mouth of the lake. Jones sent word to Patterson: "The position I am now in is the most central I know of, and the best calculated to oppose any Force which may attempt to come through Pass Mariana, Pass Christiana, or the South Pass." Patterson sent word back that as soon as he made certain of his defenses on the Mississippi, he would personally join the gunboat fleet. But things were moving swiftly now. He never had the chance.

Jones sent McKeever and Ulrick in their respective vessels to reconnoiter in the Gulf beyond the passes. They sighted the vanguard of the British armada, behind which — stretching for miles along the placid waters of the Gulf — were the white sails, the towering masts, the gleaming guns of the main body of the fleet. The following day they were still some distance off, but Jones reported a small force anchored off Ship Island — only five vessels as yet, but "all are provided with a number of large Barges, which with the schooners and Brig are always kept in such positions that we cannot approach them with the Gun vessels without first encountering one of the ships."

For the next two days, with Ulrick and McKeever back from their scouting expedition, Jones bided his time in Pass Christiana.

On December 8, a week after Jackson's arrival in New Orleans, the mightiest armada ever to approach America's shores had sailed westward through the Gulf towards the Mississippi Delta — some fifty ships, with firepower manifest in the thousand guns they carried. Aboard the flagship *Tonnant,* Admiral Cochrane spied two tidy sloop-rigged vessels running parallel to the fleet and close to shore. They carried no colors, but he knew them for what they were: American vessels keeping track of the *Tonnant*'s movements. Ah, well! He had no such fatuous hope that this expedition was a secret from the enemy. Nor did he doubt its inevitable success. In spite of the setbacks at Mobile and Pensacola, he headed, he knew, an invincible armada bearing an army that would seal with victory the termination of this war.

The Admiral's only cause for chagrin was that he was well behind schedule. Late tropical storms had raked the Caribbean and the Gulf during much of November and early December. It was soft weather as they passed the West Florida coastline, but Cochrane had promised his sailors and marines that they would spend Christmas in New Orleans, hinting at the bounteous prizes that would soon be theirs to help them celebrate. If all went well, there was still time to fulfill that promise.

By December 12 almost all the ships had come to rest off the crescent-shaped Chandeleur Island. The larger ships, the seventy-fours, remained at anchor here; it was as close as they could safely get to shore. The remaining vessels, of shallower draft, proceeded towards the entrance to Lake Borgne, anchoring off Cat Island.

They might have moved further in, into the lake itself, but Captain Nicholas Lockyer on the *Sophia,* with two other ships, had started to reconnoiter in this direction. Somewhat surprisingly, they had been fired on by a pair of gunboats lurking near the channel entrance. It was a picayune encounter: the gunboats had scored no hits and had quickly withdrawn into the lakes. But it raised the specter of a possible ambush in these unfamiliar waters.

Aboard the British transport *Fox,* as the fleet approached the passes to Lake Borgne, Lieutenant George Gleig noted in his diary: "December 13th: five large cutters armed with six heavy guns each, were seen at anchor in the distance, and as all endeavors to land, till these were captured, would have been useless, the transports and largest of the gun-brigs cast anchor, while the smaller craft gave chase to the enemy."

Cochrane had sighted the gunboats, too. A puny force to try to block the lakes. But, as he reported later, "It became impossible that any movement of the troops could take place till this formidable [?] flotilla was either captured or destroyed." Out went the order to "Clear the lakes!" Down went the barges from their cradles on the ships, while 1500 troops and sailors piled down the ladders to the waiting craft.

As the barges lined up in formation—forty-five in all, each carrying thirty to forty sailors and marines—they were joined by several pinnaces and launches from the fleet. In command of the flotilla was Captain Lockyer, still smarting from his willful treatment by the Baratarians and itching for revenge. Lockyer divided his attack force into three divisions, one commanded by himself, the other two by captains Roberts and Montressor. Instead of a unified assault upon the enemy, they would pick off the gunboats one by one, like wolves descending on a flock of sheep.

On signal, and in perfect formation, the shallow-draft vessels were rowed towards Lake Borgne.

Tac Jones had witnessed these preparations and sent the *Alligator* to report to Patterson the arrival of the British fleet at the entrance to the lakes. Patterson relayed the news to Jackson, who still regarded these enemy movements as a feint. Jones, however, knew this was no feint.

On December 13, as the line of British vessels moved slowly and inexorably towards his gunboats, he began his withdrawal to The Rigolets. But luck was against him. A strong west wind combined with an ebbing tide to ground his vessels in a foot or more of mud between Malheureux Island and the mainland. Here he had a bitter choice: either to blow up his vessels to keep them from capture by the British or to make a last, determined, suicidal stand.

He decided on the latter. Using spring cables and anchors, he forced his boats into a ragged line between the island and Point Claire. Do what he could, however, his own ship and Ulrick's were grounded somewhat forward of the others, making them dangerously vulnerable. Stout triangular nets were raised from the decks to half way up the masts to repel boarding by the enemy. Jones called his four other officers aboard his flagship and gave them their orders. They were to inflict as much damage as possible on the enemy, fight till the last man fell.

First to see action was the little schooner *Sea Horse*. She had been sent to the Bay St. Louis to guard a small American battery and arsenal maintained there. Lockyer spotted her, alone and vulnerable, and detached seven barges to capture or destroy her. In command of the *Sea Horse,* Sailing-master Johnson took a position close to shore, where the guns of the little Fort St. Louis could protect him. For half an hour he held off the enemy squadron with his ship's guns and the land artillery. When the British barges gave up and retreated, Johnson ordered his crew ashore to destroy the land battery and ammunition—then blew up the schooner to keep her out of enemy hands.

The explosion alerted Jones to his extremely hazardous position. At dawn on December 14, having rowed all night, the line of enemy barges was nine miles below his station. He watched them approach, the pairs of oars rising and falling rhythmically. On each bow a carronade, on each barge a cluster of blue-coated sailors and red-jacketed marines. Jones estimated his chances. He was outnumbered five to one, outgunned almost two to one. In addition, while the light-draft vessels of the British could maneuver at will, he was stuck in a fixed position. No retreat, no mobile strategy was possible.

Off to the west, a small white speck appeared. It was the little tender *Alligator* under Sailing-master Shepperd, returning from Chef Menteur to join the gunboat fleet. Lockyer spotted her, too. He ordered four barges under Captain Roberts to intercept the vessel.

The little *Alligator* never had a chance. Her small four-pounder hurled several balls harmlessly at the approaching enemy, but the barges, spreading out, presented a scattered target. Shepperd saw the British marines preparing to board the tender. Against several hundred English he had a crew of only eight. He ran up the white flag of surrender. Roberts sent a boarding crew to take possession of the vessel and to deliver it to the British fleet below Pass Christiana.

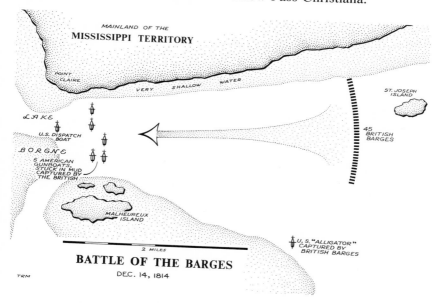

**BATTLE OF THE BARGES**

DEC. 14, 1814

Aboard his flagship, Tac Jones watched with reddened, sleepless eyes the relentlessly approaching enemy. How could they keep up that even sweep of oars, maintained for hours without a break in rhythm? Lockyer had the same thought; his men had been rowing for thirty-six hours and were reaching a point of exhaustion. In mid-morning he ordered a halt and allowed his men to enjoy a hearty breakfast. Half an hour later they were on their way, pressing towards Malheureux Island, narrowing the gap between the barges and the gunboats.

Lockyer put his strategy of divide and conquer into play. The two forward gunboats, stranded and exposed a hundred yards below the rest, would be the initial targets. Fifteen barges broke loose from the line and moved towards Jones's flagship, Captain Lockyer in the lead boat. Jones ordered his men to hold their fire till the barges were within musket range; then cannon and muskets blazed in unison. Two of the British barges rose from the water as if stricken by a tidal wave, hurling their loads of screaming wounded into the waters of the lake. A few able survivors, one of them Lieutenant Tatnerell, swam to the remaining barges.

Now it was Lockyer's turn to open fire. Jones caught a musket ball in the shoulder and fell bleeding to the deck. As he was carried below, he ordered his second officer, Lieutenant George Parker, to take over the command. "Keep up the fight! Keep up the fight!" Jones screamed to Parker. Parker barely had time to reply "Aye, aye, Sir!" before a charge of grapeshot brought him down.

In seconds the British barges bumped alongside, and the Royal Marines swarmed over the gunwales, slashing the boarding nets with knives and cutlasses. Scores of marines engaged in hand-to-hand combat with the forty defenders, using cutlasses and pistols, till the deck was strewn with dead and wounded. Both Lockyer and his second officer Pratt were severely injured in the action. Bleeding and prostrate on the deck, Lockyer ordered the captured gunboat's cannon turned on the remaining vessels. Overhead the American flag still flew over American guns firing upon American marines.

With Lockyer wounded, Lieutenant Tatnerell took over command of the English barges. A wily and ingenious officer, Tatnerell, before leaving Europe, had escaped from a French prison in the canonical guise of a monk. He now turned his division of barges on Ulrick's vessel, the second gunboat forward of the rest. Ulrick held them off till another division joined the first — close to thirty barges against a single gunboat. From all sides Ulrick's ship was boarded, with more hand-to-hand fighting on the deck, leading inevitably to the vessel's capture. Once again, American guns beneath the Stars and Stripes were trained on the remaining gunboats.

The third target in this divide-and-conquer attack was Lieutenant Spedden's ship. Spedden stood in the bow, directing the fire, when a blast of grapeshot shattered his arm. He remained standing, exhorting his men to maintain their fire, till a second blast all but severed his other arm. The British marines stormed over the gunwale, slashing and firing at the defenders. In the center of this melee, still shouting orders, Spedden stood erect with both arms limp and bleeding at his side. With respect for gallantry, in spite of the fierce confusion, no Britisher laid a hand upon him.

In less than two hours it was over. The other two gunboats, hopelessly surrounded, were subdued and captured. The Americans had
suffered losses of ten killed and thirty-five wounded, with the rest of the
gunboats' crews taken prisoner. The British had suffered seventeen
killed and seventy-seven wounded. They had cleared the lakes, but it
had taken them nine precious days, including the cat-and-mouse
preliminaries.

At that, it might have gone differently, according to Major Lacarrière
Latour, who later assumed the role of hindsight analyst. "Twenty-five
gunboats," he wrote, "might at the time have saved Louisiana." But
even apart from the numerical inequality, Latour attributed the
British victory principally to the fact that Jones's gunboats had been
mired in the mud, without enough wind for the sails to pull them loose.
"It is presumable that had not the wind died away, the gunboats under
sail would have destroyed the [British] flotilla, though numerous and
well armed."

It was a somewhat rose-colored view of the engagement, which did
not refute the consequences of an English victory. True, the British had
suffered formidable losses and much chagrin at this troublesome delay.
One British officer, quoted by Latour, decried the whole operation. "I
have always regarded this affair as a wanton sacrifice of human life,
merely to maintain the idle boast of bull dog pertinacity." But the
sacrifice was necessary, beyond the fulfillment of an idle boast. The
lakes had had to be cleared, and had been, and both Cochrane and
Lockyer magnified the enemy resistance to justify the sacrifice.
Cochrane reported to the London Admiralty that Lockyer "with determined bravery" had vanquished the enemy, "notwithstanding their
formidable force, their advantage of a chosen position, and their
studied and deliberate preparation."

Jones's position had been, of course, anything but chosen: any
studied and deliberate preparation he had made had been negated by
adverse conditions on the lake, and his tiny navy could hardly be
termed "formidable." Lockyer, however, in a separate report, was not
averse to agreeing fully with his Admiral, speaking of the "great
strength of the enemy's vessels," and describing the little gunboats as
"vessels of the largest dimensions." Perhaps uppermost in Lockyer's
mind was the fact that he had avenged the humiliating rebuff handed
him by the Baratarians. The lakes were cleared; the British would have
no need of Barataria or the Baratarians now.

That afternoon the British barges, with the captured American gunboats in tow, returned to the English fleet now anchored between Ship and Cat islands. Here the British sailors painted out the simple number on Jones's flagship and flatteringly renamed the boat *Destruction*. Here, too, the American captives were imprisoned on the warship *Gordon* and the wounded were tended by British doctors. Jones lay beside his fellow officer Spedden, trying to ignore the latter's screams as his shattered arm was crudely amputated by a British surgeon. When he was well enough, Jones drafted his report to Patterson, to be delivered when and if an opportunity presented. He made no apologies for his defeat and stuck to a meticulous recording of the facts. He enclosed "an estimate of the forces I had to contend with, as acknowledged by the enemy, which will enable you to decide how far the honor of our Country's flag has been supported in this conflict."

Actually, Jones had accomplished all that could have been expected of him. At the cost of losing his gunboat fleet he had bought invaluable time for the American defenders at New Orleans. His men had shown a stubbornness and skill in battle that was disturbing to the English. Quartermaster Surtees had witnessed the conflict from a distance and concluded that "better shots, either with artillery and small arms, do not exist than the Americans."

There had been other witnesses to the engagement. A group of Portuguese and Spanish fishermen, from their village at the west end of the lake, had watched the one-sided battle. They had noted with awe the British fleet riding in Mississippi Sound. Possibly they were aware that Spain was an ally of Great Britain. But more likely they knew a winning combination when they saw it — the armed barges, the majestic warships, the crushing of the American defenses on the lake.

It seemed to them that the Messiah had arrived, that new masters would shortly control Louisiana. That being so, it would be common sense to get in their good graces. A group of the fishermen, affecting to be about their business, approached the fleet and were fulsomely welcomed by the confident and dapper British officers. Plainly they had done right by coming. These friendly and impressive people were worth cultivating; and if that cultivation yielded a nice crop of gold, so much the better. Wisdom was always on the side of might, and clearly these white foreigners had might.

Imprisoned aboard the *Gorgon,* Jones took advantage of his position to render further service to his cause. The day following the gunboat battle he was grilled by Cochrane's aides and later by the Admiral himself. How heavily fortified were the passes leading into Lake Pontchartrain? They were well defended, Jones assured his questioners. In the "impregnable" Fort Petites Coquilles were stationed five hundred troops and over forty heavy guns.

Cochrane decided he could never squeeze through The Rigolets in the face of such potential fire power. He would have to settle for a landing somewhere on the west shore of Lake Borgne. In that case the Portuguese and Spanish fishermen, who had accosted the fleet the day before, might be useful to him. It was not until Cochrane and Keane had committed themselves to that course of action that Cochrane learned from his scouts that Fort de Petites Coquilles was held by only fifty men and mounted only eight light-caliber cannon.

It was during one of many of Jones's interrogations by Cochrane and Keane that a deck officer aboard the *Tonnant* brought some unexpected news. An American vessel, flying a white flag of truce, lay alongside the *Tonnant,* requesting permission to come aboard.

The ship had been sent, they later learned, by Commodore Patterson as soon as he had heard of the battle on Lake Borgne. Aboard the vessel were Thomas Shields, purser of the New Orleans naval station, and navy surgeon Dr. Robert Morrell. Their instructions were to obtain, if possible, a release on parole for the prisoners, while Morrell was to treat the American wounded.

Understandably the British officers were piqued at this invasion of their anchorage. They wondered if the Americans had not been sent as spies. When Shields and Morrell explained the purpose of their visit, and the doctor asked permission to attend the wounded, Cochrane flatly refused.

"We have able surgeons, sir, who will give the enemy as excellent treatment as they give our own wounded. We need no interference from American doctors."

Defeated, Morrell announced that they would therefore withdraw "reluctantly."

The Admiral was quick to reject that too.

"I hope your reluctance is genuine, Doctor, because you must remain as our guest. It was a clever device of your commander to send you here to spy on us under this pretext. But Englishmen are not so gullible. You will remain with the fleet."

Though the action violated the flag of truce, Shields and Morrell were taken aboard the prison ship *Gordon* and placed with the other captives. Cochrane had detected that Shields was slightly deaf. There could be no whispered talk between the prisoners, and it might be valuable to overhear their conversation.

Suspecting this intention, the Americans saw a chance to be of some oblique use to their cause. Shields lustily proclaimed: "These British are due for a bloody big surprise. With the twenty thousand troops he now has, plus the reinforcements on the way, Jackson will make mincemeat out of any troops this fleet can land."

It was one of many false reports fed to the British at this time. Some days later, when Morrell and Shields were invited to dine with Admiral Cochrane and General Keane aboard the *Tonnant,* both gladly discussed the strength of the American defenses. Jackson, they declared, was a military genius equal if not superior to Wellington.

Whether or not the doughty Cochrane was taken in by this, the more apprehensive General Keane was troubled. The lakes were cleared, but precious time had been lost to the betraying winds and the obstinacy of the gunboats. He would take New Orleans, no doubt about that. A well-disciplined, courageous army could not lose. But he must tread softly, very softly, until he knew what lay ahead. His first job was to find a landing spot, a bridgehead for the troops. And he must be careful not to place them in a trap. The Yankees were tricky, very tricky. God alone knew what preparations they were making now.

Twelve hundred miles away in snowbound New England the Hartford *Courant,* in its thirtieth year of publication, displayed the provocative one-word headlines, SEDITION! and SECESSION!

The news itself concerned the opening on December 15 of a convention of New England delegates to bring to an end "Mr. Madison's War." even if it meant secession from the Union. The movement marked a peak of dissension which had been festering throughout the war, alienating the New England states, especially, from Washington. Five-star, five-stripe flags were locally displayed. British victories abroad were celebrated. In one instance an attempt was made to free English captives from American prison ships.

The voices of dissent were loud and clear and couched in strong-sounding but elusive words. Boston's George Cabot, a distinguished financier, called the war "absolutely unjust" and "morally wrong." John Lowell, looking beyond New England interests, proposed a new Union of the thirteen states, ignoring much of the South and West. It was, he declared, "the last hope of our country." Great Britain naturally welcomed and approved these sentiments, the London *Times* observing: "New England allied with Old England would form a dignified and manly union well deserving the name of Peace."

Massachusetts was the center of this movement of dissent, which divided the country as never before or since. The *Boston Gazette* gave the United States six months to survive: "If James Madison is not out of office [by July 4, 1815] a new form of government will be in operation in the Eastern section of the Union." The *Columbian Centinel,* Boston's leading Federalist Journal, urged the Hartford Convention to ignore moribund commitments to the Constitution, adding: "The bond of union is already broken by you, Mr. Madison."

New Orleans, too remote for news of the convention, took little heed of this turmoil in the East. Andrew Jackson had summed up his opinion of Peace Party advocates and anti-war Federalists in a single sentence: "I would hang them all." But the East was not unconscious of the trembling fate of New Orleans. It was at this point that Senator Pickering gave voice to his dire and widely-circulated prophecy that the Union would fall asunder as soon as the British possessed New Orleans—with no qualifying thought that they might fail in this endeavor.

Engaged in fighting for its life, New Orleans never considered that its survival predicated the survival of the Union. It was not even fighting for the Union; it was fighting for its own salvation. And in contrast to the division that now threatened to dismember the United States, it was for once united in a common cause. Wrote Bernard de Marigny in his journal:

> On all sides could be heard the cry "To Arms!" The whole population arose *en masse*. It would be impossible for any detractor to mention one Louisianian, one Creole, or even a naturalized French citizen, who at the sign of danger abandoned the country or refused to serve in combat.

In spite of Louisiana's early apathy, New Orleans and New England were now separated by much more than distance.

# 9. *"Aux Armes, Citoyens!"*

> I expect at this moment that most of the large sea-port towns of America are laid in ashes, that we are in possession of New Orleans, and have com-command of all the rivers of the Mississippi Valley and the lakes, and that the Americans are now little better than prisoners in their own country.

So wrote Lord Castlereagh, British Foreign Secretary, in December 1814 on his way to the Vienna Congress, which was trying to establish peace in Europe. New Orleans was not in ashes and the Mississippi Valley was precariously free. But the guns had sounded at the gates. They had echoed over the cane fields and the Crescent City on the river and had been heard by Andrew Jackson on the accurately-named "Deception Point," or Chef Menteur, as he was reconnoitering the point's defenses.

A courier from Patterson brought word to Jackson of the outcome of the battle on the lake. It was dark news, but certainly not unexpected. The worst of it was that, as Jackson later reported to Monroe, he and the Commodore had lost their "eyes" on Lake Borgne. Hereafter they would have no way of keeping track of the enemy's maneuvers, no further warning of his preparations to attack.

Jackson quickly rode back to Royal Street, and for the next thirty-six hours, reclining on a couch and sipping brandy to keep going, he dictated rapid-fire requisitions to his aides. He needed guns. He needed powder and ammunition. Above all he needed troops, to raise the meager forces in the city to something resembling an army with at least a fighting chance. And he needed officers around him he could count on. Leaders with battle experience. Men like Coffee and Carroll with their gritty Tennesseans.

John Coffee was encamped near Baton Rouge. Jackson flashed the word to him, "You must not sleep until you reach me." (Adjutant-general Robert Butler, who transcribed the message, added the foot-note: "To you it is deemed unnecessary to say—hasten to the field of danger.") William Carroll, with three thousand raw recruits, was already on his way. He had left Tennessee by boat two months before, in spite of instructions to bring his troops as speedily as possible by land. Hurry! the General urged him. "Your presence and your brave companions in arms are much needed here. Our lakes are open to the enemy. I am prepared to die in the last ditch before he shall reach the city."

Similar urgent messages went to Hind's Mississippi Dragoons and to Major General John Thomas with his 2300 Kentucky militiamen, since the War Department had permitted Jackson to draw upon that state for reinforcements. He needed everything he could get now to strengthen his estimated force of some two thousand generally untested troops.

Jackson was enough of a strategist to maintain a broad view of the threatened invasion. He had, as he wrote to James Winchester at Mobile, "a large coast to guard," and he instructed the Brigadier General to defend his post "at every hazard." Similar do-or-die commands were dispatched to Major Walter Overton at Fort St. Philip on the lower Mississippi and to Captain Newman at Fort St. John, who was ordered "to defend his post to the last extremity." Secretary of War Monroe in Washington could probably do little for him, but Jackson nevertheless reported his precarious position. "We have no arms here. Will the Government order a supply? If it will, let it be speedily. Without arms, a defense cannot be made."

It was an almost futile appeal that he had made before. As Major Latour wrote somewhile later:

During the summer . . . General Jackson had made a requisition of a quantity of arms, ammunition, heavy cannon, balls, bombs, etc. to be sent to New Orleans; but such was the fatality that appeared to be attached to all the measures adopted for our defence, that it was not till the middle of January, 1815, that a very small portion of what had been ordered, arrived at New Orleans.

That small portion would have been invaluable now — five thousand muskets, plus tents and ammunition, which a Pittsburgh contractor had undertaken to deliver to New Orleans. He had left in early November and should have arrived by now. But to save money, the contractor had been allowed to proceed, with other marketable merchandise, by the Ohio and Mississippi rivers, with permission to trade with the riverside cities on the way.

The War Department in Washington, even with Monroe replacing Armstrong as its secretary, had done little to relieve the pressure on New Orleans. The Government, strapped by lack of credit, had sent few supplies, and what it sent was irrelevant to the city's needs. "Thus," wrote Vincent Nolte, keeping his finger on the pulse of things, "they had sent molasses from Boston by land and down the Western rivers to New Orleans, apparently entirely forgetting that Boston and the Northeastern States procured that very article by sea from New Orleans."

With Patterson and Latour, Jackson again studied the engineer's maps of the surrounding country, in the light of the enemy's confirmed position on Lake Borgne. He concentrated on three possible approaches that the British might attempt. One might be via Chef Menteur and the Gentilly Plain, though Latour considered this unlikely; the plain was narrow, pressed between marshes on either side and could be easily defended.

Another route might be by way of Lake Pontchartrain, descending on the city from the north. But that meant squeezing through the tight pass of The Rigolets under the guns of Fort de Petites Coquilles, then forcing an entrance past Fort St. John to the Carondelet canal. Again, the invasionary force would be constricted and precariously vulnerable.

The remaining and most likely route would be via one of the several bayous and their many branches leading from Lake Borgne to the plantations several miles below New Orleans. But obstruction of these bayous had been assigned to reliable officers, Colonel de la Ronde and

General Villeré, and by now the bayous should be impassable. Nevertheless, Jackson would keep a watchful eye in this direction.

If the General maintained his outward calm throughout this crisis, New Orleans' morale was badly shaken. With no news to go by beyond the British conquest of the lakes, the city was in a state of panic. Significantly, before word of the gunboat rout had been received, Jackson himself had posted a warning to the citizens not likely to promote calm and confidence. Rumors had circulated that the purpose of the British invasion was to restore Louisiana to England's ally, Spain, an aim not altogether odious to many Creole residents. Similar reports and even evidence of treason among Spanish Creoles had reached the General's ears. He issued a proclamation to the citizens which read in part:

> Believe not such incredible tales — your government is at peace with Spain — it is the vital enemy of your country, the common enemy of mankind . . . that threatens you, and has sent his hirelings amongst you with this false report, to put you off your guard, that you may fall an easy prey to him. Then look to your liberties, your property, the chastity of your wives and daughters; take a retrospect of the conduct of the British army at Hampton and other places where it has entered our country, and every bosom which glows with patriotism and virtue will be inspired with indignation, and pant for the hour when we shall meet and revenge these outrages against the laws of civilization and humanity.

He added a grim note of warning to any not readily subscribing to this sentiment.

> The rules and articles of war annex the punishment of death to any person holding secret correspondence with the enemy, creating false alarm, or supplying him with provisions; and the general announces his unalterable determination rigidly to execute the martial law in all cases which may come within his province . . . those who are not for us are against us, and will be dealt with accordingly.

The next day, December 15, according to Major Howell Tatum, Claiborne called on Jackson with charges that the Legislature, ever a bone of contention with the Governor, was in a "state of rottenness," declaring in substance that a large proportion of that body, in his opinion, as well as a great number of the inhabitants would change with the current of events, whatever they might now pretend, and that many of them could easily be prevailed on to become vehicles of intelligence to the Enemy.

On Jackson's recommendation Claiborne went before the Legislature, ostensibly to report on the outcome of the gunboat battle which had placed the city and the state in dire peril. He requested, and got, measures suspending all financial transactions during the period of the crisis; there would be no sales of property or slaves, no forced collections of interests and debts, no civil suits or actions in the courts. Then he got to the gist of his address.

> The moment is certainly inauspicious for that cool and mature deliberation which is essential to the formation of laws. Permit me, therefore, to suggest the propriety of adjourning the two Houses for fifteen or twenty days.

As Claiborne and Jackson must have expected, the move was vigorously opposed. Philip Louaillier, for one, asserted that such an abdication of responsibility would further endanger the city. It was in just such critical times as these that the Legislature should remain alert — for any unforeseen developments or "accidents" that might require instant action by the legislative body.

Louaillier took a swipe at Claiborne, declaring that the time for "issuing proclamations has passed." Whereupon Jean Blanque arose to issue a proclamation to New Orleans citizens:

> *Aux armes, Citoyens!* Your country is in danger! It expects of you the greatest efforts to repulse the bold enemy who threatens to penetrate, in a few days, to the very hearthstones of your homes. . . . Rush to arms, fellow citizens! Enlist promptly under the banner of General Jackson. . . . We must conquer or be trampled under the feet of a cruel and implacable enemy. . . .

Motions were passed to raise and allocate sixteen thousand dollars to purchase supplies for the hard-pressed militia. Citizens were asked to provide blankets and clothing. Any kinds of guns in private possession were requisitioned for the troops. A rather singular motion was passed to award a stand of regimental colors to Colonel Alexandre Declouet of the Baton Rouge militia — the only such award to any officer. Why Declouet? ("A good man," according to Bernard de

Marigny, "but lacking in intelligence.") He was popular, true, but subsequent events would not reveal him as a man of shining armor.

With his gunboats lost, Patterson desperately needed a crew to man the *Louisiana* and any other vessels he could commandeer. There were seamen of all nationalities now stranded on the waterfront, along with roustabouts and other able-bodied men made idle by the enemy blockade. He appealed to Jackson for authority to impress them in his navy. Jackson endorsed the idea and suggested to Claiborne that he ask the Legislature to suspend the writ of habeas corpus for the length of this emergency.

Ever ready to renew his battle with the Legislature, Claiborne did so. The request was referred to Philip Louaillier, Chairman of the Ways and Means Committee. Supported by Judge Dominic Hall, Louaillier asserted that only the Congress could take such action, and he would not recommend they do so.

But Louaillier projected an alternative. He persuaded the Legislature to authorize a bounty of twenty-four dollars for all volunteering for three months' service in the navy. Thirty thousand dollars was assigned to Patterson to implement this offer. Jackson, who would have preferred more forceful measures, advised Patterson to accept the money. He would take care of the Legislature in good time. As a result, some eighty seamen were added to the naval force — all that responded to the bonus bait — and the *Louisiana* at last was fully armed and manned.

No halfway measures were acceptable to Jackson now. The following day, December 16, he took the drastic step he had been contemplating since the Legislature turned down Claiborne's counsel to adjourn. He placed New Orleans under martial law. The following military regulations were imposed upon the Crescent City:

1. Every individual entering the city shall report himself to the Adjutant-General's office, and on failure shall be arrested and held for examination.

2. None shall be permitted to leave the city, or Bayou St. John, without a passport from the General or his staff.

3. No vessel, boat or other craft shall leave the city or Bayou St. John without such passport, or that of the Commodore.

4. The lamps of the city shall be extinguished at nine o'clock, after which every person found in the streets, or out of his usual place of residence,

without a pass or the countersign, shall be apprehended as a spy and held for examination.

Considering the dominant Latin temperament, it is not surprising that this move was bitterly resented. In the Legislature, Philip Louaillier spoke out in protest of the action, and again he was supported by Judge Dominic Hall, who was becoming more and more critical of Andrew Jackson. Both men felt that the imposition of martial law was a violation of civil rights.

They were not alone in their resentment. Many conservatively-minded Creoles felt that the Tennessee General was being dictatorial and arbitrary. There was a whispered rumor that, if forced to retreat, he would adopt the "Russian" scorched-earth policy and destroy the city rather than let it fall into enemy hands. Was destruction preferable to peaceful surrender? Not to many property owners. Nor to the bankers. Nor to merchants with warehouses filled with merchandise, nor to planters whose fields and manors and sugar houses represented years of labor and investment.

Yet the over-all result of the decree was to restore sanity and confidence, and even a degree of calm, to New Orleans. A decision had been made. The period of doubt was over. There was now a strong hand guiding the city's destiny.

"General Jackson had electrified all hearts," wrote Lacarrière Latour. "All were sensible to the approaching danger, but they waited its presence undismayed. It was known that the enemy was on our coast, within a few hours sail of the city, with a presumed force of between nine and ten thousand men; whilst all the forces we had yet to oppose him amounted to no more than a thousand regulars, and from four to five thousand militia."

Latour was optimistic in his estimates. Jackson had less than a third as many troops at his disposal. But the citizens were ready and eager to believe an even larger figure—up to fifteen thousand, if given an erroneous report to that effect. They believed because they wanted to believe. The swarms of men in uniform passing to and fro, the constant drilling, the trumpet calls and marching bands were all the substantiation that they needed.

Latour took note of the new atmosphere that pervaded New Orleans, the sudden confidence and optimism and dedication:

The citizens were preparing for battle as cheerfully as if it had been a party of pleasure, each in his vernacular tongue singing songs of victory. The streets resounded with "Yankee Doodle," the "Marseillaise," the "Chant du Depart" and other martial airs, while those who had been long unaccustomed to military duty were furbishing their arms and accoutrements. Beauty applauded valor, and promised with her smiles to reward the toils of the brave. Though inhabiting an open town, not above ten leagues from the enemy, and never till now exposed to war's alarms, the fair sex of New Orleans were animated with the ardour of their defenders, and with cheerful serenity at the sound of the drum presented themselves at the windows and balconies, to applaud the troops going through their evolutions, and to encourage their husbands, sons, fathers, and brothers to protect them from the insults of our ferocious enemies, and prevent a repetition of the horrors of Hampton.

Jackson began scraping the bottom of the barrel in his quest for troops. He requested and obtained the release of military prisoners in the city, on their promise to bear arms against the British.

What then, was a natural query, of the Baratarians — those jailed in the Cabildo and the others still in hiding? Livingston had been doing some spadework in his clients' behalf, out of both patriotic and professional considerations. Vincent Nolte noted that "Jackson was too keen not to see through Livingston's object at once; he found him a man who was not troubled by any scruples of conscience. Moreover, good fighting men were wanted, and Livingston represented the advantages that were to be anticipated from the cooperation of these men, from their influence with the lower classes of the French population, from their intrepidity, and their skill in handling the heavier descriptions of artillery."

Bernard de Marigny, knowing that Jackson's mind was hard to change, approached the matter more obliquely. He and his Defense Committee called on Judge Hall in an attempt to circumvent Jackson's opposition to the pirates, in a way which might save the General's face. Hall assured them, "I am General under these circumstances." He suggested that they entreat the Legislature to suspend all charges against the buccaneers.

De Marigny approached his friend Magloire Guichard, Speaker of the House, and Fulwar Skipwith, President of the Senate, who in turn sponsored a legislative resolution to grant amnesty to "the privateers lately resorting to Barataria who might be deterred from offering their services for fear of persecution." The motion passed almost unanimously.

Free to walk the streets again, Jean Laffite persuaded Jean Blanque to take him to the General. Precisely where the interview took place is uncertain. It would not do for Laffite to be seen at Jackson's quarters. Legend assigns the meeting to the Absinthe House at Bienville and Bourbon streets, which was not yet, however, a public café. Or it might have been the Exchange Café on the corner of Chartres and St. Louis streets. Who else was present is also unrecorded. But Latour, who professed to be everywhere at this time and most likely was, provides a succinct but creditable record of the interview.

> Mr. Laffite solicited for himself and for all the Baratarians, the honour of serving under our banners, that they might have an opportunity of proving that if they had infringed the revenue laws, yet none were more ready than they to defend the country and combat its enemies.
>
> Persuaded that the assistance of these men could not fail of being very useful, the General accepted their offer.

The next morning, prompted by Jackson, Claiborne issued a proclamation to the "Barratariòrs," his own suggestive title for them, to the effect that all who enlisted in Jackson's ranks would be welcomed and that those whose subsequent services met with the General's approval would be granted "a Free and Full pardon."

Jackson had gained more than a tough and militant band of skilled artillerists. Laffite was able to promise him five hundred muskets and 7500 badly needed flints, along with other arms and ammunition which Patterson's raiders had overlooked. The General wasted no time in authorizing the pirates to form their own artillery units, under their chosen commanders, to be stationed at whatever points the current strategy required. Though granted no official titles, Pierre and Jean Laffite remained thereafter close to Jackson, who could use their knowledge of the terrain and of secret approaches to New Orleans, as well as their potential skill as guides and scouts.

Among Jackson's scouts in his campaign against the Creeks had been Pierre Jugeat, son of a Creole trader and a half-breed Choctaw woman. Though well educated and of gentlemanly presence, Jugeat had spent his life by choice among the Indians and spoke their various dialects.

With Jackson's approval he organized a company of Choctaws, induced by army pay, to defend the wilderness approaches to the city. Their numbers were small, from fifty to sixty, but Jugeat felt that one lone Indian was worth a dozen white men in the swamps.

Came Sunday, that "Last Gay Sunday" of December 18 when Jackson, with an eye for showmanship as a booster of morale, ordered a full-dress review of the troops in the Place d'Armes. Some were militia he had reviewed on his arrival, but their numbers had been more than doubled by volunteers swarming in from the outlying country and the Mississippi Territory.

There were few able-bodied in the city who were not now enlisted in one branch of the service or another. Even the reluctant merchant Vincent Nolte, finding his situation "critical," had signed up with Roche's Carabiniers. He felt himself exempted from military duty, owing to a fall from a horse which had partially crippled an arm. He had wanted to remain on the sidelines. "But, as the suspicion of entertaining a secret preference for the English and English interests rested on me, I could not have done so without incurring malicious remarks and, very probably, persecution."

Such additions to the ranks relieved the repetitiousness of much of this review, as the troops again paraded through the square. First in order, two below-quota regiments of Louisiana militia "variously dressed and equipped but defiant," led by their honorary commander, W. C. C. Claiborne, proudly adorned in "an extremely high, stiff collar, heavy gold braid epaulets, a ribbon across his chest sporting a badge with a pelican on it, and a ruffled neckpiece of immaculately white linen."

Following were Major Plauché's Battalion of Orleans Volunteers and five companies — Roche's Carabiniers, St. Gême's Dragoons, Hudri's Francs, Guibert's Chasseurs, and White's Louisiana Blues accompanied by a marching band. Each wore the proverbial badge of the Creole soldier, a neat bouquet of flowers pinned to the shoulder, a gift from mother, wife or sweetheart.

Next, and receiving a remarkable ovation from the crowd, came Major Lacoste's Battalion of Free Men of Color. Dressed in motley uniforms they nevertheless looked stalwart and determined, proud of their position in the ranks. Jackson noted them approvingly; he could use more such men, regardless of some prejudice against them.

Saved for last were John Beale's freshly-organized Volunteer Rifles, most of them sons of distinguished Creole families. They were only thirty in number but sharpshooters all, with the reputed ability to shoot the eye out of a squirrel at a hundred paces. As they marched by in blue hunting shirts and wide-brimmed ebony-black hats, the crowd thundered its approval, the women waving their dotted linen handkerchiefs from balconies and windows.

For the record, and in fairness, one perhaps should note the comment of Alexander Walker in recording the event. "Here assembled the scant force which New Orleans could contribute for its defense out of its small and mixed population. . . . These troops were poorly armed — many of them having only ordinary fowling-pieces, and many being without flints."

But not as New Orleans saw them! The volunteer companies especially were their native sons, their very own. Look at those glittering uniforms! Hark to those pulsing drums and bands! Notice how smartly and with what pride the men performed their drilling! Observe the General's smile as he salutes them! In truth, the General's smile may well have come from the knowledge that this was only a token army, a fraction of the forces he would have when the Tennesseans and Kentuckians arrived.

When the troops had come to parade rest, flanking the square, Jackson presented his three prepared addresses. They were handed to Livingston to read in French, in his vibrant voice and flawless diction. The first was directed to the Louisiana Militia. It hailed "the noble ardour that has animated you in the hour of danger" and the unity of spirit that had overcome racial prejudices, surmounted the barriers of language and the differences in nationalities.

It appealed separately to each of the major nationalities present, calling on Americans to remember that they, the enemy, "are the oppressors of your infant political existence . . . the men your fathers conquered. . . ."; calling on Frenchmen to remember that "they are the English, the hereditary, the eternal enemies of your ancient country, the invaders of that you have adopted, who are your foes." And, "Spaniards! remember the conduct of your allies at St. Sebastian, and recently at Pensacola, and rejoice that you have an opportunity of avenging the brutal injuries inflicted by men who dishonor the human race."

To the Battalion of Orleans Volunteers the General addressed his appreciation of their increased numbers in the face of peril. "This is true love of country!" He praised their evident skill and discipline, and the high character of their officers. Then, acknowledging their presence for the first time in his ranks, and no doubt aware of the lingering prejudices of the Creoles, he turned his attention to the Men of Color.

*Soldiers!* From the shore of Mobile I collected you to arms; I invited you to share in the perils and to divide the glory of your white countrymen. I expected much from you for I was not misinformed of those qualities which must render you so formidable to an invading foe. I knew that you would endure hunger and thirst and all the hardships of war. I knew that you loved the land of your nativity, and that, like ourselves, you had to defend all that is most dear to man; but you surpass my hopes. I have found in you, united to those qualities, the noble enthusiasm which impels great deeds.

*Soldiers!* The President of the United States shall be informed of your conduct on the present occasion, and the voice of the Representatives of the American Nation shall applaud your valor, as your General now praises your ardor. The enemy is near; his sails cover the lakes; but the brave are united; and if he finds us contending among ourselves, it will be for the prize of valor, and fame its noblest reward.

The troops dispersed, some repairing to their homes for a last reunion with their families, others to the cafés and bordellos for an hour's fleeting pleasure, a brief interval of wine and roses before Armageddon broke. In Royal Street, Jackson plunged into a period of feverish anticipation. New Orleans was now an armed camp, and he would see that it remained that way — armed to the teeth with every available weapon, every able-bodied man.

A general order went out to "all officers commanding detachments, outposts, and pickets, on the approach of the enemy, to remove out of his reach every kind of stock, horses, provisions, etc., oppose the invaders at every point; harass them by all possible means." The veteran guards and the fire brigade were instructed to occupy the barracks, hospitals and other posts as soon as the defending troops should be engaged. Captain Thomas Butler, elder brother of the adjutant-general, would be in charge of the policing of the city.

Joseph Savary, a colored refugee from Santo Domingo, proposed raising another regiment of black militia from among his fellow countrymen. This time there was no hesitancy or objection. By all means! Jackson could use all the free colored he could get, even though Savary was suspected of having once been one of the Baratarian outlaws. The regiment was formed and put under the over-all command of Colonel Fortier, to serve beside the colored troops of Major Daquin and Pierre Lacoste.

Jackson gave Savary the rank of colonel. But at this confused point, Savary was also referred to as major and captain. With a dearth of standard uniforms and insignia, many officers found themselves saluted by whatever title their popularity, or the inclination of their troops, suggested.

The once-reluctant militia was also growing, as volunteers poured in from the outlying districts. A third regiment was mobilized and assigned to Colonel de la Ronde. A fourth, still being assembled in Acadia, would go to General Jacques Villeré. Several new volunteer cavalry units were formed, a type of service appealing to frontier Americans. Among them were Captain Peter Ogden's Company of Orleans Dragoons and Llewellyn Griffith's Company of Feliciana Mounted Riflemen. The state's Adjutant General took a dim view of some of these sports-minded cavalry, describing them as "well mounted, handsomely dressed but deficient in discipline." Perhaps so — but they promised mobility, especially in reconnaissance, to troops otherwise rooted in the damp Louisiana soil.

Bit by bit, like some sprawling protoplasmic body propagating cell by cell, the somewhat makeshift army grew. It was hard to keep track, precisely, of its numbers. The volunteer troops were especially bothersome in this respect, considering themselves independent of ordinary regulations, free to act on whim and preference. When Claiborne undertook to supply General Jackson with a dossier of their numbers, he complained it was nearly impossible to do so. They switched too fast from company to company and commander to commander.

"Indeed the practice of leaving one company to join another," the Governor asserted, "has of late become so common that to prevent the total destruction of some Corps and much derangement to others, I have deemed it proper to forbid it in General Militia orders."

Jackson ignored the issue. He was little concerned about propriety. He wanted men on the line, equipped to fight, regardless of what unit they belonged to. The only thing he would not tolerate was desertion or neglect of duty. He was ready to shoot a man for that, as he had threatened to do in his wilderness campaigns against the Creeks.

Among Jackson's papers, marked *Private* and dated December 22, appears the following note with Claiborne's signature:

> Sir: *The times perceive no Union,* nor is there anything I more desire than to maintain with you the most friendly understanding, and a cooperation zealous and cordial. With this Object in view, I request of you a private Interview on this Day, at such hour as may suit your convenience.

Whatever was on Claiborne's mind — perhaps no more than a friendly wish to heal the breach — this is the first admission in writing of the growing discord between the Governor and General Jackson. There is no record that Jackson formally acknowledged it or submitted to the interview. In fact his next letter to Claiborne, written only two days later, waspishly takes the Governor to task for failure to place two small pieces of field artillery, "as was my perticular [*sic*] direction," on the Chef Menteur Road.

That third week in December brought fresh hope, new optimism to the stricken city. After a forced march of 135 miles in three days, John Coffee arrived with his picked advance of eight hundred mounted Tennesseans. The rest of his force was close on his heels and would raise the number to over 1200 men. They encamped on the Avart plantation four miles above New Orleans.

His spirits lifted, the commander-in-chief rode out to greet the battle-hardened frontier general. They met with all the sentiment of old companions. Perhaps even a tear could be detected in the hawk-like eye of Jackson as he clasped his comrade's hand. The tall, broad-shouldered Coffee, "gentle in manner, but brave and intelligent," meant a great deal to the commanding general — a man after his own heart, one above all he needed in this crisis.

The forty-three year old Coffee was not only a kinsman, having married Rachel Jackson's niece, but he had twice served under Jackson with distinction. His was the decisive action that routed the Creeks at the Battle of Horseshoe Bend in March of 1814. Eight months later, after a hard-pressed march of 470 miles in eighteen days, he had, by the sheer weight of numbers, forced the surrender of Pensacola.

Now they rode together to Jackson's quarters in Royal Street, watched from the balcony of his home by Governor Claiborne, who took a dim view of the husky protégé so highly favored by the General. Here was another Johnny-come-lately to stand between himself and Jackson. New Orleans itself was torn between admiration and alarm at the sight of this backwoods army from the north. In truth, wrote Alexander Walker:

> Their appearance was not very military. In their woolen hunting shirts and copperas dyed pantaloons; with slouched hats made from the skins of raccoons or foxes; with belts of untanned deer-skin in which were stuck their hunting knives and tomahawks—with their long unkempt hair and unshorn faces. . . . But [they] were admirable soldiers, remarkable for endurance and possessing that admirable quality in soldiers of being able to take care of themselves.

Of Coffee himself, Walker noted with unqualified approval, "their gallant leader, a man of noble aspect, tall and herculean in appearance, mounted upon a fine Tennessee thoroughbred, was stately and impressive." As for the Tennesseans with their tomahawks and hunting knives, well, their battle cry was a familiar one: "War to the knife, and knife to the hilt."

Coffee's arrival was not the only heartening event. Hard on his heels came Major General William Carroll with three thousand Tennessee militiamen. Vincent Nolte, witnessing their arrival, reported: "These men carried nothing but their Cartouch-boxes and powder-horns— their bullets were usually in their pantaloons pockets—they had no idea whatever of military order and discipline; they paid attention only to the more important part of their calling, which, according to their notions, was quietly to pick out their man, fix him in their aim, and *bring him down*."

As directed by Jackson, Carroll's troops also encamped on Avart's plantation and were riotously welcomed by their fellow Tennesseans. But what had delayed them? Both Governor Blount and General Jackson had instructed Carroll to hasten by land to New Orleans. But the twenty-six-year-old Carroll, tough and independent, had had other ideas. His volunteers were raw and untrained. His arms and ammunition had been damaged by rain. He needed time to correct these deficiencies.

He hired the necessary flatboats, and while half his troops poled and rowed, the other half were rigorously drilled and put through their maneuvers on the shallow decks. To the inhabitants of the river banks this floating show of marching men and beating drums was fascinating entertainment. "As fine looking men as ever we saw," remarked one observer, noting that they were well armed with muskets and rifles (provided, it so happened, at their own expense).

The trip had taken five long weeks, but on greeting him Jackson made no mention of Carroll's tardiness. That the time had been well used was evident. The troops looked spirited and disciplined. And the voyage had brought an unexpected benefit. The barges had overtaken a keelboat carrying 1100 muskets and had taken them aboard. They were part of the dilatory shipment that had left from Pittsburgh. Carroll had found blacksmiths among his troops who had put the guns in order and manufactured cartridges to fit them. As to his tardiness, he had tried to keep Jackson informed of his progress, but the messen ˙rs had been delayed by storms and flooding.

Nor were these all the reinforcements to arrive. That same day, December 22, Major Thomas Hind galloped into the city with his blue-coated Dragoons, sabers rattling from their white belts, representing the pick of aristocratic young bloods from the Mississippi Territory. With the detachment was Captain Jebediah Smith's Feliciana Troop of Horse.

Among these cavalry, tall in the saddle, lanky, arrogant and carelessly groomed, Jackson spied Reuben Kemper. He knew Kemper's reputation, and his presence was a welcome one. Reuben was one of seven sons of a Virginia minister who had moved into the Mississippi Territory when the Spaniards held the borders of Louisiana. A vigorous fighter for freedom, Kemper had made life miserable for the Spanish authorities, engineering raids on Mobile and the Texas area of Mexico, suffering capture and torture, and retaliating with some violent measures of revenge. A born guerrilla fighter, independent and reckless of human life, his own included, he was the sort of warrior Jackson needed and admired.

All that was missing now, which he could reasonably hope for, were the Kentucky militia, estimated at roughly 2300 men under Major General Thomas. Supposedly, they were somewhere in the wilderness near Natchez, but nothing had been heard from them. There was no time, however, to worry about the missing. Jackson had lightly told Coffee that he expected to "have a fandango" with the British during the Christmas holidays. Christmas was three days away. He would make do with what he had.

That evening, with his aides at Royal Street, Jackson assembled his principal commanders — Coffee and Carroll, Patterson, Hind and Ross — for what was to be a final briefing. Latour's well-studied maps were once again spread out for scrutiny. Every point of possible attack, every seeming hole in the defenses, must be made secure.

The Mississippi River, a forbidding approach because of its length and tortuous course, was well protected. Patterson's remaining gunboat had been stationed at Fort St. Philip, and the fort itself was adequately garrisoned by U.S. Regulars under Major Walter Overton. On the river below New Orleans rode the *Carolina* and *Louisiana,* their magazines loaded with grapeshot, ball, and powder — much of it provided by the Baratarians.

Between these two points on the river, at the English Turn, were stationed General David Morgan with Colonel Alexandre Declouet and five hundred troops of the Louisiana militia. They were to guard both the Turn itself and the Bayou Terre aux Boeufs leading westward from Lake Borgne. Morgan, a man of inflated self-importance, and Declouet, obsessed with imaginary fears, were uninspiring leaders, and their green militiamen might well grow restless under their command. It was a chance one had to take with fledgling troops.

The lakes and riverways of Barataria were being watched by Major Michael Reynolds posted at Grande Terre, aided by handpicked members of the "hellish banditti" now enrolled as allies. Jackson sent Jean Laffite to make sure all was well. In view of Laffite's past reputation, he gave him a covering letter for Reynolds:

Mr. Jean Laffite has offered me his services to go down and give you every information in his power. You will therefore please to afford him the necessary protection from Injury and Insult and when you have derived the information you wish, furnish him with your passport for his return, dismissing him as soon as possible as I shall want him here.

The Rigolets leading to Lake Pontchartrain were guarded by Fort de Petites Coquilles. It was a flimsy structure, not even completely finished; but beyond it lay Fort St. John, well-garrisoned by U.S. Regulars under Major Hughes, while the Bayou St. John was commanded by batteries manned by Dominique You and Renato Beluché and their buccaneer artillerists.

On the Plain of Gentilly leading to the Chef Menteur, which Jackson still considered a likely point of attack, though Major Latour continued to belittle it, the General stationed Lacoste's Free Colored—a measure of his confidence in the black brigade. Also on Gentilly he posted Hind's Dragoons, whose mobility could keep him constantly informed of what developed in this quarter.

So much for the city's many-mouthed perimeter. The bulk and muscle of his army, Coffee's and Carroll's Tennesseans, Ross's two regiments of Regulars and Plauché's Uniformed Volunteers, along with much of the militia, he would keep beside him at New Orleans—ready to be summoned instantly in an emergency.

Finally, Jackson let his fingers trace the concourse of the Bayou Bienvenu, following its several branches leading to the cane plantations along the river. This obvious invasion route must be made secure. He had, of course, ordered the bayous blocked with fallen trees and other obstacles. To make doubly sure, he directed young Gabriel Villeré, the general's son, to take a corps of militia to the bayou's mouth and establish a picket at its junction with Lake Borgne.

Promptly Major Villeré sent a dozen militiamen to the fishing village at the mouth of Bayou Bienvenu. Aside from a few stray dogs, they found the village practically empty. An ailing Spaniard was sleeping in one of the huts. They let him be, and chose one of the larger dwellings for their quarters. After reconnoitering the lake and seeing nobody abroad, they posted a picket on the shore and settled down for a long and boring vigil. Nothing was going to happen here.

That night the lights burned late in New Orleans. In their homes, in the cafés and coffeehouses, the people had much to talk about, and they talked with voices hushed. A proclamation had circulated through the city, distributed by a British spy. It read, in both French and Spanish, "Louisianians! Remain quiet in your houses. *Your slaves shall be preserved to you,* and your property respected. We make war only against Americans." It was signed by Admiral Cochrane and Major General Keane.

There was no doubt but that the enemy was at the gates. Was Jackson ready for them? How many troops did he have—ten, fifteen, twenty thousand? Exaggeration, optimistically repeated, helped ease the tension. But in the convent the black-cowled Ursuline nuns knelt on the cold floor of their chapel to pray to Our Lady of Prompt Succour for the salvation of their city.

At dawn on the morning of December 23, Pierre Denis de la Ronde rode with his groom from the stables of Versailles and cantered across the stubbled cane fields to inspect his property. War or no war, Versailles could not be permitted to run down; he had kept the slaves busy with make-work, strengthening the levee, clearing the canals. At the point where the Bayou Mazant joined the Bayou Bienvenu, he scanned the marshes to the east. Even from this slight elevation he could see to the far edge of Lake Borgne. He noted "several sail of vessel" visible above the trees.

It might mean nothing, but he took no chances. He sent the groom galloping back to Jackson's quarters to report the sighting of vessels on the lake. It suggested that the enemy might be striking towards the English Turn and the Bayou Terre aux Boeufs. The only other possibility was an attempted landing near one of the plantations. But Villeré's pickets were keeping watch at the Bayou Bienvenu, and Colonel de la Ronde himself would have ample warning if anyone dared set foot on his estate.

Rising early that morning, Jackson had already received a message from the cavalry at Chef Menteur. Two Americans, a white man and a Negro, had landed from a pirogue and reported a vast enemy armada stationed on the lake, with 350 barges being filled with troops. Three hundred and fifty barges! Ridiculous! The men were suspected of being spies engaged in spreading false alarm.

But de la Ronde's message regarding the threat to the Bayou Terre aux Boeufs could be accepted as reliable. Jackson dispatched Lacarrière Latour to reconnoiter and check on de la Ronde's report. Then, seizing a moment of calm, he composed a letter to the family in Nashville. Previously, in a note to Rachel, he had asked her to join him in New Orleans—"your presence is worth several regiments to me." Later he advised against her coming; the city was in jeopardy. Now, however, he reported that since the capture of the gunboats, "the British have made no movement of importance."

He added a footnote to the letter, "All's well."

At that moment the first British soldier to trespass on this corner of America in fifty years, set foot on Louisiana soil.

# 10.   Lion at the Gates

By mid-December the last of the wild geese had traveled south across Lake Borgne. Where their arrowhead formations and nostalgic bugle calls had filled the air, there were only gray clouds covering the sky, with here and there a slice of sunlight shining through. Rain was almost certain before nightfall, followed by freezing temperatures and a chilling frost at dawn. A bleak, forbidding seascape in the dead of winter.

Admiral Cochrane's order to "Clear the lakes!" had been only a first step in his master plan to invade Louisiana. New Orleans had always been his goal. As the crow flies, he was within easy striking distance. But the crow flew over shallow, treacherous waters, all but impassable marshlands and dense cypress forests. Somewhere, preferably at the west end of the lake below New Orleans, he must find an acceptable place to put the troops ashore and establish a solid bridgehead. After that, if the troops moved forward quickly, the taking of New Orleans should be easy.

He and General Keane were not without some knowledge of the region. They had charts — possibly those made by Lacarrière Latour when, at an earlier date, the Spaniards had commissioned him to map the area. From these they were familiar with the waterways and bayous

153

that connected with Lake Borgne, and also the islands in the lake itself. It would be risky to throw their troops ashore directly from the fleet in Mississippi Sound, some eighty miles away. They would need an intermediate point at which to land the infantry and to which they could withdraw if necessary, before committing the entire army to a bridge-head on the mainland.

They decided on the Isle aux Pois, so named because Bienville's sailors had found a cache of peas there during their early explorations. It was near the mouth of the Pearl River — sixty miles from the fleet's anchorage and another sixty to the west shore of the lake where the many bayous stretched their tentacles to the Mississippi River and the outskirts of New Orleans.

Here was a chance to make use of the Spanish and Portuguese fisher-men who had approached the fleet and seemed eager to make friends. Cochrane and Keane had them brought aboard the *Tonnant* to be ques-tioned as to how the land lay in the western quarter of the lake. Yes, there were many bayous there. But the handsomest of all was the Bayou Bienvenu, easily navigable by small boats. The fishermen knew, because they had used it constantly themselves. Cochrane wasn't sure of their reliability. But if they spoke the truth, they would make valuable guides and useful pilots.

On December 15 Cochrane and Keane began moving the troops from the fleet anchorage to Isle aux Pois. There were not enough small, shallow-draft boats to transport more than two thousand at a time. It would take them five days to carry the entire army to the island — only the troops; wives and civilian personnel would remain aboard the fleet.

That day began a marathon ferry service scarcely equaled in the annals of amphibious operations. Back and forth from anchorage to island and from island back to anchorage, Cochrane's two thousand sailors rowed unceasingly. Twenty-eight hours, thirty-six hours, seventy-two hours, and finally five whole days, with little sleep and little time for food.

Lieutenant George Gleig with the 85th Light Infantry marveled at their endurance. Hunger, fatigue and want of sleep, "three as fearful burdens as can be laid upon the human frame." But Gleig's own en-durance was soon tested. After ten hours in an open boat, cramped and shivering beneath a freezing rain, he was dumped on the island while the weary sailors rowed back for another load. Gleig looked about him. Ship Island had been bad enough — but this!

"It is scarcely possible to imagine a place more completely wretched," Gleig noted in his journal. "It is a swamp, containing a small space of firm ground at one end, and almost wholly unadorned by trees of any sort." William Surtees, arriving later with the 95th Rifle Corps, found it "a complete desert." On top of that dismal outlook, there was miserable weather. They had no tents (there had not been room for them in the boats), no huts or shelter, no fuel for fires. With rain by day and frost by night, their clothes froze to their bodies. As a consequence, noted Lieutenant Gleig, "many of the wretched Negroes, to whom frost and cold were altogether new, fell fast asleep and perished before morning."

The diary of an unidentified British officer, left among the scattered litter of a passing army, gave a succinct tabulation of those dreary days.

16. Disembarked on a small island, the whole of which except about 6 acres was a complete swamp, passed a cold night. 17th. Remained on the Island, a wet day, and the night colder than the last. 18th, 19th, 20th. Remained on the Island. Suffered more from cold Since landing in this place than I did in all my Spbr [probably "Spanish-British"] campaigns. 21st. Embarked on board the Gun Vessels, where we remained all night.

For five days the number of troops increased with each arriving ferry, until the island had all the appearance of a crowded concentration camp. Food was scarce—again for lack of cargo space. Some salt meat and ship's biscuits were washed down with a draught of rum. On the boat that brought William Surtees to the island some sailors settled for the rum alone. "Poor devils, they were exhausted," Surtees wrote forgivingly. Consequently they became, as he expressed it, "rather in the wind, and did not manage the craft so well. Our boat was several times on the point of being swamped. . . ."

While the shuttle service continued and the army on the island grew in numbers trip by trip, Keane and Cochrane made preparations for alighting on the mainland. Cochrane dispatched a scouting party headed by Captain Robert Spencer of the navy and Lieutenant John Peddie of the quartermasters' corps. They were to reconnoiter the shores of Lake Borgne in search of a suitable landing place, not too far from the Mississippi River or the city. They would try to enlist the Spanish and Portuguese fishermen as guides.

Meanwhile there would be the Negro slaves, the Indians, and the

French and Spanish Creoles who were counted on as allies when the chips were down. The slaves and Creoles would have to wait until the British had reached the city's gates, or at least had made their presence known. But the Indians could be rallied in advance. Colonel Nicholls had already established an alliance with the Choctaws during his visit to Apalachicola. Now a mission should be sent to round them up. George Gleig was one of the emissaries, "and a most amusing expedition it turned out to be."

The Choctaws welcomed the British ambassadors with a ceremonial banquet, "lumps of warm buffalo flesh still dripping blood." The English responded with gift flasks of rum. Soon, recorded Gleig, the Indians "began to jump about and exhibit such feats of activity that I was afraid this riotous banquet would end in bloodshed." The "King" and chief warrior, however, remained sober enough to pledge their assistance to the British cause. The next morning, two chiefs in scarlet jackets and nothing below, wearing cocked hats and tomahawks, returned with the emissaries to the British fleet as guests of Admiral Cochrane on the *Tonnant*.

Meanwhile, Spencer and Peddie had scouted the west shore of Lake Borgne and discovered the Spanish fishing village at the mouth of the Bayou Bienvenu. As ever, the fishermen were friendly and eager to be of service, especially if a little gold changed hands. Two of them offered to guide the Englishmen up the Bayou Bienvenu, to study its condition for themselves. With tarpaulin and blue shirts covering their uniforms, the British officers were piloted up the creek to its junction with the Bayou Mazant bending west towards the Mississippi.

Here the view quickened their enthusiasm. Vast, level cane fields, from a half mile to a mile wide, stretched towards the river. Flanking the river were the silent mansions of the planters, promising food, horses and supplies. There were no soldiers in sight, no sign of fortifications, nothing between them and the Cathedral spires of the city. Fearless now of detection, they followed de la Ronde's canal clear to the Mississippi. Here Spencer, just to make sure this dream was real, scooped up a hatful of Mississippi water and he and Peddie drank a toast to victory.

They had found the perfect approach, the perfect battlefield if there need be a battle. Returning to the fishing village, they not only paid off their guides, but persuaded the entire colony—except for one invalid asleep in a hut—to return with them to Isle aux Pois.

Back on the island, Peddie and Spencer reported their findings to General Keane, painting a glowing picture of the welcoming plantations, the easily navigable bayous and canals, the unobstructed plain to New Orleans. The ever-cautious Keane received the news with reservations. Why, he asked himself and others, was the bayou unobstructed? Why was so obvious an approach not fortified? Could it be the setting of a trap?

Cochrane pooh-poohed such fears with scorn. When a thing was handed to you on a silver platter, why reject it? Perhaps the Americans were not so smart after all, or not sufficiently alert. Perhaps they had too few men to spread around as guards and pickets. If Keane refused to seize this opportunity, Cochrane would take his two thousand sailors and capture the city on his own, and the army could remain behind.

The Admiral, Keane knew, was not altogether joking. He himself would prefer to wait until the third wave of troops from England, under General Lambert, had arrived. But time was running out, and the troops on Isle aux Pois were getting restless. His own reputation might be tarnished if he showed timidity. He agreed that the Bayou Bienvenu should be the invasion route, and set the time of embarkation for the fishing village as 9 A.M., December 22.

Two full days remained for planning and preparations. The chief problem was the boats. As before, they could carry only two thousand troops at once. The army would have to move by segments, the vanguard running the risk of being overwhelmed before the next detachment could arrive and come to their support. A clumsy but unavoidable procedure was decided on. The heavier, larger vessels, with as many troops as possible, would follow the vanguard of the lighter boats. When they got stuck, as they surely would, the boats would return for the stranded troops. At least they would not have to row all the way back to Isle aux Pois to pick up their next load.

Keane chose as his vanguard some 1800 veterans of the 85th and 95th regiments, along with portions of the King's Own, under Colonel Thornton — since Thornton had already expressed himself as impatient with delay. With them would be a corps of artillerists and engineers, a few field pieces and a handful of marines. Keane himself, with Admiral Cochrane, would proceed to the mouth of the bayou by a light-draft schooner and supervise the operations. When the first wave was ashore, Keane would follow and join them at their probable encampment at the site the scouts had chosen – de la Ronde's plantation. The second detachment, the 21st Regiment of Fusiliers, the 44th and the 93rd Highlanders, along with the two black regiments, would follow as fast as the boats could bring them to the landing.

While these preparations were continuing, Surtees recorded that "five or six French Americans from New Orleans arrived as friends and told us that there were scarcely any troops in the district; so that we had nothing to do but land on the opposite side, and march right to the town, and that the inhabitants would welcome us most cordially, and that no resistance might be expected."

Quartermaster Surtees was inclined to be suspicious of their information and believed they might be spies. But Lieutenant Gleig and his companions listened with avid interest as their informants described the abundant stores and government supplies that could be captured in the town – millions of dollars' worth of merchandise, and banks well stocked with gold and specie.

December 22 dawned cold and rainy. In spite of the careful planning, there was considerable confusion as the troops embarked. The barges had been lined up in numbered order and the sailing vessels readied. Yet the troops boarded the wrong boats, officers contradicted one another, vessels became mired in the muddy shallows. It was noon, three hours late, before the more than fifty vessels headed out into the lake.

It was a long, hard haul to the fishing village sixty miles away. The troops shivered in the open boats. As Surtees wrote, "We were completely wedged in, so that there was no moving, let the call be ever so urgent. I suffered from a severe pain in my side, from being obliged to remain so long in the same position. But we endeavored to divert the tedium in the best manner we could, by amusing stories, etc."

In another boat Lieutenant Gleig likewise complained of the "cutting north wind, sleet and ice. The boats were so much crowded that the soldiers had no room to move, but were compelled to sit still, cramped and half-frozen, for twelve, eighteen and almost twenty-four hours together."

But to Gleig, the dedicated soldier, the chief complaint was not of discomfort. He worried about the distance from Isle aux Pois to the mainland and from the mainland to the fleet – in short, the military wisdom of this operation.

In case of defeat not only would re-embarkation of any kind be most difficult and hazardous, but it would be impossible to find sufficient small craft to carry the whole of the military force at once. There are times and circumstances in which such risks must and should be taken by commanders. But to put the country to the expense of sending thousands of men across the Atlantic for so mad a venture was little short of criminal.

As expected, some of the heavier vessels, including Admiral Cochrane's schooner, became stranded ten or twelve miles from the appointed landing, their tall sails fluttering like beacons in the sky (and seen by Colonel de la Ronde at dawn the following morning). It was dusk by the time the flotilla reached the fishing village. The troops were ordered to extinguish the charcoal fires in the boats, by which they had endeavored to keep warm. An advance guard under Captain Travers, guided by the Spanish scouts, crept ashore on both sides of the fishing village. Belatedly, a solitary picket challenged their approach. He was captured without a shot being fired.

Five more landing craft entered the Bayou Bienvenu before Villeré's militiamen, asleep in their hut, were alerted. They had heard no shots, and no dog had barked; the dogs, as it happened, had been rounded up the night before by the "ailing" fisherman, who had kept them locked up in his hut. As the guards rushed from their barracks, they were quickly surrounded and overcome, although one or two, according to Surtees, escaped into the wilderness, "where they not improbably perished."

One of the prisoners, Joseph Ducros, the volunteer son of a respectable New Orleans planter, was selected for questioning and taken aboard Cochrane's schooner to be interviewed by General Keane.

"How many men has General Jackson in New Orleans?" Keane demanded.

"Maybe twelve, maybe fifteen thousand," Ducros told him. "He has about four thousand at the English Turn."

Ominous news! The information dovetailed with what Keane had heard from Dr. Morrell and Thomas Shields, as well as that learned from Lieutenant Jones and the other gunboat prisoners. These separate sources could not possibly have been in collusion. Twenty thousand men, at least, were ranged against him. He would have to move with caution.

One by one the landing craft entered the Bayou Bienvenu. They moved slowly because of the darkness and the shallowness of the water. Proceeding up the Bayou Mazant to de la Ronde's, they found that the water in de la Ronde's canal had evidently fallen since Peddie and Spencer had found it navigable. With considerable difficulty they withdrew the boats to Lacoste's canal, a short distance below de la Ronde's. Suprisingly they found the canal completely blocked with timber framework and felled trees — the first suggestion that possibly the Americans had not been as lax as first expected. But why this waterway, and not the others? They withdrew once more to Villeré's canal, which they had passed originally. It was clear and the water sufficiently deep, and they started poling up it through the marshes to the cane fields.

Considerable time had been lost, and the position of the boats was scrambled, so that, as Quartermaster Surtees noted, "had the enemy been aware of our intention, and had they had a force of a few hundred men hid in the high reeds which grow in this marsh, they might, I am persuaded, have cut us off in detail, for no two boats were sufficiently near to assist each other."

As solid ground appeared on both sides of the canal, the troops sprang ashore and pressed on by land, the engineers rapidly clearing the way of reeds and obstacles. They moved at double time across the cane field, with files extended to twice the usual distance, "in order to magnify the appearance of our force, should any concealed American be looking on."

No concealed American was looking on. No pickets, no troops, no sign of any fortifications. Ahead they could see an innocent plantation manor embraced by groves of orange trees, surrounded, too, by the customary barns and storage houses and the mud huts of the slaves. At that early hour all appeared to be sleeping. Colonel Thornton, now at the head of the landed troops, ordered the column to disperse, move forward quietly and surround the house.

It had been cold, but now the winter sun was spreading its customary midday warmth across the cane fields and plantations. On the gallery of the single-story manor young Gabriel Villeré, in the smart uniform of a militia major, was smoking a cigar. Beside him, his worshipful younger brother Jules was cleaning his rifle. A handful of militiamen were discussing with Gabriel the possibility of an invasion. It seemed unlikely to Gabriel and would certainly be doomed to failure with fifteen thousand troops in Jackson's army.

A militiaman challenged the figure of fifteen thousand, saying ten thousand would be closer. Gabriel bridled. "Fifteen thousand, and more arriving every day," he insisted. By silent assent the group agreed on fifteen thousand.

At about that moment, Gabriel's eyes were distracted by a flash of red among the orange groves. He peered intently through the closely-clustered trees. More flashes of red, with here and there an ominous glint of sun on steel and polished leather.

With a sudden premonition of catastrophe, Gabriel leaped from his chair and raced through the house to the gallery in back. His fears were confirmed. Beneath the oaks and the pecan trees, erect and wary, stood the British soldiers in their scarlet tunics and plumed leather helmets, with their rifles at the ready. The house was surrounded! The correct British officer, stepping forward, informed Gabriel that he and his men were prisoners.

The captives were herded into the parlor of the house, where Gabriel unwillingly played the gracious host. He invited the British to sample his cigars and to enjoy a bottle or two of vintage wine. They talked politely together, while Gabriel's mind explored this cruel predicament.

There was no doubt as to how the British had arrived—the canal, the bayous Mazant and Bienvenu. But how had they got past the pickets at the fishing village? He quickly recognized the danger implicit in his situation. The blocking of the bayous, the guarding of the fishing village, these had been his and his father Jacques' responsibility, along with Colonel de la Ronde. How would it look for him to be closeted, perhaps discovered, with the British?

He had to escape. He had to get word to Jackson.

Young Jules was watching him, secretly urging him to take some action. But what action? The front of the house was picketed by guards, and beyond them lay the river. His only hope lay in a dash across the cane fields to the cypress marshes half a mile away.

Picking his time, he plunged through the guards, smashed through a window, bowled over the pickets in his path, and hurdled the high fence that enclosed the yard. Cries of "Stop him! Kill him!" followed him across the open fields. Bullets rained about him as he raced towards the woods. Then he was in the cypress marshes, his feet sinking deeper and deeper in morasses threatening to trap him. Grace King, a perceptive observer of this facet of New Orleans history, picks up the narrative:

> The Britons were gaining; had reached the swamp! He could hear them panting and blowing, and the orders which made his capture inevitable. There was but one chance; he sprang to a cypress tree, and strove for the thick moss and branches overhead. Half way up, he heard a whimpering below. It was the voice of his dog, his favorite setter, whining, fawning and looking up to him with all the pathos of brute fidelity. There was no choice. It was her life or his, perhaps the surprise and capture of the city! Dropping to the earth, he seized a billet of wood, and aimed one blow between the setter's devoted eyes — with tears in his own eyes, as he related. To throw the body to one side, snatch some brush over it, spring to the tree again, was the work of an instant. As he drew the moss around his crouching figure, and stifled his hard breathing, the British floundered past.

When it was safe to move again, Gabriel dropped from his tree and twisted through the wood to the edge of de la Ronde's plantation, then raced to the manor of Versailles. De la Ronde had returned from the inspection of his property and paled at the dreaded news with all its implications. Together they rowed across the river in a skiff and borrowed horses from Dusseau Delacroix to take them to the city. Since Villeré and de la Ronde spoke only French, Delacroix rode with them as interpreter.

It was noon when the excited trio burst into Jackson's house on Royal Street. The General was pale and visibly shaken. News had arrived which he found unbelievable. While Latour had not returned from his reconnaissance, he had sent a companion, Augustin Rousseau, to carry the dread word to Jackson. The British were coming up the Bayou Bienvenu!

With grim foreboding he inquired of the trio, "What news do you bring, gentlemen?"

Delacroix could hardly get the words out. But even his excited, garbled English made their meaning clear. The British were at Villeré's! En masse!

So it was true! What had gone wrong? How had he, Jackson, been betrayed? Who could have been so direly derelict? He had ordered the bayous blocked and guarded. He had counted on de la Ronde and Villeré to carry out those orders. Here they were before him now—harbingers of disaster. What had gone so irreparably wrong?

No time for questions, much less answers. No explanation, however justifiable, could be of comfort now. It is parenthetical to note that, writing more than half a century later, historian Henry Adams at least sympathized with his predicament. "The record of American general-ship offered many examples of misfortune, but none so complete as this," wrote Adams, adding that no previous commander in this or any other war, "had allowed a large British army, heralded long in advance, to arrive within seven miles unseen and unsuspected, and without so much as an earthwork, a man, or a gun between them and their object. The disaster was unprecedented, and could be repaired only by des-perate measures."

The General's voice was hoarse with anger. "By the Eternal, they shall not sleep upon our soil!"

It was too early, in the British camp, to bed down for the evening. The infantry stacked its rifles beneath the pecan trees and started breaking up the cypress fence for firewood. Others brought water from the river, while still others ranged over the nearby plantations like a band of curious and amiable tourists. Most of the occupants had evi-dently left. But the slaves were cordial and glad to sell them food or direct them to the wine and liquor closets.

The propriety-conscious Gleig was pleased to note that the British paid well for whatever they appropriated—"hams, fowls, and wines of various descriptions." He himself purchased a turkey and returned to the slave hut where his companions of the 85th had settled down and were trying to coax their fire into flame.

All around Villeré's house the troops were relaxing in their separate ways, lighting fires, cooking food, sharing their new-found provisions. Some of the more sporting-minded, now that the sun was overhead, stripped for a swim in the Mississippi. They had not bathed or taken off their clothes for days. Between the two levees, the old and new, there was a sheltered area like a sunken fortress, pleasant for basking in the sun.

A reconnoitering British officer prowled through the mansion of Monsieur de la Ronde, admiring its elegant furnishings, its admirable

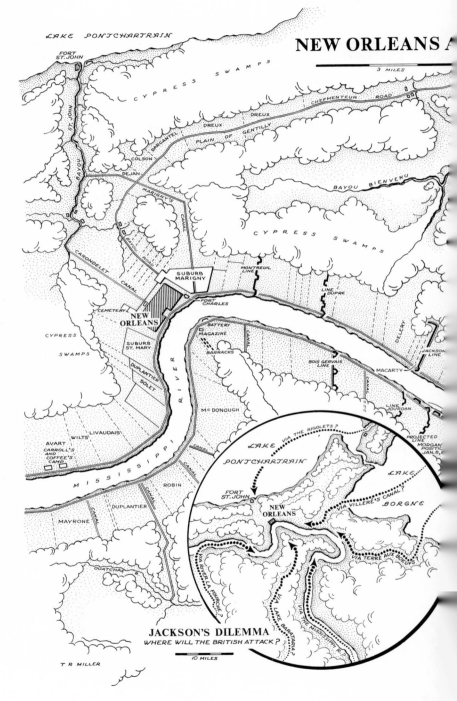

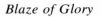

**NEW ORLEANS A**

3 MILES

JACKSON'S DILEMMA
*WHERE WILL THE BRITISH ATTACK?*

10 MILES

T R MILLER

NITY IN **1814** AND **1815**

BRITISH
LANDINGS
ON LAKE BORGNE
(AFTER LATOUR)

10 MILES

rack of vintage wines. They lived well, these planters! In what he took to be a lady's dressing room he found a copy of Ronsard's poems propped up against the mirror, as if left there in a hurry. It was opened on the marked lines, *Si périssable est toute chose née, Que songes-tu, mon âme imprisonnée?* He admired the lady's taste and wondered about the reference to her imprisoned soul.

Having appropriated Villeré's house as his headquarters, General Keane pondered his situation. It had all been too easy. He had arrived unchallenged with almost two thousand men, just nine miles from New Orleans. Between him and the ultimate goal were only open fields, and along the river an unobstructed roadway leading to the city. It was as if it had been made to order for this expedition. Too good to be altogether true.

The impetuous Colonel Thornton, when consulted, was all for pressing their luck and marching at once on New Orleans, before the Americans had time to brace themselves for the attack. They could take the city by nightfall, and the rest of the army, as it arrived, could bring up the supplies. The spies and deserters had promised that they would meet with little opposition; the Creoles were ready to welcome them with open arms.

While Thornton and the many other officers who supported him miscalculated the reception they were likely to receive, they may well have been right about the strategy of immediate attack. Some years afterward, no less an authority than J. W. Fortescue, official historian of the British army, noted: "Had he [Keane] advanced at once, he would probably have surprised Jackson before the American concentration had been accomplished."

But the hesitant Keane was not so certain. He was inclined to discredit the reports of the deserters, remembering that Ducros at the landing, Morrell and Jones at the Isle aux Pois, had separately confirmed that there were from fifteen to twenty thousand troops with Andrew Jackson. Discounting the advantage of surprise, the present British force would be outnumbered ten to one. He would wait at least until the second wave of troops arrived from Isle aux Pois.

He checked the deployment of his men. Half were encamped at Villeré's; the rest had settled on Lacoste's. He sent a small detachment down to Jumonville's to protect their rear and posted an advance guard under Captain Travers on the road near de la Ronde's. The light artillery pieces rested in the yard of Villeré's. They would not be needed until the troops began their march upon the city.

At three o'clock a bugle sounded an alarm, and shots were heard at Travers' outpost. The troops dashed for their arms and fell in line, until it was learned that a corps of American cavalry, apparently on reconnaissance, had discovered the British position and engaged the advance in random fire, after which they had speedily retreated.

Surtees and his companions turned back to their cooking "with great glee." But the sound of guns had jolted their complacency. As the quartermaster noted in his journal:

> Considerable discussion now began to take place amongst the knowing ones, as to the merits and demerits of our situation, in point of security. One officer of ours . . . did not hesitate roundly to assert that we were in a most unprotected and dangerous position. I do not remember the reasons he advanced. But certainly, could he have foreseen what yet remained in the womb of time, he would have had much stronger reasons for his opinion.

Some yards away, Lieutenant Gleig and Captain Grey were finishing their turkey dinner—"a most hearty meal indeed, after which we took each a tot of grog to comfort us." The sound of the shots disturbed them little, although Gleig believed "that our situation hardly deserved the title of a military position." A companion reassured him that, "since the Americans were not given to attacking first, there was little likelihood that they would do so on this occasion."

The day passed without further alarm, "and as darkness set in, the fires were made to blaze with increasing splendor . . ." In voices stimulated by anticipation, the weary troops discussed what lay ahead. Tonight the second division would arrive from Isle aux Pois. Tomorrow they would be in New Orleans, "where beauty and booty," which some translated as "lust and loot," awaited them.

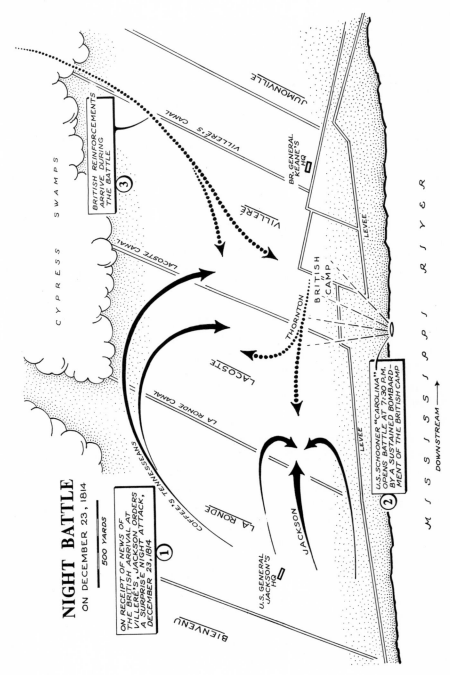

NIGHT BATTLE
ON DECEMBER 23, 1814

500 YARDS

① ON RECEIPT OF NEWS OF THE BRITISH ARRIVAL AT VILLERE'S, JACKSON ORDERS A SURPRISE NIGHT ATTACK, DECEMBER 23, 1814

② U.S. SCHOONER "CAROLINA" OPENS BATTLE AT 7:30 P.M. BY A SUSTAINED BOMBARDMENT OF THE BRITISH CAMP

③ BRITISH REINFORCEMENTS ARRIVE DURING THE BATTLE

CYPRESS SWAMPS

JUMONVILLE

VILLERE'S CANAL

VILLERE

BR. GENERAL KEANE'S HQ

LACOSTE CANAL

LACOSTE

THORNTON

BRITISH CAMP

LEVEE

LA RONDE CANAL

LA RONDE

COFFEE'S TENNESSEANS

BIENVENU

U.S. GENERAL JACKSON'S HQ

JACKSON

LEVEE

MISSISSIPPI RIVER

DOWNSTREAM

# 11.   Decision in the Dark

"I will smash them, so help me God!"

This was not the vengeful boast of a madman goaded to fury by surprise and the knowledge that he had somehow been betrayed. It was the calculated though swift decision of a battle-minded veteran who knew that one countered surprise with surprise, and that the best defense was often to attack.

Then, in a voice more self-composed, Jackson calmly told his aides: "Gentlemen, the British are below. We must fight them tonight."

He was not prepared for such immediate action. Neither were the troops, many of them only just arrived after taxing marches, many others green and not yet fully disciplined. But Jackson was not a man of caution; nor was this a time for caution. He felt certain that the troops at Villeré's, whatever their numbers, could be no more than the British vanguard, and that reinforcements must be on their way. He could not afford to wait.

At 1:55 that afternoon the signal gun at Fort St. Charles resounded in alarm, scattering the pigeons in the Place d'Armes, bringing anxious housewives to their windows, alerting the troops around the city that their time, to their surprised delight, had come. Seconds later the bells of the Cathedral tolled in answer to the triple cannon blast. Couriers

169

sped from Royal Street, west, north and east, to summon the outlying troops to Fort St. Charles and thence to the Montreuil plantation three miles above Macarty's.

Down from Avart's came Coffee's and Carroll's Tennesseans, fumbling with their powder-horns and buckling their belts. They were quickly passed by Hind's Dragoons, trailing clouds of dust as they galloped through the city. From the Bayou St. John came Plauché's Orleans Volunteers, running all the way as if they meant to keep on running till they met the enemy. The two regiments of Regulars poured out of the barracks, to be joined by Jugeat's Choctaws and Daquin's Battalion of Free Colored, trotting to the beat of Jordan Noble's drum.

The Commanding General watched them arrive and pass down the Esplanade on their way to Montreuil's. They were a motley crew, their officers shouting commands in French and English, but he found them strangely reassuring. There was not a dragging foot among the lot.

Jackson hastily moved his field headquarters to Macarty's, a two-story mansion with double balconies, now vacated by its ailing owner. From there, overlooking Chalmette's and de la Ronde's, he had a distant view of the British bivouac at Villeré's. How many were there? It was hard for him to tell, even with the enemy's fires plainly visible.

The Americans had one asset which the British were without, and would, in fact, remain without, and that was cavalry for reconnaissance. Jackson sent Colonel Hayne with twenty of Hind's Dragoons to scout the British position and report. After a brief encounter with Travers' outpost, in which one horse was killed, two men were wounded and the enemy was alerted, the Dragoons took shelter at de la Ronde's. Hayne boldly rode as close as he dared to the British lines, and calmly studied the invaders through his glass. He returned to Macarty's with the extraordinary information that there were "only two or three hundred" British on the field.

Fortunately, Major Latour, ever scurrying about like a beaver seeking a weak point in the dam, had made his own close-quarter survey of the enemy encampment. He came back with the far more accurate estimate of their numbers — between sixteen and eighteen hundred. And what did Jackson have to throw against them? In his report to the Secretary of War he appraised his forces as "not exceeding in all fifteen hundred." He seems to have been overly conservative. Other sources, including the generally reliable Latour, set the figure closer to two thousand.

Jackson was still not certain that the British landing at Villeré's was not a feint, screening a second landing at the Chef Menteur. Having recalled Daquin's blacks from the Plain of Gentilly, he now dispatched the Louisiana militia under Claiborne to that post. They would be supported by a detachment of Carroll's Tennesseans, with the rest of Carroll's men remaining in the city as reserves.

Characteristically, Claiborne complained bitterly of this assignment. He told Colonel Bartholomew Shaumburg, his aide-de-camp, that "this was part of a System decided on to keep me in the background." Shaumburg did not agree. He held with Jackson that the pass should be strongly guarded, since the enemy approach below the city might be simply a diversion. Somewhat mollified, Claiborne began to think that he might be a hero yet, if Jackson's fears of a second landing should be realized.

At Macarty's, Jackson consulted Patterson as to what the Commodore could do with his two vessels on the river. The larger *Louisiana,* though armed and partially manned with impressed seamen, was not fully ready yet for action. In what state was the *Carolina?* Under the command of Captain John Henley she had recently been fitted with stronger fire power, five six-pound guns on either side and two long-range twelves on bow and stern. Her crew of ninety was disciplined and skilled.

It was agreed that Patterson would board the *Carolina,* taking Livingston with him as an observer well acquainted with the river's landmarks. The ship would move downstream to a position opposite the British camp. At precisely seven thirty she would open fire, softening up the enemy with a sustained bombardment. Half an hour later, successive red, white and blue rockets would be Jackson's signal to attack.

Towards dusk, Jackson watched the *Carolina* weigh anchor and start her downstream drift, sails slack, for there was little wind and she rode on the strength of the current. Then Jackson led his assorted army, with the two pieces of field artillery, down the field to the avenue of oaks that stretched from de la Ronde's manor to the river. Here they waited; their movement in the darkness had been undetected.

At seven, well after nightfall, Pierre Denis de la Ronde stood beside the General on the borders of his own plantation. With mixed emotions Pierre realized that his beloved Versailles was to be the site of battle, possibly of destruction, and that he himself, at Jackson's request, was to be an instrument of the holocaust. He knew the lay of the land as no one else, and although a general of militia, he was now relieved of that command to serve as battlefield adviser to the General.

Nothing had been said of his failure to block the Bayou Bienvenu and the canal, nor would the oversight ever be thoroughly investigated. A charitable and likely explanation was that these waterways were vital to the life of the plantations and, once obstructed, would require long and costly work to make them usable again. Possibly Jackson, recognizing this conflict of interests, chose to ignore the matter at this point of crisis. De la Ronde was here beside him, eager and able to be of service, and should have this chance to make amends.

Behind them, like phantoms in a pall of mist and darkness, stood some 1800 troops, silent and motionless, awaiting orders for deployment. Jackson's strategy had been decided. It would be a three-pronged offensive, with the *Carolina's* guns harassing the British left, while Jackson and Coffee attacked the front and right.

On signal, de la Ronde and Coffee led the six hundred mounted Tenneseeans across the field below Lacoste's canal to the edges of the swamp. They were accompanied by Hind's Dragoons and John Beale's Rifles. De la Ronde rode ahead of them as guide. Near the swamp, they paused and waited for the signal rockets.

Jackson formed the remaining troops, a thousand of them, in a line from de la Ronde's house to the river. On the right, close to the levee, were the 7th and 44th Regulars under Colonel Ross. Next to them, Plauché's company of Orleans Volunteers. To the left of Plauché, Daquin's Battalion of Free Colored, with Jugeat's Choctaws on their flank. A team of horses drew the field guns up to de la Ronde's canal and stationed them on the river road. They were manned by a corps of artillerists commanded by Lieutenant Samuel Spotts. With this force, plus a small detachment of marines, Jackson would attack the British left.

Almost seven thirty. The hushed troops waited for the thunder of the *Carolina's* guns.

In Major Plauché's battalion, the Major whispered to Vincent Nolte, "I scarcely feel I have the courage to lead fathers of families into battle."

Captain Roche of the Carabiniers overhead him. "That's no way to talk, Major," he rebuked. Then, setting an example, Roche called softly to his brother in the ranks: "Sergeant Roche!"

The sergeant stepped forward.

"Let us embrace, brother," said the captain. "It may be for the last time."

In Creole fashion they embraced, then: "Sergeant Roche, to your post!" the captain ordered.

In New Orleans, where Captain Thomas Butler had been left in charge, strange scenes were played in counterpoint to the drama on the plains of de la Ronde. At the home of Mrs. William Christy, née Cenas, wives, sisters, and sweethearts had assembled to knit and keep one another company. The women were anxious and uneasy with the absence of their men. Since the clarion calls had sounded from the fort and the Cathedral, they had known what was going on below the city. They had seen Coffee's cavalry and Plauché's Creoles racing through the streets towards the battlefield. Earlier they had sent a member of their group to Jackson, asking what they were to do, in case the city was attacked?

Jackson sent back the reply that there was no cause for uneasiness. "No British shall enter the city as an enemy, unless over my dead body."

But what if the English entered the city over Jackson's body, in the wake of his retreating troops? Hushed voices spoke of the horrors of Hampton, of British soldiers on the rampage, of plunder and arson and rape. Wives bravely displayed the daggers their husbands had given them, and boasted of how they would choose death before dishonor. Tremulous maidens shuddered deliciously at thoughts they scarcely dared to entertain.

Strange dialogues, and what Charles Gayarré called "suspicious nocturnal meetings," went on in the cafés and the coffeehouses of the city. And New Orleans had its share of courtesan informers. Fulwar Skipwith, patrolling the streets with the city guard, took time off for a brief engagement with an open-minded woman of the town. She had had earlier visitors. Now she asked:

"Is it true that General Jackson will destroy the city, rather than let it fall into the hands of the British?"

Skipwith assured her it was not. At least, not to the best of his knowledge.

"But that's what the soldiers are saying," said the lady. "Some were here earlier this evening."

On leaving, Skipwith ran into Captain Thomas Butler, in charge of policing the streets. He reported, without revealing the lady's name, the gist of this disturbing conversation. It was indicative, he thought, of the temper of the city. Where the matter went from there is hard to trace in the confusion of that evening. But it started a chain of rumors and events that would trouble New Orleans for days and weeks to come.

Shortly after dark, the *Carolina* drifted past the British outpost, where Captain Travers had been relieved by the aggressive and determined Captain Hallen. Hallen sent a messenger down the road to inform General Keane of the vessel's approach, but the runner was outdistanced by the swiftly-moving schooner.

At Villeré's and on a portion of Lacoste's plantation, the British troops remained relaxed around their fires, which were plainly seen aboard the *Carolina* and by the Americans at de la Ronde's. Since the earlier skirmish at the outpost, there had been no further reason for alarm. The incident had been dismissed as insignificant. Some enemy cavalry had stumbled by accident on the outpost and been readily repelled.

Though normally apprehensive, General Keane himself was not worried about anything so "barbarous" as a night attack. True, certain savages might resort to such unprincipled action, but it was hard to believe that the partially civilized Americans would do so. Night fighting violated all the rules of European warfare and sophisticated military tactics—like playing cricket when one could not see his opponents on the field.

But what of the strange and silent schooner that suddenly made its appearance on the river? As the *Carolina* approached the encampment, a British picket challenged her, and getting no reply, sent a musket shot across her bow. Still no response. A hundred yards or so off shore she was seen to drop anchor and slowly swing around until her bow was headed upstream, her starboard facing the encampment. The slack sails dropped and were furled methodically by the silent crew who moved like ghosts around the deck.

More curious than alarmed, some of the troops climbed the outer levee to inspect the vessel and speculate on her purpose there. Was she a partisan ship bringing hoped-for allies from New Orleans? Was she part of a planned naval attack upon the city? Strangely enough, neither Keane nor Thornton, dining by candlelight at Villeré's, seemed bothered by her presence. They would wait and see what the ship's intentions were. Right now they were more concerned about the prompt arrival of the second wave of troops, the Highlanders and the 44th, which would give them the necessary power for a mass offensive in the morning.

Seven thirty now at Villeré's. The British had stacked their rifles. It was time to bed down for the night. And the night, as Lieutenant Gleig observed, "was now dark as pitch, the moon being but young, and totally obscured with clouds." Fatigued as they were, the men were reluctant to leave the cheery fires, around which they discussed the promise of tomorrow — New Orleans, riches, glory, and pale-skinned beauties in abundance. Nothing could stop them now. The path ahead was broad and clear. There was not an enemy in sight.

Clear on the night air, amplified by the surrounding silence, came a command so loud that it seemed intended for their ears alone.

"Now, boys, give it to them, damn their eyes!"

Before they had time to turn their heads toward the river, the broad-side guns of the *Carolina* broke loose in a thunderous, flame-spitting roar. The echo had barely died before the air was charged with the screams of a hundred stricken men. In the eerie, smoke-filled twilight, grotesque, writhing figures sprawled among the still forms of the dead.

In an instant all was chaos, as the stunned men ran for their muskets, and officers shouted orders from all directions. Then the great guns blazed again. More screams, more tortured figures on the ground.

Recorded Infantry Captain John H. Cooke, the barrage was "like so many thunderbolts, the balls boring down whole piles of arms, knocking kettles off the fires, scattering blazing beams of wood about, maiming some soldiers, and sending others whence no traveller returns . . ."

Round after round, and ball after ball, were vomited forth, driving the troops into the most dire confusion, causing a ten-fold panic in the darkness. No mob could be in a more utter state of disorganization . . . Officers were buckling on their swords, and throwing down knives and forks, and calling to their soldiers. Soldiers were looking after their arms or buckling on their knapsacks, and calling to their officers. Bugle-calls were sounding, while the soldiers strove to get together . . . .

In that murderous hail of ball and grapeshot it seemed impossible to hope for sanity and order. But these soldiers of Wellington were veterans. Somehow they managed to find their units and form a ragged line. Certain quick-witted men started stamping out the fires which had treacherously served as beacons, but the screams of the wounded and their own shouts helped to mark the target for the *Carolina's* guns.

Lieutenant Gleig with the 85th was in dead center of that target.

"Against this dreadful fire we had nothing whatever to oppose. Our artillery was too light to bring into competition with an adversary so powerful." Nor, Gleig observed, could muskets reach the enemy on the ship. "Our sole object was to shelter the men as much as possible from this iron hail. With this in view they were commanded to leave the fires, and to hasten under the dyke." Lying there they "listened to the shrieks and groans of those who lay wounded beside them."

Out of range and out of sight of the *Carolina,* Quartermaster Surtees, with a detachment of the 95th at Hallen's outpost, was astounded at the sound of heavy cannon. He had heard an order shouted from the river, followed by cheers, but he couldn't figure out what it meant.

I at first imagined it was some of our men-of-war that had been able to pass the forts down the river, and that they were firing a salute and cheering in consequence; and yet this seemed a strange conjecture. But we did not long remain in suspense, for we were soon after informed of the real state of the case, that it was a large American schooner, with at least fourteen guns which she had been enabled to bring to bear upon our unfortunate bivouac with the most deadly precision, great numbers having fallen at her first broadside.

As Surtees and his companions of the 95th debated the significance of this attack, a young soldier in an unfamiliar uniform walked into their midst and stopped abruptly at sight of the green jackets of the riflemen.

"Where are the Regulars?" he asked.

"What Regulars?"

A look of alarm crossed the soldier's face. These were not his troops, but British!

He was quickly pounced on and disarmed. Surtees, for one, came to an obvious conclusion. The American soldier was looking for his regiment, which meant the American Regulars were on their way. Hallen's outpost would need reinforcements. The units below the outpost must be warned. General Keane must be informed.

Hardly noticing the colored rockets blistering the sky, Surtees raced to Lacoste's, where the 85th was bivouacked. He was surprised to find the encampment empty, the embers of the fires scattered over the demolished campsite. He found an officer looking for his troops and warned him of Hallen's predicament. The officer agreed to summon reinforcements.

Further down towards Villeré's, Surtees met a sergeant of the 93rd and with him ran into a detachment of Americans, whom he recognized by their voices. They seemed to have come from nowhere.

"Accordingly," recorded Surtees unashamedly, "we took to our heels and ran like heroes."

Jackson's attack on the British left was well launched. The two field pieces had been towed by horses up the road, and the marine artillerists were adding their shells to the *Carolina's* cannonade. The 44th Infantry was leading the advance, with Plauché's battalion struggling over the ditches to keep pace with them. The gap between the units widened. Plauché's trigger-happy Creoles started firing at the shadowy figures ahead of them and the American 44th fired back.

With Plauché's Carabiniers, Vincent Nolte coolly observed the action by the light of flashing British muskets. "I thus observed the peculiar method of firing adopted by the English, who still kept up the old custom of three deep; one row of men half-kneeling, and the other two ranks firing over their shoulders. This style of firing, along with the darkness of evening, explained to me the reason why the enemy's balls, which we heard whistling by, mostly flew over our heads . . ."

In the confusion there was one solid center of British resistance. Captain Hallen stood his ground at the outpost with only eighty rifles. Faced with the two artillery pieces firing at them, Hallen's men made a gallant charge to seize the battery. The horses reared, overturning one of the guns. General Jackson suddenly appeared beside the wavering marines.

"Save the guns!" he shouted. "Save the guns!"

The 7th regiment, still in the rear, raced forward to aid the marines in dragging the field guns out of danger. Jackson stood by till the artillery was safe, oblivious of the rain of lead around him. Years later he was asked about the practiced graciousness of his bows when in the company of ladies. "I learned that dodging British bullets on December twenty-third," he told his inquirers.

Unable to overcome Hallen's outpost, the U.S. 7th and 44th bypassed it and pressed on towards the British left. Plauché's excitable Creoles charged recklessly ahead. *"Aux baionnettes!"* was now their battle cry. Colonel Ross wisely held them back. They would have little chance in hand-to-hand contact with Wellington's veterans, skilled and experienced in bayonet fighting.

Quartermaster Surtees had finally joined a section of his own battalion near Lacoste's canal. He was not a combat officer; he wanted no part of this madness; but he stayed to observe "as strange a description of fighting as has ever been recorded."

> The enemy soon discovered from some men, whom they had unfortunately taken, what the regiments were that were opposed to them. With all that cunning which the Yankees are famed for, they instantly turned it to best account. In several places they advanced in bodies, crying out, "Come on, my brave 85th!" or "My brave 95th!" and thus induced several of our small detached parties to go over to them, when of course they were instantly made prisoners.

As the Americans pressed on towards the British left, the *Carolina*'s guns fell silent. The target had become too mixed; the Americans were in the range of fire. Lieutenant Gleig with the 85th could leave the shelter of the levee to join the battle. "In the whole course of my military career I do not recollect any scene at all resembling that which followed," Gleig recorded.

Since this was before the days of smokeless gunpowder, the smoke merged with the mist and darkness to cover the field with an impenetrable pall. Since both sides, excepting the Creoles, spoke the same language, there was no distinguishing of friend from enemy. Men fired at rifle sparks, or swung the butts of their muskets at the sudden flashing of a bayonet. Americans fired on Americans, British on British, and both sides took prisoners from among their own, releasing them in fury at their own mistakes.

It was a battle of a hundred small, confused engagements. "All order, all discipline were lost," wrote Gleig. "Each officer, as he was able to collect twenty or thirty men around him, advanced into the middle of the enemy, when it was fought hand to hand, bayonet to bayonet, and sword to sword . . ."

Gleig stayed close to his friend Captain Grey, anxious to have someone beside him whom he recognized. The two officers managed to round up some thirty members of the infantry and advanced towards an indistinguishable band of troops ahead of them. Gleig gave the order to attack. Grey countermanded with, "Hold your fire! Those are *our* men!"

"They're Americans," insisted Gleig.

"They can't be. Americans could never get this far."

They settled the debate by separating. Grey stayed with half the men behind the shelter of a cane stack. Gleig took the other half on an encircling movement to trap the opposing unit. It was the last time they saw one another alive.

Towards the marshes, opposite the British right, Coffee and his Tennesseans had been slow in getting started. They found the terrain, with its frequent ditches, difficult for cavalry maneuvers. Coffee ordered his men to dismount at de la Ronde's canal and to proceed on foot. The horses were turned loose, some to be reclaimed later, some to drift over to the British lines. Hind's Dragoons with de la Ronde were left behind at the canal to protect Coffee's flank and rear as he moved towards the river.

Commanding the British 95th, Major Samuel Mitchell led his men in the direction of the swamp. The second wave of English troops, he knew, had landed and was making its way to Villeré's. Perhaps he could make contact with them. Now he thought he had. From the darkness emerged a band of men whose dark shirts closely resembled the jackets of the Highlanders.

"Are you the Ninety-third?" he called.

"That's right!" shouted one of Coffee's Tennesseans.

Mitchell pushed confidently forward and was slapped on the shoulder by Captain John Donelson, Andrew Jackson's nephew.

"You're my prisoner, Major," Donelson declared, and asked for the officer's sword. Mitchell couldn't believe it. He uttered a battlefield oath and reached for his sword, but with no intention of releasing it.

A dozen rifles were leveled at him, and a chorus of voices ordered, "Hand it over!"

Mitchell did. Still swearing violently he was led back to the rear.

It was only natural in this game of hide-and-seek that the tricks should be ironically reversed. Minutes later Donelson's company stumbled on a corps of infantry and demanded that they identify themselves. "We are Coffee's men," came the reply. Donelson approached till he heard the command, "You damn Yankee rebels, drop your arms!" Donelson himself escaped the trap, but lost six men who were either killed or captured.

Beale's Rifles, protecting Coffee's flank, became separated from the main division and suffered near catastrophe. Hoping to close the gap between themselves and Jackson's troops, they stumbled blindly towards the river and ran into a group of Highlanders, whose unfamiliar uniforms a sergeant mistook for Tennessean hunting clothes. "Where's the first division?" he called out. "*Richt* here!" was the reply. Before the sergeant could identify the Scot's brogue, a good half of Beale's Rifles were surrounded and captured.

After this general free-for-all, however, the rest of Beale's men returned to Jackson's line with over thirty British prisoners. The score was approximately tied.

Completing their wide encirclement of the British right, Coffee's men plunged through the outskirts of the British camp at Villeré's and pressed toward the river. This brawl in the darkness with fists and rifle butts and tomahawks was as much meat to them as it was poison to the

British. It was Colonel Thornton who brought order out of chaos in the English camp. Having absorbed innumerable bullets in his lifetime, his mind surmounted the panic and confusion. He ordered the men around him to take shelter in the fort-like trough between the old and new levees. From behind these solid earthworks Thornton would not budge, and his rifles began to take a heavy toll among the Tennesseans.

For two hours the hit-and-miss fighting in the dark had raged without decision. British reinforcements had arrived, were still arriving, but were moving cautiously towards the sound of battle for fear of exposing their sole line of communication, the bayou and the land around it.

Only one American unit had not been heard from and. in fact, was not expected. Down at the English Turn the five hundred troops under David Morgan had been itching to get into the fight ever since news of the British landing had arrived. Up to this moment Morgan had been able to restrain them. He had been wise to do so, if one opinion can be accepted, since "raw levies, who clamor for action, invariably run away under fire and generally shoot their leaders." Now they could be restrained no longer.

Led by their Colonel Alexandre Declouet, beneath his spanking-new regimental colors awarded by the Legislature, the troops double-timed towards the sound of battle, moving up to Jumonville's plantation to attack the British rear. Had the attack been pressed, they might have been overwhelmed by the British division stationed at Jumonville's against just such an emergency. As it was, they did not reach the battle zone till well after midnight and were met by a half-drunk British artilleryman who mistook them for an English regiment.

"Come on, my lads, the Yankees are getting the licking of their lives!" the cheerful inebriate proclaimed.

It was this dire announcement, according to Surtee's notes, that caused Morgan's contingent to abandon the attack, though the quartermaster confessed that he was not sure of this deduction. More than likely Morgan realized, from the marked reduction in the firing at the front, that he and his men had arrived too late to be of value. Exhausted from their forced march, cursing and grumbling at their luck, the troops straggled back towards the English Turn.

Unable to dislodge Thornton's troops from their position behind the old levee, Coffee reported his situation to General Jackson. He re-

ported, too, the continued arrival of British reinforcements from Lake
Borgne. By now the Americans were clearly outnumbered, though it
was hard to make any accurate assessment in the dark.

Jackson ordered a general withdrawal to de la Ronde's plantation.
But such was the nature of the fighting that it took hours for the troops
to disengage. There were too many trigger-happy soldiers looking for
a chance at one last shot, too many Choctaw Indians who, though
forbidden by Jackson to take scalps, were hoping to kill a few more
enemy and seize a few more rifles.

For the balance of the night, Jackson established provisional headquarters at de la Ronde's. Sprawled in an overstuffed armchair in the
parlor, the exhaustion of battle needling his dysentery-racked body, the
General debated his next move. Two British deserters were brought in,
who reported that almost all the English advance had landed and that
Keane's army now numbered five thousand men. It was close to the
truth. Three fresh regiments plus additional artillery had raised Keane's
effective fighting force from 1,800 to nearly double that amount.

As troops and officers drifted back to de la Ronde's with their reports of dead and wounded, it was hard to make a clear appraisal of the
action. But of this much Jackson was certain. He had caught the British
off balance and delivered them a stunning blow. While he had not dislodged them, as he'd hoped to do, they would think twice before advancing on the city without further preparation. And what he needed
most was time.

Moreover, the lines had been drawn; the battlefield had been defined. There was less need now to worry about attack from other directions. By pouring their reinforcements into Villeré's, the British had
committed themselves to this position. They might be able to open a
second front at Chef Menteur, if they had the necessary troops, but he
began to doubt that possibility. He could concentrate on the plain
between Chalmette's and de la Ronde's, dig in behind one of the
canals and prepare for the British offensive that was bound to come.

Keane, too, had been given thought in the ferocity and recklessness
of the American attack. A general who would commit so many troops
so flagrantly must have plenty in reserve to count on. The British
general had more reason to believe the exaggerated figures he'd
received regarding the strength of Jackson's forces. Beale's captured

riflemen (whom British officers were amused to find were "no more than a bunch of clerks and businessmen") had been interrogated. "They would give but one answer—that Jackson had almost 30,000 men," including those stationed at points along the coast.

There was substantiation in the many different uniforms encountered on the field and among the prisoners. If each uniform represented a division, and each division was up to strength, the Americans certainly numbered more than fifteen thousand. Keane found this perversely consoling. It vindicated his earlier decision not to attack till reinforcements had arrived, in spite of Thornton's urging him to do so. Many French voices and French commands had been overheard, indicating that the Creole population, far from defecting to the British side, were engaged in the defense of New Orleans.

All things considered, losses had been surprisingly light on both sides, due to the uncertain marksmanship imposed by darkness. When a final tally could be made, Jackson recorded twenty-four killed, 115 wounded and seventy-four missing, or total casualties of 213. British casualties had been higher, compounded of forty-six killed, 167 wounded and sixty-four missing. But the fury and disruption of the battle caused the English to magnify those figures. "Our loss," wrote Lieutenant Gleig, "had been enormous. Not less than 500 men had fallen, many of whom were our finest soldiers and best officers." As to the effect of the *Carolina's* deadly guns, Keane reported to his superiors in London that he had been bombarded by three ships at once!

The highest-ranking British prisoner taken had been Major Samuel Mitchell. Out of deference to his rank, Jackson sent a courier to New Orleans, where the captives had been detained, to inquire if the major needed anything to make him comfortable. "Thank the General for his courtesy," said Mitchell haughtily, "but my army will be bringing up my luggage in the morning." Jackson decided he could do without the major's presence in the city and sent him up to detention quarters in the hinterland.

In many ways the battle might have been considered a draw, though John Fortescue, writing from the British point of view, gave an edge to the Americans. Jackson recorded in his journal that, all things considered, it was "the best fought action in the annals of military warfare." One thing was certain, though no one would know it for weeks to come: the fight in the darkness on December 23 was the last "official" battle of the War of 1812.

British resistance had owed much to Hallen's incredible fight at the outpost, in which he had lost more than half his men and had himself been severely wounded. Had he not held fast, had he allowed the Americans to reach the British camp at its moment of disruption by the *Carolina's* guns, Keane might have found his forces overwhelmed before any reinforcements had arrived. In such an event, the entire assault against New Orleans might have had to be abandoned.

At three o'clock, that twilight hour of the soul, Jackson thought briefly of renewing the attack. But the men were tired now, and by daylight their meager numbers would be apparent to the enemy. As he wrote to Monroe, "As the safety of the city will depend on the fate of this army, it must not be incautiously exposed." He ordered his troops to rest on the field at de la Ronde's for the remainder of the night. They were to build as many fires as they could find wood for, to suggest the encampment of a mighty army. At dawn he would pull them back closer to the city to form a line of permanent defense.

No campfires glowed at Villeré's during the balance of the night. The *Carolina's* guns still dominated the plantation. Those who had fought slept fitfully on the damp ground, while their newly-arrived comrades tried to reconcile this scene of near disaster to their preconceptions of an easy victory. Lieutenant Gleig wandered among the prostrate forms, looking for his companion Grey. He was shocked by the number of dead bodies in so small an area. "Friends and foes lay together in small groups of four or six, nor was it difficult to tell by whose hand some of them had fallen. Nay, such had been the deadly closeness of the strife that in one or two places an English and American soldier might be seen with the bayonet of each fastened in the other's body."

Moving further afield, Gleig came to the stack where he and Grey had parted, and found the captain's body "shot through the temple by a rifle bullet so remarkably small as scarcely to leave any trace of its progress. I threw myself on the ground beside him, and wept like a child."

*Major General Andrew Jackson, commander-in-chief of the American forces at New Orleans, engraved from a contemporary portrait by John Vanderlyn.*

*Sophronie Claiborne, wife of Governor Claiborne of Louisiana.* (Collection of the Louisiana State Museum)

*Governor W. C. C. Claiborne, commander of the militia during the siege of New Orleans.* (Courtesy, Louisiana National Guard)

*Edward Livingston, lawyer and spokesman for the American colony at New Orleans, and Jackson's aide throughout the invasion crisis.* (New York Public Library)

*Jean Laffite, pirate leader of the buccanners of Barataria, allied with General Jackson's forces in the defense of New Orleans. From a contemporary sketch.* (Collection of the Louisiana State Museum)

*Pierre Denis de la Ronde, wealthy planter and militia colonel, on whose plantation much of the battle action centered.* (Collection of the Louisiana State Museum)

*Versailles, the de la Ronde mansion, with its avenue of oaks leading from the Mississippi River to the entrance.* (From Lossing's Pictorial Field Book of the War of 1812)

*The Place d'Armes (now Jackson Square) in the early nineteenth century, with St. Louis Cathedral in the background, flanked by the Cabildo and the Presbytere.*

*Villeré's plantation manor, though single-storied, was typical of the French "chateaux" on the Mississippi below New Orleans.*

*Major General Jacques Villeré whose plantation manor became the British headquarters throughout the campaign.* (Collection of the Louisiana State Museum)

*Bernard de Marigny, wealthy and aristocratic leader of French society in New Orleans.* (Special Collections Division, Tulane University Library)

*Commodore Daniel Todd Patterson, commander of U. S. naval forces at New Orleans, 1814-1815.* (Courtesy of Chrysler Museum, Norfolk, Va.)

*Defeat and capture of the American gunboat flotilla on Lake Borgne, December 14, 1814. Painting in oil by T. L. Hornbrook.* (Courtesy, Chicago Historical Society)

*Lieutenant Thomas Catesby Jones, commanding the gunboat flotilla in the battle for Lake Borgne.* (Official U. S. Navy photo)

*Major Jean Baptiste Plauché, commander of the Battalion of Orleans Volunteers.* (Collection of the Louisiana State Museum)

*Colonel Michel Fortier, organizer and commander of the Negro battalions.* (Collection of the Louisiana State Museum)

*Brigadier General John Coffee, commander of Tennessee troops and Jackson's "right hand," from a portrait in the Hermitage at Nashville.*

*Major General William Carroll, serving beside Coffee, was later elected Governor of Tennessee.* (Courtesy, Tennessee Historical Society)

*Brigadier General David B. Morgan, commander of the ill-fated American troops on the right bank of the Mississippi.* (Collection of the Louisiana State Museum)

*Admiral Sir Alexander Cochrane, commanding the British fleet at the siege of New Orleans, as painted by William Beechy.* (Courtesy of the Hon. Mrs. Hastings, photo by National Maritime Museum)

*Sir Edward Michael Pakenham at Salamanca, two years before he assumed command of the British troops at New Orleans.* (Courtesy of His Grace the Duke of Wellington)

*The ramparts of Jackson's line today. Behind this earthwork the General's heterogeneous army repelled the repeated British assaults.* (National Park Service)

*Jackson rides to the aid of the hard-pressed artillery during the night battle of December 23. From a painting by W. A. C. Pape.* (Collection of the Louisiana State Museum)

*Death of General Pakenham at the last great battle for New Orleans, from a contemporary engraving.* (New York Public Library)

*Jackson, right, commanding the American troops behind the ramparts during the British assault of January 8.* (New York Public Library)

*Macarty's house behind the Rodriguez canal, Andrew Jackson's field headquarters, survived British artillery fire as this post-war daguerrotype indicates.*

*Hailed by a grateful citizenry, General Jackson is crowned with laurel beneath an arch of triumph erected at New Orleans in his honor. From a contemporary sketch.*

*Rachel Jackson, wife of the commanding general, joined her husband at New Orleans after the victory.* (New York Public Library)

*General Jackson acknowledges the plaudits of his rugged army after the victory at New Orleans. From a painting by Howard Pyle.* (Howard Pyle Collection, Delaware Art Museum)

*Contemporary allegorical drawing depicts the Peace of Ghent. The treaty itself, which settled very little, was signed before the Battle of New Orleans.* (From Lossing's Pictorial Field Book of the War of 1812)

*Statues of Generals Pakenham and Gibbs, both killed at New Orleans on January 8, 1815, stand in the South Transept of St. Paul's Cathedral, London.* (Courtesy, Warburg Institute)

# 12. *"God Rest You Merry, Gentlemen"*

Earl Bathurst, Minister of War, wrote to the Lord Mayor of London:

> My Lord, I have the honour to acquaint your Lordship . . . with the intelligence that a Treaty of Peace was signed between his majesty and the United States of America by the respective Plenipotentiaries on the 24th Inst. It is at the same time my duty to acquaint your Lordship that hostilities will cease as soon as it Shall have been ratified by the President of the United States as well as by the Prince Regent in the name and in behalf of his majesty.
>
> > I have the honour, etc.

Five thousand miles from New Orleans the Belgian city of Ghent awakened to a frost-bound Christmas Eve. Rivers and canals were frozen solid. In the air was a hint of the snow that blanketed the rest of Europe. At the medieval Citadelle Chartreux the five American commissioners had met for the last time with the three representatives of the Crown to sign the treaty of peace that culminated eleven months of fractious negotiations.

185

It was a "treaty of the status quo." Two and a half years of bloodshed, the blundering defeats and costly victories, had brought little of
significance to either side. Conquered lands would be returned to their
original possessors. The Indians would be neutralized. Disputed
boundaries with Canada, the matters of fisheries and sailors' rights,
were tentatively settled. Over the fields of Flanders the bells of St.
Bavo's Cathedral pealed their messages of Peace on Earth.

But there was no Atlantic Cable then to inform New Orleans of that
message—no thought of peace on the plains of Chalmette-de la Ronde.
True, the treaty made Jackson's "Christmas fandango" of the night
before the last battle of the War of 1812. But who was to know that
in Louisiana? As the troops awoke to a chilly dawn, their thoughts
were beamed at battles yet to come. And there was plenty to remind
them.

"That day dawned gloomily for the invaders," wrote one British
commentator. "The events of the 23d had greatly depressed their
spirits, and the soldiers had lost confidence in Keane, their commander.
The sky was clouded, the ground was wet, the atmosphere was chilly,
and shadowing disappointment was seen in every face."

In the British camp at Villeré's, where daylight at last permitted the
burial of the dead, spirits were as heavy as the early morning fog. From
the cane stack where Charles Grey had fallen, Lieutenant Gleig carried
the young captain's body back to Villeré's manor, now converted to a
hospital. "Here, having dug for him a grave at the bottom of the garden,
I laid him out as a soldier should be laid, arrayed not in a shroud but in
his uniform."

It was not the end of Gleig's compounded shock and grief. Seemingly
compelled to share in the misery of his comrades, he wandered through
the halls of Villeré's, seeing not the glory, but the inhumanity of war.

> Every room in the house was crowded with wretches mangled, and ap-
> parently in the most excruciating agonies. Prayers, groans, and I grieve to
> add, the most horrid exclamations smote the ear everywhere I turned. Some
> lay at length upon straw, with eyes half closed and limbs motionless; some
> endeavoured to start up, shrieking with pain, while the wandering eye and
> incoherent speech of others, indicated the loss of reason and usually fore-
> told the approach of death. But there was one among the rest, whose appear-

ance was too horrible ever to be forgotten. He had been shot through the windpipe, and the breath making its way between the skin and the flesh, had dilated him to a size absolutely terrific. His head and face were particularly shocking. Every feature was enlarged beyond what can well be imagined; while his eyes were so completely hidden by the cheeks and forehead, as to destroy all resemblance to a human countenance.

He found things no better in the rooms reserved for wounded officers, many of whom were acquaintances or friends, and was shocked to find a fellow lieutenant "in the most dreadful agony, screaming out, and gnawing the covering under which he lay." No, he thought, hearing the distant "Angelus" tolled by the bells of the Cathedral, it was hard to realize that this was Christmas Eve, heralding the day when mankind's thoughts and prayers were turned to Peace on Earth.

Shortly before dawn Jackson had pulled his troops back to Macarty's, two miles closer to New Orleans. He left Hind's Dragoons and a portion of the 7th Infantry at de la Ronde's to serve as lookouts keeping track of British movements. Macarty's mansion, screened by its orange groves, would now be his field headquarters and its second-story balcony his observatory.

A retired Creole planter whose twilight years were engaged in studying the stars sent the General a seemingly eccentric Christmas present, his astronomical telescope. Jackson had it mounted on the railing. It gave the field commander a greatly magnified view of the opposing enemy.

Below the house, bordering Chalmette's, ran the Rodriguez canal, extending to the cypress swamp some half mile to the east. It had been mentioned previously as a likely margin of defense if the city should ever be threatened or assaulted. Here the General resolved to make his stand, telling his troops, "This position will not be abandoned till we drive those redcoats off our land."

New Orleans was canvassed for spades, picks and shovels. A thousand Negro slaves were solicited from the plantations, and they joined the troops in a hard-pressed effort to deepen and widen the canal. Mud from the bottom was piled on the upper bank and secured there by staves and branches from the swamp. The ditch was widened to a good ten feet and deepened until it contained two feet or more of water.

The troops grumbled at this menial task; it was work for Negroes only. But they recognized the need for the rising parapet along the ditch and kept digging till their muscles ached and they were relieved by successive waves of diggers.

While this work was going forward, Jackson ordered Major Latour to cut a crevasse in the levee along the Mississippi just below the ditch, to flood the fields between this point and Villeré's plantation. He sent a message to Morgan at the English Turn to have the engineer Major Lafon do the same at Jumonville's below the British line. He would have the enemy trapped in a morass of mud and water in which the movement of troops and artillery would be impeded.

The levees were cut and for a while the Mississippi waters swirled across the plains to a depth of several inches. But there was a back-lash to this strategy. The almost dry canals at de la Ronde's and Villeré's were filled to a point that greatly aided the navigation of the barges bringing troops and ammunition and provisions to the British camp. And after three days the plains were effectively drained of water, though the ground stayed treacherous and sodden.

Throughout all of Christmas Eve and Christmas morning, there was little peace at Villeré's plantation and the huddles of huts and British tents around it. From the river the schooner *Carolina* kept up her intermittent cannonades, sending the exasperated soldiers scampering for shelter. Quartermaster Surtees recorded a providential escape the morning of the 24th, "for we had scarcely left a little wooden hut, behind which we had take up our abode, and slept for a few hours after the fight, when Bang! comes an eighteen-pound shot right through the house, just at the very spot where we had a minute or two before been sitting."

Surtees complained that the schooner's captain "fired into every house within reach of his guns, although he saw as plainly as we did that most of them were filled with wounded." One of the shots neatly removed, from beneath the head of an injured soldier, the knapsack which he was using as a pillow. Another struck a fleeing corporal in the breast, passing completely through him, "upon which he gave himself a sort of a shake, and fell lifeless to the earth."

Nothing could exceed the great annoyance this mischievous schooner continued to be to us all that and the next day, for they not only saw everything we did, but we could not move in any number without being saluted with an 18 lb. shot, and we had no means of retaliation.

Actually, Captain Henley had become anxious about the position of the *Carolina* since Jackson's withdrawal up the river. Well below Macarty's, it no longer afforded support for Jackson's line. He wanted to move further up-river, adjacent to the new American position, but the wind was against him and the current strong. The only immediate alternative was to slip down-river, past the British camp, before enemy artillery arrived to intercept him. That, however, would remove his vessel from the scene of action altogether. Henley decided to hope for a change of wind and, with plenty of ball and powder taken from the Baratarians, continued his bombardment.

Meanwhile the *Louisiana,* commissioned at last and manned by a conscripted crew, had moved downriver to a position just one fateful mile above the *Carolina*—partly to protect the open field in front of the Rodriguez canal, partly to add her firepower to the *Carolina's* cannonade. Under the command of Lieutenant Charles Thompson of the U.S. Navy, her sixteen twenty-four-pound cannon had a range of nearly two miles, bringing in range any British troops who sought shelter between the new and old levees.

In fact, there was little security anywhere along the British front. From their position at de la Ronde's, Major Hind's pickets worried and fired on their British counterparts throughout the day. After dark the Tennesseans engaged in "rabbit hunts," creeping along the cane fields to pick off British sentinels with their unerring marksmanship. It had all the sport of a squirrel shoot. Occasionally groups of backwoodsmen, stifling their snickers, would creep close to the British line, shout commands and discharge their rifles, inciting the British to fall in to meet the impending attack—and, after the onslaught of December 23, the British were easily convinced of such a possibility. The Americans would hug the ground, convulsed with laughter.

The Choctaw Indians were uniquely adapted to this sport of night-time terrorism. One of Jackson's Choctaws named Poindexter did a flourishing business during this interval, ambushing and killing British sentries and bringing their weapons back to sell to the Americans as souvenirs. American officers were especially interested in the British rifles, which fired a much heavier ball than their own, with barrels, however, only thirty inches long. Plainly they would inflict a mortal wound at close quarters, but had nowhere near the range of the long American rifles firing a smaller shot. It was something to remember in the future.

The British, especially those assigned to picket duty, complained bitterly about the tactics of the Choctaws and the Tennesseans. Such sneaky nighttime killings violated every rule of "civilized" warfare, could only be branded as "assassinations."

"Those savages have no knowledge of how war should be fought," one officer protested. "In Europe, when two armies face each other, the outposts of neither are molested. Nay, so far is this tacit good under-standing carried out that I myself have seen French and English not more than twenty yards apart. These 'dirty shirts' entertain no such chivalric notions."

It was a stark and joyless Christmas Day for the men from Merrie England. Officers clubbed together for their Christmas dinner, sharing their small stock of provisions, eating in huts or barns without benefit of plates or knives and forks. They did their best to make light of their misfortunes and tried to ignore the volleys of ball and grapeshot from the *Carolina* which shook the ground around them, sometimes crashing through the roofs and walls. But as George Gleig wrote, "At so melancholy a Christmas dinner I do not recollect at any time to have been present."

While we were thus sitting at table, a loud shriek was heard after one of these explosions, and on running out we found that a shot had taken effect in the body of an unfortunate soldier. I mention this incident, because I never beheld in any human being so great a tenacity of life. Though fairly cut in two at the lower part of the belly, the poor wretch lived for nearly an hour, gasping for breath, and giving signs of excruciating pain.

It was little wonder that camp conversation contained little of that note of optimism, the boastful confidence, that had accompanied their uncontested landing. It was sorely evident to Gleig and others that "the American deserters had purposely deceived us, or been simply misinformed. Instead of an easy conquest, we had already met with vigorous opposition; instead of finding the inhabitants ready and eager to join us, we found houses deserted, the cattle and horses driven away, and every appearance of hostility."

But that afternoon a thunderous salvo—this one from within their lines—proclaimed a reversal of their fortunes. Spirits soared and hope was born anew. General Sir Edward Pakenham had landed and was on the field to take command of the British expeditionary force.

Some may have guessed but few had known the identity of the awaited General. Rumors had circulated ever since the rendezvous at Negril Bay. For a while Lord Hill had seemed a likely choice, having been one of Wellington's chief lieutenants in the Peninsular campaign.

Then speculation focused on the Iron Duke himself. Wellington had, in fact, been offered the assignment and had turned it down. He was needed too greatly in Europe. Furthermore, he had been ever critical of the war in America and was opposed to Admiral Cochrane's motives of pecuniary gain.

"I shall do you but little good in America," he told the British ministry, "and I shall go there only . . . to sign a peace which might as well be signed now."

The Duke, however, readily recommended his brother-in-law, Lord Pakenham, as an able substitute. Sir Edward, a major in the army at the age of sixteen, had had a distinguished career of military service, five years of it under Wellington himself. As division commander at Salamanca in July of 1812 he had broken and routed the French army in what the Duke considered "the most decisive and brilliant maneuver of the battle."

"He may not be the greatest genius," Wellington had said, "but my partiality for him does not lead me astray when I tell you he is one of the best we have."

At thirty-seven, Lord Pakenham was everything that Andrew Jackson, forty-eight, was not. Of high birth and aristocratic breeding, he had been educated in the refinements of military discipline. Tall and conventionally handsome, he was punctilious about dress and deportment. He would no more have appeared with boots unpolished than with hair unpowdered or improper regimental facings on his cuffs or collar. In contrast to Jackson's shattered and abused physique, he was at the peak of health, having suffered only two minor wounds in his career, the first in an assault against the French on Martinique. A bullet had damaged a muscle at the base of his neck, giving his head what he considered a "comical" tilt. A later bullet, striking in the same place, had put it right again.

Like Wellington, Pakenham had little regard for the war with the United States. "I think I have escaped America," he wrote in June of 1814, "and shall consider myself vastly fortunate to have been spared such a service." But he hadn't escaped. Four months later, in October, he was aboard the frigate *Statira,* sailing to join the expeditionary force against New Orleans, with specific instructions to act without regard for any talk of peace negotiations or treaties signed at Ghent.

There was a rumor that Sir Edward brought with him a commission as governor of Louisiana, along with the promise of an earldom if he conquered New Orleans. A more intriguing rumor claimed that the future "Lady Pakenham" was aboard the *Statira,* waiting to marry the General when he re-embarked victorious. Neither story was ever corroborated. But it gave the new leader a halo of glamor with the troops, to whom he was a distant though respected figure. Even the officers felt overshadowed in his presence, excepting Admiral Cochrane, twenty years his senior, and his adjutant Harry Smith who spoke of him as "dear Sir Edward . . . one of the most amusing persons imaginable, a high-minded and chivalrous fellow in every idea."

His appointment had come too late for him to join the first wave of the expedition. Stopping at Jamaica he had accompanied General John Lambert's third division to the Gulf and to the anchorage below Lake Borgne. With Pakenham were Major General Samuel Gibbs as second in command, artillery Colonel Alexander Dickson, and as chief of engineers, Colonel John Fox Burgoyne, illegitimate son of "Gentleman Johnny" Burgoyne of Revolutionary War repute.

It was a stalwart staff of officers, all veterans of Wellington's campaigns, much decorated, much experienced, generally outshining those who had preceded them across the ocean. Only they were arriving late. The lines of battle had been drawn and crucial decisions had been made.

The General reached the landing at the Bayou Bienvenu on Christmas morning, and on his way to Villeré's was briefed on the events of December 23. He made no comment, but was obviously impatient to assume command. Up to now, he realized, everything had been in Cochrane's hands. It was not as he would have wanted it.

To greet their new commander-in-chief, General Keane had lined up the troops in full dress uniform with regimental colors flying. Against the drab background of the cane fields they presented a colorful, almost majestic spectacle, brass buckles gleaming on the crossed white belts of green and scarlet tunics; the facings of each tunic matching the colors of the regimental flags; emblems and epaulettes lending a touch of gold in contrast to the black sheen of leather boots and plumed caps.

As Pakenham rode up the line with General Gibbs to accept command from Keane, the bugles sounded, officers' swords flashed in salute, and the cannon boomed a welcome. Tall in the saddle, Sir Edward forced a polite smile as his keen eye swept across the disposition of the camp and the terrain. J. M. Fortescue's comments bear the ring of truth.

> When he realized the situation into which the Admiral had decoyed the army, he was with good reason furious. To all intents his force was cooped up on an isthmus three-quarters of a mile broad between the Mississippi and the swamp. In front was Jackson's fortified position; on the river were the enemy's armed vessels, flanking the only possible line of advance; and in the rear was [sic] the lake and the sea. The only base of supply was eighty miles distant, and accessible only in open boats; and the last four miles of this waterway were so narrow that it could hardly admit two boats abreast.

The position, Pakenham realized, was precarious, either for supplying munitions and supplies for an effective siege, or for retreat if retreat were necessary. It was twelve miles over rough terrain by a hastily-constructed road from the mouth of the Bayou Bienvenu to the encampment. If that extended line of communication should be cut by the enemy, the army would be stranded. Even with the line kept open, the far-distant fleet had not enough supplies for a prolonged siege, and the plantations could hardly supply enough food to supply the British troops for long.

Immediately after the reception ceremonies, Pakenham conferred with generals Keane and Gibbs and Admiral Cochrane. It was a moment of truth for Keane. As he tried to explain the developments to date—the difficulties in ferrying troops across the lake and up the bayou and over the marshes to Villeré's, his decision to withhold attack until reinforcements had arrived, the unexpected battle of December 23—he sensed behind Pakenham's instinctive courtesy a festering disapproval. More, he sensed the silent scorn of Admiral Cochrane, who had helped to create this situation in the first place, but who felt that he, Keane, had not made the best of it.

Although Pakenham had listened considerately to Keane's veiled apologies, he took exception to them. It was a mistake, he averred, not to have attacked at once on landing. It was a mistake, too, not to have considered the Plain of Gentilly more seriously, at least with a view to making a second beachhead at that point. And he quite bluntly referred to the battle of December 23 as a "defeat."

This brought Cochrane vocally to Keane's side. It had not been a defeat, but a successful holding action, the Admiral insisted. Moreover, New Orleans was still invitingly within their grasp, since the "dirty shirts" were hardly a match for veteran British troops. If the General was unwilling to risk his army, he, the Admiral—repeating his earlier boast to General Keane—would "take the city with my marines and sailors, and the army can bring up the baggage."

Pakenham winced at this. Cochrane was technically his equal on this expedition. But it was the navy's duty to transport the army and supplies and counter American naval maneuvers. As to land operations, that was his department. To himself, the General may well have considered withdrawing and establishing another, more convenient beachhead. But shifting troops at this point and on this terrain was too hazardous a risk. He was in a cul-de-sac and would have to make the best of it. He had no doubts about ultimate victory, but it would be more difficult and more costly than anticipated.

On top of it all, the British General had no sources of intelligence regarding the enemy in front of him, no cavalry for effective reconnaissance. During the Peninsular campaign the Spanish guerrillas had penetrated French lines and had brought back valuable information. Who was there here to keep him so informed? American captives and deserters? The wily Spaniards from the fishing village? Not for a moment would he rely on them.

And where were the disaffected citizens of New Orleans who were supposed to flock to the British side at the first sign of the Union Jack? Where were the slaves who were supposed to rise to their support? His own West India troops, whose black complexions were expected to strike terror among white Louisianians, were lying generally indisposed from unfamiliar hardship in this unfamiliar climate, with many even dead.

But—first things first.

With the constant shelling from the vessels on the river making further operations hazardous, Pakenham's first decision was to silence those destructive guns. Cochrane readily agreed. For the next forty-eight hours the overworked sailors were assigned to hauling up artillery from Lake Borgne. To aid in this, the Indians from Pensacola were sent to round up horses on the plantations below Villeré's. They were fired on mistakenly by British pickets, but returned with thirty animals too small to be of use. The few British officers with mounts of their own were ordered to turn them over to be put to work. They did so reluctantly, keeping the better horses under cover.

For the most part the marines and sailors did the job with brawn and sweat. The canals which the enemy had temporarily flooded were now empty; the barges had to be pushed through the mire till they bogged down altogether. Guns were then wrestled to more solid land and hauled by horses and sailors across the difficult terrain.

By evening of the 26th more than a dozen pieces of artillery had been brought from the fleet to Villeré's and erected on the river bank—six heavy cannon, four lighter guns and several howitzers. Two of the heavy guns were for firing hot-shot, and furnaces were built beside them. Launching equipment for the new-type Congreve rockets was made ready.

The rockets, designed as much to terrify as to destroy, were Britain's secret weapon in this last year of the American war—a six-centuries old Chinese invention that Sir William Congreve had developed for use by Wellington against the French. They had been employed in the Chesapeake against Fort McHenry, inspiring Francis Scott Key to write his lines, "And the rockets' red glare, the bombs bursting in air . . ." In previous use they had been inaccurate and unpredictable, but had caused some panic among green Yankee troops.

All this had been distantly observed by the Americans behind their rising ramparts and from Jackson's crow's nest at Macarty's. When the Christmas salute to Pakenham had echoed across the plains of Chalmette-de la Ronde it was clear that the British were welcoming a new commander. Major Latour, with an uncanny nose for news, correctly identified the British viscount. The name was confirmed when a British deserter slyly boasted that Lord Pakenham expected to enjoy his Christmas dinner in New Orleans.

"If so," Jackson remarked dryly to his aides, "he will find me at the head of the table."

The arrival of the British General honed Jackson's almost fanatical determination to destroy the enemy. Presaging the words of Winston Churchill, he would fight in the ditches and the fields, he would fight behind the ramparts, he would fight in the streets of New Orleans, he would fight in the ruins and retreat to fight beyond them if he had to. He ordered Captain Thomas Butler to keep a tight hold on the city, alert the guard, arrest anyone abroad without a pass. "Before two days," complained Mayor Girod, "the guard house will be full."

The British, now reinforced and with a new commander, would not wait long before attacking. Jackson looked to the strengthening of his earthworks, now rising five or six feet along the upper bank of the canal. Half a mile in length between the river and the cypress swamp, they were a naturally foreshortened line—the cane fields narrowing towards the city like the center of an hour glass. Jean Laffite, still close to the General as an unofficial aide, surveyed it knowingly. He recommended that the fortifications be extended further, into the swamp and back towards the Chef Menteur, "to prevent the enemy from flanking your left."

Jackson concurred, and Carroll's division was summoned from the Plain of Gentilly, presumably no longer threatened, to help with the digging and to occupy that section of the line. At the same time, most of the Louisiana militia at Gentilly was called in to be placed among the Regulars in the new line of defense, leaving the disgruntled Claiborne once again without command.

Operating from de la Ronde's, Hind's Dragoons kept a careful watch on British movements. The ubiquitous General Humbert, whose reckless eagerness appealed to Jackson, was sent on spying missions of his own invention. Reuben Kemper and his guerrilla-minded band of mounted Tennesseans ranged down the Bayou Mazant and Bayou Bienvenu and observed the additional troops and artillery arriving from the fishing village. They might be headed for Villeré's or even up the main branch of the Bayou Bienvenu towards Gentilly.

Word came from Pierre Lacoste at the Chef Menteur that the British had made a landing at that point and that he was retreating to a new position. It was what Jackson dreaded most—a second front! He sent Major Latour to verify Lacoste's report. Latour returned with reassuring news. According to his interpretation, a group of fun-loving British sailors had indulged in some Halloween amusement—setting fire to the dry grass of the peninsula and forcing Lacoste to withdraw from the intimidating smoke and flame.

The prank appealed to Major Hind, who retaliated by setting ablaze the sedge grass in front of Villeré's canal. It burned out harmlessly, and the British were grateful to him for clearing the land and bettering their vision.

Most of the available American artillery was on the *Carolina* and *Louisiana*. The two light field guns which had featured in the battle of December 23 were placed on the right end of the new "Line Jackson," commanding the river road, and two heavier guns were mounted to the left of them, batteries Two and Three, directed on the plain below.

The troops which had participated in the Battle in the Dark were distributed approximately as before—the Regulars and militia near the river on the right end of the line, Plauché's Creoles and Daquin's colored near the center, Coffee on the left and Carroll's Tennesseans holding down the new, oblique extension in the swamp. This time Jugeat's Choctaws were positioned on the far left under General Coffee.

At nightfall the Americans spread out on the damp ground in a chilly drizzle with their arms beside them. There were no tents, few blankets.

Exposure was something they would have to get accustomed to. But there was plenty of food, one of the blessings of being near the city, and on that suspenseful night of December 27 fires were kept smoldering for heating coffee.

Jackson and Butler rode along and behind the Rodriguez canal to inspect the defenses. The half-mile rampart looked solid enough, six feet high and twelve feet deep in places. But it had yet to stand the test of enemy bombardment. Could it withstand the shock of the heavy guns which the British had been seen installing on Chalmette's? Where the line bent backwards through the cypress swamp the barricade was sketchier, twin rows of fallen logs with earth and branches piled between, barely high enough to protect a marksman lying prone. That seemed sufficient to the Tennesseans, who relied on the swamp itself, marked "impassable" on contemporary charts, to frustrate and impede the enemy.

As he passed among the troops Jackson exchanged easy banter with the men whose names and faces were familiar, something his counterpart Lord Pakenham would never think of doing. Often the General would dismount, preferring to mingle with the troops on foot, but walking was as tiring to his overtaxed physique as was sitting in the saddle. Among Carroll's troops he nodded cheerfully to the middle-aged James Henderson, a retired colonel from Tennessee, who had ridden all the way from Natchez, offering to enlist as private. Jackson had promptly accepted him and restored him to his former rank. Near the bend in the swamp, he came upon his ward and nephew Captain John Donelson. They exchanged news from home and Jackson teased him about the girl he'd left behind him.

"I see you have the extreme left of the line," said Jackson. "I suppose you know that's the place of honor here."

"No, General. Jugeat and his damned Choctaws are still to the left of me."

"Don't say 'damned Choctaws,'" Jackson rebuked avuncularly. "They're good fellows, every one of them. But where are they? I don't see them."

"Oh, they're always out in the swamp, basking on logs like so many alligators."

Jackson was gratified to hear it. That was where the Indians belonged, where their penchant for wilderness fighting might be useful.

In fact his whole line from the Choctaws on the far left to Ross's Regulars near the river seemed as well deployed as he could arrange it. If only the barricades would hold. . . .

He rode back with Butler to Macarty's, hoping for a good night's sleep. He badly needed it.

# 13.   Bring up the Guns!

For once the dawn, on December 27, was bright and clear and free of fog. Since early morning hot-shot had been glowing in the furnace at the British battery beside the river. Watching through his telescope at Macarty's, Jackson realized the danger to the *Carolina*. He sent word to Captain Henley to move further up the river, out of range. Henley had already tried that. With the northwest wind too scant to fill the sails, and the current too strong for warping, the ship could not be budged.

As aboard the *Louisiana,* a mile above and a little safer, seamen with lighted matches took their battle stations at the guns. Before they could fire, an ear-piercing blast from the five guns of the British battery shook the air and rippled the waters of the Mississippi. Shells and hot-shot raked the deck of the *Carolina*. Both vessels returned the fire, but only the twelve-pound gun on the schooner's bow could reach the enemy. A second blast from the shore dropped a red-hot ball in the center of the *Carolina*'s hold close to the magazine. Wedged between cables, sputtering and gnawing at the timbers of the hull, the festering shot could not be reached. The fire spread.

Henley gave the order to abandon ship. Marines and sailors lowered the boats or plunged in the river to swim ashore. One seaman, for reasons never to be known, swam back to the ship and climbed aboard. He had reached the deck when the flames struck the magazine and the ship exploded in a burst of flaming timber that showered on both sides of the river. Witnessing the ship's destruction Quartermaster Surtees wrote, "This of course deserved and obtained three as hearty cheers as I believe were ever given by Britons."

The British battery now trained its guns on the *Louisiana*. Aroused by the initial blast American and English soldiers flocked to the levee to view the contest and cheer their respective teams, indifferent to one another's presence. Among the spectators on the English side were the Indian chiefs from Pensacola, delighted with their role of audience in this diverting white man's war. In New Orleans citizens climbed to their roofs and balconies to watch in fascination as the "flaming comets" soared towards the vessel.

Manning the *Louisiana* were the derelicts of the New Orleans waterfront, idle seamen rounded up two weeks before. They were men of all races and nations ("excepting Britons") two thirds of whom could not speak English. If there were ever a time a crew might break and panic under fire, this was it. But somehow Lieutenant Thompson had shaped them into a disciplined smooth-running outfit, responding like veterans to his command.

The longboat was quickly lowered. Half the men slid aboard, grabbed a hawser from the *Louisiana*'s bow and started tugging at the oars. The other half jumped ashore and tried to haul the ship upstream with cables. As shells and hot-shot rained around them and the schooner's hull began to smoke, the separate crews strained every muscle in this tug of war against the current. Inch by inch, as the cheering Americans egged them on, the *Louisiana* was hauled to safety opposite Dr. Flood's plantation.

From the charred wreck of the now neglected *Carolina*, divers and crew began to salvage many of her heavy guns. In that respect her humiliating fate was not a total loss.

With one American ship destroyed, though he had hoped to eliminate both, Pakenham felt more certain of his boast that "the American war should terminate with a brilliant success on our part." Like Cochrane he had received instructions that if reports or rumors reached him regarding a peace settlement at Ghent, he should continue hostilities "to the end that its final ratification might be governed by more favorable circumstances." He interpreted those circumstances as the capture of New Orleans and possession of the Mississippi Valley.

It was time now for the mass assault that would carry his troops into the city. He planned his attack for the following morning. The enemy lines would first be pulverized by an artillery bombardment. Throughout the rest of the day Colonel Dickson and Captain R. N. Hill of the artillery directed Cochrane's sailors and marines in bringing up more heavy guns from the fleet and the beachhead at the Bayou Bienvenu. As Captain Hill recorded,

> The guns and their carriages were brought ashore separately in ships' boats and were then assembled and mounted for transport by land to the position of the Army . . . Our lack of transport-animals hampered all our efforts. It at once became apparent that our plan of relying on the invaded country for horses or oxen or mules was visionary, because all belonging to the plantations within our zone of operation had been driven off inside the enemy's fortified lines as soon as our presence in Lake Borgne became known.
>
> Under these circumstances the transport of heavy guns and their ammunition over the Bienvenu road became exceedingly slow and toilsome. In some cases the guns and tumbrils were hauled by the soldiers, manning long drag ropes. The road itself was very bad; passing most of the way through dense cypress swamps, soft and miry everywhere, and frequently "corduroyed"—as the Americans called it—in places where the swamp would otherwise be impassable.

In spite of the difficulty, three mortars and six medium cannon were hauled up to Villeré's along with rockets and launchers. During the operation troops of the second division continued to arrive at the landing, fearful they had missed out on the capture and occupation of New Orleans. Hill assured them they were not too late and recounted the night battle of December 23 when the unorthodox Americans had fought like savage Indians. From this "I gave them my honest opinion that we should find more difficulty in the conquest than we had anticipated."

At sundown strong detachments of British infantry drove the American pickets from Lacoste's and de la Ronde's and established advanced positions midway between Jackson's line and Villeré's. Here they waited out the night, while Dickson brought up the Artillery.

Pakenham's plan for the assault was simplified by the destruction of the *Carolina;* he would not have to worry excessively about his flank. After the opening barrage had silenced the American artillery and reduced the enemy earthworks to rubble, the army would advance in two divisions. Keane would attack near the river with three regiments, the 85th, under Colonel Thornton, the 95th, and the 93rd Highlanders along with the 1st West India. General Gibbs would attack on the right with the 21st under Colonel Rennie, the 44th, and the 5th West India. Pakenham would lead and direct at the center with the Duchess of York's light dragoons. The troops were ordered to fill their knapsacks with emergency rations for the subsequent occupation of New Orleans.

Meanwhile the Americans girded for the attack they knew, through spies and deserters, would come on the morning of the 28th. Jean Laffite supervised the placement of another battery on Jackson's line and urged the General to send for Dominique You and Renato Beluché stationed along the Bayou St. John. They were the best artillerists, Laffite insisted, in the whole United States. Jackson agreed and also summoned Lacoste's Free Colored from the Chef Menteur, where he felt they were no longer needed, to take their place beside Daquin's blacks in the center of the line.

As a precaution the General ordered the slave battalion and part of the militia to start erecting a second defense position at Dupré's canal a mile closer to the city. It would be something to retreat to if he had to retreat, and it would keep the slave laborers occupied and out of mischief.

Perhaps it was this precautionary act, along with the destruction of the *Carolina,* that reinfected New Orleans with anxiety. Was Jackson already contemplating a withdrawal? The optimism which had followed the American heroics on December 23 was wearing thin. Faith in their backwoods General began to wane. Jackson, to whom their safety was committed, became again a stranger to them, "a commander who had never faced an enemy but Indians."

Vincent Nolte, with an impish inclination to pour fuel on festering fires, spread the word that Jackson had "openly declared" that, if forced to retreat, "he would imitate the sample of the Russians at Moscow, and consign the whole city to flames," rather than let it fall to British hands. Certain members of the Legislature were reported as favoring surrender to the English to avoid destruction of the city.

Abner Duncan, one of Jackson's more unstable aides, had informed the General that many Creoles favored this idea.

Judge François-Xavier Martin, a firsthand observer of events in New Orleans and more reliable than Vincent Nolte, noted: "A report was spread that . . . Jackson had taken measures and given positive orders for blowing up the magazines and setting fire to various parts of the city, in case the British succeeded in forcing his ranks. His conduct in this respect was considered by some as an evidence of his deeming his defeat a probable event."

Older residents remembered the slave uprisings in the past and the incendiary epidemic of some years before when a number of planters' houses had been burned by Negroes. Should Jackson set fire to the city it would be a signal for the slaves to rise again, spreading terror and death among the population. "The idea," wrote Martin, "of thus finding themselves with their wives, children, and old men driven by the flames of their houses towards a black enemy bringing down destruction, harrowed the minds of the inhabitants."

A committee of four from the Legislature, headed by Bernard de Marigny, called at Macarty's to inquire what Jackson's plans were for New Orleans in the event of an enforced retreat. Miffed by the query, Jackson told them: "If I thought the hair of my head knew my thoughts I would cut it off or burn it." The emphasis on "burn it" seemed suggestive. The General added, "Tell your honorable body that if disaster does overtake me and the fate of war drives me from my line to the city, they may expect to have a very warm session indeed." In other words, de Marigny thought, New Orleans could look forward to a hot time. An incendiary time, perhaps?

> (Later Jackson confided to an unnamed friend his secret intentions if he met with an initial setback. "I should have retreated to the city, fired it, and fought the enemy amid the surrounding flames." He would further have ordered the destruction of the riverside plantations. "Nothing for the comfortable maintenance of the enemy would have been left in the rear. I would have destroyed New Orleans—occupied a position above on the river—cut off all supplies, and in this way compelled them to depart from the country.")

On leave from David Morgan's troops at Dr. Flood's, Alexandre Declouet paced the ill-lighted streets of New Orleans. He could not sleep. His over-heated imagination saw the city in flames, the citizens fleeing for their lives. Then the picture changed. New Orleans had been handed over to the British by the Legislature. Its women were ravaged, its houses plundered, its citizens enslaved. Declouet felt he had suddenly seen the light! It was for that purpose, the negotiations for surrender, that the Legislature had remained in session!

He noted a light still burning in the home of Magloire Guichard, Speaker of the House. Guichard was a friend of Fulwar Skipwith, who was a knowledgeable man-about-town. Between them they must know what was going on. Declouet knocked on the door, and Guichard, in his night clothes, admitted him. The Speaker found Declouet something of a bore and fell asleep while his guest was talking. When Declouet kept waking him, he gave him a guest room and retired.

The next morning—early, for great events were pending—Declouet resumed the talk where he had been cut off the night before. According to Guichard's diary of the conversation, his guest repeatedly asked why the Legislature was still in session. Why had it not disbanded according to Governor Claiborne's earlier suggestion?

"I don't know," said Guichard. "I wish they had, for my own affairs suffer as a consequence."

"Say, my friend," persisted Declouet, "do you think the British mean to keep the country for themselves, and that they'll be able to do so?"

"I do not," said Guichard.

"But—tell me frankly what you think would take place, should the English succeed."

"I think the country would be lost. I know what the English did to me in France."

Declouet then repeated the question: Why did the Legislature remain in session? Guichard lost his patience.

"You are constantly asking me why this and why that. Now let me ask you: Why, with General Morgan on the night of the twenty-third did you not attack the enemy from below his camp? To do so, would have caused him to lay down his arms, and would have saved the city— instead of exposing it to this anxiety and peril."

Declouet "made as if he wanted to tear his hair off," Guichard noted. He *had* urged the attack, he said, but Morgan would not agree. What could *he* do, as second in command? Then Declouet reverted to the question, Why did not the Legislature adjourn? What was the meaning of its nightly, secret meetings? "There is in that damned Legislature so many intriguers who would either seize all authority or see the country overturned, that I place no reliance on them. The Legislature can have none but *suspicious intentions* in continuing their sessions, that is my opinion!"

Guichard rose from the table. "Monsieur Declouet, you will always be the same; your suspicions never abandon you." With that he dismissed his guest, who took his unallayed suspicions with him.

Back on the street Declouet had the fortune or misfortune to run into Abner Duncan, Jackson's highly-suggestible aide-de-camp. He explained that he had just come from the home of Magloire Guichard, Speaker of the House. Was it true, he asked excitedly, that the Legislature was conspiring to surrender to the British?

Stunned by the question, Duncan interpreted it as fact. He would have to check with Skipworth, talk to Claiborne. In any event, General Jackson must be told of this.

Behind the Rodriguez canal the troops were sleeping fretfully beside their rifles. But the British on the plains below were promised little sleep that night. Time and again, under cover of darkness, Hind's Dragoons and units of Coffee's cavalry would charge the pickets, shouting and firing their rifles. Time and again the troops encamped at Villeré's would rise to the alarm, seize their muskets and fall in for attack, only to realize they were victims of a prank—"than which," complained Lieutenant Gleig, "nothing is more trying, both to the health and spirits of the army."

In the swamp the Choctaws crept forward to pick off a picket or two; then waited for his replacement to arrive, and picked him off as well, gradually adding to their marketable reservoir of British rifles. As the casualties among the pickets mounted, Pakenham drafted an indignant note to the American commander; such actions were not compatible with civilized military operations.

The next morning dawned clear, cold and sunny. Pakenham noted with satisfaction that the ground would be firm after the long night frost. As the eastern sky turned pink, the bugles sounded for the troops to take their places, Keane on the left, Gibbs on the right. On the field since early morning, the twelve pieces of artillery waited to be hauled into position. They were not heavy guns; two nine-pounders were the largest. But they would be sufficient to shatter the enemy earthworks, which seemed from there to be no more than piles of mud.

But—what if those earthworks proved more solid than they now appeared? Pakenham began to hedge his bets. If the mud held, his troops would still advance and make a closer observation of the barricades, with a view to scaling them and routing the enemy at bayonet point. If, on closer inspection, this should seem inadvisable, he could always withdraw and consider this offensive merely "a reconnaissance in force"—a test of the American fortifications, their artillery and firepower.

Behind the American ramparts, in response to the distant trumpet calls at Villeré's, the bugles sounded reveille and Jordan Noble's drumhead called the Regulars to battle stations. As Jackson mounted the line he could see the *Louisiana* edging down towards Chalmette's, her broadside cannon leveled at the plain.

A commotion behind the General announced new arrivals. Dominique You and Renato Beluché with thirty of the "hellish banditti," their colored shirts stained with sweat and mud, had run nearly all the way from Fort St. John to take their places beside the guns. Behind them came the crew of the defunct *Carolina* under U.S. Artillery Lieutenant Charles E. Crawley. Dominique's men, with the renegade Gambi, were put in charge of one of the twenty-four-pounders; the crew of the *Carolina* manned the other.

Precisely at eight o'clock the British troops received the order to advance. In straight, tight columns they marched with the mechanical precision of toy soldiers, as if imaginary keys protruded from their backs. The green and scarlet jackets and the Highland tartans formed vivid patterns against the dun-colored background. Handsomely mounted and caparisoned, Sir Edward rode in their center, feeling certain of the enemy's disintegration at "the stunning sight of an unyielding undaunted British army marching relentlessly upon him."

Step by step, metering out their growing claim to Louisiana soil, the troops moved forward—"in a merry mood," observed Lieutenant Gleig, though the proper subaltern was somewhat shocked by the coarse jokes and ribald conversation that passed back and forth. A hundred yards. Two hundred yards. Three hundred yards. They had crossed Lacoste's and de la Ronde's and were now at Bienvenu's. No fire from the enemy or from the river.

Aboard the *Louisiana* Patterson stood beside Lieutenant Thompson and watched them come. The seamen stood with lighted matches by the cannon. "Not yet," Patterson cautioned. "Not yet. Wait till they get directly opposite." A British battery had opened fire on the ship, the shots creating harmless whirlpools in the river.

George Gleig with Colonel Thornton and the 85th were within six hundred yards of the American entrenchment. Gleig studied the enemy line and noted with some consternation the intervening ditch and formidable parapet behind it.

Eight twenty-five. Lieutenant Thompson signaled: Fire! The broadside guns of the *Louisiana* paralyzed the air with shock. As if detonated by the blast, the batteries on the American defense line let loose with what Quartermaster Surtees called "as destructive a fire of artillery as I have ever witnessed." Ball and grapeshot raked the British column near the river, one shot killing fifteen men at once.

But the British troops were not the only target of the guns. Shells plunged into the barns and houses of Chalmette and Bienvenu which Colonel MacRae had booby-trapped the night before. The plantation buildings smoked and flamed and then exploded. A British officer with Keane was in the center of the target and recorded:

> Scarce a bullet passed over, or fell short of its mark, but all striking full into the midst of our ranks occasioned terrible havoc. The shrieks of the wounded, the crash of the firelocks, and the fall of such as were killed, caused at first some little confusion; and what added to the panic was, that from the houses beside which we stood, bright flames suddenly burst out. The Americans expecting this attack, had filled them with combustibles for the purpose; and directing one or two guns against them, loaded with red-hot shot, in an instant set them on fire.

Lieutenant Gleig, too, was caught in the barrage and shocked by the knowledge that "the Americans are excellent shots, as well with artillery as rifles." He added: "A tremendous cannonade mowed down our ranks, and deafened us with its roar; while the two large châteaux and their out-buildings almost scorched us with the flames, and blinded us with the smoke that they emitted."

Gleig, who had witnessed the burning of Washington and called the spectacle "very sublime," found this holocaust "sublime" as well. But Pierre de la Ronde on Jackson's line was heartbroken at the sight. His own house was out of range of the American guns, but how long would it be before it suffered the same fate? If Versailles should be destroyed his life was ended. Gone would be the dream of a flourishing new city on the Mississippi. The passing minutes aged him by as many years. He was too old, now, to start again.

With the houses destroyed, denying the British any refuge, Patterson and Jackson trained their fire on the British field artillery. Knock out the guns and let the backwoods riflemen take care of the advancing infantry. Dickson's field pieces were overturned, their carriages knocked out from under them. Keane's column broke; the troops had not counted on this fierce barrage from the *Louisiana*. The men took shelter in the drainage ditches or lay prone in the sedge grass.

From the center of Chalmette's, Dickson and Hill released their vaunted "secret" weapon: the Congreve rockets, still unfamiliar to this theater of the war. At the rate of two a minute the viper-like missiles soared towards the American ramparts with a banshee shriek intended to terrorize their targets.

"Pay no attention to the rockets, boys," Jackson shouted. "They're nothing but toys to amuse children."

After their first suprise the Americans ignored the screaming, twisting rockets which proved highly inaccurate in aim. A few men were burned, some horses frightened. That was all.

Dominique's and Beluché's deadly fire tossed the advancing troops into the air "like old bags." Two more enemy field pieces were dislodged and silenced, and the British rushed forward to try to drag them to the rear.

In the heat of battle Abner Duncan rode up to Jackson, panting with excitement.

"The Legislature is going to give up the country to the British," he shouted. "Governor Claiborne wants to know what to do!"

"Who told you this?" asked Jackson grimly.

Duncan started to mention Colonel Declouet, and then thought better of it.

"A militia colonel."

"The colonel should be immediately apprehended," Jackson said. "If his information proves false, he should be shot."

"But what do I tell Claiborne?"

"Tell him to investigate," said Jackson curtly. "If he finds it's true, tell him to blow up the Legislature."

Duncan whirled his horse and raced back to the city. Jackson returned to the business at hand. The British advance along the river had been halted; the troops were trying to save the few remaining guns. He turned his attention to the left, the weakest section of the line, becoming much less formidable as it stretched into the cypress swamp.

General Gibbs had met little opposition. No heavy guns had halted his advance. As he approached within range of the American line, Coffee's trigger-happy Tennesseans climbed to the top of the parapet for better shooting, and nine were picked off by British rifles.

But now Gibbs had a close view of the enemy offenses. No puny mud piles these, but solid ramparts that could be scaled only by ladders, while the canal in front of them was wide and deep and would have to be filled or bridged before his troops could reach the barricade itself. He noticed, however, that the line diminished as it approached the outward-curving cypress swamp.

The field here was quartered by canals and drainage ditches, some rimmed with cypress fences and tall sedge grass providing protection for maneuvers. Gibbs sent Rennie with men of the 21st to circle through the protruding swamp and try to outflank the American left. Carroll saw the maneuver and ordered Colonel James Henderson with two hundred Tennesseans to counter Rennie's move.

Henderson's heart was bigger than his battle tactics. Instead of advancing deep into the swamp to wait for Rennie he tried to outflank him on the outer edges of the forest. Rennie was in good position to receive him. The British rifles barked, and Henderson won that moment of glory he had come so far to find. He fell dead beside the bodies of twenty of his men.

From deep in the swamp the Choctaws rallied to the rescue. There were sixty of them against six hundred British. They shot behind trees and logs and from the swamp holes. Rennie later complained that he couldn't even see his enemy. But he was within two hundred yards of the American defenses. In minutes more he would reach their rear and have the Americans outflanked.

A courier from Gibbs and Pakenham raced up with a startling message: Withdraw!

Rennie could not believe his hears. With victory at hand he should retreat? But in the ironbound tradition of "Theirs not to reason why," he obeyed the order and pulled back his men.

Gibbs as well as Rennie was bitter at the order to retire. But the situation as viewed by Pakenham, unable to see the extent of Rennie's penetration, was hopeless. The artillery had failed. The American gunners had proved far more skillful than anticipated. The enemy ramparts, though indeed they had been made of soft Louisiana mud, had swallowed the British cannon balls as if they hungered for them. The canal below the parapets was something else to reckon with.

It was not an orderly withdrawal. The arrogant Tennesseans climbed to the top of the earthworks to jeer and shoot at the retreating troops. Dominique You observed a tartaned Highlander striding erect and proudly to the rear. He fired a single shot that knocked the man's head off and sent it spinning like a football down the field.

To Lieutenant Gleig the collapse of the British offensive was a heart-breaking spectacle. By candlelight in his hut that night he wrote:

> Thus, without as much as one effort to force through them, was a British army baffled and repulsed by a horde of raw militiamen, ranged in line behind a mud wall which could hardly have protected them from musketry, far less from round shot. There was not a man among us who failed to experience both shame and indignation when he found himself retreating from a force for which he entertained the most sovereign contempt.

Another officer shared Gleig's feeling of humiliation. "In spite of our sanguine expectations of sleeping that night in New Orleans, evening found us occupying our Negro huts at Villeré's, nor was I sorry that the shades of night concealed our mortification from the prisoners and slaves."

Losses had been light on the American side with sixteen killed and wounded. British casualties totaled sixty. Pakenham spoke no more of his original hopes for splitting the earthworks and marching to the city. He would regard the engagement as a "reconnaissance in force" (the Americans called it a "battle," while later historians considered it a "demonstration").

Regarded as a reconnaissance, the affair had proved revealing. The American earthworks were stout, and it would take much heaver guns to break them down. The ditch in the foreground would have to be filled and spanned, an operation to be executed at the moment of attack. Right now Pakenham's orders to Dickson were, Bring up the siege guns. Batter down those ramparts. It would take some days to bring the heavier artillery from the fleet. Meanwhile his troops would remain on the occupied lands of Chalmette, Bienvenu and de la Ronde.

There, however, they had little peace. Nighttime raids and sniping at sentinels, according to British historian Fortescue, "never gave [them] five minutes rest, caused not a few casualties, and contributed materially to wearing down the strength and endurance of the invaders." Quartermaster Surtees, who was actually present, took a charitable view of this harassment, noting in his journal that the Americans "did all they could to annoy and weary us, of which we ought not to complain, as they were defending their own country, and allowances ought to be made in such a case that would not be tolerated in an army having no interest in the soil. I trust Englishmen will be equally zealous and bitter to their enemies should our country ever be invaded."

Under a flag of truce Sir Edward dispatched the letter of protest he had composed the night before. He requested that Jackson refrain from his barbaric nighttime forays and assassination of the sentries. It was not commensurate with gentlemanly warfare. Jackson laconically replied that he was repelling an invasion of his country and was not concerned with ethics.

"It would not be safe," he replied, "for our respective sentries to drink out of the same stream."

The British, he implied, should keep their heads down.

Abner Duncan had meanwhile returned to the city in haste, reporting to Claiborne's aide that, "The governor is to place a strong guard at the door of the Legislature and employ armed force to prevent it from meeting." Claiborne accepted this garbled interpretation of Jackson's earlier outburst and placed a detachment of militia at the State House entrance. No one was allowed admittance.

Bernard de Marigny arrived for the morning session of the Legislature and was stopped on the steps by Magloire Guichard with tears in his eyes.

"We are accused of treason," Guichard told him. "The doors of the Legislature are closed on orders of General Jackson."

De Marigny, according to his own account, at once confronted the General "with a heart enraged." What was the meaning of this insult?

Jackson, who was sympathetic to just wrath, tried to appease de Marigny's indignation. "Return to the city," he told Bernard. "Reassure your colleagues. It is all a misunderstanding. I was occupied in fighting when I sent word to Governor Claiborne to blow up the Legislature if he thought it wanted to capitulate."

The explanation of "misunderstanding" was accepted and the Legislature resumed its sessions. But the gap between that body and the General widened. To Jackson this was just as well. Let the Legislature stay behind its doors and he would carry on the war. They were a fractious bunch; he did not need them.

But Abner Duncan deserved a little hell for stirring up the matter in the first place.

# 14. Ring out the Old, Ring in the New...

Rain, mud and discontent established the mood of the British bivouac on December 29. The artillery skirmish, the *grande reconnaissance* — call it what you will — had been a dismal failure. The wounded, their numbers increasing, were now transferred from Villeré's to Jumonville's, a half mile below the camp, where units of the disheartened West India regiments were posted to stand guard.

General Pakenham called for a council of war. If Sir Edward had been loath to listen to his somewhat condescending naval counterpart, Admiral Cochrane, he listened to him now. The army field artillery had scarcely dented the enemy lines; several guns had been damaged or destroyed. "Since the infantry has failed to scare the Americans from their line," said Cochrane, "we must bring more heavy artillery from the ships." With the fleet was a train of heavy siege guns that had cleared the way for Wellington's troops in Europe. These could hardly fail to pierce the enemy earthworks and clear a passage for the army.

General Gibbs disagreed. "And if the cannon fail," he argued, "how are you going to make regular approaches in this ground where you cannot dig more than two feet without making a well of water? How can parallels and zigzags be pushed in such soil?"

Pakenham thought he had the answer. "The operation can be accomplished by sap-rolling. We will use hogsheads of sugar for the saps."

Gibbs excused himself from the meeting in disgust. He was heard by Dickson to mutter, "Oh, for the days of the Grand Duke!" But Dickson did not repeat this bit of heresy to Pakenham.

Cochrane estimated it would take three days to bring up the guns. Colonels Dickson and Burgoyne were put in charge of the operation. The former recorded in his journal, "From the 26th to the 31st every exertion was made to get up from the ships ten 18-pounders and four 24-pound carronades with ammunition. These were brought up the canal in boats to within a quarter of a mile from the main road, and thence transported on carriages of the country or our own limbers by the seamen with incredible labour." With the guns saved from the battle of the 28th this would give the army thirty pieces of artillery, including mortars, howitzers and rocket launchers.

Jackson had willing scouts to keep him informed of enemy operations. Hind's Dragoons were ever on the move. They reported that, to protect his communications, the enemy was building strong redoubts at the junctions of the different bayous and the entrance to Villeré's canal. Reuben Kemper kept watch over the protruding cypress swamp. He discovered a group of British engineers at work. Apparently they were surveying the possibility of clearing a passage through the morass to attack the Americans from the rear—a project suggested by Rennie's successful penetration of this area. Kemper later gathered that they had given up.

General Humbert was a hard man to keep down. He was ready to volunteer for anything, and at a moment's notice. He insisted on making a daily inspection of the British line, galloping back and forth oblivious to bullets. What he had to report came out in a torrent of incomprehensible French. Jackson, developing a fondness for this reckless general, finally gave him an escort of mounted Tennesseans.

It was Humbert's moment of glory. He was the leader of an army!— albeit an army of only twenty men. The Napoleonic veteran led his cavalry across Chalmette's to Bienvenu's, where they alerted a group of British pickets who promptly opened fire. While Humbert replied with a chain of Gallic oaths, the Tennesseans wheeled their horses and galloped out of range. Humbert remained to calmly survey the pickets through his glass and then return to complain bitterly to Jackson about the behavior of the cowardly Tennesseans.

Routinely, Jackson queried their sergeant as to why the Tennesseans had retreated.

"Well, General, it was this way," drawled the sergeant. "Not understanding French and believing our commander was a man of sense, we construed his orders to retire out of reach of the muskets, and so we just kind of countermarched."

While the British were obviously getting ready for another major effort, the Americans used these last days of the year in strengthening the earthworks. Carroll's segment on the left was sketchy, and under Jean Laffite's direction more logs and earth were piled along the modest ridge. The half-mile stretch from swamp to river had stood up well, but needed patching. The batteries, which had been a target for the British guns, had suffered from lack of adequate protection. As more guns were brought up from the naval arsenal, some salvaged from the *Carolina,* Jackson asked Latour about using cotton bales for platforms and embrasures.

"Well, General," the major told him, "it's not in any military manual I know of."

"We'll rewrite the book," said Jackson.

There were hundreds of bales of cotton in sheds along the levee, but the nearest source was the merchant vessel *Pallas,* owned by Vincent Nolte and lying idle on the river. She was loaded with high-quality cotton hopefully bound for Pensacola as opportunity permitted. Some 250 bales were confiscated, brought ashore and packed in embrasures around the batteries.

Nolte, on the line with Plauché's volunteers, could hardly miss recognizing his own merchandise.

> I was somewhat vexed at the idea of their taking cotton of the best sort, and worth from ten to eleven cents, out of a ship already loaded and on the point of sailing, instead of procuring the cheaper kind, which was to be had in plenty throughout the suburbs of the city, at seven or eight cents, and said as much to Livingston. He, who was never at a loss for a reply, at once answered: "Well, Mr. Nolte, if this is your cotton, you at least, will not think it any hardship to defend it."

Nolte also made note of Jackson's intensified effort to round up additional arms and men before the enemy's next offensive. He had had no word from the 2500 Kentuckians still in transit or the shipment of muskets due from Pittsburgh. Accordingly, wrote Nolte:

A general order was now issued, requiring every one who had super-
fluous arms in his possession to bring them to the arsenal, and all able-bodied
men between the ages of eighteen and fifty to hold themselves in readiness.
No distinction was made between regular inhabitants of the city and strangers who had just come down the river and lodged in various taverns. They
were armed and enrolled in the second regiment Louisiana militia.

Even the veteran guards assigned to policing the city were asked
to relinquish their sidearms. They did so reluctantly, insisting that this
transaction be recorded in writing as "only a loan." General Jacques
Villeré arrived from Acadia with another regiment of militia and was
assigned to the secondary defense line at Dupré's. A third line of earthworks, behind Dupré's and two miles closer to the city, was begun
along the canal at Montreuil's.

During the next two days Lieutenant Thompson maneuvered the
*Louisiana* down the river and peppered the enemy encampment with
ball and grapeshot, hampering the British preparations for new batteries at de la Ronde's and Bienvenu's. By December 30, however,
Patterson decided that the ship had served its purpose as a floating
battery. The British were moving their field guns further up the river
road and would soon be able to reach the ship with hot-shot. He had
the *Louisiana* permanently moored at Dr. Flood's. Here she would
serve as a depot for powder and ammunition, while her guns would
be brought ashore to supplement the ground artillery.

The Commodore now began construction of his famed marine battery on the right bank of the Mississippi. It was placed directly opposite Chalmette's, where the river was a mile wide, and would eventually cover a good mile of the embankment. He started with one
twenty-four-pounder and two twelves, manned by his sailors and the
motley crew of the *Louisiana*. As fast as they were installed, the guns
opened up on the enemy position, forcing the troops, as Patterson
wrote, "to retire from the levee and shelter behind houses, etc."

In his account of this action Alexander Walker marveled at the skill
and dedication of the gunners, many corralled from the waterfront
saloons and brothels and impressed into service on the threat of arrest
if they did not volunteer. Portuguese, Greek, Italian, German, Arab,
Hindu, Swede — they could not understand the orders given in a different tongue; they could not even understand each other. Yet they
might have been brothers of a single family answering a common call.

Miraculously they made the marine battery one of the deadliest in the history of modern warfare.

Plagued by the guns across the river, the British troops were equally harassed by the slippery Yankees in Jackson's line, whose methods they could not comprehend. The crack-shot Tennesseans were the nighttime terror of the English pickets, their long brown hunting shirts making them almost invisible as they stalked their prey. In his journal Lacarrière Latour recounted the operations of one backwoodsman permitted to leave the lines for a "hunting party."

> He stole along through ditches and underwood, till he got near a British sentinel, whom he immediately killed; and having seized his arms and accoutrements, he laid them at some distance from that place, and went to post himself in a different direction. When it was time to relieve the sentinel, the corporal of the guard, finding him dead, posted another in the same place. The guard had hardly left him when the Tennessean shot the second sentinel, deposited his arms with those of the first whom he had killed, and returned to await his next victim. The corporal, in his next round, had again to relieve a dead sentinel, and the next man who took his place soon shared the fate of the two others. His arms were added to the Tennessean's cache. At last the corporal, amazed to see that in one night three sentinels had been killed at one post, determined to expose no more men in so dangerous a spot.

The Tennessean returned to camp with his cache of arms, to receive the congratulations of his comrades.

Meanwhile Jackson undertook to strengthen the artillery along the earthworks. There were guns to be had from Patterson's arsenal and ships, but not always the necessary shot and powder—since powder deteriorated fast in the damp Louisiana climate. Claiborne being rendered idle, the General gave him the perverse assignment of keeping the gunners supplied with powder and shot—a role which the Governor regarded as equivalent to that of water boy.

In addition to the five batteries mounted on December 28, two more were added and the others shifted to make for even spacing on the line. On the right Captain Enoch Humphrey, a veteran Regular addicted to cigars, commanded a twelve-pounder designated Battery Number One. On the extreme left Brigadier General Garrigues de Flaujeac, the only member of the Legislature to volunteer for significant duty in the campaign, commanded Battery Number Seven. The other five batteries, from right to left, were manned respectively by Lieutenant Otho Norris of the U.S. Navy, Dominique You and the Baratarians, Lieutenant Crawley, Captain Henry Perry and Lieutenant William Kerr of the U.S. artillery, and Lieutenant Samuel Spotts of the artillery.

There were a few more touches to make the American defenses as complete, under the circumstances, as they could ever be. Far up the river from his marine battery Patterson assigned Captain Henley of the sunken *Carolina* to a small battery constructed in an abandoned brick kiln on the right bank opposite the city. With Morgan's troops still awaiting deployment at Dr. Flood's, Major Latour crossed the river to begin construction of breastworks along the Bois Gervais canal. Morgan sulkily considered it too far behind Jackson's line. He wanted a position opposite Macarty's or even further down the river. He did some reconnoitering of his own in this direction.

On New Year's Eve Pakenham and Dickson completed preparations for the artillery assault that would precede the army's advance the following morning. American pickets were driven behind their lines to leave the plain from Villeré's to Chalmette's clear for British troops who could protect the men working on advance redoubts and batteries. De la Ronde's was occupied by Briggs and Thornton and the house used as an ammunition depot.

After nightfall the siege guns were dragged into position, and the engineers went to work on platforms and embrasures. It was exasperating toil. The field was so mushy that the spades struck water nine inches below the surface, and the piled-up mud refused to hold. Because of the need for any material of relatively solid substance, scores of kegs from de la Ronde's sugar house, containing thousands of dollars' worth of sugar, were rolled up as foundations for the platforms and embrasures for the batteries.

In the center of Chalmette's, six to eight hundred yards from the American earthworks, two strong batteries of seven and ten guns, respectively, were established. Under the supervision of Colonel Burgoyne the troops were called to the field to construct earthworks and redoubts to protect the advancing infantry. In strict silence they worked furiously, "knowing as we all knew," wrote Lieutenant Gleig, "that we worked for life or death." Again, de la Ronde's sugar kegs were used to strengthen the redoubts.

By 2 a.m. the preparations were completed. The two main batteries facing the American line were interspaced with mortars and rocket launchers. On the levee and river road two batteries of field artillery were positioned to counter the American guns across the river and command the right of Jackson's line. With the work completed, the entire British army, except for the West India guards at Jumonville's were mustered on the fields of de la Ronde's to await the attack at dawn.

Pakenham kept to a nearly standard disposition of his forces, which were posed at the center and left of the American defenses. Again it would be Gibbs on the right with the 21st and Mullin's 44th, Keane on the left with Thornton's 85th and 93rd Highlanders, with small detachments at both extremes of right and left to make diversionary feints at Jackson's flanks. No units would move till the American earthwork had been breached by the artillery — then a charge through the gaps to take the line at bayonet point. The army should be in New Orleans by nightfall, a reasonable assumption based on the massive firepower of the naval guns which the enemy breastworks could not be expected to withstand.

A hundred miles to the south, in the Gulf near the mouth of the Mississippi, British ships, too, were on the move. A fleet carrying the third wave of the expeditionary forces — General John Lambert with 2700 troops of the 7th, 40th and 43rd regiments — was cruising in search of Cochrane's anchorage.

Meanwhile a six-ship squadron had left the anchorage and sailed to the mouth of the Mississippi, preparing to capture the pickets and pilots stationed at Balize. It was Cochrane's more-or-less secret plan that this flotilla should sail up the Mississippi, destroy Fort St. Philip and proceed upriver to give support to Pakenham's infantry. If the infantry had already reached New Orleans, the ships would be available to carry off the immense amounts of plunder that the navy had been promised.

Three thousand miles away the British sloop of war *Favorite* sailed from London for America with the peace treaty signed at Ghent now ratified by the Prince Regent and the cabinet. Weather permitting, it would take the vessel six weeks to reach its destination.

Even more than Christmas, New Year's Day in French New Orleans was an occasion for exchanging gifts and hospitality and sharing the city's provisions which had still escaped the ravages of war. Homes were decked with greenery and scented with rum-flavored pastries, and many a toast was drunk to the dawn of Eighteen Fifteen, year of decision for the Crescent City and the Mississippi Valley. To console his troops for their commitment to the battlefield, Jackson agreed to their request for a full-dress parade on New Year's morning, to which any citizens inclined to risk the chilly dampness were invited.

At nine o'clock the following morning, with a thick fog smothering the plantations, the American troops fell in, Coffee's and Carroll's mud-stained Tennesseans contrasting sharply in appearance to the smart and colorful uniforms of Plauché's Creole volunteers. For a while they waited for the mist to clear, the band fingering its instruments, the standard-bearers clinging to their regimental colors. Then, providentially, a fresh breeze tore the fog to scattered fleeces, the bugles sounded, Jordan Noble beat a drum roll, and the troops moved forward to the rhythms of the "Marseillaise" and "Yankee Doodle."

On the plains of Chalmette and de la Ronde the British artillery had waited for the mist to clear. Through rifts in the fog the British ground troops, "confidently anticipating that they would be snugly housed before sunset in the city of New Orleans," caught glimpses of the enemy's festive review. As if no danger threatened! Or as if they were celebrating in advance a bold resistance. Lieutenant Gleig noted that "the different regiments . . . being dressed in holiday suits, presented a really fine appearance. Mounted officers were riding backwards and forwards through the ranks, bands were playing and colours floating in the air. In a word, all seemed jollity and gala; then suddenly our batteries opened, and the face of affairs was instantly changed."

One of the initial targets of the British batteries was Macarty's house in which Dickson's gunners hoped to bury the American commander beneath a pile of rubble. With Jackson's staff in the General's apartment was Major Latour, who recorded: "In less than ten minutes upwards of one hundred balls, rockets and shells struck the house . . . bricks, splinters of wood and furniture, rockets and balls, were flying in all directions." Dust and plaster showered on the startled group, but no one was injured, though Colonel Butler was bowled over by a flying beam.

Outside was momentary panic. The dress parade turned into a stampede. Spectators fled. Troops scrambled to the parapet for safety. The artillerists leaped to their guns. Almost instantly Jackson was at the ramparts. He found no orders were needed. Every man was at his post, every unit in position. He saw Captain Humphrey, "with that eternal cigar," standing coolly at the foremost battery.

"Ah," said the General. "We have nothing to fear. Humphrey is at his post."

Humphrey was leveling his guns. Satisfied that the aim was right, he laconically gave the order, "Let 'er off."

Humphrey's blast was the signal for all seven batteries to open up, with Patterson's guns across the river joining in. The fire from both sides, deafening and unremitting, blanketed the field with smoke. "I have never before witnessed so severe a cannonade," wrote Major Tatum, "even in the 6-weeks siege of Charleston in 1780."

Nolte's cotton bales became a treacherous hazard. Knocked right and left and catching fire from the muzzle blasts, they obscured the gunners' aims with clouds of black, eye-smarting smoke. Volunteers dragged them to the rear or hurled them into the canal, where contact with the water made them smoke more fiercely.

Dominique You with the Baratarian artillerists was seared in the arm by a passing ball. "You'll pay for that!" he shouted at the enemy. He ordered his crew "to cram their gun to the mouth with terrible chain-shot and ponderous ship cannister, and every description of destructive missile," and blasted to pieces the carriage of an English cannon, sending seven gunners to their doom.

Dickson's artillerists, veterans of many a naval battle in European waters, were far more accurate and able than those employed at the guns on December 28. In ordnance and bulk of ammunition fired they outweighed the Americans by a ratio of two to one. But the unstable ground, the hasty planning and the speed with which the naval guns had been installed, now worked against them. The recoil of the heavy cannon sent them hurtling off their platforms. Gun carriages slithered in the mire and destroyed the aim. Intended for the solid decks of warships, the guns were ill-suited for service in the field.

At the start, however, the American and English batteries seemed deadlocked in a mortal duel. "For the first half hour the weight of execution was undoubtedly in our favor," wrote British Artillery Captain Benson Hill. "But the American defenses—a heavy solid earthwork—soon proved far superior to our flimsy protection from hogsheads of sugar. The latter were soon knocked to pieces." Lieutenant Gleig, in the batture near the river, also complained that "The hogsheads filled with sugar proved to be of little or no value as defenses against cannon shot."

In the clouds of smoke now covering the plain neither Hill nor Gleig could have noticed the similar foozle of Jackson's cotton bales. Actually, the "Battle of the Bales and Hogsheads" was a draw.

The British battery on the levee was first to go, soon crippled by the fire from Patterson's cannon. Resignedly the English officer in command remarked, "The howitzers could not throw their shot across the river anyhow. So that the American commodore who commanded that battery and his sailors who served it could knock the poor howitzers about at their leisure in perfect security." Patterson, however, gave the English guns more credit for their range. "Many of their shells went immediately over my battery, and their shots passed through my breastwork and embrasures, without injuring a man."

It was far from one-sided in that first and fateful hour. Wrote Major Latour, "Justice obliges us to acknowledge that the fire of the British was for a long time vigorously kept up and well-directed." The carriage of Beluché's twenty-four-pounder was shattered, Crawley's thirty-two-pounder was damaged by an enemy ball, and Flaujeac's battery was silenced. A lucky hit by enemy rockets blew up two artillery caissons loaded with powder. At the explosion the British infantry, believing this marked the destruction of the earthworks and preparing to storm the line, rose from their ditches to give "three lusty cheers." The cheers were answered by a blast of American cannon that sent them scampering to shelter.

On the American line not only the commander-in-chief but every man at every gun was aware that upon the outcome of this duel of cannon hung the fate of New Orleans, the Mississippi Valley, possibly the war itself. Jackson was seen tirelessly riding back and forth behind the lines with Reid and Butler, checking on the batteries. Noting that Dominique's gun was silent, he galloped over.

"Dominique!" he shouted. "By the Eternal, why aren't you firing?"

"It's the powder, Zhénéral," said Dominique in Gallic rage. "It's rotten! It's only good for shooting crows, not redcoats."

Despite Dominique's indecipherable French, the General got the message. He whirled on Captain Reid.

"Tell Claiborne," he shouted to his aide, "that if he does not send balls and powder instantly, I shall chop off his head and have it rammed into one of these field pieces!"

Reid rode off to locate Claiborne, who, according to Vincent Nolte, "was so frightened he could scarcely speak." Minutes later Dominique's battery was back in operation.

For all the romanticizing of the pirates' role in the Battle of New Orleans, the deadly effectiveness of their artillery could hardly be exaggerated. Testifying for the British, Captain Hill admitted: "The battery of theirs that did us by far the most injury was the 3d one from their right, which brought it about opposite to the center of our formation. This battery . . . fired with great deliberation and unvarying effect." Quartermaster Surtees affirmed Hill's observation:

> Their gun, a 32-pounder, was a most bitter antagonist to our principal battery. This happened to be erected in front of that part of the line where this gun was situated, and when it fired, its shot always struck the battery at the first bound, then ricocheted into the redoubt where I had taken up my post . . . any of the other guns seemed like child's play to the unceasing and destructive fire of this heavy piece of ordnance. I could distinctly see that they were sailors that worked it — one of whom, a large mulatto with a red shirt, always sponging her out after firing.

Surtees kept tabs on Dominique's battery through his field glass. "I could distinctly perceive the ball from this gun every time it was fired, it appearing like a small black spot in the midst of the column of white smoke, which gradually grew larger in appearance as it approached us . . . Seeing which way the ball was coming, I told the men when to lie down; and on one occasion was the shave so close, that it actually carried away one of the men's pack as he lay on the ground."

While essentially it was a duel of flying lead, of cannon against cannon, small human tragedies took place among the troops. A group of British infantry were pinned down in a shallow trench by the bombardment. They drew lots to see who would watch for enemy shells. Since one among them had a wife and child he was exempted from the lottery. Yet he alone, succumbing to curiosity and just for a second raising his head, was struck by enemy fire.

Vincent Nolte saw one man of his company bend over to light a cigar, just as a bullet passed over his neck and severed the head of the man immediately behind him. By what strange accidents did war select its victims! Nolte later saw one of his officers hit by a Congreve rocket and asked permission to escort the wounded captain to the rear. He came upon an intimate, revealing tableau.

"As we reached the low garden wall behind Jackson's headquarters, I saw to my great amazement two of the General's volunteer adjutants, Duncan the lawyer and District Marshall Duplessis, lying flat on the ground to escape the British balls. Livingston was invisible — the writing and reading of proclamations kept him out of sight."

With scarcely a second's pause in the intense barrage the balance of firepower shifted, minute by minute, to the Americans. Captain Hill, a highly impartial and credible witness, noted:

> Our men, both those working the guns and the infantry lying down in the rear, suffered heavily. By half past eleven or after the enemy's fire had been maintained about forty minutes, five of our guns were dismounted completely. They had to be left on the field. Eight more were so disabled in their carriages that they could not be pointed. This left us with only nine serviceable guns and of these but one was a 12-pounder.

Crouched on the field, awaiting that glorious moment when the ramparts should be breached and they should take the American line by storm, the British troops grew restless. They discovered that the redoubts in which many were sheltered "were not nearly so strong as they ought to have been made, had there been more time, and the enemy's shot penetrated into every part of our works."

But while respect for the American artillerists was mounting, contempt for the "dirty shirts" was fomented by delay. Why not storm the enemy line without waiting for the siege guns to reduce it? "What are we waiting for?" Surtees heard the infantry call to one another. "What's holding us back?"

On the far left, where Colonel Thornton and Lieutenant Gleig had reached to within six hundred yards of the embankment, the impatience was equally apparent.

Yet with ten thousand men engaged on both sides there was only one sortie of troops that morning. Pakenham sent the intrepid Colonel Rennie, with a company of riflemen and Lieutenant Wright of the engineers, through the swamp in another attempt to flank the American left. The movement was perceived, and a detachment of Coffee's Tennesseans plunged into the cypress wood to counter the attack. The resulting skirmish put the kiss of death on British hopes that afternoon. As summarized in an eloquent sentence by Latour:

"Wellington's heroes discovered that they were ill qualified to contend with us in woods where they must fight knee deep in water and mud, and that the various kinds of laurel which abound in Louisiana, in the cypress swamps and prairies, were not intended to grace their brows."

Quartermaster Surtees, reporting the action as pressed by Lieutenant Wright of the engineers, was more specific. "Both himself and nearly all his party perished; for it seems they fell in with a body of American riflemen who, being much better acquainted with traveling in the woods than our people were, fell on them and . . . nearly cut off the whole party."

Around noon General Pakenham, "seeing that our position was not tenable and that any attempt at further holding out would merely expose our men and guns to further destruction," gave the order to withdraw. Bitter as that decision must have been, Captain Hill for one confirmed its wisdom. In contrast to the loss of nearly half the British batteries, "we could not see that we had silenced so much as one of their guns; and their fire grew more and more accurate with every discharge." Casualties among the English during the hour-and-a-half exchange had come to twenty-six killed and forty-one wounded.

Because of the incessant fire from Jackson's line and Patterson's battery across the river, the withdrawal could not take place till after nightfall. The cramped, disheartened troops were obliged to stay in the ditches and redoubts throughout an afternoon of drenching rain. The sugar kegs had burst, exuding what Captain Hill observed as "a thick, sticky mass of black stuff, full of grit and little splinters of cane." Having had nothing to eat since dawn, the men swallowed it by the handful and, said Hill, "it always made them sick, producing nausea and diarrhea . . ."

In midfield, on his way back to the British camp, Hill came upon a group of West Indians huddled and shivering in a transverse ditch. He ordered them back to the lines.

"No sir, Boss," their self-appointed spokesman said. "No more Jamaica. No more white man's orders. We die here."

Unable to budge them, Hill left them to their fate.

As soon as darkness fell, the British artillerists began salvaging the guns. Five were regarded as hopeless and left for the enemy (although Tatum insisted that eight or ten pieces of ordnance fell into American hands). The troops were called from their ditches to help. When they refused to obey the order, disgusted with the artillery's performance, Pakenham was forced to send an aide to make the command imperative. In the mud and rain Hill found the task "a very rough experience." The gunners had been on short rations and had not slept for three days and nights. The infantry had fared little better. Working beside them, Gleig recorded:

> The labour of dragging a number of huge ships' guns out of the soft soil into which they had sunk, crippled, too, as most of them were in their carriages, was more extreme by far than any one expected to find it. Indeed it was not till four o'clock in the morning that our task came to a conclusion, and even then it had been very imperfectly performed.

Adding to the misery was the mood of failure. The troops complained of the abortive planning and stupidity of their leaders. The officers shared their disillusionment. A naval commander called the duel of cannon "a blot on the artillery escutcheon." An infantry officer reported the engagement as a futile display of "fireworks and pop guns such as has been seldom witnessed even in Lord Wellington's great action on the Peninsula . . ."

In New Orleans, however, the New Year's Day festivities interrupted by the thunder of the guns resumed with new éclat, heightened by a sense of rescue from disaster. In homes throughout the mercurial city, toasts were drunk to the valiant commander, General Jackson, who hours before had been regarded with distrust and ridicule. Bars and brothels on the waterfront did a thriving business. Troops along the Rodriguez canal paid little heed to regulations and were absent without leave en masse.

Jackson and his aides remained in the relative comfort of Macarty's house. The roof had been badly damaged, but the structure was still livable. On the hearth they built a fire of splintered beams and broken furniture, and discussed the day's events. All things considered, losses had again been light, eleven killed, eleven wounded—about half the casualties suffered by the British.

The General complained lightly of a personal misfortune. In the rain of British shells upon the house he had lost an overcoat, and overcoats were hard to come by in the army. He wondered where he would get another. Meanwhile he dictated a proclamation to young Captain Reid:

"The Major General tenders to the troops he has the honor to command his good wishes for a Happy New Year. Watch word, Fight on! The quartermaster will issue half a gill of whiskey all around."

# 15. The Eye of the Storm

An American soldier wrote a letter:

> Although New Orleans troops are constantly under arms, such is the spirit which prevails among them, that they submit to the fatigues of the camp with the greatest cheerfulness, and it appears more like a party of pleasure than the encampment of an army in hourly expectation of being led into battle . . . Indeed, an aide-de-camp of the general said he could not get a man of them to keep clear of the shot and rockets which were flying among them. They volunteer and go out in parties of 20 or 30 men, and pick off the British when they get a chance . . . The deserters say there would be many more coming over to our lines, if they were not afraid of "those fellows with the dirty shirts."

A British soldier wrote a letter:

> It was a sad day for men who, a year before, had marched through France from the Pyrenees to the sea. We retired not only baffled and disappointed, but in some degree disheartened and discontented . . . All our plans had proved abortive. Even this artillery attack, upon which so much reliance had been placed, was found to be of no avail . . . Provisions are scanty and coarse. Cannon and mortar from the enemy's position play unremittingly upon us day and night . . . With such experience the army almost as one man has settled down to the conclusion that nothing short of a grand assault at any cost of life can extricate us from our difficulties.

229

If there was reason for gloom in the British camp after more than a week of discouraging setbacks, there was cause for rejoicing on Jackson's line. The superior marksmanship of the rifles and artillery, especially the latter, had resisted two successive onslaughts with remarkable success. There was confidence of doing so again. Meanwhile, though the weather was cold and damp, the troops were well supplied with food and whiskey. Unlike the long supply line of the British, seventy to eighty miles from anchorage to camp, the Americans were only a few miles from the city. Along the open road came beef and bacon, corn for bread, eggs and vegetables — supplies that kept flowing down the Mississippi from the war-free territory to the north. The scorched bales of cotton, which had proved so treacherous a substance in the ramparts, were hauled to the rear and converted to comfortable mattresses for nighttime sleeping.

Jackson, too, was inspired with confidence, though far from ready to relax his guard. He expected the British to attack again shortly and was puzzled when they didn't. He used the lull to strengthen his breastworks, repairing any damage done by the British barrage of New Year's day. The earthworks were now from twelve to twenty feet deep and roughly nine feet high, though less solid towards the swamp. No cotton bales in sight, thank God! Nothing but good elastic Mississippi mud, shatter-proof, puncture-proof, guaranteed to cushion the enemy shot like swan's-down. An eighth battery, consisting of one small carronade, was added to the extreme left of the line, in Carroll's segment of the swamp.

Some of the General's "more scientific minded officers" suggested erecting an advance redoubt across the Rodriguez canal to protect the right of the line and enfilade its front. It would be constructed of three embrasures, commanding respectively the river road, the river bank and the front of Jackson's defenses, and would be surrounded by a shallow ditch or moat.

Jackson took a dim view of the rising of this "demi-fort." Being below the canal, he felt that it was too exposed. Besides, he doubted that it could be finished in time to meet the next British onslaught. But he told the men to go ahead, although he was overheard muttering to himself, "That will give us trouble."

From time to time Jackson went up to the now-splintered balcony of Macarty's house and leveled his telescope at the British-occupied plantations. It appeared that more reinforcements from Lake Borgne were beginning to arrive, doubtless with more naval guns and ammunition. Were it possible, he thought disconsolately, he would like to attack that supply line and cut the enemy's vital artery leading up from the Bayou Bienvenu. But, as he wrote to Secretary Monroe, he did not want to risk his inexperienced troops in such a hazardous mission. They could fight behind ramparts, he was sure, and in nighttime skirmishes and forays. But he did not trust them in the open field against disciplined veterans skilled in bayonet fighting.

He did, however, keep the supply line and the British camp under constant surveillance. For this purpose General Humbert, with his lack of English, was not altogether satisfactory. He detailed Reuben Kemper to reconnoiter the swamp and the Bayou Bienvenu and report on British activity in that sector. Also, Kemper should observe, was there any chance that the British might still launch a flanking attack through the swamp?

Kemper returned with the reassurance that no major assault could be directed through the marshes. He also reported that the British, to protect their communications, had erected a stronghold just above the fishing village, another at the junction of the Bayou Mazant and the Bayou Bienvenu, and a third at the entrance to Villeré's canal. Kemper believed these forts were held by upwards of a thousand men. It was an unlikely assumption, but the presence of such strongholds further discouraged an attack on the supply line.

Jackson received cheering word on January 3 that the long-delayed Kentuckians were on their way, that they were now just below Baton Rouge. Not so cheering was the fact that the majority were without guns and would have to be supplied on their arrival. He acknowledged this news with what Livingston referred to as "his peculiar dry wit." Said the General:

"I don't believe it. I have never in my life seen a Kentuckian without a gun, a pack of cards, and a jug of whiskey."

Yet he ordered a canvass of the city for any firearms, new or old, that could be had. Many were antiquated Spanish muskets with rusty hammers; they could be discharged only by firing a pistol in the breech.

A similar problem was presented by the arrival from the upper valley of the second division of Louisiana militia, five hundred in strength, but none of them armed. Jackson placed them temporarily in his second reserve line on Montreuil's. They would make a good showing in numbers if they accomplished nothing else.

Like a wounded giant, mired in mud and licking his wounds, the British army remained supine on the five plantations bracketed by Bienvenu's and Jumonville's. In one of the mud huts occupied by officers at de la Ronde's, George Gleig recorded in his diary: "It must be confessed that something like murmuring begins to be heard through the camp. And in truth, if ever an army might be permitted to murmur, it was this. In landing, they had borne great hardships . . . their hopes had been inspired by false reports . . . and now they found themselves entangled amidst difficulties from which there appeared to be no escape."

While the American batteries across the river and Jackson's night raiders made sleep impossible, the specter of hunger haunted the inadequate shelters. Foraging parties had exhausted what the neighboring plantations had to offer. There was little meat for the officers and none whatever for the men. Reduced to damp ship's biscuits, the troops scraped up the sugar scattered from the broken kegs and tried to sweeten the unpalatable chunks of dough.

On top of it all, dysentery, the concomitant of armies in the field, swept through the ranks, adding to the misery and the list of noncombatants. Yet Gleig observed that, though desertions had increased, there was no talk of surrender or retreat. Rather, the grumbling of the infantry was "like the growling of a chained dog when he sees his adversary, but cannot reach him."

Disconcerted by the failure of the artillery to breach the American ramparts—a failure which Dickson attributed to the clumsiness of naval guns indifferently installed on land—Pakenham debated his next move. One thing was certain. He would not attack again until General Lambert arrived with his fresh, as yet undisillusioned troops. Word had reached Villeré's that this third wave of the expedition had reached the anchorage in time to hear the roaring guns at Chalmette usher in the third year of the war. But it would take several days to bring the contingent across the lake and through the forest to the camp at Villeré's.

Pakenham briefly considered shifting his main attack to the west bank of the Mississippi, where his scouts along the levee could detect no major preparations for defense. He discussed this move with Cochrane. The Admiral, impatient as he was for action, shook his head. There were not enough barges to ferry an entire army to the other bank in any single operation. They would be like sitting ducks to American artillery. Besides, it would take too long; the element of surprise could not be realized; the enemy would have ample time to cross the river and counter the attack.

The Admiral offered an alternative. He suggested that, before the next frontal assault on Jackson's line, a substantial force of, say, a thousand men be ferried across the river in the hours around midnight, to take Patterson's batteries by surprise. The captured guns could then be turned upon the enemy.

Depending on how things went, this might become more than a diversionary thrust. At the least it would silence Patterson's batteries and offer flanking cover for the British troops advancing on the left bank. Then, if successful to this extent, the division could continue up the right bank towards New Orleans and join Pakenham's forces in a pincer thrust against the city.

Cochrane elaborated on the plan. His seamen and naval engineers would deepen and widen the Villeré canal. A crevasse would extend it to the Mississippi. The canal could then be flooded to the level of the river, creating a mile-long lock. A dam at the far end, near the cypress swamp, would keep the water from draining into Lake Borgne. At the crucial moment, the barges could breast the river in darkness, with an escort of gunboats to protect them as they crossed.

Pakenham liked the idea. But he questioned whether a single dam could contain the rushing waters of the Mississippi once the canal was opened to the river. He suggested a second dam, just below it, to make sure. It wasn't necessary, Cochrane said; his engineers knew their business.

As a witness if not a participant in this project, Quartermaster Surtees was duly impressed. "Nothing could exceed the grandness of this conception," he wrote enthusiastically.

> All hands were set to work to widen and deepen the rill of water which flows into the creek at the landing-place and, continuing it up past Monsieur Villeré's house, to let it enter the river a little above that point. This, as may easily be conceived, was most laborious and dirty work; and lest the health and spirits of the troops should suffer from such incessant fatigue, they were told off into four watches or spells, each of which followed the other in regular succession, so that the work never stood still. When it reached near the house and highroad, screens were put up on the latter, to prevent the enemy on the opposite bank of the river from seeing what was carrying on . . .

The same British officer whose captured diary revealed his discomfort at Isle aux Pois, also recorded, with consistent brevity, the fatigue assignments of those days.

1st of January, 1815. On picquet all night.
2d. Halted, on fatigue from 12 to 6 pm.
3rd. Do. on Do. from 6 to 12 pm.
4th. Do. fine weather.
5th. Do. on picquet on the Right flank of army.


Closing in on the action from a hundred miles to the south, Cochrane's expeditionary fleet had passed the Balize — easily capturing the pilots stationed there — and had entered the mouth of the Mississippi. Battling the current and maneuvering with difficulty around curves and shallows, it was making slow progress and was still some fifty miles from Fort St. Philip, where Major Overton's small garrison awaited its arrival.


General Jackson had heard the rumor that British warships were headed up the Mississippi from the Gulf. It seemed a credible maneuver. If the report were true, Overton would need additional supplies and ammunition. He summoned Captain Shreve of the *Enterprise,* who had been shuttling food and material from the city to the army at Macarty's.

"Captain, could you get by the British line to take supplies to Fort St. Philip?"

"If you give me time," Shreve told him.

"How much time?" the General asked.

"Twenty-four hours."

Shreve used the twenty-four hours to hang bales of cotton along the port side of his vessel, as a cushion against British cannonballs. It is doubtful if he realized he was making history. Never before had a steam-driven vessel shared in a military operation.

That night, concealed by fog, the *Enterprise* slid down the river past the British batteries as officers and seamen held their breaths. She was not detected until making the return trip, when enemy guns were hastily trained against her. But before they could fire, the *Enterprise* was out of range. Shortly she was safe back in the city. Here, mission accomplished, Shreve volunteered to serve as artillerist on Jackson's line and was assigned to Humphrey's battery.

The next morning, January 4, the 2300 Kentuckians under General Thomas began arriving on their flatboats. They encamped by the river behind Jackson's secondary Line Dupré. Thomas himself was seriously ailing and relinquished his command to the capable Brigadier General John Adair.

Jackson was stunned to find that the earlier report on their predicament was true: only seven hundred of the Kentuckians had firearms. Not only that, but they looked like refugees from a hobo jungle, ill-clothed, ill-fed, dirty and unkempt. New Orleans, however, had revised its opinion of these backwoods ruffians, after noting the courage and resourcefulness of Coffee's and Carroll's Tennesseans. A Creole belle, twitted by the captive Major Mitchell regarding the "dirty shirts," told the British officer: "I'd rather be the wife of one of those hardy and coarsely clad but brave and honest men, who have marched through two thousand miles of wilderness to fight for the honor of their country, than wear an English coronet."

To provide for the hapless Kentuckians, the city subscribed, and the Legislature voted, over six thousand dollars to purchase blankets and woolens which, Major Latour recorded, "were distributed among the ladies of New Orleans to be made into clothes."

> Within one week twelve hundred blanket cloaks, two hundred and seventy-five waistcoats, eleven hundred and twenty-seven pairs of pantaloons, and a great number of mattresses, were made up or purchased ready made, and distributed among our brethren in arms, who stood in the greatest need of them.

Adequate clothing boosted the Kentuckians' morale, but did not solve the problem of their lack of firearms. Jackson sent another blistering letter to Monroe. Where were the barges from Pittsburgh with the muskets promised two months ago? Unless they were received at once, the contractor might as well continue dawdling, trading with river towns en route, as he was no doubt doing anyway.

The protest, Jackson knew, was useless. He and John Adair approached New Orleans Mayor Girod and asked him to release the guns which the mayor was keeping in the city arsenal against a possible slave insurrection. Girod agreed to hand over the arms if the transaction could be made at night and the citizens could be kept in ignorance of the transfer.

By this means Jackson and Adair succeeded in putting a thousand armed Kentuckians in business. Seven hundred who had brought their own rifles were placed under General Adair on Jackson's line between Carroll's and Coffee's Tennesseans. Three hundred more under Major Harrison, with assorted arms from the city's arsenals, were placed behind Adair as a reserve. Among these was a private named John Richard Ogilvy, who, noting the rusty muskets of his comrades, cheerfully observed, "the worst of these ancient weapons made a good club in the hands of a stalwart young Kentuckian!"

The rest of the Kentuckians Jackson placed with the unarmed Louisiana militia in his secondary line at Dupré's, where they might add "a show of numbers without, however, increasing strength." The two rear defense lines, at Dupré's and Montreuil's, had become a sort of repository for those men the General didn't know what to do with.

Using his standard measure of an enemy's intentions — "What would I do if I were in his place?" — Jackson continued to worry about an attack on the right, or west, bank of the river. The terrain there was somewhat similar to that which stretched below his own line — level cane fields varying in width between the river and the cypress swamps. If the British could effect a crossing, they could flank the Rodriguez defenses and would face only Morgan's militia if they advanced upon the city.

He dispatched Latour to the right bank to provide an entrenchment for Morgan's five hundred Louisianians now encamped on Dr. Flood's plantation. Latour had already chosen a position behind Morgan's camp along the Bois Gervais canal and had begun work on it. But before he could finish the breastwork, Jackson asked him to prepare a more advanced position, one that more closely paralleled his own defenses.

Latour selected a second point below Jourdan's plantation, where the plain between river and woods was only nine hundred yards in width. He mapped out a projected line that could be adequately manned by Morgan's limited militia with the help of light artillery.

General Morgan — a double-chinned, obstinate Massachusetts Yankee with little military training or experience — considered Latour's proposed line and rejected it. He wanted a position further down the river, closer to Patterson's batteries. With extraordinary lack of sense he chose a point where the plain, between river and woods, was two thousand yards wide—twice the length of Jackson's line. While his own militia sat by and watched indifferently, Morgan impressed a band of slaves to erect a breastwork two hundred yards long behind the shallow Raguet canal, leaving 1800 yards across the plain protected by only a trifling ditch.

Jackson knew of Morgan's decision, but time was running out and there was little time for juggling positions. He was more concerned with his own defenses, still convinced that the main attack would come on this side of the river. Patterson, however, was deeply concerned. The entire defense of the west bank rested solely upon him and Morgan, the latter's new position being downriver from his batteries. The batteries, now greatly strengthened, extended for almost a mile along the bank, and mounted nine twelve- and twenty-four-pound cannon trained on the British camp across the river.

Already the harassment of Patterson's guns had forced the British to withdraw from their advanced positions, and plagued their efforts to erect redoubts and batteries close to Jackson's line. In the event of attack, this enfilade would be invaluable in protecting Jackson's right. That was the batteries' fixed, inalterable purpose. They would be of little use and would also be highly vulnerable if the enemy crossed the river in appreciable force. In such a contingency Patterson counted on Morgan for protection.

With this in mind he furnished Morgan with two light field pieces from his naval arsenal, plus a twelve-pound gun for the left of Morgan's line. He then sent word to Jackson requesting that Morgan's troops be reinforced. Jackson had few men to spare. But in this extremity he ordered Colonel John Davis to take five hundred unarmed Kentuckians across the river to Morgan's aid. Passing through New Orleans on his way, Davis managed to collect arms for 180 of his hapless crew and left the rest behind. The muskets he had found in various abandoned arsenals were of ancient Spanish vintage and assorted calibers. They could shoot pebbles if they had to, or the Kentuckians could use them as clubs.

By the end of that first week in January, Jackson was as prepared as he would ever be to meet the enemy attack. On both sides of the river he had altogether 5400 troops of one sort or another. Less than one thousand were posted on the right bank—Morgan's militia, some of the Kentuckians, Patterson's sailors and artillerists.

With nine guns, twelve- and twenty-four-pounders, in his batteries across the river from the British camp, Patterson hoarded enough ammunition to level a murderous fire on the British flank when it advanced. "Come when they may," he sent word to Jackson, "my Guns shall roar long and loud, depend upon it." Just below New Orleans, also on the right bank, Captain Henley of the ill-starred *Carolina* manned the smaller battery in the abandoned kiln, to defend the city if the British ever reached that point.

The only thing still worrying Patterson was the threatened British crossing just below his batteries. His guns could not be swiveled to face an army coming up the bank. He contemplated reactivating the *Louisiana* some of whose guns had been transferred to land, to intercept the crossing. But he did not want to risk his one remaining ship; it could be useful in covering an enforced retreat if this were necessary. He would rely for now, as Jackson recommended, on Morgan's troops to hold the line below his fixed artillery.

On the east bank, behind the Rodriguez canal, Jackson had some 4400 troops in his command. Discounting those stationed as pickets at strategic points around the city, and others inadequately armed or in reserve, there were just under four thousand men on his main line of defense.

On the extreme right, facing Chalmette's, were Beale's Rifles and the 7th U.S. Infantry, units of which were placed in the advance redoubt. Next came Plauché's uniformed volunteers, Lacoste's and Daquin's two colored battalions, and the 44th regiment of Regulars. This whole section, a third of the line, was under the command of Colonel Ross.

In almost dead center of the line were Carroll's Tennessee Rifles supported by Adair's Kentuckians stationed slightly to their rear; then Coffee's troops extending to, and well into, the cypress swamp. On the far left, deep in the swamp itself, were Jugeat's Choctaws keeping watch among the alligators. They made up for their paucity of numbers by their canny guerrilla knowledge of the swamp and forest. This whole left section of the line was under the command of General Coffee.

Of the eight batteries mounted on the ramparts at varying intervals, Captain Enoch Humphrey, chewing on his unlit cigar, commanded that closest to the river. Near the center, Battery Number Three was manned by the Baratarians, two twenty-four-pounders attended by Dominque You and Renato Beluché. Furthest to the left was Battery Number Eight, by far the weakest, consisting of short-range carronades. Coffee's artillery support was weak, but he counted on his musketry to make the difference.

On January 6 a group of Patterson's sailors, still keeping watch on Lake Borgne with what few vessels they could commandeer, intercepted a British gig carrying rum and provisions to the army. The ten-man crew was captured and taken to General Jackson at Macarty's. The prisoners revealed that the British were preparing for a mass attack on January 8 that would involve a crossing of the river. Several deserters from the British line, nerves shattered by the constant fire of American artillery, brought similar advice—along with the report that fresh troops were arriving from the anchorage under the command of General John Lambert.

General Lambert's arrival at Villeré's on January 6 brought to the field two of the finest regiments in the British army, the 43rd Light Infantry and the 7th Royal Fusiliers, totaling 1700 fresh and eager troops. A third contingent, the 40th Sommersetshires, would shortly follow, as fast as the boats could bring it from the anchorage. Lambert himself, at forty-two, was one of the more highly decorated army officers, had distinguished himself under Wellington on the Peninsula, in the advance through France and at the capture of Toulouse.

While the troops were in top condition, they had had a rough time of it coming from the landing through the swamp. Because of Cochrane's pressing need for ammunition, each soldier was ordered to carry a cannon ball inside his haversack or shirt. Looking like pregnant hermaphrodites, they had trudged through the treacherous morass, the weight of the cannonballs sinking them deeper and deeper with each step.

The next morning, however, lined up for review, they looked like the fresh and disciplined veterans they were: boots polished, gray pants spotless, their scarlet tunics with multicolored regimental facings crossed by the white belts anchored by shining buckles just below the heart. "Every eye sparkled with hope at their appearance," Surtees observed, while George Gleig noted: "By this reinforcement . . . our numbers amounted now to a little short of eight thousand men; a force which, in almost any other quarter of America, would have been irresistible."

Gleig's comment reflected the general exaggeration of the forces defending New Orleans:

> Of the numbers of the [American] enemy, various reports were in circula-
> tion; some stating them at 23, and others at 30,000; but perhaps I may come
> nearer the truth if I choose a middle course, and suppose their whole force
> to be about 25,000 men. It is at least certain that they exceeded us in
> numbers as much as they did in resources . . .

General Pakenham did not attend the review of Lambert's troops.
He left that ceremony to General Keane. In frontier fashion peculiar
to a British general, Sir Edward had climbed a pine tree at the edge of
de la Ronde's plantation and was training his glasses on Jackson's
line, to form his own appraisal of the enemy. He noted the eight batteries stationed behind the canal, and the crescent redoubt just forward
of it, by the river. Most of the heavier guns seemed concentrated on
the American right and center, leaving the left towards the swamp
defended by rifle-bearing infantry — the much-disparaged "dirty shirts."

It confirmed what he already knew. According to Captain Benson
Hill of the artillery:

> Previous operations and reconnaissance had developed the fact that no
> artillery was mounted on that part of the American lines; also that the ditch
> was narrower and the parapet lower than elsewhere. Besides, two Spanish
> residents of New Orleans, who made their way out of the American cordon
> during the night of the 6th had informed General Pakenham most positively
> that the whole left half of the works was held by militia imperfectly organ-
> ized, not regularly armed *and totally unprovided with bayonets!*

The Spanish informers, Señores Galvez and Alzar, were real enough.
But an apocryphal story grew up around their defection to the British —
namely, that the English troops were smarter than Pakenham in spot-
ting the self-styled "deserters" as spies dispatched by General Jackson
to lure the redcoats to disaster. Whereupon "they seized the poor
wretches and hanged them on a tree within plain sight of the Americans."

It is doubtful if any such ostentatious execution did take place. Sir
Edward would hardly have permitted it. In fact, the information brought
by the Spaniards was accepted by Pakenham as reasonably accurate.
And reasonably accurate it was.

From the *grande reconnaissance* of December 28, as well as from
subsequent observations, it was plain that equipment would be needed
to bridge the Rodriguez canal and scale the ramparts rising on the
further bank. During the days of January 6 and 7 the engineers were
engaged in preparing fascines, or bundles of cane, to throw into the
ditch, along with ladders by which to climb the breastworks. These

would be hidden on the field the night before, ready to be picked up in the morning in advance of the attack.

On the evening of the 7th, Pakenham assembled his officers at Villeré's for final briefing on the grand assault that would begin at dawn. The key to success of the operation, or a vital part of it at any rate, would be the "surprise" attack on the right bank of the Mississippi — the unexpected second front which, Pakenham felt sure, the Americans were ill-prepared to meet.

Colonel Thornton, one of the more enterprising officers, would cross the river with what would be known for this operation as the Light Brigade — the 85th Infantry, one West India regiment, plus sailors and marines, all totaling 1400 muskets. With them would be a corps of rocketeers, while three barges with carronades would patrol the river to protect the flanks. They would cross as soon as it was dark, storm the marine battery and command its guns, then proceed up the river towards New Orleans before dawn, surprising any American troops that might be stationed in their path.

As to the operation on the left bank, Pakenham divided his army into three divisions. Gibbs would storm the American left, believed to be a vulnerable point. Keane would attack the American right, with Rennie advancing on his flank along the levee and river road. General Keane would be prepared to swing to the support of Rennie or of General Gibbs, depending on which would profit most from reinforcement. Lambert, with most of the 7th and the 43rd, would remain in reserve at Villeré's, to attack as the progress of the battle indicated.

To make sure that all orders were understood, they were entered in the regimental books and read by the commander to his staff and officers:

> The troops will be under arms two hours before daylight tomorrow morning, when the army will form in two columns in the following order: The right column, consisting of the 4th, 21st, and 44th, will take post near the wood, the 44th leading and bearing the ladders and fascines; the left column, composed of one company from the 43rd regiment, one from the 7th, the 93rd, and the fifth West India regiments, shall station itself on the left, and on the road, and with the 95th extended, shall keep up communications between the heads of the two columns. A general assault will then be made on the two enemy's lines, and the commander of the forces places the fullest reliance on the gallantry of the troops and the skill of their officers; that arrangements have been made to secure success; and that he confidently expects that tomorrow will add an additional laurel to the many which already adorn the brows of his brave followers.

The 44th regiment under Colonel Mullins was selected for the tricky task of getting the scaling equipment into position ahead of the advancing troops. Half the regiment would provide covering fire, while the other half rushed the fascines and ladders into place. It would require split-second timing, but this was a common exigency of battle.

When Colonel Mullins was summoned for briefing, he was shocked and mortified by this assignment. Asked if he thoroughly understood his orders, he replied:

"Nothing could be clearer. You are sending my regiment to execution. Their dead bodies are to be used as a bridge for the rest of the army to march over."

Pakenham eyed the colonel with sudden misgiving. But it was Gibbs who delivered the scathing answer.

"I can hardly have patience with one who argues that British veterans can be halted by, much less repulsed from, a low log breastwork manned by a backwoods rabble."

Mullins sulkily retired, brooding on the "forlorn hopes of the Forty-fourth," while word of his disaffection spread among the troops. "In all my campaigning," wrote Quartermaster Surtees, "I have never yet heard of a commanding officer who did not look upon the post of danger as the post of honour, and who did not rejoice, as if a favor was conferred on him, when appointed to an arduous or hazardous duty."

Back in his tent, Mullins reflected on his orders: *The officer commanding the 44th regiment must ascertain where the fascines and ladders are this evening, so as there may be no delay in taking them forward tomorrow morning.*

Mullins directed one of his subordinates, Lieutenant Johnston, to find out just where the ladders and fascines would be secreted. Johnston returned with the information: "They will be in the advance battery. There will be an engineer there to distribute the equipment. It's written on this memo."

Mullins shoved the memo into his pocket. There were several batteries on the field, built for previous artillery engagements. Some had since been stripped of their guns and were being used as redoubts by British pickets. The instructions were ambiguous, but Mullins would not reveal to his subordinates that he was puzzled. He would rely on the engineer to advise him when the time came—if he could find the engineer. Meanwhile he gave a critical assignment to an officer whom he especially disliked, Lieutenant Knight.

"You, sir, commanding the grenadiers, will take the ladders."

Knight regarded his superior with some contempt. He hated Mullins, and Mullins hated him; in fact the colonel had disciplined Knight a few days earlier for insubordination. Now the lieutenant acknowledged the order with a curt nod.

"That will be easy," he said. "We'll pick them up in the redoubt."

If Mullins noted a discrepancy between the words *redoubt* and *battery,* he refused to show it. Actually, Knight knew precisely where the ladders were. He had helped secrete them earlier that evening. But he was not going to enlighten Mullins; let the colonel think anything he liked. The disgruntled 44th bedded down for a sleepless night, convinced that their leader was a pompous fool who had committed them to a suicidal venture.

That evening the British officers and troops dined well. The boats which had brought up Lambert's division had also brought up fresh provisions. Pakenham, Keane and Gibbs sat down together at Villeré's, attended by the owner's slaves, who had served them with transmuted loyalty from the beginning.

Down the river road came an elegant, solitary figure on a roan mare. He wore the civilian clothes of a Louisiana planter and carried no side arms. Challenged by pickets, he addressed them in cultured French they could not understand. A spy? An American deserter? One of the Creole leaders who the British hoped would join them? The pickets led him to Pakenham at Villeré's, where he introduced himself: Pierre Denis de la Ronde, owner of property further up the river. Another place was set at the table, and Pierre sat down to dine with the British generals.

The siege of New Orleans will ever hold its mysteries, and this was one of them. Of this strange visit, only Vincent Nolte – who, though sometimes unreliable, kept a close ear to the ground – left a brief account:

> One of the guests was the planter, de la Ronde, who had visited the English on their landing. They supposed him to be inimical to the American government, and therefore spoke freely before him, and drank to the toast of "Booty and Beauty," as they had heard of the great beauty of the fair Louisianians. De la Ronde returned that night to his plantation, and at daybreak crossed the river in a canoe to travel, most of the way on foot, to the American defenses. He reached Jackson's Camp about 1 o'clock, and told the whole plan to the General. Jackson instantly took measures for stubborn resistance.

It seems hard to believe that Nolte's story was entirely a fabrication, but equally hard to believe that General Pakenham would have discussed his plans before a total stranger, regardless of that stranger's sympathetic attitude or innocent appearance. And whatever information de la Ronde took back to Jackson, it could hardly be anything that the General did not already know.

Throughout that night, under cover of darkness, Pakenham's troops and engineers continued to drag up the heavy guns for the morning's opening bombardment. They were placed at strategic points to cover the infantry's advance. But, as before, it was almost impossible to dig proper embrasures or emplacements for the cannon. The spades and shovels struck water just inches below the surface; the mud was too soft to work with. Even with cypress planks for underpinning, the guns were insecurely mounted.

While most of the British troops and officers, including Pakenham, slept soundly, content that every measure to insure success had been attended to, Quartermaster Surtees and a major of the Rifle Corps tramped over and back across the field on which the army would march to victory next morning. "I was sadly disappointed at our not meeting with any other commanding officers engaged in this most necessary duty," he observed. He remembered how, in the Peninsula campaigns, commanders went over every inch of ground before an impending battle, to become familiar with its obstacles and opportunities, "but here all seemed apathy and fatal security, arising from our too much despising our enemy."

> I own I did not at all feel satisfied with what I had seen and heard, and retired to rest with a considerable degree of despondency on my mind; and as I knew I could render little aid to the service in a case like the present, I determined I should not take any part in it, for I almost felt confident of its failure.

Colonel Thornton was another who was haunted by foreboding that night. He stood on the bank of Villeré's canal, where it penetrated the levee, with Lieutenant Gleig, the Light Brigade, and the sailors and marines. It was nine o'clock, long past the appointed hour for their embarkation for the crossing of the Mississippi. The dike had been opened and the water had coursed into the canal to raise the boats — but it raised them only slightly. What Pakenham had feared, had happened. The dam at the far end of the lock had given way and the water was coursing towards Lake Borgne. The few boats closest to the river stood in shallow water, with those below them hopelessly mired in the mud.

Thornton had been in a state of mild exasperation since the landing, when Keane had refused to advance at once upon the city. He was in no mind to be balked again. He knew that his mission on the right flank of the Mississippi was decisive to the outcome of the battle. He would use the few boats at hand to take as many troops as possible across the river and leave the rest behind. His force would be reduced to 340 men along with some sailors and marines, compared with the 1400 he had counted on, and there would be no room for field artillery.

There was little sleep for anyone in Jackson's camp that night. While half the troops cat-napped beside their arms, the other half manned the breastworks, later alternating with their comrades. No one was allowed to leave the line, and Jackson had posted sentries on the plantations in the rear with orders to shoot would-be deserters or wayward soldiers seeking a last night of illicit pleasure in the city.

In Macarty's house, Jackson stretched out on blankets on the ground floor with his aides Davezac, Reid and Butler. Edward Livingston was there, too, sword and pistol by his side. But, the General wryly reflected, Livingston had a knack of disappearing when the action became hot. Sometimes he pleaded ignorance, at other times a sudden illness. The General prized his shrewd advice and canny wisdom, and forgave Livingston his lack of military fortitude.

At one o'clock they were aroused by the sentry who announced a courier from Patterson. An urgent message. Enemy boats were crossing the river, seemingly headed for Morgan's camp. General Morgan pleaded "most earnestly" for a quick dispatch of reinforcements to bolster his defense line.

Jackson reacted with irritation. He had sent five hundred Kentuckians to Morgan's camp that afternoon, presumably raising his forces to a thousand men. He had not been informed that only a token company had got there, poorly armed at that.

"Tell General Morgan," Jackson ordered, "that I have no men to spare. He must maintain his position at all hazards."

Then, noting the time, the General told his aides: "Gentlemen, we have slept enough." It was time for a last inspection of the barricades.

Ill with dysentery and exhausted as he was, Jackson preferred the intimacy of reviewing his troops on foot. But he allowed his horse to follow in case he gave out, and handed the reins to young Billy Phillips, a protégé of the General's, who, at the outbreak of war, had ridden 860 miles in nine days to bring the news to the Hermitage, Jackson's home in Nashville.

Starting at the levee, the General observed the forward redoubt at the far right of his line. "I never did like that redoubt," he grumbled. "I didn't want it in the first place. I told my officers it wouldn't hold." But it was manned now by Beale's Rifles, as well as portions of the 7th regiment, and he had come to admire those "Gentlemen Johnnies" who, since the battle of December 23, had shown such surprising spirit under fire

Passing on, the group reached the battery of the Baratarians, where the French buccaneers were brewing coffee with ritualistic reverence. ("It was black as tar and its aroma could be smelled twenty yards away," recalled Colonel Butler.)

"That smells like better coffee than we can get," the General told Dominique You. "Where do you get such coffee? Smuggle it, perhaps?"

"Mebbe so, Zhénéral," said the grinning Dominique, handing him a cup. Jackson drank it with gusto, and as he moved out of earshot remarked to Butler: "I wish I had fifty such guns on this line, with five hundred such devils as those fellows behind them. I could storm the gates of hell with Dominique as my Lieutenant." The "hellish banditti" had soared in his estimation.

The General and his aides moved on slowly behind the ramparts, greeted with smiles of appreciation by the troops. Butler was surprised at the way Jackson seemed able to call each man by name, addressing him familiarly without loss of respect on either side.

Reaching Carroll's troops, Jackson noticed a youngster named Robertson from Nashville. "How are they using you, Joe?" he asked. "Wouldn't you rather be with your Aunt Lucy than with me?"

"Not by a damn sight, General!" Joe averred. "But I wouldn't mind if Aunt Lucy was here a little while."

Jackson laughed and patted the young man's shoulder. "Stick to it, Joe. We'll smash hell out of 'em and then you can go home to Aunt Lucy."

As he moved among the Tennesseans huddled around their little fires and breakfasting on corn bread, bacon and whiskey, his salutations bore a special note of warmth. These, in his estimation, were the elite of his assorted army. Unshaven, dirty, they had lived for seven days waist-deep in mud, chilled by the intermittent rains, surrounded by the stench of the decaying marshlands, threatened by lurking danger in the shadows of the cypress trees. Yet they'd had only one complaint: "If only we could see the redcoats within fair buck-range."

There was a frontier camaraderie between the General and these men, and they crowded around him as around an old, familiar friend. Intuitively he suspected they would bear the brunt of the impending onslaught, luring the enemy by their deceptive lack of discipline and unimposing breastworks. But he had no doubts about them.

Returning to Macarty's, Jackson sent Billy Phillips for his telescope. It would start getting light soon; he would want to see what was going on out there. Far to the left two shots rang out. They seemed to come from the edge of the swamp, some distance forward of the line.

"Some of my Choctaws, I reckon," Jackson said contentedly. "That's where they ought to be by now."

Then, dismissing his aides, he sat down on a log to wait for day to break—a day, his biographer Marquis James observed, to which all his life till now had been a preface.

# 16.   Armageddon

Sunday, January 8, 1815.

Long before dawn the bells of St. Louis Cathedral summoned the devout to early mass. On the cold floor of their chapel the Ursuline nuns knelt in prayer before the altar of Our Lady of Prompt Succour. On the streets of New Orleans the veterans made their rounds while the fire brigade stood shivering at their stations. The citizens slept fitfully and wakened early, conscious of a sense of doom that hung like a pall above the city.

From the river a chill fog spilled over the banks to blanket the plantations, limiting visibility to a hundred feet. The plain of Chalmette, seen fragmentarily, was coated with a silver frost. At four o'clock as scheduled, generals Keane and Gibbs moved their columns forward. Five hundred yards from the American line Keane veered to the left towards the river, with his Rifles and Highlanders, and soon vanished in the mist. The West Indians obliqued towards the forest on the right. The main columns moved towards the center of the field and halted just behind the British batteries.

Forbidden to light fires, the men had breakfasted on rum and cold ship's biscuits. They were forbidden to move or talk or even beat their arms to dispel the cold. But their spirits were high. Their knapsacks had been filled with provisions from the night before; their arms and uniforms had been carefully tended for the victory march on New Orleans. Silently they waited for the sound of rifle fire from Thornton's forces across the river that would signal their advance.

Colonel Mullins of the 44th led his men forward across the field to pick up the scaling equipment for the regiments to follow. The ground was slippery and treacherous; visibility was so poor that the men had only the backs of those ahead to guide them. As they reached the first of the redoubts Mullins saw no sign of the fascines and ladders. And where was Captain Tapp of the engineers who was supposed to meet him with instructions?

Mullins waited ten minutes for the engineer. When no one appeared, he signaled his troops to advance. The scaling equipment must be up ahead. Or perhaps the plans had been changed and he had not been properly informed.

Barely fifty feet away the dozing Captain Tapp awoke to see ghost-like figures moving through the fog. He had been expecting them and was surprised when they passed on.

As the rear of the column passed the redoubt, Subaltern Knight exclaimed to his companion, Lieutenant-Colonel Debbeig:

"Mullins is forgetting the ladders and fascines!"

Debbeig smugly shrugged. "That's his business."

Knight ordered a sergeant to hurry forward and politely inform Colonel Mullins that he was forgetting the scaling implements. Did Mullins want Knight to pick them up? The sergeant raced up to Mullins with the message. The colonel bridled.

"Tell the lieutenant to go about his business," he said sharply.

Reaching the next redoubt, still seeing no sign of the ladders or the engineer, Mullins cursed his superiors for their faulty information. He led his troops to their assigned position just forward of the British batteries, behind the first of two intervening ditches.

At Villeré's Pakenham breakfasted with his aides. Then, in full dress uniform, sword sashed to his side, he walked out to inspect the disposition of his army. The first thing that caught his eye was a line of thirteen barges mired in Villeré's canal, with two-thirds of Thornton's infantry stranded on the bank. One of the boatmen who had crossed the river and returned, informed the General of Thornton's plight. Only 450 of the 85th had made it to the other bank, and they had disembarked some miles below their intended landing.

The General had not been told earlier because, as his adjutant Major Harry Smith confessed, such news "was as bad as the loss of a leg." One vital facet of Pakenham's master strategy had gone awry.

"Smith," Sir Edward said, "most commanders-in-chief have many difficulties to contend with, but surely none like mine. Thornton's people will be of no use whatever to the general attack."

Smith argued that, since possession of the right bank was essential to secure success, the main attack should be postponed. "There is still time before daylight to retire the columns now," he recommended. "We will be under the enemy's fire as soon as discovered."

"That may be," said Pakenham. "But I have twice delayed the attack. Further delay will only cost more men."

At that moment, Smith recorded, the fog began to break.

"Go to General Lambert," Pakenham ordered. "Tell him to fire the rockets, now!"

Twin rockets soared and sputtered in the sky. With faultless precision the troops began to move, in columns sixty men abreast and four men deep. They marched as on dress parade, in perfect step, led by the wind-whipped regimental colors of white, gold and scarlet. All that was needed to enhance the spectacle was the sound of military bands and martial airs. But the British musicians had not, since landing, unpacked their instruments. The troops kept step to the roll of drums and maneuvered to the mellow tone of bugles.

On his chestnut charger, with Duncan MacDougall mounted at his side, General Pakenham watched the columns advance with the old thrill of remembered victories. They were magnificent! These were the cream of the British empire; history was in the making. The mightiest army to cross American soil was on the march. The setback to Colonel Thornton on the right bank suddenly seemed of small significance — and the enemy troops a mile away of even less significance. They would crumple at this awesome sight.

But already, in the center of the field, Gibbs's column seemed to be in trouble. Word had swept back from the foremost ranks that the 44th had failed to advance the ladders and fascines. Controlling his rage Gibbs ordered Mullins to return for the equipment. The rattled men of the 44th stumbled back through the advancing troops to the overlooked redoubt. The bundles of green sugar cane seemed to weigh a ton. The ladders were heavy and difficult to carry. Breathless and exhausted, the men labored back over the slippery terrain, trying to catch up with

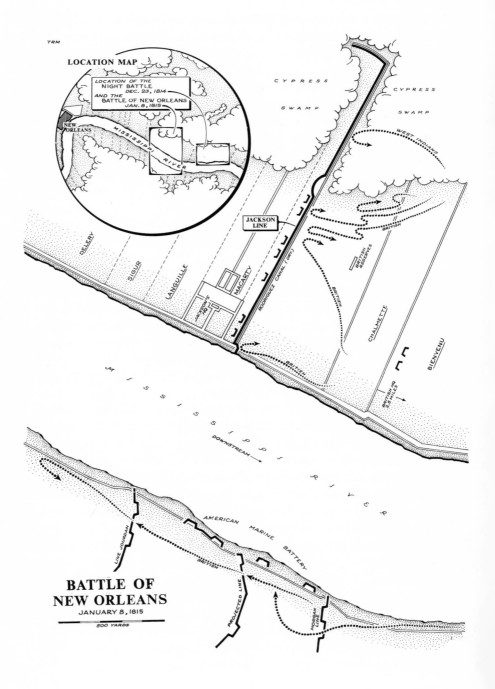

**BATTLE OF NEW ORLEANS**
JANUARY 8, 1815
500 YARDS

the 21st. But the 21st was already nearing the ramparts, cursing the lack of fascines and ladders, cursing the 44th and firing their rifles wildly at the unseen enemy behind the breastworks.

Assured by Major Latour that the mist would break with the rising sun, General Jackson had mounted the parapet with Colonel Butler in time to see the fog lift and the rockets streak across the sky.

"That is their signal for advance, I believe," he said.

He ordered Butler off the parapet, but remained himself on the ramparts, keeping his field glass trained on the advancing enemy. Behind the breastworks, from Beale's Rifles on the right to Coffee's Tennesseans on the left, the men were silent, tense and cool — watching in fascination the mechanically advancing troops. Jackson sent word along the line. Keep down! Pick your target among the British ranks. Don't fire until told. Aim for the buckles on the crossbelts.

As the seconds ticked by, no artillery, no rifle sounded. A cathedral-like silence hung like a benediction over the advancing army. One impressionable Kentuckian saw in the clouds "the wings of the Angel of Death above Chalmette." But the excitable French artillerist Flaujeac, commanding the central twelve-pound gun, saw only the tempting scarlet jackets presenting a perfect target from five hundred yards away. He gave the order, "Fire!"

"Then," noted Butler, "all the guns opened. The British batteries . . . replied, directing their aim by the sound of our guns." In Adair's company the young Kentuckian Richard Ogilvy saw how the flames of the enemy cannon "lit up in a wonderful way, though the guns themselves could not be seen. The enemy's infantry did not fire a shot, but came on with fixed bayonets."

The British columns never broke step although the initial blast tore frightful holes in their forward lines. True to ironbound tradition they stepped over their fallen comrades, closed ranks and marched with measured step towards the thundering cannon. Coffee and Adair sent word to Jackson that the settling smoke of the artillery was spoiling the aim of the tautly-awaiting riflemen. Jackson signaled the batteries to hold their fire.

In the sudden lull Ogilvy witnessed "a comical thing." Among Carroll's Tennesseans was a grizzly sergeant named Sam Williams who, around the campfires, had led the men in singing Negro spirituals. Now, "seeing General Jackson standing straight as a ramrod, all alone on the top of the breastworks," Williams leapt to the crest of the parapet. There, waving his arms like a choirmaster, he burst into song:

> Dere's Gabriel standin' at de gate . . .
> Just one mo' minute fo' to wait
> To heah dat Trumpet blow!

"Old Sam didn't get any further," Ogilvy observed. "Jackson, turning, looked at him benignantly." But Carroll exploded at this reckless clowning.

"Get down and shut up, Sam!" he shouted. "If the redcoats hear you singing, they'll run like hell! And we want them to keep coming!"

Sam stepped down to hear, not a trumpet blow, but Jackson's steady voice saying to Carroll and Adair: "They're near enough now, gentlemen. Fire when ready."

General Adair moved forward and tapped the shoulder of one of his marksmen, pointing to a British major riding in front of the English columns.

"Morg, see that officer on the gray horse?"

Morgan Ballard nodded, tightening his finger on the trigger.

*"Snuff his candle!"*

Morgan's rifle cracked, and Major Whitaker of General Gibbs' division tumbled, mortally wounded, from his horse.

From the balcony of de la Ronde's the British Quartermaster E. N. Burroughs saw Major Whitaker shot from his horse and marveled at the marksmanship that brought him down.

> At a distance of nearly three hundred yards! As if to warn us of the fate in store! . . . The bullet cut about half its diameter in the upper rim of his left ear, passed through his head, out at the right temple and went on. Instantly the whole American line, from the swamp to a point past its center was ablaze.
>
> In less time than one can write it, the Forty-fourth Foot was literally swept from the face of the earth. In the wreck and confusion that ensued within five minutes the regiment seemed to vanish from sight — except the half of it that lay stricken on the ground. Every mounted officer was down at the first fire. No such execution by small arms has ever been seen or heard of.

On the far left of the field, along the river, Burroughs saw Rennie's column pressing forward, sheltered by the levee from Patterson's batteries and eager to reach the forward redoubt on the right of Jackson's line. From across the field General Carroll saw their swift advance. He sent a detachment of riflemen racing behind the lines to fire on them. "The right flank of Rennie's column seemed to sink into the earth," said a British lieutenant who witnessed the counterattack.

Two out of three men in the cólumn fell. The remainder hesitated only briefly. Then, led by Rennie, they charged up the glacis of the demibastion and fell on the defenders. In sixty seconds of furious fighting with rifle butts and bayonets the Americans were overcome, a few escaping across a plank laid over the canal. The advance redoubt, about which Jackson had been skeptical, was firmly in the enemy's possession.

Now fifty feet from the main American line, with only the canal between, Rennie looked around for Keane's battalion. With reinforcements they could storm the American flank and be behind the Yankee lines. Keane, it had been understood, was to move wherever he was needed most. But inexplicably Keane's column now was veering to the right, towards General Gibbs. Rennie ordered his men to keep under cover until reinforcements hopefully arrived.

Keane's decision to move to Gibbs's support may have doomed the most promising British penetration of the American defenses. But it seemed at the time to be called for. Over the sprawling bodies of Colonel Mullins's 44th, the 21st was pressing forward, aware that no scaling equipment awaited them at the ramparts, but determined to scale them nonetheless. They were four hundred yards from the canal. Three hundred yards. Two hundred . . .

The American ramparts exploded in a burst of flame and smoke. "The whole line," wrote Butler, "from Carroll's Tennesseans to the swamp was almost one solid blaze." Four men deep, the ranks of the Tennesseans and Kentuckians never stopped for breath. As fast as one man fired he stepped back for the next to take his place. By the time the fourth line had discharged its rifles, the first was taking aim again. "There were barely fifteen hundred rifles in the line," wrote Alexander Walker, "yet scarcely a rifle failed to find its mark."

The redcoats fell "like blades of grass beneath the scythe," a British officer recorded. "Never before had British veterans quailed," wrote Quartermaster Burroughs from his observation post at de la Ronde's. "But there was something in that leaden torrent that no man on earth could face. In minutes the entire column was broken and disorganized . . . in full retreat that lacked little of precipitate flight."

The field before Jackson's line was a scarlet carpet of dead and wounded. By the time more than half the enemy column had fallen, Colonel Butler noted that "no officer on horseback could be seen, and such as had escaped death or wounds were running as fast as their legs could carry them to the rear—anywhere to get out of reach of those awful rifles." Among the British commanders lying on the field were Colonel Francis Brooke of the King's Own and Colonel William Patterson of the 21st. Lieutenant-Colonel Debbeig had fallen, relieved of his chagrin at the failure to advance the ladders.

His face scarlet with fury, General Gibbs rode forward to rally his stricken troops. Officers smote the retreating soldiers with the backs of their swords. The 44th was past all hope; the ladders and fascines lay scattered helter-skelter on the field; those who had survived the butchery were huddled in the ditches or the swamp. Gibbs yelled for Colonel Mullins. The colonel was nowhere to be seen.

"If I live till tomorrow," Gibbs shouted, "I'll hang Mullins to the highest tree!"

Briefly, under their general's exhortation, the second column rallied. A handful of men under Lieutenant Leavock of the 21st reached the Rodriguez canal and looked in vain for a plank or ladder to throw across it. A few leaped into the ditch and were shot from above like salmon in a barrel. Only Leavock himself, clawing his way up the slippery breastwork, reached the top and came face to face with two American officers. With extraordinary gall he called on them to surrender, then realized his lone position and handed them his sword.

Following Leavock's example, Major Thomas Wilkinson of the 21st, shouting to his men to follow, charged almost alone across the canal and up to the top of the parapet. A dozen Kentucky muskets riddled him with bullets. He pitched to the feet of his executioners, where Major Smiley, moved to compassion by his courage, bent over to console him.

"Bear up, Major. You're too brave to die."

"I thank you with all my heart," murmured Wilkinson. "But do me a favor. Tell my commander that I died here on your parapet."

He did, in fact, die as he was carried to the rear, and the Kentuckians covered his body with their regimental colors.

There were other gallant attempts to scale the earthworks, an effort impossible without ladders. A British officer reported:

> Some few, indeed, by mounting one upon another's shoulders, succeeded in entering the works, but these were instantly overpowered, most of them killed, and the rest taken; while as many as stood without were exposed to a sweeping fire which cut them down by whole companies. . . . They fell by the hands of men whom they absolutely did not see; for the Americans, without so much as lifting their faces above the rampart, swung their firelocks by one arm over the wall, and discharged them directly on their heads.

Not all the Americans remained behind the parapet. One spirited Tennessean mounted the breastwork for a better shot at the oncoming enemy. His gun jammed. Swearing lustily, he seized the rifle by its barrel and hurled it butt-first at the nearest redcoat. An English officer, taken prisoner, told of another impetuous Tennessean who seemed to be fighting a personal battle of his own.

> Instead of firing from behind the breastwork, he would stand on top of it where, balancing himself, he would bring his rifle to his cheek, throw back his broad brim, take sight and fire as deliberately as though shooting a herd of deer.
>
> Though the grape whistled through the air over our heads, for the life of me I could not help smiling at his grotesque, demi-savage figure as he threw back the broad flap of his castor to obtain a fair sight—shut his left eye, and blazed away at us. I verily believe he brought down one of my men at every shot.

Far to the left, in the captured American redoubt, Rennie's men were pinned down by the close-range fire of Ross's Regulars. "Indeed," observed Quartermaster Surtees, who true to his vow remained on the sidelines of the battle, "they were in a most critical situation. For, being within a few yards of the enemy's main body, they could not move without being shot through the head by their riflemen." One taller-than-average sergeant removed his peaked hat to wipe his brow and counted five bullet holes in the crown. As Quartermaster Surtees further noted:

> It was not till they threatened to shoot the prisoners they had taken, that they induced the Americans to desist from attacking them. . . They were obliged at last to adopt a very singular but politic expedient, which was to

make one of the American prisoners embrace one of their own, and thus to stand up together to see what was going forward . . .

What Rennie's men perceived by this "politic expedient" was Gibbs's division in full flight and no sign of Keane's forces coming to their aid. Rennie had two bitter choices. He could attempt an inglorious retreat or storm the ramparts with the few men left to him. Waving his sword and shouting, "Come on, boys, the day is ours!" the colonel led his men over the walls and across the narrow plank that spanned the ditch. Jostling one another in a frantic rush towards the breastwork, some were pushed into the canal to drown, others fell to American bullets.

Only Colonel Rennie, clawing his way in frog-like fashion up the slippery glacis, reached the top of the rampart, where one of Beale's riflemen shot him through the forehead. His body, spread-eagled like a scarecrow, slid into the ditch.

Keane's column, having left Rennie's Rifles to their fate, was approaching in support of General Gibbs. The tall Highlanders, a hundred men abreast, "their muskets glittering in the morning sun and tartans waving in the air," marched with measured tread into the hail of cannon shot and bullets. One officer remembered, "The first objects which we saw, enclosed as we were in this little world of mist, were the cannon balls tearing up the ground and crossing one another and bounding along like so many cricket balls through the air. Coming on our left flank from the Americans on the right bank of the river and also from their lines in front."

General Keane felt a sharp sting in his neck. Raising a hand to explore the wound, he toppled senseless from his horse.

With their leader down, the Highlanders hesitated briefly, waiting for an order. Automatically Colonel Dale assumed command, but all about was nothing but confusion. The survivors of General Gibbs's shattered division were fleeing in every direction, throwing aside their muskets and knapsacks to be rid of all impediments. A captain in the rear was so confounded by this panic that he asked a retreating soldier, "Have we or the Americans attacked?"

"The Americans have attacked," the soldier told him, racing on.

Mounted on his charger beside Lambert in the rear, General Pakenham watched the decimation of his legions with stunned disbelief. "That's a terrific fire, Lambert," he remarked, concealing his mortification. These were men he had led to victory at Albuera and Salamanca.

They had never faltered under fire, had never known the meaning of the word fear. Yet here they were, scattered in panic, crouched in ditches or prostrate on the ground. He saw Gibbs vainly trying to rally them for a renewed attack. It was time to take a hand.

Accompanied by his aide, Duncan MacDougall, Sir Edward galloped up the field. Approaching from the left came the Highlanders, a thousand strong, their ranks as yet intact. There was cause for hope in these stalwart, tartaned giants. Pakenham spurred his horse on. "Brave Highlanders!" he cried, waving them on with his hat.

As he galloped forward with MacDougall, Gibbs came to meet him.

"I cannot control my men," Gibbs shouted. "They won't obey me!"

Pakenham turned on the scattered troops around him, crouched in ditches or supine among the dead and wounded.

"Shame! Shame!" he called to them. "Remember you're British! Forward, Gentlemen, Forward!"

Briefly the troops took heart, throwing off their heavy knapsacks to resume the charge. Pakenham rode to their lead, tall in the saddle, his plumed hat like a beacon in their midst. Out of some curious respect that men in battle have for one another, even though enemies, the American riflemen withheld their fire. But the artillery still thundered. A ball struck the General in the shoulder, while another knocked his horse from under him.

MacDougall dismounted to come to the aid of his wounded chief. Pakenham waved him away, swung himself up on MacDougall's pony and pressed on toward the enemy's line. From the center of that line two shots rang out. One bullet struck the General below the ribs, another pierced his throat. Stiffening briefly in the saddle, blood gushing from his wounds, Sir Edward slid from his horse. He collapsed in the arms of Duncan MacDougall, as General Ross had collapsed in the Scotsman's arms six months before.

The dying General gave a final order. "Have Lambert bring up the reserve," he whispered.

As Pakenham was carried off the field and laid in the shelter of an oak at de la Ronde's, a bugler, informed of the General's order, raised his trumpet to summon the reserves. At that instant a shell from across the river all but severed his arm. The signal to call up the reserves was never sounded.

Stunned and enraged by the signs of defeat around them, the Highlanders followed Colonel Dale in a last magnificent charge towards the ramparts. At the start of the battle, Dale had handed his watch and a letter to his adjutant. "Give these to my wife," he said. "I shall die at the head of my regiment."

His prophecy came true as a thunderous volley brought down almost half the regiment and left him dying on the field. A second volley took another dreadful toll. Flight was not familiar to the men from Scotland, but now they broke and fled as they had never done in any battle in their long and glorious careers.

Riding in circles like a man demented, unwilling to accept disaster, General Gibbs was stopped by Major Shaw of Pakenham's staff.

"They have killed the General, Sir," the Major said. "You are now in command."

But in command of what? This scattered, formless rabble?

"Where are the Highlanders?" roared Gibbs. "What's the matter with the Highlanders?"

"They cannot be urged to go further," Shaw said. "They are nearly destroyed already."

"Then get them out of my way!" bellowed Gibbs, and spurred his horse in a lone charge towards the enemy. He would storm the ramparts singlehanded.

Four bullets brought him down, a fifth piercing the forehead of his horse. Cursing his fate, cursing Mullins, and even, some reported, damning Pakenham, he was carried to the rear to linger long in agony before he died.

Helplessly witnessing the carnage, General Lambert could stand by no longer. He ordered the 43rd Infantry and Royal Fusiliers to take the field. But it was more to cover the retreating troops than to launch a new attack. Beyond range of the American artillery he halted and ordered the remnants of Gibbs's regiments to remain where they were, under cover. As a last expedient he sent a detachment of West Indians through the swamp to see if it were possible to flank the enemy line.

Jugeat's Choctaws, leaping from log to log, caught the unit mired knee-deep in the mud. Seeing themselves surrounded, and noting the swarthy color of the Choctaws, the West India blacks were not averse to surrendering "to men of our own race."

With the rest of his regiments intact, Lambert rode back to de la Ronde's. There Admiral Cochrane asked him: "What do you intend to do, General?"

Lambert inclined his head towards the corpse-strewn fields of Chalmette. "I do not think it prudent to renew the attack, Admiral."

"Why not?" Cochrane protested. "Rennie almost made it. Rally the
troops, General, and we'll have this battle, yet."

Lambert felt no answer was required. A third of the army were dead
or wounded on the field, another third disabled by hysteria and shock.
Already the constricted plains of Chalmette-de la Ronde had gained the
sobriquet of "Suicide Alley" with the troops. To renew the attack
would be to send his men to certain death. He turned and left the room.

A few yards away, beneath one of the oaks which Pierre de la Ronde
had planted to celebrate his offspring's birthday, General Pakenham
lay dying. An aide bent over to catch his final whispered words.

"Lost for the lack of courage."

Pacing behind the left and center of his line, which bore the brunt of
the British assault, Jackson had witnessed with a mixture of compassion and astonishment the wholesale slaughter of the enemy. In every
direction the ground in front of the canal was strewn with dead and
wounded. Yet still the thin red lines had kept on coming. Butler's
voice spoke beside him.

"Magnificent, isn't it, General?"

Jackson nodded grimly. "Magnificent. But is it war?"

While some of the men behind the ramparts exulted in the carnage,
there were those among the grizzly frontiersmen who could not conceal
their tears. Officers' voices choked or trembled as they gave the orders
to fire. Among the emotional Creoles many turned their faces from the
sight, immobilized by shock, fingers frozen on the hammer locks.

But as the red-coated targets disappeared, or melted beyond range, it
was hard to restrain the Tennesseans and Kentuckians. One by one and
then in groups, they sprang to the top of the parapet, shouting and waving their hats in glee, discharging their rifles at anything that moved.
Officers grabbed at their legs to pull them down. Jackson, angered, repeated his order for the men to remain behind the breastworks.

"What I fear now, Robert," he said to Butler, "is that some of these
youngsters may get out of hand, go over the works to get after the
the enemy."

He was right. With nothing to shoot at, the young backwoodsmen began fingering their knives or hefting their rifles to be used as clubs.

Young Robert Polk, of his father's company, sprang to the top of the breastwork, waving his Indian tomahawk and shouting:

"Come on, boys! Let's charge 'em!"

*"Down, sir, down!"* roared Jackson. *"Back to your post!"*

He turned to Butler. "Lend me your pistols for a moment, Colonel."

Butler unstrapped the rifled pistols on his belt and passed them over.

"Now," Jackson thundered, "I'll shoot the first man who goes over the works. We must have order here!"

The General's voice was not easily ignored. Order prevailed in the center, but to the far extremes of the line, beyond the reach of his command, men chose danger over prudence. They scrambled over the breastworks and canal to capture wounded British officers, carrying them back as trophies. One subaltern, barely able to stand, refused to surrender his sword to "a dirty chimney sweep." His insulted captor raised his rifle and seemed about to drill him through when a companion advised, "Forget it. His wound entitles him to decent treatment." The subaltern was allowed to keep his sword.

Dead officers who had fallen on the parapet were also hauled behind the lines, where riflemen vied for the credit of having brought them down. Rennie's body was a matter of dispute. Said a zealous marksman named Swithers, "If he is not shot directly above the eyebrows then it wasn't my rifle that did it." Impartial inspection revealed that Rennie had died of a single bullet just above the eyebrows.

Many of the prostrate enemy, wounded or not, seemed content to be claimed as prisoners. Among these were a number of Irish who swore they had never wanted to fight Americans in the first place.

"Then why did you charge our lines with such determination?" they were asked.

"'Faith, we had no choice — with the officers sticking and stabbing us with their swords."

In substantiation they displayed the slashes in their trousers and the flesh cuts on their rumps.

One of the prized captives was an unsung hero of the battle. While drummer boy Jordan Noble had aroused the Americans with his ceaseless, rhythmic beat ("Listen to Jordan, boys, keep firing!"), a fourteen-year-old British bugler had climbed a tree two hundred yards from the canal. Throughout and above the din of battle, ignoring shells and bullets, he had sounded the call to "Charge! Charge!" — continuing long after there were no men left to charge.

Now he was seized by the heels and dragged down by a group of admiring Creoles who took him behind the lines, where, to his bewilderment, he was feted as a hero.

In half an hour it was over. With no more standing targets on the field the American musketry fell silent. While the artillery continued blasting, there was one chord missing. The roar of Patterson's battery had ceased. From the right bank came the sound of rifle fire, but not from where it might have been expected.

Jackson trained his field glass on the plain across the river.

"What's the matter with Morgan?" he exclaimed to Butler. "He's retreating!"

There was no doubt about it. Sparks from what was obviously an exchange of fire appeared just across the river from his own position. Morgan's line was supposed to be a little below that point.

The General might well have echoed Napoleon's words on hearing the news of Trafalgar: "I cannot be everywhere at once." It was a helpless feeling. The battle which minutes before had seemed decided, still hung in a precarious balance. He sent for Jean Laffite. Someone must determine just how serious Morgan's situation was.

# 17.  *Disaster on the Right Bank*

It was not until the first light of dawn, eight hours behind schedule, that Colonel William Thornton and his 340 troops of the Light Brigade, with detachments of sailors and marines that raised his total force to some 450 men, pushed off from the levee at Villeré's and started their fateful crossing of the Mississippi.

They had been supposed to embark the night before, to overcome Patterson's battery by midnight, and thereafter coordinate their advance with Pakenham's main attack upon the American breastworks. The delay in bringing up the boats, the inadequate number of barges, had held them back. Now the small flotilla of six barges, three with carronades at their bows, was being driven downstream by the current, past their intended point of landing on the right bank.

Crouched in one of the boats that were loaded to capacity, Lieutenant George Gleig and his fellows of the 85th exchanged messages to be delivered to their families should any of them perish. Their mission seemed doomed, for, as Gleig gloomily reflected, "nothing could repair the loss of time."

It was in vain that they rowed on in perfect silence, and with oars muffled, gaining the point of debarkation without being perceived. It was in vain that they made good their landing and formed upon the beach, without opposition or alarm; day had already broken, and the signal rocket was seen in the air while they were as yet four miles from the batteries, which ought hours ago to have been taken.

The contingent landed at the plantation of Manuel Andry five miles below Morgan's main position behind which stretched Patterson's batteries across the river from Chalmette's. Andry's son, Hortane, was asleep in the house, having just returned from a nighttime reconnoitering of the Terre aux Boefs, where the British were foraging for supplies. He was awakened and taken prisoner, and grilled by Colonel Thornton as to American forces on the west bank. Yes, there were Louisiana militia at the English Turn some miles below, Hortane told his captors, with "several thousand" stationed up the river to intercept the landing party..

Taking this with a grain of salt, Thornton left a picket at Andry's to guard the prisoner, and started his small force moving up the river. They saw the twin rockets exploding over Pakenham's army on the left bank, signaling the main assault, and "this unwelcome sight added wings to our speed." The three cannon-bearing gunboats moved with them up the river to cover their advance with flanking fire when they met the enemy.

Behind the Raguet canal, a mile below Jackson's line across the river, General Morgan awaited the approaching English whose landing had been sighted by Patterson and reported to him and Jackson. There was no guessing how many there were. His defense force consisted of five hundred infantry concentrated along the shallow breastwork which he reported as high enough to "cover a man's head when kneeling on one knee."

The line extended only two hundred yards from the Mississippi River, though the plain itself was two thousand yards in width. Of his three militia regiments, the First Louisiana was stationed nearest the river, then the Second, then Alexandre Declouet's regiment of drafted militia on the right—leaving 1800 yards from that point to the cypress swamp protected by only a shallow ditch. Patterson had supplied him with three pieces of artillery. A twelve-pound cannon was mounted near the river with two six-pounders to the right of it.

Having received Jackson's order to oppose the British landing,

Morgan had, the night before, sent Major Paul Arnaud with a hundred men to Morin's plantation three miles below his main defense, there to establish an outpost and to check the enemy's advance. Arnaud's troops, according to Latour, "were very ill armed, most of them having only fowling-pieces and musket cartridges too large for them. Several of them were even without any arms, and not one of them, I believe, excepting their commander, had ever been exposed to any enemy before."

Possibly Morgan considered them expendable. He could hardly have expected them to put up any effective resistance to an enemy attack in force. They reached Morin's plantation before midnight, spread out their blankets and promptly fell asleep, leaving a lone sentry to stand watch. Before long he as well dozed off.

Early the following morning, between four and five, Colonel John Davis arrived at Morgan's position with his 170 weary Kentuckians, dispatched by Jackson to Morgan's aid the evening before. Out of the five hundred Davis had started with, these were all that he had found arms for as they shambled through New Orleans. He had left the rest behind. The contingent was in poor shape, "faint for want of food." As Latour recorded:

> They had marched five miles, from the ferry near the powder magazine to the line, on bad roads, sometimes knee deep in mud. It appears also that their arms were in an ill condition, their ammunition bad, and several of their muskets without flints, some having but pebbles in their stead. What could be expected from men thus dispirited, ill armed and exhausted with inanition and fatigue?

What to expect of them, what to do with them, were troublesome questions for Morgan. Finally, as Davis was arranging his men along the unfortified section of the line, he galloped over and ordered the Colonel to take his men down the river and join Major Arnaud at the outpost. Davis was outraged.

"Forward!" he shouted indignantly. "General, these men are tired. They can't move hither and yon on someone's whim."

It was Morgan's turn for indignation. "Take them forward. If necessary, we can bring them back again. Jackson's orders — oppose the landing."

Reluctantly Davis marched his grumbling troops downriver. Half

way to Morin's they met Arnaud's detachment hurrying towards them
in confusion. They had been wakened by grapeshot from gunboats on
the river, directed at their camp, and without waiting to fire at the
unseen but obviously nearing enemy, had fled. Davis and Arnaud jointly
decided to make a stand along Mayhew's canal a mile and half below
Morgan's line. There was a sawmill offering some protection, and from
it they gathered planks with which to make a sketchy barricade.

Meanwhile Colonel Thornton's British troops were advancing in a
single column up the right bank of the river. Arnaud's outpost had
scarcely caused them to break step. "To dislodge them was the work of
a moment," George Gleig wrote. "A boat with a carronade in her bow
got upon their flank, gave them a single discharge of grape, whilst we
advanced at double quick time. But they scarcely waited till we were in
range, when they fled in confusion."

From the Raguet canal, Morgan had witnessed the flight of Arnaud's
militia, and his confidence was badly shaken. It had been a mistake to
expose them far below his line. Now he doubted that Davis's impro-
vised barricade at Mayhew's canal, already being shelled by gunboats
on the river, could be held. Better to get them back to the main defense
position. He sent word to Davis and Arnaud to withdraw.

Some said it was Arnaud's faulty English that caused the subsequent
confusion. The French-speaking troops may have misunderstood the
order to withdraw as *"sauve qui peut."* After firing only two rounds at
the advancing enemy, Arnaud's contingent took to the swamps, while
Davis's Kentuckians fled in disorder to the rear towards Morgan's
breastwork. "I assert positively," Morgan afterwards protested, "that
they withdrew to my lines in a great hurry and confusion, without returning a shot after they commenced their retreat."

With Arnaud's men it was a total rout. Through the swamp they bypassed Morgan's line and fled toward the city. Colonel Davis halted his
Kentuckians behind Raguet's canal. Here, with the Louisiana militia
and Declouet's regiment lodged behind the breastworks, Davis positioned his men three hundred yards to their right, with only the shallow
ditch as a shield—leaving an open gap between the two defending units.

Patterson's batteries on the river bank just above Morgan's position
were pouring a murderous fire on the British army advancing across
Chalmette's towards Jackson's breastwork, oblivious to Thornton's
troops now threatening their flank and rear. With Thornton, Lieutenant
Gleig surveyed the American line and overestimated the defenders as

totaling 1500 men, outnumbering the Light Brigade by three to one. He further noted:

> Like their countrymen on the other side, they were strongly entrenched, a thick parapet with a ditch covering their front; whilst a battery upon their left swept the whole position, and two field-pieces commanded the road. Of artillery we possessed not a single piece, nor any means, beyond what nature supplied, of scaling the rampart. Yet nothing daunted by the obstacles before us, or by the immense odds to which we were opposed, dispositions for an immediate attack were made.

Thornton disposed his troops in double columns stretching clear across the field. The 85th would attack near the swamp where Davis's Kentuckians were scantily deployed. The sailors would charge the American left near the river, hoping to outflank the defenders and reach Patterson's destructive batteries behind them. The bugle sounded and both columns advanced with loud "Huzzahs!"—their offensive covered by a shower of rockets from the gunboats on the river.

Then Morgan's batteries spoke. A discharge of grape and canister splattered the sailors' uniforms with blood. Momentarily they reeled back. To their right, Patterson saw this sudden peril to Morgan's line. His guns were positioned to shell the enemy across the river, but now he ordered his marines to tussle them around and direct their aim at Thornton's troops. Then he realized the danger of hitting Morgan's men and told the gunners to withhold their fire.

Along the breastworks behind the canal General Morgan galloped nervously back and forth among his kneeling troops, who "glanced darkly at this nervous old man."

"Wait till they're close," the General shouted, "then fire, and load and fire again!"

Thornton's columns were rapidly closing in on the breastworks. They knelt for a moment, leveling their rifles, and Morgan gave the order: "Fire!" It was a ragged volley, coming from troops unevenly dispersed, and the British infantry charged towards the gap between the units.

One lone fatal voice broke through a second's interval of silence. "Every man for himself!" a Kentuckian shouted and darted for the swamp. It was all that was needed to cause panic in the ranks. To a man, the Kentuckians broke and started fleeing to the rear.

Desperately Morgan rode among the stampeding men who fleetly dodged his horse's hoofs.

"Kentuckians!" he shouted. "Remember your valor—your patriotism! Kentuckians! Your country has confidence in you! Is this how
you requite it? Shame on you! Shame on you! You're not Kentuckians!
You dastards! Shame on you! Kentuckians—shame!"

To Davis, whose men had joined the flight, he shouted hoarsely:
"Stop those men!"

"Nothing can stop them," Davis said and jogged on behind his
troops.

Only one officer rallied to Morgan's importunities. He was Adjutant
Jansen Stephens, who, though badly wounded in the head, pulled himself bloodily from the ground to run after the retreating troops.

"Shame on you, boys!" he cried, echoing Morgan's words. "Shame
on you! Come, let's follow the General!"

His courage had a brief effect. The men stopped in their tracks for an
instant; and Morgan, seeing them hesitate, seized the moment to raise
his sword and impel them forward.

"Follow me!" he shouted, swinging his horse towards the enemy.
"Follow! Follow!"

He had gone no more than fifty yards when he found himself alone.
Behind the canal the men were streaming over the fields of Jourdan to
the rear. He was moved to despair and almost to compulsive suicide.

Deserted by men in whom I had placed the most unbounded confidence,
the bullets of the enemy flying thick around me; unable to endure the dis-
tracting thought, my first impulse was to rush headlong into the enemy's fire,
sword in hand, cut down all before, until overpowered by numbers, I should
be compelled to surrender.

Overcoming this impulse, he turned and galloped after his retreating
troops. It was just such a rout that Jackson had feared and later found
"strange and difficult to account for." At the very moment when a show
of resistance might have thrown the enemy off balance, the General
believed, "the Kentucky reinforcements, in whom so much reliance
had been placed, ingloriously fled, drawing after them, by their example, the remainder of the forces; and thus yielding to the enemy that
most formidable position."

Commodore Patterson also witnessed with horror the wild retreat of the Kentuckians. They would leave his batteries undefended, to be taken by the British. In a moment of fury he ordered one of his marines beside a cannon: "Fire your piece into the damned cowards!" The marine leveled his gun at the Americans, when Patterson controlled his anger and revoked the command. His battery was lost, but he would see that it did the British little good. As he reported to Secretary Jones of the Navy:

> Finding myself thus abandoned by the force I relied upon to protect my battery, I was most reluctantly and with inexpressible pain, after destroying my powder and spiking my cannon, compelled to abandon them, having only thirty officers and seamen with me. A part of the militia were rallied at a saw-mill canal, about two miles above the lines from which they had fled, and there encamped. I ordered the *Louisiana* to be warped up for the purpose of procuring a supply of ammunition, and mounting other cannon remained myself at the aid of General Morgan.

Thornton had lost three men killed and over thirty wounded in the assault on Morgan's line. He himself had been wounded, and although he protested that it was nothing, his men persuaded him to put Major Gubbins in command and accompany the other casualties back to Villeré's. Gubbins, who had served with Thornton in the attacks on Washington and Baltimore and found this engagement a jolly excursion somewhat similar to the American rout at Bladensburg, lost no time in pressing his pursuit of the distracted enemy.

Morgan had hoped to make another defense at Jourdan's canal, where Latour had formerly erected the beginnings of a breastwork. But the British were hard on his heels, and the Americans fled again. To show he meant business, Gubbins set fire to Jourdan's sawmill, providing a smoke screen for his troops as they pressed on after the Americans. Above Jourdan's, Morgan vainly tried to make another stand at Flood's canal. As before, a single volley from the British sent the Americans scampering back towards the next plantation. The incendiary-minded Gubbins set fire to Flood's house and mill.

There seemed no stopping of Thornton's forces, stimulated to enthusiasm by success. The misleading word had reached them that "things were going well" across the river, which further inspired them to press the attack. At the plantation next to Flood's they stumbled on the fallen standard of one Louisiana regiment—the colors which the

Legislature had bestowed on Alexandre Declouet — and carried it ahead of them to taunt the foe. Years later these colors were hung (and hang today) in London's Whitehall with the inscription, "Taken at the Battle of New Orleans."

Morgan's position, in fact the whole situation on the west bank, was becoming desperate. Between the British and New Orleans there was little more than a six-pound battery across the river from the city. All available men were either fighting on Jackson's line or tied down at defense posts many miles away. The General decided on a final, do-or-die stand at the Bois Gervais canal where Latour had started, a week before, to prepare a secondary breastwork. But could he force his troops to halt at that position?

Riding in advance of his retreating regiments Morgan came upon a body of twenty Dragoons on reconnaissance. He attached them to his dwindling forces and led them by a wooden bridge across the Bois Gervais canal. Then, as he related, "I ordered the Dragoons to form, draw their swords, and cut down every man who refused to form a line on the canal." Caught between cavalry sabers and British bayonets, the Louisianians, with thirty-two Kentuckians who still remained, fell in as ordered. Of Arnaud's men and the rest of the Kentuckians there was no sight. They had shown no sign of stopping till they reached the city.

In the massive town house of Étienne de Boré at the corner of Chartres and Conde streets in New Orleans, young Charles Gayarré, de Boré's grandson, stood on the second-floor balcony to watch the battle raging on the plains of Chalmette. He was witnessing history in the making, history he would some day put between the covers of enduring books. Earlier that morning he had seen Abner Duncan galloping through the streets and shouting above the din of the artillery, "Up! Up! The foe is upon us. To the field! To the field!" It was a puzzling performance, since every able-bodied man in New Orleans was on the field.

His grandfather Étienne de Boré, furious at being deprived of military duty at the age of only seventy-four, had ascended to the balustrade roof to view the battle from a higher level. Young Charles was alone with his mother and sisters, but this female company put no restraint on his reactions. "At every volley of artillery or musketry," he wrote,

"I flung myself on the floor, exclaiming 'Ten Englishmen killed!' 'Twenty Englishmen flat on the ground!' and so on."

He kept these gymnastics up until, as he relates, his grandfather came down from his post of observation to face the inquiring looks of the anxious women.

"Dismiss your fears," he told them. "The Americans are victorious."

"But Father, how do you know?" Mrs. Gayarré asked.

"You forget, my dear child," said the old *mousquetaire* with a smile, "that I have some military experience. My practised ear has not been deceived, I am sure. The American guns have silenced the English guns. The enemy is defeated."

The words were hardly spoken when down the long avenue of pecan trees leading to the river there appeared a band of about a hundred men apparently headed for the shelter of the house.

"The English!" Charles's mother and sisters cried. "Here come the English!"

But young Charles knew better. These were a band of fugitives, muddy, disheveled and without arms. Even from a distance he had determined that the English soldier was an ornate model of military elegance. The men below looked and talked suspiciously like Kentuckians. Étienne de Boré, speaking only French, couldn't understand a word they said.

"Who are they, and what do they want?" he inquired of his daughter, who acted as interpreter.

The Americans had been completely routed, Mrs. Gayarré told her father. These were fugitives from the battlefield. They begged for food. They had not eaten since the day before.

Blood rushed to the cheeks of the old soldier. His eyes flashed. He shouted to the men in French:

"You lie! The Americans are victorious. You have run away; you are cowards. Never shall it be said that I gave a hospitable welcome to dastardly fugitives from the battlefield. Hence, all of you, or I will call my Negroes to drive you away."

This time it was the baffled fugitives from the right bank rout, who failed to understand. But there was no mistaking the tone of voice, the indignation or the cause and meaning of the old man's fury.

One of the rabble sought to gain his sympathy. He took off his hat and pointed  with his index finger to the bullet hole — proof that he had faced danger, even narrowly missed death. The result was not what the Kentuckian expected. Now the old gentleman leaned forward on the railing, directing scathing eyes on the suppliant below.

"In thy hat!" he bellowed. "In thy hat!" Then striking his breast violently: "*There* is where the ball should have been received, and not through thy hat, when probably thy back was turned to the enemy. No! No food for cowards! There is food in the British camp — go and get it."

He was superb at that moment, young Gayarré recalled, turning his back on the postulants, pacing the balcony like an angry lion in a cage.

"Father," Mrs. Gayarré protested. "They look so miserable."

"No! No food for cowards. I have said it."

"Father, they're shivering with cold. They haven't eaten since yesterday."

"No! No food for fugitives from the field of honor."

"But Father," continued the compassionate lady, "they may not have fled at all. They may have been ordered to retreat."

Then, as Gayarré concludes the episode:

> Grandfather, wheeling around, with a smile on his lips, and with the usual expression of benevolence on his face, said: "Daughter, I am inflexible. No food shall *I* give those wretches. But I am going away, and in my absence *you* may deal as you please *avec ces héros de la retraite.*" True to his word, he disappeared and was not seen for the remainder of the day.

On the left bank Jackson had noted the silencing of Patterson's batteries. Now he followed the retreat of Morgan's forces by their sporadic rifle fire and the flashing guns of the pursuing British. "No words can express the mortification I felt at witnessing the scene," he wrote to Secretary Monroe. "This unfortunate rout had totally changed the aspect of affairs. The enemy now occupied a position from which they might . . . be able to defeat, in great measure, the effects of our success on this side of the river."

There was ready communication with Morgan's officers by ferry from New Orleans, and Jackson drafted a message for Jean Laffite to take to the General and his troops. Considering the pressure he was under and his shock at their behavior his words, for him, were moderate. Citing the valorous opposition that his own troops had presented to the enemy, "it must be a source of eternal regret, that a few moments' exertion of that courage you certainly possess, was alone wanting to have rendered your success more complete than that of your fellow citizens in this camp."

He continued: "The want of discipline, the want of order, a total disregard to obedience, and a spirit of insubordination, not less destructive than cowardice itself . . . must be eradicated or I must cease to command." He concluded:

> Soldiers! You want only the will, in order to emulate the glory of your fellow citizens on this bank of the river. You have the same motives for additional interest from past events, to wipe off the stain and show . . . that you will not be inferior in the day of trial to any of your countrymen.

But words alone were insufficient. It was imperative, he told his aide Robert Butler, that Morgan receive reinforcements. But no men could be spared from Jackson's line. Who knew but that the British might attack again? This was a job for the ever-eager General Humbert. Humbert was ordered to assume command of the Louisiana reserves on the secondary Line Dupré and take them to the right bank. Meanwhile Butler instructed Claiborne to round up every available man in town to take to Morgan's aid.

There were no able-bodied men left in town, insisted Claiborne. Butler then suggested taking some of Villeré's militia encamped behind the line. But Villeré refused to release any of his troops, He had been posted there, he said, "by the express orders of General Jackson," and had hundreds of prisoners to guard. "All right," said Claiborne, "but take note that I delivered the request."

The Governor rode to New Orleans, rounded up the necessary boats and took Humbert and his men across the river. Humbert rode ahead to Morgan's line and announced to the commander that he had instructions from Jackson to destroy the enemy below. Morgan would be relieved of his command.

"Do you have that in writing, General?" Morgan asked.

No, said Humbert in French that Morgan could barely understand, it was a spoken order.

"I will not relinquish the command without a written order," Morgan said.

As Claiborne rode up with the militia, the three men, all of equivocal authority, argued violently as to who should take command. Morgan remained intractable. He resented especially Humbert's interference. His men would not take orders from a foreigner, he asserted. "Monsieur Humbert was then displeased and went off," leaving his men to be deployed on Morgan's line to brace for the renewed attack that all believed was imminent. That it never came was due to unforeseen developments.

When Thornton returned with the wounded to Villeré's, reporting the British successes on the right bank, Lambert asked him if Gubbins could hold his position or, better, clear the path of enemy troops for a march upon the city. Thornton believed he could. Lambert sent Colonel Dickson to confirm this opinion. Dickson returned with the advice that at least two thousand troops with the support of naval vessels would be required to consolidate and extend the victory already gained.

Reluctantly, Lambert decided not to make the effort. There had been no decisive word from Cochrane's naval expedition against Fort St. Philip — only that the vessels were in position and preparing to besiege the fort. Were he assured of its success and of the subsequent support of Cochrane's ships, he might have taken the risk of a renewed offensive. Now, with the plains of Chalmette strewn with the unburied dead, with hundreds of newly-wounded crowding the halls of de la Ronde's and Villeré's, he felt he had no choice but to call off the expedition.

Only Admiral Codrington, in charge of supplying the troops and looking forward to plundering the city, raised strong opposition. The capture of New Orleans was imperative if the army was not to starve.

In other words, Harry Smith sarcastically observed, "Kill more men, and the navy won't have to worry about bringing up the supplies."

Lambert sent word to Gubbins to withdraw his troops to the east bank, leaving a picket to cover the retreat. The order was "melancholy news" to Lieutenant Gleig, who nevertheless admitted that had the Americans stood firm in their entrenchments, "it is hardly conceivable that so small a force [as ours] could have wrested an entrenched position from numbers so superior; at least it could not have been done without much bloodshed."

Even retreat was risky at this point since, if such a movement became apparent, the outnumbering Americans might easily upset the operation. Gubbins ordered a picket to cover their rear. As George Gleig noted:

It so happened that the picket in question was this day under my com-

mand. As soon, therefore, as I received information that the main body had
commenced its retreat, I formed my men and made a show of advancing.
The Americans, perceiving this, fled; when, wheeling about, we set fire to
the château and, under cover of the smoke, destroyed the bridge and retreated. Making all haste towards the rear, we overtook our comrades just
as they had begun to embark. Whereupon the little corps being once more
united, entered their boats and reached the opposite bank without molesta-
tion.

Simultaneously with his order to Gubbins to withdraw, Lambert sent
a flag of truce to Jackson asking for a cease-fire to allow the burial of
the dead and the collection of the wounded. The flag was fired on,
according to Fortescue, by both artillery and musketry, but the message
was received by Jackson. It was signed simply, "Lambert."

The proposal rescued Jackson from a critical dilemma. He needed
time. Morgan's defeat on the right bank had given the British an imposing tactical advantage. Should the enemy exploit it, the whole victory
on the left bank would be meaningless and New Orleans would be
once again endangered. But who was the man who signed his name
simply "Lambert"?

He sent Butler across the field with a truce detachment and a message stating that General Jackson would deal only with one of equal
rank on the British side, and inquiring who Lambert was. The reply
came back:

"John Lambert, commander-in-chief of the British forces on particular service in America."

This was the first indication Jackson had received that General
Pakenham was no longer in command and could be presumed either
dead or seriously wounded. To protect the American position on the
right bank, the General sent Butler back with a qualified acceptance of
the armistice: the truce would apply to the left bank only. It would
be observed for twenty-four hours, until noon the following day, during
which time neither side would send troops across the river.

Lambert, worried about Gubbins's men on the right bank who had
not yet returned to Villeré's, and concerned, too, that he might have to
send troops to his rescue, stalled for time. He sent Harry Smith to
Jackson requesting until ten o'clock the following morning to think the
proposition over.

Meanwhile, though artillery fire from both sides was continuing, attempts were made to retrieve the dead and wounded. For a quarter of a mile in front of the American line the field was serried by three compacted lines of bodies marking the three successive waves of the attack. The carnage had indeed been frightful — the worst ever suffered by a British army in proportion to the troops engaged. According to estimates given Jackson by his Inspector General Hayne, British losses had totaled 2600, a good third of the troops involved — seven hundred killed, 1400 wounded and five hundred taken prisoner. In contrast the Americans· had thirteen killed and thirty-nine wounded. Most of the American casualties had been among Coffee's Tennesseans, and among the colored regiments who, wrote Vincent Nolte, "were so anxious for glory that they could not be prevented from advancing over our breastworks and exposing themselves."

More serious losses and probably more accurate figures were recorded by the Medical Director of the British Army:

| | |
|---|---:|
| Killed on the field ............................................................ | 381 |
| Died of wounds ............................................................ | 477 |
| | 858 |
| Wounded and permanently disabled .................................. | 1,251 |
| Wounded and temporarily disabled .................................. | 1,217 |
| | 2,468 |
| Total | 3,326 |

To the British the casualties became more eloquent when related to the individual companies involved. The gallant Highlanders who had charged the enemy guns with over one thousand men, withdrew with only 132 still on their feet — a far more heartbreaking loss than that to be suffered forty years later by the Light Brigade which charged the Russian guns at Balaklava. Gibbs's Light Infantry lost all but 212 of its original 862. The 7th Fusiliers, 780 in number, got out with 266 still fit for duty. The King's Own lost 397 out of 796. Mullins's 44th went into action 816 strong and returned with 134, with only five out of thirty-one officers remaining.

Many of the English wounded were still dying on the field, hastened to their deaths by the continuing artillery fire. Sergeant Jack Cooper, clinging to the ground for safety, saw the man next to him split asunder by a cannon ball. Pieces of the man's brain splattered the sergeant's uniform. Not far away an infantryman was trying to hold back his intestines. Behind Cooper a West Indian sat upright on the ground, his face shot away, his eyes gone, his features defined only by the blood cascading from his shattered forehead.

Captain John Cooke, who would leave his memoirs of this nightmare, also crouched among the fallen. He observed:

> Some of the wounded managed to crawl away; but every now and then some unfortunate man was lifted off the ground by round shot, and lay killed or mangled. . . . A wounded soldier, who was lying amongst the slain two hundred yards behind us continued without any cessation, for two hours, to raise his arm up and down with a convulsive motion, which excited the most painful sensations amongst us; and as the enemy's balls every now and then killed some soldiers, we could not help casting our eyes toward that moving arm, which really was a *dreadful magnet of attraction.*

As volunteer units darted onto the field to rescue or give succor to the wounded, both sides fired on the good Samaritans. "With horror I record the atrocity," wrote Latour, noting that British troops hovering in the ditches fired on the unarmed units, while Quartermaster Surtees observed the same deplorable conduct among the riflemen in Jackson's line. American opportunists plundered the dead and wounded for their personal possessions, arms and souvenirs. Wrote Surtees:

> An American soldier came within about 150 yards of our line, and began to plunder such of the killed or wounded men as he thought possessed anything valuable. He at length commenced upon a poor wounded man belonging to my battalion, which being perceived by Corporal Scott of ours, he asked permission from his captain to take a shot at him. This being granted . . . he took up his rifle and, taking a steady aim, he fired, and tumbled the plundering villain right over the body of the poor wounded man.

To capture a wounded British officer was a signal feat. Lieutenant William Wickliffe, a Kentuckian, recruited several of his buckskinned comrades to seize and bring behind the lines Lieutenant-Colonel Francis Brooke, who was severely wounded. Brooke, the son of a lord and nephew of a duke, surveyed his ill-groomed captors with disdain.

"Are there no regular officers in your army?" he demanded. "I would like to be attended by gentlemen."

"Let's leave the conceited bastard to wallow in his own blood," suggested one of Wickliffe's comrades.

"No," said Wickliffe, "don't mind his impudent tongue. His wound makes a gentleman of him. Nothing else could!"

As dusk fell over New Orleans and the battlefield slaughter became known, there was little celebration of the victory, only muted feelings of gratitude and relief. Forty wagonloads of British wounded wound into the city, along with five hundred prisoners under guard. The small boys of the town, among them young Charles Gayarré, watched with sympathy and pity the sad cortege, expressing begrudging admiration for "the great, tall, handsome prisoners in their fine uniforms." Since the city's hospitals were crowded with American sick and wounded, many were taken to the barracks, others to private homes thrown open to them.

The warmhearted Creoles offered their aid to the stricken enemy, contributing mattresses, pillows, linen and lint for dressing their wounds at a time when, Latour observed, such articles "were extremely scarce in New Orleans." The Quadroon nurses, famous for their attendance to the sick, offered their services in caring for the injured, "without any compensation but the pleasure of relieving suffering humanity." By the light of candles flickering on the altar, the Ursuline nuns knelt with prayers of thanks before Our Lady of Prompt Succour. One again she had not failed them.

On the plains from de la Ronde's to Villeré's the decimated British army hovered around tiny fires, fearful that larger blazes might attract the enemy artillery. They were somewhat heartened by the news that General Lambert had placed Colonel Mullins under arrest. At Macarty's General Jackson drafted a second message to David Morgan on the right bank. "Every exertion must be made to dislodge the enemy or our position will be delicate here. The force I have sent you is competent to this end." As yet no word of the British withdrawal across the river had reached the General.

He sent by courier to Nashville a message to his wife Rachel, urging her to join him at New Orleans. He had missed her greatly during the trials of battle. Somehow he needed her even more in this moment of triumph — more, in fact, than he could know.

# 18.  Requiem and Retreat

Dawn of January 9 brought little peace to the British on the left bank of the Mississippi. With the retreat of Thornton's forces from the right bank, Patterson had repossessed and reactivated his battery opposite the English camp. He now began a continuous shelling of the enemy, supported by the artillery on Jackson's line.

Beneath this torrent of terror, the British began to take stock of their frightful losses. In addition to the over three thousand casualties among the troops, Generals Pakenham and Gibbs were dead, and General Keane was seriously wounded. The British camp was a charnel house. Captain Benson Earle Hill, making a tour of inspection, reported:

> The scene now presented at de la Ronde's was one I shall never forget; almost every room was crowded with the wounded and dying . . . I was the unwilling spectator of numerous amputations; and on all sides nothing was heard but the piteous cries of my poor countrymen, undergoing various operations . . . and I cannot describe the strange and ghastly feelings created by seeing a basket nearly full of legs . . .

On one occasion, as Quartermaster Surtees witnessed, a shell which landed in the bivouac carried off both legs of an Irish lieutenant named

281

Darcy who was sleeping in a hut. "Poor fellow! He was thus awakened
in a rough manner indeed." As Surtees later attempted to console the
victim, the lieutenant assured him that no sympathy was called for. Had
he lost only one leg, there would be little financial recompense. But having lost two, he would be entitled to a double pension. "I shall live now
like a prince," he told his visitor.

At ten o'clock that morning, Lambert sent his promised reply to Jackson's edict for a truce. He requested a six-hour suspension of hostilities.
Having gained the time he needed to repossess the right bank, Jackson
agreed. A truce line, marked by a row of hedge grass, was established
three hundred yards in front of the American breastworks, which no
British soldier was to cross. American troops were detailed to assist
the English in gathering up the dead and wounded, employing as
stretchers the ladders that lay scattered on the field.

Though this grim cooperative task was generally carried on in silence,
occasional comments passed between the rival armies. An American
who, sympathetically, exclaimed at the piles of English dead was
sneered at by a British private. "That's nowt, man; if you'd been wi' us
in Spain, you would ha' seen sommat for war!" Another American
officer, also expressing words of sympathy, was assured by his British
counterpart that the battle had been "a mere skirmish." "One more
such skirmish," the American replied, "and devilish few of you will
ever get back home to tell the story."

George Gleig mounted his horse and rode to the truce zone, later to
report: "Of all the sights I ever witnessed, that which met me there was
beyond comparison the most shocking, and the most humiliating. Within the narrow compass of a few hundred yards were gathered together
nearly a thousand bodies, all of them arrayed in British uniforms. Not a
single American was among them; all were English; and they were
thrown by dozens into shallow holes, scarcely deep enough to furnish
them with a slight covering of earth. Nor was this all. An American
officer stood by smoking a cigar and apparently counting the slain with
a look of savage exultation; and repeating over and over to each individual that approached him, that their loss amounted only to eight men
killed and fourteen wounded . . ."

> I confess that when I beheld the scene, I hung down my head, half in sorrow
> and half in anger. With my officious informant I had every inclination to pick
> a quarrel; but he was on duty, and an armistice existed, both of which for-

bade the measure. I could not, however, stand by and repress my choler, and since to give it vent would have subjected me to more serious inconvenience than a mere duel, I turned my horse's head, and galloped back to camp.

Vincent Nolte witnessed the return of the corpse of Major Whitaker, who had been brought down by Morgan's bullet. He recorded that many of the stalwart English infantry openly wept at the sight of their fallen leader. "Poor Whitaker, he was a worthy fellow," was their collective dirge. Similar grief accompanied the return of Colonel Rennie's body to the British. Among the lost heroes of that battle, his single-handed charge upon the battlements had won him a place in their Valhalla.

Most of the dead were buried on the field in ditches so shallow that subsequent rains would exhume them, sprouting a crop of protruding arms and legs and heads. The bodies of officers were carried to Villeré's or de la Ronde's to be buried in the gardens. Those of Pakenham, Gibbs and Rennie were disembowled and preserved in casks of rum to be delivered to the anchorage and taken back to England for burial. The viscera of General Pakenham, according to legend, were buried beneath a pecan tree which forever after refused to bloom.

Along with the collection of the dead and wounded went the scramble for souvenirs, an inevitable war phenomenon. Pakenham's field glasses were brought behind the lines, along with trumpets, bayonets, and a sword allegedly belonging to General Keane. A "very pretty fowling piece," said to be General Lambert's, was recovered by Jacques Villeré and presented to his children, who learned to shoot with it and referred to it familiarly and tenderly as "*le petit* Lambert." But important to General Jackson was the immense collection of firearms retrieved from the field, including 1500 British muskets. These the commander distributed among the unarmed Kentuckians; his forces were better armed after the battle than before.

As the hours of truce drew near to a close, the commanding officers of both sides faced decisions as to what came next. Jackson's nature was one that demanded complete destruction of an enemy. But according to Vincent Nolte, Livingston counseled him against continuing the fight. "What do you want more?" asked Livingston. "Your object is gained—the city is saved—the British have retired." There would be considerable risk in attacking an army stung to desperation by defeat, with little to lose by fighting to the death.

Lambert's decision, no longer contested by admirals Cochrane and Codrington, who for the time being were becoming realists, was to call off the expedition and evacuate his troops as speedily as possible. His army had suffered heavy numerical losses and a near destruction of morale. True, reinforcements had been promised, and his own 40th Regiment of Sommersetshires was now coming from the anchorage. But they were too late to outweigh other considerations. To avoid further tying-up of transportation facilities, he ordered that they be withdrawn as fast as they arrived.

In contrast to his precarious position, the Americans, he knew, were well entrenched behind their seemingly invulnerable breastworks. Their numbers were believed to be increasing as fresh troops arrived. And, as the British infantry admitted, the "dirty shirts" had proved to be exceptional marksmen. Some three-fourths of the English killed and wounded had been brought down by the small-bore rifles of the Tennesseans and Kentuckians, an enemy they had barely seen as they advanced toward the ramparts.

The withdrawal of the army would, as Lambert was well aware, be a precarious operation — covering the same difficult terrain, with the same shortage of boats, which had impeded the delivery of troops below New Orleans in the first place. There were only enough barges to carry a part of the army at a time. This separation meant that while half the army might be intercepted en route, the other half would be well outnumbered by Jackson's forces if the Americans decided to attack the camp.

The surviving army, Lambert decided, would have to be evacuated, and in secret, in a single move. This ruled out transportation by boat along the various bayous to Lake Borgne — too slow, too obvious, too open to the enemy. He directed his engineers to start construction of a passable overland route across the fields and through the cypress marshes to the landing place at the mouth of the Bayou Bienvenu. The time was limited; supplies were becoming increasingly low; it seemed like an impossible task — but no other choice was left.

While the engineers went to work with creditable vigor, the troops languished in a Gehenna of idleness. "Now gloom and discontent everywhere prevailed," wrote Gleig. "Disappointment, grief, indignation, and rage, succeeded each other in all bosoms; nay, so completely were the troops overwhelmed by a sense of disgrace that, for a while, they retained their sorrow without so much as hinting at its cause."

Understandably they blamed their leaders: Pakenham for ordering the attack before Thornton's position was assured across the river, Keane for hesitating to advance before the Americans were prepared, Mullins for failing to see that the ladders and fascines were brought up properly in time to storm the ramparts. "To the Americans they would allow no credit," Gleig reported, "laying the entire blame of the failure upon certain individuals among themselves; and so great was the indignation expressed against one corps, that the soldiers of other regiments would hardly exchange words with those who chanced to wear that uniform."

Indeed, the Forty-fourth was ostracized, but to some extent that ostracism was directed at the other regiments who retreated from the field. The Highlanders, who had performed valiantly and futilely and taken heavy losses, walked around the bivouac with heads averted so as not to see the huts now emptied by their dead and dying fellows.

Throughout that week, as Gleig and Surtees both reported, life in the British bivouac was living hell. There was not enough food, and some officers were reduced to eating horsemeat from their slaughtered mounts. There were no comfortable shelters for the troops. The men slept in clothes they had not changed or taken off for weeks. "Besides all this," wrote Gleig, "heavy rains now set in, accompanied with violent storms of thunder and lightning which, lasting during the entire day, usually ceased towards dark, and gave place to keen frosts. Thus we were alternately wet and frozen; wet all day, and frozen at night."

On top of this raw discomfort was the constant bombardment from both sides of the river. Before the grand assault of January 8 the British had occupied some five square miles of the cane belt and the better part of six plantations, from Jumonville's to portions of Chalmette's. Now abandoning de la Ronde's and Lacoste's to consolidate their position, they were confined to Villeré's and Jumonville's. Though this constricted area was easier to defend, it made a more compact target for the enemy. Shells fell upon Villeré's, passed through the roof and intervening floors, and buried themselves in the foundations. Though Lambert had hoped to sustain morale and discipline by regular drill and review of his troops, he did not dare expose them to this fire.

"Every night also," wrote Quartermaster Surtees, "the piquets were kept in a state of agitation and alarm by the continual attacks of small parties of our skulking enemy, and my battalion, as did others also, lost considerable numbers by this petty warfare. In short, the men's lives began almost to be a burden to them." According to Gleig this pressure of night attacks compelled the British to "maintain their ground by dint of hard fighting. In one word, none but those who happened to belong to this army can form a notion of the hardships which it endured, and the fatigue which it underwent."

The Americans, according to Surtees, adopted a form of propaganda warfare directed at "the mental powers of our soldiers. Every day almost they assembled in large bodies on the parapet of their line, with flags of various descriptions, some with 'sailors' rights' and numerous other devices, etc., painted on them, using the most insulting gesticulations towards those who were near enough to see them, a band playing Yankee Doodle, and other national airs, all the while, and sometimes ironically favoring us with Rule Britannia."

Taking up the complaint, George Gleig amended: "Nor were these the only evils which tended to lessen our numbers. To our soldiers every inducement was held out by the enemy to desert. Printed papers, offering lands and money as the price of desertion, were thrown into the picquets, while individuals made a practice of approaching our posts, and endeavoring to persuade the very sentinels to quit their stations. Nor could it be expected that bribes so tempting would always be refused. Many desertions began daily to take place, and became before long so frequent, that the evil rose to be of a serious nature."

One incident in this campaign to induce desertions was recorded by Lieutenant Gleig with satisfaction. A private of Gleig's 85th rifles was approached, while standing sentinel, by an American officer who offered him one hundred dollars to come over to the other side, giving him at the same time a lecture on the advantages of democracy. The Britisher, feigning deafness, asked the officer to step a little closer — whereupon he shot him in the shoulder and dragged him triumphantly back to de la Ronde's plantation as a prisoner.

While the British guns in whatever batteries remained below the fields of de la Ronde lay silent, the distant sound of cannon on the Mississippi, forty-five miles below, reminded New Orleanians that the siege of their city had not ended. In a last gesture of fury and frustration, units of Admiral Cochrane's navy were assaulting Fort St. Philip.

Perhaps the fort's defense seemed something of an anticlimax after the heady triumph of Chalmette. Actually, it was critical. Were St. Philip to be subdued and passed, possession of the Mississippi would not only aid Lambert in the successful evacuation of his army, but might pave the way for a second assault upon the city.

In command of the fort was Major Walter H. Overton, in whom Jackson placed much confidence, with Captain Charles Wollstonecraft, a native of England and now with the U.S. Army, in charge of the artillery. In addition to the artillery units, numbering 120, were portions of the U.S. 7th Infantry, a battalion of Louisiana volunteers, and a company of free colored — making a total garrison of 366. Major Lacarrière Latour was present to aid in strengthening the fortifications.

Overton had had ample time to prepare for the attack. All combustible material had been removed from the interior of the fort. Magazines had been strategically distributed and protected. Batteries further up the river bank, never satisfactorily fortified, were withdrawn as too vulnerable to seizure by the enemy. Gunboat No. 65, with forty marines under Captain Cunningham had arrived on January 8 and been warped to the bank of the Rio Mardigras behind the fort to guard its rear. As a gesture of defiance the British Union Jack was run up the flagpole beneath the Stars and Stripes to taunt the enemy.

On the afternoon of January 9 Cochrane's flotilla appeared below the fort. Three sloops, the *Herald, Nymph,* and *Thistle,* with the schooner *Pigmy,* took up positions well downriver, out of range of Overton's guns, while the two bomb-ships, *Aetna* and *Meteor,* anchored close to the right bank protected by a slight bend in the river.

At three o'clock the enemy opened fire, and throughout the afternoon and night shells fell every two minutes on and over the fort. "No injury was done to the men or works," Latour reported, "as the shells, from the nature of the soil, sunk in the ground without bursting, or burst under the ground at so great a depth as to produce no other effect than a tremulous motion."

That night, Latour believed, the enemy had intended to sneak past the fort. At least they resorted to a ruse in that direction, sending several small boats as decoys to draw the fire of the batteries. The boats themselves were regarded as expendable. They drew so close the taunting voices of the sailors could be heard. Had Overton's guns fired on them the heavy smoke they would have thus created would have screened the passage of the flotilla as it pressed on to the city. Since Overton suspected a trick, the American guns remained silent and the boats withdrew.

For a week, from January 10 to 18, the British fleet maintained an almost continuous bombardment of the fort, making a shambles of its interior, but killing only two of the garrison. A chance shot dislodged the American flag from its pole, and a sailor volunteered to replace it. Shinnying up the flagstaff, he spent almost an hour on the crosstrees securing the flag to the staff, while enemy fire was concentrated on bringing him down. He descended safely, brushed off his hands and went back to his battery.

Throughout the siege, due to almost constant rains, the interior of the fort became a millpond, and there was little sleep for the besieged. The British now fused their shells so that they would explode above the fort and not on landing. "The troops," reported Latour, "were on the battery nine days, five days without cover; and exposed to the rain and weather which was extremely cold." In general, Overton's guns could do little but hold the enemy at bay; they could not reach the distant target. The mortars of the fort, which might have driven off the enemy, could not be fired for want of fuses.

Until dawn of January 18 the bombardment continued without intermission. During that time, Latour estimated, "the enemy threw more than one thousand shells and cases, expending upwards of seventy tons of ammunition, and more than twenty thousand pounds of powder, besides small shells and round and grapeshot from their boats."

On January 15 there were signs of some relief as supplies began arriving from New Orleans. The ships unloaded upriver from the fort, and their cargoes were brought to the besieged by land under cover of darkness. With fuses now for the mortars, the American fire began to take effect. One of the bomb ships was silenced and the other driven out of range. On the morning of the 18th, the enemy ships fired a last salute and started slipping down the river. As on the plains of Chalmette a small outnumbered garrison, entrenched behind the elastic Mississippi mud, had held fast.

"After the enemy left us," wrote Latour, "we had the time to examine the interior, and the ground in the neighborhood of the fort. Upwards of one hundred shells had fallen and buried themselves within the fort. The surrounding buildings, workshops, stores, and the hospital, were almost in ruins; and the ground for half a mile around was literally torn up in every direction."

For nine days the defenders had got little sleep, little rest from the terrible pounding they had taken. Yet Major Overton expressed the nature of their discontent in his report to Andrew Jackson: "The only thing to be regretted is that the enemy was too timid to give us an opportunity of destroying him."

Meanwhile, steps to evacuate the British troops were moving forward. By January 17, after nine days of grueling labor, the engineers had completed a seven-mile road of sorts from Villeré's, across the field and through the swamps, to the fishermen's village on Lake Borgne. It was at best a makeshift highway, with a roadbed of reeds where the ground became soggy, and log bridges over the intervening creeks. The reeds, as fast as they were trampled on, sank into the morasses; the bridges veered and sank into the mudbanks.

Secrecy was of the utmost importance. For that reason Lambert decided to leave all heavy artillery on the field, ten guns in all. To retrieve them would have been a betrayal of his intentions. Likewise, tents were left standing, fires were ordered to be maintained, and pickets stood their watches to the last. According to Nolte, "scarecrow" sentries built of poles and straw were dressed in British uniforms and posted around the British camps to fool the Americans until the last man left.

First to be evacuated were the wounded—all who could be moved at all. Next followed the baggage and stores, then all civilian personnel who had been imported for the occupation of New Orleans, and finally what light artillery could be transported without discovery.

On the evening of the 18th the mass evacuation was begun. With fires trimmed and pickets commanded to stay at their posts until the last man had left, regiment after regiment stole away under cover of darkness. Strict silence was maintained; the soldiers even tried to muffle their foot-treads.

The road from Villeré's to the edge of the swamp was on generally solid ground, but in the pitch-black darkness of the swamp itself, the going became hazardous—and the road all but disappeared beneath the footsteps of the army. As Gleig recorded: "Being constructed of materials so slight, and resting upon a foundation so infirm, the treading of the first corps unavoidably beat it to pieces; those who followed were therefore compelled to flounder on in the best way they could; and by the time the rear of the column gained the morass, all trace of a way had entirely disappeared."

The soldiers began to sink up to their knees, unable in the darkness to detect solid ground from treacherous morass, unable to call advice or warning to each other, or to offer any guidance to those following. Many who had so far survived the ill-fated campaign now disappeared in the quagmires of the swamp. Reported George Gleig:

> At one of these places I myself beheld an unfortunate wretch gradually sink till he totally disappeared. I saw him flounder in, heard his cry for help, and ran forward with the intention of saving him. But before I had taken a second step I myself sunk at once as high as the breast. How I contrived to keep myself from smothering is more than I can tell, for I felt no solid bottom under me, and continued slowly to go deeper and deeper, till the mud reached my arms. Instead of endeavouring to help the poor soldier, of whom nothing could be seen except the head and hands, I was forced to beg assistance for myself; when a leathern canteen strap being thrown to me, I had hold of it, and was dragged out, just as my fellow sufferer became invisible.

When they reached the fishermen's village, where they had disembarked with such high hopes six weeks before, there was no surcease from their misery. The officers occupied the now empty huts, while the troops sank to the ground to sleep in exhaustion on the marshy earth. There were only reeds to use as fuel for fires which flared and died briefly, never adequate for warmth. And there was little food; most of the men existed on dried biscuit crumbs and a tot of rum.

George Gleig considered himself lucky. He still had a little ammunition, and with this went foraging for game. He managed to bring down two ducks, which dropped in the water twenty yards off shore. Taunted by hunger, Gleig took off his clothes and waded through ice to swim in bitterly cold water to secure the ducks and bring them back to camp.

With a mixture of amusement and dismay, the troops at daylight found they had been followed, not by hostile pursuers, but by an army of slaves from Villeré's, de la Ronde's, Lacoste's and other plantations that the troops had occupied. Wrote Surtees: "These, male and female, often amused us with their native dances, the men generally have a number of rings or bells about them, which sounded as they kept time to the tune. Some of their dances were, however, far from decent, particularly on the part of the females, which . . . highly delighted some of our young and thoughtless countrymen."

With a shortage of food, the slaves were hardly welcome. Attempts at persuading them to return to their owners were generally unsuccessful. One slave assured Captain Hill that if he should be obliged to go back, his master would "lash his back raw and then rub it with pickles." Reluctantly, for now, the blacks were allowed to remain with the army and to board the fleet anchored off Cat Island.

In spite of British efforts at secrecy, the withdrawal of the enemy's forces was suspected by Patterson, Jackson and observers at Macarty's. On January 18, the day the siege of Fort St. Philip was lifted, Jackson wrote to Governor David Holmes of the Mississippi Territory: "Their army is at present conducted by Major General Lambert who, if I mistake not, finds himself in a very great complexity. To advance he cannot: to retreat is shameful. Reduced to this unhappy dilemma, I believe he is disposed to encounter disgrace rather than ruin, and will, as soon as his arrangements for this purpose are affected, return to his shipping."

One indication of British intentions to withdraw was the start of negotiations for an exchange of prisoners. This was conducted through a series of courteous notes — Major Smith acting for the English, Edward Livingston for the Americans. In equal rank and in equal number, the British would bring their American captives to The Rigolets, while the Americans would deliver their British prisoners to Balize, at the mouth of the Mississippi.

On the morning of the 19th Jackson trained his telescope on the British camp, where fires had blazed brightly through the night. Though there was little movement, he could see no change from previous days. The flags were still flying, the sentinels were at their posts. He sent Hind's Dragoons to investigate, and meanwhile asked the eagle-eyed General Humbert for his opinion. Humbert put his eye to the glass and exclaimed, "They're gone!" Asked how he could be sure, Humbert pointed to one of the sentries where a crow was perched on the figure's shoulder. The picket was plainly a dummy, Humbert expounded; no bird would settle so comfortably on a human being.

Major Hind, returning from his reconnaissance, confirmed the veteran's opinion. The British had left, and the last of their troops were moving slowly down the Bayou Bienvenu. Hind asked permission to pursue them and, if feasible, attack their rear. Jackson approved, with reservations. He assigned Reuben Kemper and Colonel de la Ronde to the Dragoons, to act as guides, and advocated caution. He could not afford a major engagement with the possible loss of additional men. The party returned an hour later, having heeded the General's advice. The retreating enemy was still strong in numbers, and the bayous Mazant and Bienvenu had been well fortified to cover their withdrawal. Beyond capturing a few stragglers, the Americans had not risked a provocative attack.

' That afternoon a British army surgeon, under a flag of truce, appeared before the American line with a letter for Jackson from General Lambert. In it, the English commander announced the withdrawal of his army and solicited care for some eighty wounded he had been obliged to leave behind at Villeré's.'Jackson dispatched his surgeon general, Dr. David C. Kerr, to attend to this mission and bring the wounded back to New Orleans. Then with his aides he rode across the plains of Chalmette-de la Ronde to inspect the deserted British camp. Scattered everywhere, like the ruins of an abandoned city, were the wrecked outbuildings and battered redoubts, shattered artillery, spent and unused ammunition, personal possessions of the once-proud army of invaders.

He was satisfied that the enemy had abandoned this phase of the expedition, but not at all sure that New Orleans was relieved of danger. From spies and deserters he knew that the British were withdrawing to West Florida — perhaps intending an overland attack from Pensacola or Mobile to Baton Rouge — and that the British fleet had received fresh reinforcements. Though badly damaged, the enemy was still a formidable army.

Jackson at once dispatched a message to General James Winchester in command of the district of Mobile, expressing the verdict, "Major General Lambert is said to have went crazy," and adding: "Should this crippled army attempt to visit you on their Passage home you will give a good account of them." He followed this up with a confirming letter: "I have no idea that the enemy will attempt Fort Bowyer, or your quarter. Still you cannot be too well prepared or too vigilant. Admiral Cochrane is sore and General Lambert crazy, so they may in this situation attempt some act of madness — if their Panic does not prevent it."

He was worried about Fort Bowyer, a key point in Mobile's defense and now inadequately garrisoned under Major William Lawrence. He had no men to spare, to send to Lawrence. But the veteran General Humbert suggested a unique expediency. There were several hundred British deserters now in the American encampment. Why not organize them into a sort of foreign legion, to be led against the army they had disavowed?

With Jackson's approval, Humbert took steps to round up the deserters. But he had no place to put them, apart from the barracks where the military prisoners were detained. There, when he issued his proclamation inviting the deserters to enlist in this American expedition, the entire contents of the barracks stepped forward in response. Plainly, prisoners still loyal to the British army saw this as a chance to rejoin their comrades, and there was no way of distinguishing the deserters from those conspiring for freedom. Jackson forthwith canceled the whole idea. The deserters would be returned with the regular prisoners to General Lambert.

In one of his typical acts of humanity, that so often contrasted with his military ruthlessness, the General undertook to intervene in behalf of the deserters, fearing retributions once they were returned to their commanding officers. He wrote a note to Lambert expressing the belief that the deserters were victims of "improper allurements" and hoping that no punishment would be inflicted on "those who may, under such circumstances, have swerved from their duty." To this Lambert replied with equal humanity: "You may rely upon it, I shall take no retrospective view of the conduct of the men returned, and shall find no reason for discountenancing this conduct should it be brought before me, or come to my knowledge through any other channel."

General Humbert's abortive "foreign legion" was the only serious proposal for attacking the retreating British. However, with the release and exchange of prisoners, personal vendettas were engaged in. Purser Thomas Shields and Dr. Robert Morrell, still smarting from their detention at the British anchorage following the gunboat battle on Lake Borgne, organized an expedition of six small boats and fifty-three armed volunteers, to intercept the retreating British on the lakes. On January 20 they surprised and captured a barge containing a similarly-numbered force of British troops and officers, and returned with their prisoners to The Rigolets. It was the final engagement in this last stage of the Battle of New Orleans.

For a long and bitter week, from January 19th to the 26th, Cochrane's sailors and marines tugged at the oars, carrying regiment after regiment across Lake Borgne to the anchorage below Cat Island. Here they were stranded by unfavorable winds. So many men had been lost that the ships were far less crowded than before, a condition that revived among the survivors the general sense of depression and indifference to their fate. No one seemed to care what happened next. Even the thought of returning home inglorious, was smothered in despondency.

But they were not going home. When the weather cleared, the transports moved the army to Dauphine Island at the western entrance to Mobile Bay. Two more regiments had arrived, the vanguard of 5,600 additional troops that had embarked from England. With this fresh muscle, Cochrane and Lambert conferred on a second attempt to take New Orleans, this time via the inland route from Mobile, which Sir Edward Pakenham had once declared far preferable to the route of the original invasion.

On Mobile Point, across the bay from Dauphine Island, Fort Bowyer presented the only obstacle to the successful launching of this new campaign. General Keane, recovering rapidly from his neck wound, was consulted. What would it take to subjugate Fort Bowyer? Give him a thousand men, said Keane, with gun support from warships in the harbor, and he would take the fort in less than half an hour — after which the army could be on its way.

The battle for New Orleans, it was optimistically agreed, had just begun.

# 19.  Triumph and Tribulation

For some days after the British evacuation Jackson and his army kept to their watchful posts behind the ramparts. Then, on January 20, the General returned briefly to his Royal Street quarters after four weeks on the field. He was all but mobbed by the enthusiastic crowds which swarmed the streets at word of his appearance, and had difficulty staying in the saddle. "The first display of popular feeling," wrote Alexander Walker, "was too wild to be controlled by any regular method or system."

Jackson, too, felt that this public demonstration should be programed. He sent a note to the Abbé Dubourg, head of the Catholic Diocese, noting that "emotions of the liveliest gratitude require some external manifestation of those feelings." He suggested that a Service of Solemn Thanksgiving should be held at the Cathedral "in token of the great assistance we have received from the Ruler of all events." The good Abbé forthwith declared January 23 as the date for this formal celebration.

On that memorable Monday the Place d'Armes and the Cathedral facing it were decked with greenery and flowers. Virtually the entire population pressed around the square or jammed the balconies and rooftops. An eyewitness present at the time described the carnival setting in the square:

295

The scene was splendid and delightful — it was perhaps the most unmixed
triumph that ever occurred on this globe; so few men had fallen in the contest that private regret did not impair public joy. Every eye beamed, every
heart beat high. Parents and children, husbands and wives, brothers and
sisters were again united, rendered dearer to each other by the peril and
the danger past.

Young Charles Gayarré was among the spectators, and he recorded
the event for history. Temporarily erected in the center of the square
was a triumphal arch supported by six Greek columns and festooned
with flowers. On either side awaited two of New Orleans' Creole
beauties costumed respectively as Liberty and Justice. On pedestals
beneath the arch stood two nymph-like children (Gayarré wasn't sure
if they were boys or girls) each holding a crown of laurel. Beside them
Miss Louisiana, loveliest by election of the city's ladies, waited to
greet the anticipated hero.

Between the arch and the Cathedral steps a double line of young
girls represented all the States and Territories of the Union. Dressed
in white, with a blue transparent veil, each wore a silver star upon her
forehead and carried a flag in one hand and basket of flowers in the
other. Beside each, too, stood a lance and shield symbolic of the region
represented. These in turn were linked with festoons circumscribing
an avenue between the arch and the Cathedral.

Along the rear of the square and in columns leading to the arch were
ranged the companies of Plauché's volunteers, resplendent in parade
dress; behind them was a sea of human faces packed as solidly as
pebbles on a beach. As, precisely on time, Jackson and his retinue
approached from the side of the river, artillery boomed and martial
music blared; the square and buildings became alive with fluttering
handkerchiefs and flags. Passing beneath the arch, Jackson was greeted
by Miss Louisiana and crowned with laurel by the two awaiting cher-
ubs; then he moved on between the rows of silver-starred beauties,
who strewed flowers in his path.

Vincent Nolte, with Plauché's Carabiniers, occupied a viewer's
point of vantage in the ranks and later noted that, as the General
reached the steps of the Cathedral, "Madame Livingston, with studied
enthusiasm, did herself the pleasure of setting a laurel crown upon
his head, which, however, the destroyer of Indians, unused to similar
marks of honor, somewhat unwillingly put away." Nolte's vision may

have been faulty, or more likely he could not resist this chance for a sarcastic jab at Livingston through his wife, for there is no record of Mrs. Livingston performing such a rite.

At the door of the Cathedral the General confronted Dubourg and his clergy, and the Abbé addressed him in fervent terms as the savior of Louisiana and as "God's right hand." Another crown of laurel was added to the weight of greenery on Jackson's head, after which the Hero of New Orleans made "a modest and felicitous reply." Organ music swelled from within the church, the choir began the majestic measures of *Te Deum,* and a thousand voices in the square took up the chant. The bells tolled and the cannon boomed again, and New Orleans' proudest day was consummated.

Behind the scenes another event went justifiably unnoticed. The long-awaited barges from Pittsburgh, bearing muskets and ammunition for the defense of New Orleans, arrived down the Mississippi, and John Pollard, the contractor, proud of having thus fulfilled his obligation, later joined the nightime celebration of that joyous and illuminated city.

It was a shock to New Orleans that, after this extravagant ovation and excessive demonstration of good will, the city should return forthwith to its preceding state of siege. Had they not just declared, with thanks and a *Te Deum,* that the war was over? Yet their dour-faced General, who immediately resumed his stiff role of military disciplinarian, was evidently going to run things as if peril still existed. Martial law was still imposed, troops drilled and slept beside their arms as if the enemy were still outside the gates.

Actually, Jackson was far from satisfied that the war in the Gulf had been decided. He was well-informed now. Spies who had served the British quickly switched allegiance to the winning side, and the Baratarian scouts missed little that transpired in the Gulf. Jackson knew and reported that the British fleet was "steering for Mobile"; that the enemy had been reinforced on January 20 by two new veteran regiments—bringing his total army up to fifteen thousand; that the British were surely still smarting for revenge and a chance to redeem their military honor. He would keep a tight rein on the city till he knew that it was safe. Meanwhile, he wished that he had men to spare to send to Colonel Lawrence at Fort Bowyer below Mobile.

But the still-encamped troops were weary of war and the very sight of arms. Among the once-united army subsurface jealousies and rivalries arose anew. The Tennesseans boasted of their major role in the enemy's defeat while the Louisianians, they alleged, had been little more than spectators. The Louisianians more than ever resented the continued presence of these interlopers on their soil. "Craven" Creoles flung epithets at "barbarian" backwoodsmen. Charges of cowardice and even treachery were hurled around without discretion. Livingston, Duplessis, Duncan, even Claiborne, were accused of being derelict of duty.

On top of it all, the troops were severely plagued by dysentery, that common scourge of armies in the field. More than five hundred were stricken and disabled in the marshy miasma permeating Chalmette's. The battlefield, eroded by late winter rains, was yielding a horrendous crop of swollen arms and legs and even decaying heads that were erupting from the shallow graves. As a single concession, Jackson removed the troops to bivouacs on higher ground, in the Faubourg de Marigny closer to the city. But their life was not much better than a concentration camp existence.

The exchange of prisoners continued smoothly, accompanied by correspondence between Jackson and General Lambert which was flavored with rare courtesy and mutual esteem. But the reclamation of fugitive slaves was another matter. Cochrane refused to send any back by force, and few offered to return voluntarily. The Admiral announced vaguely that they would be released in the West Indies when he stopped there for supplies, but he did not indicate when this would be. He had, in fact, more pressing plans.

De la Ronde's neighbor, Pierre Lacoste, was unwilling to wait or work through diplomatic channels. He boldly arrived at Dauphine Island to reclaim his property. Asking to speak to his slaves alone, he told his surprised hosts: "Since British officers cannot but be gentlemen, surely you will spare me the humiliation of coaxing my slaves to return to me, in your presence. You can understand how painful this would be to me."

Lacoste, observed Charles Gayarré, "was a man of commanding presence, having a striking military air, and really looked superb in full uniform." The British were evidently impressed by his appearance. They agreed that he should be allowed to use persuasion on his slaves.

"But there must be no force used, major. The slaves must express clearly their desire to return."

"Force!" exclaimed Pierre. "What force can I use in the circumstances, other than persuasion?"

With this understanding Lacoste was escorted by a guard of honor to the barracks where the slaves were lodged. Here he gestured for the guards to leave, then turned upon the apprehensive blacks.

"So, *cochons!*" he bellowed in French. "You thought you could escape me! I'll flog you, by God, as I flogged the British! You see how they treat me! With respect! They will shoot you in your tracks if I give the word. But follow me, two by two, to my schooner and I'll lead you safely through their lines. Close on my heels now, and no stragglers!"

With that he lined them up and led them out. As they passed the hesitant guards, Lacoste shouted: "Don't fire! They follow me willingly." Then turning to his slaves he said in French: "You see? They wanted to shoot you and I stopped them. Now, say the word. Do you want to come with me, or stay here at their mercy?"

"With you! With you!" the slaves shouted, crowding in fear around the major. There was no denying such obvious evidence of assent. The bewildered British let them go. "I taught those thick-witted Englishmen a thing or two," Pierre said later to his fellow planters.

In general, however, such transaction followed diplomatic channels. On February 4 Jackson sent a delegation to Admiral Cochrane with the fleet off Dauphine Island. The emissaries were Edward Livingston, Maunsel White and Patterson's naval aide, R. R. Shepherd. They were to arrange for the further and final exchange of prisoners and the return of the remaining slaves to their impatient owners.

The American trio was received aboard the *Tonnant* with traditional Old World courtesy bordering, at times, on warmth. Livingston had brought with him General Keane's sword, which the latter had lost on the field of Chalmette. Keane had written Jackson ("with surprising lack of pride," the American commander thought), requesting its return. No military ethic required the restoration of an enemy's weapons. But, as Jackson wrote Monroe, it seemed the "American" thing to do. Now Livingston handed it over, and the wounded General's eyes were moist with gratitude.

During this moving episode certain young naval officers could not resist twitting the army commander for having lost his sword in battle. Keane took the joshing good-naturedly.

"My young friends," he told them, "if you had been where I was on the eighth of January, you would have lost your heads as well as your swords."

Unexpectedly, and certainly unintentionally, Livingston and his two associates were unwanted witnesses to the last chapter of the British campaign in the Gulf. They had arrived on February 7, when Cochrane advised them frankly that their presence was "most inopportune." They would be welcome aboard the ship so long as they stayed out of sight, below.

The reason for Cochrane's embarrassment was later evident. While half the diminished British army remained aboard the transports, Lambert landed units of three regiments — 1200 strong, with 450 artillerists along with sappers, miners and marines — on Mobile Point behind Fort Bowyer. Once the fort was reduced, Lambert and Cochrane would move on to Mobile and there establish a bridgehead for a second assault on New Orleans, this time via the land route to the Mississippi, which Pakenham probably would have chosen to begin with.

The capture of Fort Bowyer, with its 360-man garrison, was bloodless and easy. It required little more than the landing of the troops with heavy naval guns, and the building of trenches and redoubts. During these preparations, Major William Lawrence, who had defended the fort so staunchly and successfully six months before, discharged his frail batteries at the invaders, doing little damage, while the British replied with musket fire only. When the siege was ready to begin in earnest, Lambert sent a flag to Lawrence demanding the fort's surrender.

Staring at the formidable enemy that was entrenched with field artillery below the fort's flimsy ramparts, and that was supported by several warships in the bay, Major Lawrence summoned his officers for consultation. All agreed there was no chance of defending their position. To attempt to do so would only lead to useless loss of life. They were virtually surrounded by the fleet and outnumbered a hundred to one. There was little hope for reinforcements or supplies. The fort was not bombproof; it was structured of combustible materials that would ignite with the first descending shell. Ranged against it were sixteen pieces of heavy siege artillery, about which Lacarrière Latour later observed: "Those pieces in less than half an hour would have battered down the parapet of the fort, which, on that side, was not more than three feet thick above the platforms."

Replying to Lambert's ultimatum, Lawrence agreed to capitulate if the terms were honorable.

The negotiations were conducted with the utmost propriety and courtesy. The written terms provided that the surrender would be handled with dignity and respect for the Americans, "the troops marching out with colors flying and drums beating . . . officers retaining their swords . . . all private property to be respected." The reason for these niceties, readily agreed to by the British and in fact promoted by them, became apparent later. No surrender in history has been so elaborately staged for the sake of its effect upon a truly captive audience.

It was an extravaganza timed, produced and directed with a fine flair for showmanship. While Cochrane and Lambert joined the cast on shore, Admiral Codrington, to lend dignity to the performance, arranged an elaborate dinner at sundown for the Americans in the cabin of the *Tonnant*. Codrington was at the head of the table, the Americans on his right. After the dessert and vintage wines, a bugle sounded and the curtains of the main saloon were drawn.

Framed in the proscenium like an animated backdrop was Fort Bowyer in the last glow of the setting sun. At that moment the Stars and Stripes slid down the flagstaff while the Union Jack was raised to take its place. Guns thundered. The American troops marched out in full dress uniform while the British stood at attention. The band played "Yankee Doodle" and "God Save the King" as a finale.

Codrington regarded his guests with smug satisfaction. This would be something for them to report to Jackson! This was how the British did things! He turned to Livingston on his right.

"Well, colonel, you perceive now that our day has just commenced."

Livingston, deeply troubled by this spectacle, was never at a loss for words. He raised his glass to the exultant victor.

"Congratulations, Admiral!" he said. "Please be assured that we Americans do not begrudge you this small consolation."

Small consolation it turned out to be. While the Americans were detained aboard the *Tonnant* and the British staff debated the next move that would consolidate its gain, a swift frigate approached the anchorage. A lowered gig was rowed toward the flagship. Shepherd was standing on deck beside Admiral Malcolm when an officer approached with a message from the gig. Malcolm read it, threw his hat in the air with an un-British shout, and turning to Shepherd wrung his hand with uninhibited warmth.

"Good news, my friend," he said. "The treaty has been signed at Ghent. We are enemies no longer." Then, *sotto voce,* the Admiral added: "To tell you the truth I have hated this war from the beginning."

Now released by their British hosts with tokens of warm friendship, the three Americans returned to New Orleans, arriving on February 13 and reporting at once to Andrew Jackson. On hearing of Fort Bowyer's capitulation, Jackson typically exploded. Surrender! Monstrous! He dashed off a letter to Monroe, protesting: "This is an event which I little expected to happen but after the most gallant resistance. That it should have taken place without even a fire from the enemy's batteries is as astonishing as it is mortifying." An inquiry would later be held under the supervision of Major General E. P. Gaines, resulting in Lawrence's acquittal of any stigma in the matter.

As to Livingston's report from Cochrane that the treaty of peace had been signed at Ghent, Jackson dismissed this cavalierly. He would not accredit it until he received word from Monroe that the treaty had been ratified in Washington. In a proclamation to the citizenry, he warned them not to be thrown "into a false sense of security by hopes that may prove delusive . . . To place you off your guard and attack you by surprise is the natural expedient of one who, having experienced the superiority of your arms, still hopes to overcome you by stratagem."

In other words, he would keep New Orleans in a tight state of preparedness. His efforts were somewhat undermined, however, when the *Louisiana Gazette* leaked the information that "a flag has just arrived from Admiral Cochrane to General Jackson officially announcing the conclusion of peace at Ghent." It was the signal for further grumbling and dissension in the ranks. The war was over; the men wanted to go home, and none more than the Louisianians whose families were so temptingly close. Bernard de Marigny became their spokesman and apologist. "They were eager to see anew their wives and mistresses," he noted. "They wanted to relate what they had seen and done . . . Such is the character of the men of southern Europe; they like war, particularly against the English, but after the battle is over they like their amusements."

The Abbé Dubourg also appealed to Jackson in the troops' behalf, writing that starving and unhappy wives "fall at your feet to redemand you their husbands." Officers among the volunteers requested that their men be released to tend their farms and businesses lest they suffer undue privations in the months ahead. Desertions became frequent, one AWOL soldier writing the commanding general, "Dear Sir, My wife was turned into the street by the landlord, and she asked me to come home."

There were other sources of discontent. "It is painful to note," wrote Charles Gayarré, "that . . . there were hearts which still remained deeply ulcerated by that military interference with the Legislature of Louisiana on the 28th of December, which many attributed to General Jackson." This became evident when, before adjourning in early February, the Legislature considered a proposal to award a silver sword to the commanding general in gratitude for his services to the State. Put to a vote, it was roundly defeated, with Bernard de Marigny leading the opposition.

At the same session of that august body, resolutions of thanks were extended to Coffee, Carroll, Thomas Adair, and others for their self-less services during the siege, with Jackson's name pointedly omitted. It is to Coffee's credit that he took exception to that glaring omission, noting in his reply to this citation, "We should be guilty of great in-justice . . . if we withheld from the Commander-in-Chief, to whose wisdom and exertions we are so much indebted for our success, the expression of our highest admiration and applause."

From Nashville into this troubled scene, on February 19, came Jackson's wife Rachel with their adopted son, bringing the General a momentary surcease from harassment. He had missed her greatly dur-ing the weeks of siege. Somehow he found her presence still more comforting in this unhappy aftermath. And surprisingly enough New Orleans took kindly to this frank and lovable but dumpy hausfrau. Re-garding her plump figure an old French saying was revived: "She shows how far the skin can be stretched."

Rachel stayed, naturally, with the Livingstons, and on February 22 a Washington's Birthday ball was given in her honor. Rachel, whose horizons had never extended much beyond Nashville, was duly im-pressed with "The Splendor, the brilliant assemblage [and] the mag-nificence of the supper . . . there was a gold ham on the table." Vincent Nolte was one of the arrangers of the event, and he recorded: "After supper we were treated to a most delicious *pas de deux* by the con-queror and his spouse . . . To see these two figures, the General a long, haggard man, with limbs like a skeleton, and Madame la Generale, a short, fat dumpling, bobbing opposite each other like half-drunken Indians, to the wild melody of *Possum up de Gum Tree,* and endeavoring to make a spring into the air, was very remarkable, and a far more edifying spectacle than any European ballet could possibly have furnished."

Two days later Claiborne sided openly with the restless and rebellious troops. He appealed to Jackson to release at least part of the state militia not immediately required for the safety of the city, these to return to their families and normal occupations.

Jackson, regarding this touchily as unwarranted interference, summarily rejected the appeal, whereupon the Governor circulated a rather extraordinary blast at the General. The broadside commended his qualities as a military leader, "but the violence of his temper casts a shade upon them all, and in this capital he has observed a course which cannot easily be excused, much less justified, by those who feel a proper regard for the rights of others."

Claiborne had been heard to utter prophecies of dire consequences for New Orleans if the General's dictatorial reign continued, and there were impromptu meetings of protest in the coffeehouses and cafés. Minor but significant acts of violence broke out. A portrait of Jackson hanging prominently in the Exchange Coffee House was torn down and destroyed. Aides loyal to Jackson demanded that it be immediately replaced with a similar portrait over which they kept a careful watch, threatening to arrest any would-be depredators. "New Orleans," wrote Charles Gayarré, "had become like a magazine of gunpowder; the least spark might have produced an explosion."

Meanwhile there was no containing the French Creoles still under conscription in the city. They applied to the French Consul Tousard in New Orleans for certificates of nationality proving that, as citizens of France, they were no longer subject to Jackson's law and were entitled to their freedom. Tousard, encouraged by Claiborne's attitude, was happy to comply. At first Jackson went along with this evasion. But when the number of applications came to over forty, he reacted violently. Tousard and all the dissident French were ordered to leave the city within three days, to be exiled to a point not nearer than Baton Rouge.

The outcry was immediate. Jackson, it was charged, hated the French, had never treated them with proper consideration, "had always kept himself aloof from the French and Creole population, whose language he did not understand." Philip Louaillier published an unsigned letter in the *Courrier de la Louisiane,* virtually calling for defiance of the General's order. "Are we to restrain our indignation when we remember that these very Frenchmen who are now exiled, have so powerfully contributed to the preservation of Louisiana?" It was time, the writer said, to refuse to bow to military law.

Jackson had Livingston translate the letter for him and identify its author. The following day, on the steps of the Exchange Coffee House, Louaillier was arrested on a charge of treason and confined, still shouting protests, to the military barracks. His lawyer promptly secured a writ of *habeas corpus* from Judge Dominic Hall. Jackson ruthlessly countered this move by arresting Judge Hall, unfortunately an Englishman by birth, on charges of "aiding and abetting and exciting mutiny."

U.S. District Attorney Dick intervened with a writ of *habeas corpus* for Hall's release, and was thrown into the barracks with Louaillier. Hall was later banished fom the city.

New Orleans was now at war again, an internal, nasty war of character assassination and intemperate retaliation. "It was lamentable, and a sad specimen of human infirmities," wrote Gayarré," to see New Orleans, in the hour of triumph, suddenly transformed into an arena of strife and angry passions, where the citizens seemed ready to fly at each other's throats." In general, Livingston and the Americans sided with Jackson, though troubled by his intransigence. The Creoles were almost unanimously up in arms. Who did Jackson think he was, a self-crowned King? Vincent Nolte's partner, Edward Hollander, openly branded as "a dirty trick" the General's exile of the French. He was tossed into the barracks with the rest.

As in the purges of modern dictatorial regimes, Jackson was throwing around orders for detention right and left. An unfortunate neighbor of Antoine Bienvenu, a planter named Garic, was taken to the barracks for having sold produce to the British army—the fact being that the British had appropriated everything within their zone of occupation and had often paid for it. A "poor unfortunate tailor" named Hortz, also trapped in the occupied zone, was arrested and condemned to death for spying, though he had never left his house throughout the siege. Jackson wisely stayed his execution.

A truce of sorts prevailed when, on the morning of March 13, the signal gun of Fort St. Charles boomed once again. Citizens swarmed into the street where a sweating courier had just arrived, after a cross-country trip, with news that the treaty of Ghent had been ratified in Washington. The cry of "La paix! La paix!" was relayed through the city. This time, though the actual documents had been somehow omitted from the courier's saddlebag, Jackson accepted the information as authentic.

Strangely enough, one of his first acts was to re-establish amicable relations with his former enemy. In his several letters to General Keane he had sedulously asked about the latter's health; in notes to General Lambert he had shown respect and warmth. Now he dispatched a letter to Lambert assuring him, "I have little doubt in my mind that the treaty has been ratified . . . I pray you to receive the satisfaction I feel in reflecting that our correspondence, begun as commanders of hostile armies, should terminate as officers of nations in amity."

Then, in a proclamation issued by his Adjutant-General Robert Butler, he included the citizens and troops of New Orleans in his recognition and acceptance of official peace. Martial law was abrogated, immunity granted to all military offenders. Judge Dominic Hall, Louaillier and the others were at liberty again.

With civil authority restored, Judge Hall's first act was to issue a warrant for the arrest of General Andrew Jackson for contempt of court, with orders to appear before him on March 24. Jackson took the summons calmly and turned to the dismissal of his troops.

On March 16 he once again assembled his gallant army, minus most of the militia, on the battlefield at Chalmette's. Like Washington's farewell to his troops, it was a ceremony charged with deep emotion, though Jackson's address was "dignified in tone, tender and affectionate in sentiment."

You have secured to America a proud name among the nations of the earth, a glory which will never perish . . . Go, then, my brave companions to your homes, to those tender connections and those blissful scenes which render life so dear—full of honor and crowned with laurels which will never fade . . . The expression of your General's thanks is feeble; but the gratitude of a country of freemen is yours; yours the applause of an admiring world!

Plauché's Battalion of Uniformed Volunteers replied with a written address to the General, signed by its seventeen senior officers. It is interesting to note that, such being the camaraderie and bonds of battle, all but two of these were French-born Creoles — a fact that helped to some extent in clearing the record of past animosities.

> We have delayed until this moment the expression of our feelings toward you, lest the honest emotions of our hearts be ascribed to a desire of propitiating the favor of our Commander. At this moment, when neither hope nor fear can be supposed to have influenced us, we pray you to receive the sincere tribute of our thanks: as soldiers for the confidence you have reposed in us, for the paternal care with which you have watched over our comforts, and above all for that justice you have done to our zeal in assigning us on every occasion a post of *danger* and of *honor*. . . .

Unfortunately Jackson, instead of letting matters rest, felt that this tribute called for some apology for his restrictive moves against the French. He addressed to the predominantly French battalion a lengthy explanation of past actions and the circumstances leading up to them. "Under these circumstances, fellow soldiers, your resolution to *let others declaim about privileges and constitutional rights* will never draw upon you the charge of being indifferent to those inestimable blessings."

On March 24, faultlessly attired in civilian dress, Jackson appeared as ordered before Judge Hall in the red-tile Spanish courthouse on Royal Street. As Charles Gayarré described that long-awaited moment: "The General, followed by a numerous escort of officers, entered the hall of judgment which was crowded to suffocation. The dense multitude had opened before him as he advanced and then closed again in deep silence; but when he reached the bar where he was to stand as a culprit, one wild yell of defiance, which was echoed by the multitude outside, swept over the building and seemed to shake the roof and walls against which it reverberated."

The core of that defiance seemed to be the red-sashed Baratarians who had filled the hall in disproportionate numbers. Dominique You pushed forward through the crowd.

"Zhénéral!" he shouted. "Say the word and we will pitch into the river the judge, the lawyers, and the courthouse itself!"

There was a near riot in response, quelled by the General himself. Jackson, wrote Gayarré, "looked round with an expression of calm and august majesty, which was long remembered by those who saw his commanding features on that occasion; he only waved his hand in rebuke, and instantly order and silence were re-established. Then, turning to the Judge, he slightly bowed his head as if to say: I am here in obedience to your command."

The clerk called the case: "The United States versus Andrew Jackson."

District Attorney Dick read the charges against him. Interference with the Legislature was not stressed, except as it related to the imprisonment of the legislator Philip Louaillier. But obstructing justice through the medium of martial law, when martial law had ceased to be deemed necessary, was the issue; and Jackson's highhanded enforcement of the measure was the crux of the dispute. "Despotism is not martial law," the district attorney argued. "It is the absence of all laws." He concluded:

> We are compelled, therefore, to attribute the arbitrary proceedings of the defendant, not to his conviction of their necessity, but to the indulged infirmity of an obstinate and morbidly irascible temperament, and to the unyielding pride of a man naturally impatient of the least show of opposition to his will.

Edward Livingston was there to plead the General's case, but Jackson would not take the stand. "You would not hear my defense," he told the court. "Under these circumstances I appear before you to receive the sentence of the court, and have nothing further to add." With no alternative, Judge Hall pronounced the sentence, modified by respect for Jackson's services. He fined the General a thousand dollars. Jackson paid it, bowed to the judge and left the hall.

Outside, a turbulent crowd awaited his reappearance, eager for this last chance to pay him homage and express their still unflagging loyalty. Led by more than fifty of the Baratarians, ever the General's staunchest supporters, they escorted him to Maspero's Exchange. ("American citizens blushed to see this procession," wrote Nolte, truthfully or not, "and the General himself seemed to dislike it.")

At Maspero's, over many a *petite gouave,* Jackson told his followers: "Considering obedience to the laws, even when we think them unjustly applied, as the first duty of every citizen, I did not hesitate to comply with the sentence you have heard, and I entreat you to remember the example." The assembly responded by soliciting contributions to make up the amount of Jackson's fine. The General expressed his gratitude, but asked that the fund be donated to the widows and orphans of those who had died on the battlefield.

This intimate coffeehouse gathering, crowded with the "hellish banditti" whom Jackson now referred to as his "comrades in arms," was virtually the General's last public appearance in the Crescent City. There was still unfinished business to attend to, mostly concerned with the war claims of civilians. Vincent Nolte gave him a hard time over the appropriated cotton until Jackson shut him up with a glass of whiskey: "You must be damned thirsty after all that argument."

On April 6 the General departed for Nashville with his adopted son and Rachel. His last official act was to turn over command of the military forces of Louisiana to Major General Edmund P. Gaines, hero in the gallant defense of Fort Erie six months previously. Once again Claiborne, coveting that position of authority, was ignored.

Too short of food to undertake the long voyage back to England, the British troops remained encamped on Dauphine Island while ships were sent to Havana for supplies. On this barren stretch of sand and stunted pine groves the veterans found a new foe in the swarms of snakes and alligators that terrified their women, made bathing hazardous, and invaded their tents and flimsily constructed barracks. Against these they waged an all-out war with muskets, knives and bayonets.

Nor was this their final battle on these inhospitable shores. George Gleig recorded another conflict in which,

> . . . the officers of the 7th, 43rd, and 14th dragoons made an attack with pine cones upon those of the 85th, the 93rd, and 95th. For the space of some days they pelted each other, from morning till night, laying ambuscades, and exhibiting, on a small scale, all the stratagems of war; while the whole army, not even excepting the Generals themselves, stood by and spurred them on.

*Sic transit gloria mundi.*

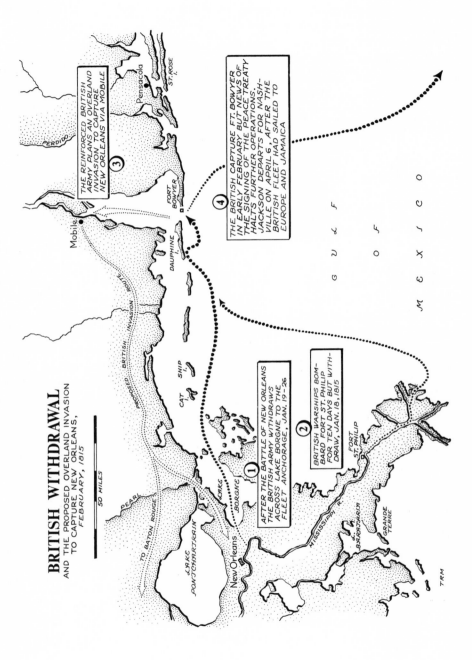

BRITISH WITHDRAWAL
AND THE PROPOSED OVERLAND INVASION
TO CAPTURE NEW ORLEANS,
FEBRUARY, 1815

50 MILES

GULF OF MEXICO

PERDIDO

Pensacola

ST. ROSE I.

Mobile

FORT BOWYER

DAUPHINE I.

CAT I.

SHIP I.

PROPOSED BRITISH INVASION ROUTE

TO BATON ROUGE

PEARL

LAKE PONTCHARTRAIN

New Orleans

RIGOLETS

FORKS

BORGNE

LAKE BORGNE

MISSISSIPPI R.

FORT ST. PHILIP

BARATARIA

GRANDE TERRE

T.R.M.

① AFTER THE BATTLE OF NEW ORLEANS THE BRITISH ARMY WITHDRAWS ACROSS LAKE BORGNE TO THE FLEET ANCHORAGE, JAN. 19-26

② BRITISH WARSHIPS BOM-BARD FORT ST. PHILIP FOR TEN DAYS BUT WITH-DRAW, JAN. 18, 1815

③ THE REINFORCED BRITISH ARMY PLANS AN OVERLAND INVASION TO CAPTURE NEW ORLEANS VIA MOBILE

④ THE BRITISH CAPTURE FT. BOWYER IN EARLY FEBRUARY BUT NEWS OF THE SIGNING OF THE PEACE TREATY HALTS FURTHER OPERATIONS. JACKSON DEPARTS FOR NASH-VILLE ON APRIL 6, AFTER THE BRITISH FLEET HAD SAILED TO EUROPE AND JAMAICA

# 20.  L'Envoi

"Great is the change which the return of Peace has already made in this Capital," wrote W. C. C. Claiborne to an unnamed correspondent. "Our harbor is again whitened with canvas; the Levee is crowded with Cotton, Tobacco and other articles for exportation. The merchant seems delighted with the prospect before him, and the agriculturist, in the high price for his product, finds new incitements to industry."

New Orleans was, in fact, at the dawn of what historians would call its Golden Age—an era of prosperity and glittering growth that would continue for a century, as the Siren City became again a mecca for ambitious fortune seekers, traders, speculators and promoters.

Captain Shreve of the *Enterprise*, whose ship had eluded the British batteries at Villeré's, not only broke the Fulton-Livingston monopoly of steamboat traffic on the river, but set the pace for a whole new floating empire on the Mississippi. The Kaintucks and their flatboats still arrived to tangle with the gendarmes. But en route they were busy dodging the swift, gaudy, brightly-illuminated palaces named *Princess, Duke of Orleans, Paragon, Diana, Aetna,* and *Vesuvius* and *Belle Key.*

The great new era of steamboats on the river added to the sudden fame and soaring commerce of the Crescent City. A year after the Battle of New Orleans, forty stern-wheelers deposited more than eight

311

million dollars' worth of merchandise on the levee. Within five years both these figures doubled, and in the next decade steamboat commerce reached the then-astronomical figure of $37,000,000. Lloyds of London settled on New Orleans as the choice place to do business in America — surely one of the great crossroads of the world.

But this presage of a golden future held no promise for Pierre Denis de la Ronde. His château at Versailles still stood, fortunately, but with the spent look of a once-loved mistress ravaged by strangers. The scars of battle marred its northern side; balls were buried in the walls and in the trunks of oaks; the picket fences and some of the outbuildings had been torn down for firewood. Horses, cattle, chickens, carriages and harnesses — all were gone. Hundreds of kegs of sugar and molasses had been confiscated for the British ramparts.

Taking inventory, he applied to the U.S. Senate for compensation, noting that the British during their occupation of the property had paid for what they had taken and done little damage, while "nearly the whole of it may be fairly attributed to the conduct of the American army." Among his losses he listed "66 acres of cane plant burned for want of fuel by Con'l Hind and General Coffee: $7,290." Missing or damaged were 800 bottles of vintage wines, "25 robes for my wife and daughters, 12 beautiful engravings," marble and mahogany furniture, paper hangings for eight rooms, agricultural tools and "a quantity of medicine."

His most highly prized possessions appeared to be his slaves and his books. He lumped them together in his inventory: eight slaves missing and four hundred volumes, including the works of Voltaire and Racine, valued at $7,200 — bringing his total claim for damages to over $40,000.

De la Ronde received only a fraction of this amount, about one-seventh, more, however, than any of his neighbors (Villeré and Jumonville got nothing for their losses). But perhaps Pierre was past caring. More important to him was that, despite his failure to see to the blocking of the Bayou Bienvenu as ordered, General Jackson presented him with a certificate praising "his attention to the public concerns during the invasion of the enemy, to the detriment of his private ones." To Pierre the testament was "more valuable than compensation for my losses."

Failure to seal off and guard the Bayou Bienvenu was not, however, lightly passed over. Young Gabriel Villeré, who had participated in the battle of December 23, was afterwards deprived of his sword and tried by a board of inquiry for "harboring and protecting the enemy" and "neglect of duty." Major Hind of the Mississippi Dragoons presided over the court. Perhaps it was Gabriel's youth, or perhaps the general euphoria that followed victory, but Villeré's peers took a lenient view of the affair and he was readily acquitted. Jacques Villeré, Gabriel's father, was, like de la Ronde, cited by Jackson for gallant conduct during the conflict and in 1816 succeeded W. C. C. Claiborne as Governor of Louisiana.

Most of the other planters on the left bank, after filing claims for damages up and down the line, carried on as before; but the gracious days of the old plantation life along that section of the river became a casualty of the war. Ignace de Lino de Chalmette died (of a broken heart, they said) within weeks of the destruction of his château in the New Year's Day bombardment. The plantations of Macarty and Lacoste and Jumonville survived for not much more than a single generation, becoming victims of urban and industrial expansion.

Several officers among those commanding the troops on the Rodriguez line were, on the strength of sudden popularity, drafted into political careers. William Carroll was elected Governor of Tennessee in 1821 and again in 1830. Walter Overton, who successfully repelled the siege of Fort St. Philip, served as Congressman from Louisiana. John Adair became Governor of Kentucky in 1821 and also served in Congress. Coffee withdrew from military life and became Jackson's partner in real estate speculation in Tennessee.

Colonel Hind of the Dragoons continued to serve with Jackson in later military operations and also spent a term in Congress. Major Plauché of the Orleans Volunteers became Lieutenant-Governor of Louisiana in 1850. Daniel Patterson remained with the navy, becoming commander of a squadron in the Mediterranean in 1835 and subsequently commander of the Washington navy yard until his death in 1839.

Edward Livingston, becoming more and more prominent in New Orleans, was elected to Congress in 1823 and to the Senate in 1829. In Andrew Jackson's administration he was appointed Secretary of State, and in 1833 was sent as minister to Paris, where he successfully settled American claims on France for Napoleon's wartime depredations.

David Morgan appeared before a court of inquiry investigating the American debacle on the right bank. Affixing the blame for the catastrophe on Colonel Davis and his irresolute Kentuckians, he was cleared of responsibility in the matter.

Although the rout of the Kentuckians — more specifically, Jackson's denunciation of them, with its charge of cowardice — caused a temporary rift between John Adair and the Tennessee General, the over-all reputation of the tough Kentuckians did not suffer. (New Orleans' only complaint against those remaining in the city devolved on their habit of cracking walnuts in the theater.) After the war, one of the most popular ballads of the century was sung and circulated from New England to the Gulf. The tune, ironically, was lifted from an earlier English ballad (somewhat as The Star-Spangled Banner's melody was stolen from an English drinking song), but the words of The Hunters of Kentucky were pure American. One stanza:

> I suppose you've read it in the prints
> how Pakenham attempted
> To make Old Hickory Jackson wince,
> but soon his schemes repented;
> For we with rifles ready cock'd
> thought such occasion lucky.
> And soon around the hero flock'd
> the hunters of Kentucky!

It was only one of many popular songs and ballads hailing the victory at New Orleans. Young Richard Ogilvy, who had witnessed Sam Williams trying to lead the singing on the ramparts at Chalmette's, was inspired to compose an epic of his own. He too did not slight the Kentuckians — naturally, being one himself. A typical verse, one of thirty-six, was preceded by salutes to England's might:

> Her Lion-flag Flew
> And her Bugles Blew
> From Cathay to the Zuyder Zee,
> But Never as Yet
> Had her Legions Met
> Old Kentucky and Tennessee!

Already the challenge of Mexican-Spanish rule in Texas had begun to arouse the United States. It would be kindled when Andrew Jackson became President. Right now it provided a cause and outlet for many

New Orleans veterans seeking action. Reuben Kemper, Jackson's trusted cavalry scout, was among the first to organize a raid on Texas. The crusade was shared by the quixotic General Humbert.

In spite of the failure to enlist British deserters in his "Foreign Legion," Humbert continued to dream of glory for his private army, numbering 150 men by early March. Like Kemper, he set out to liberate Texas from its Spanish overlords. But the expedition collapsed for lack of provisions and lack of funds to meet his payroll. Aged by both years and experience, Humbert returned to his chess and brandy at the Hôtel de la Marine and died in relative poverty eight years later.

Michel Fortier, champion of the colored militia, died short of his seventieth birthday in 1819, after a life devoted (said his obituary) to *"amitié, bienfaisance, et humanité."* His son Florent, who had fought with Michel at New Orleans, suffered more from the war than his father. According to his historian descendant Alcée Fortier, Florent was typical of those Creole planters "whom war had ruined but who to the last were noble."

Many veterans of the battle took to writing personal accounts of the event. Bernard de Marigny's monograph was filled with defensive arguments regarding the gallant conduct of the Creoles, waspishly attacking Yankee claims and renewing the conflict between French and Americans in New Orleans. "The fact remains," wrote de Marigny, "that the Anglo-Saxons have tried to give themselves credit for these glorious days. . . they want to monopolize everything and refuse to share anything with other nations."

Vincent Nolte, growing richer in the rising cotton market, settled down from time to time to write his deservedly famous *Memoirs*. "The motto of my book," he noted, "was always present to me. . . ."

> There are wanderers o'er eternity,
> Whose bark floats on, and anchored
> Never shall be.

Though Nolte anchored himself to a wife and children and a home in New Orleans, his complex commercial deals and his peripatetic nature took him back and forth between America and Europe. Published in 1854, his memoirs and character became, in 1933, material for an immensely successful American novel, *Anthony Adverse* by Hervey Allen.

Jackson's handsome young military secretary, John Reid, who had accompanied him on his first arrival at New Orleans, started at once to write a biography of the General. Reid died halfway through the task, and Jackson urged a fellow Tennessean, John Henry Eaton, to finish the book, offering to advance the money for its printing. Reid's and Eaton's *Life of Andrew Jackson* was published in Philadelphia in 1817.

The erstwhile *mousquetaire* and aging sugar baron, Étienne de Boré, died at age 78 in 1829. Alone at his bedside, by exclusive request, was his grandson Charles Gayarré, to whom his last words were addressed: "Keep your conscience free of self-reproach, so that your death may be as calm as mine." But the days ahead were anything but calm for Gayarré. Tormented by ill health, he traveled many roads, becoming lawyer, politician, then historian; haunting the health resorts of France and debating with such literary figures as de Tocqueville, de Lamartine and Balzac. He was influenced most in his later work, however, by Judge François-Xavier Martin — both writing voluminous histories of Louisiana.


Of the many veteran chroniclers of the Battle of New Orleans, the subsequent career of Arsène Lacarrière Latour was perhaps the most extraordinary. True to his vow, he tracked down and published, in his memoirs, the names of the Spaniards at the Lake Borgne fishing village who had betrayed their country to the British. Let them live in infamy! Then Latour himself turned traitor and enlisted in the Spanish secret service, betraying his country's conspiracy to undermine Spanish rule in Florida.

Bernard de Marigny, the golden son of Creole aristocracy, served briefly in the Louisiana Legislature as his fortune continued to diminish through reckless gambling and speculation. By 1860 he had retired into a world of poverty and memories.

But he never ceased to be revered in New Orleans, which treated him with sentimental kindness. Even the horsecab drivers would refuse his fare. "No, no. Not from you, Monsieur de Marigny." If, passing a familiar house, he heard music from within, he would rap on the door and instruct the servant, "Tell them it is de Marigny." Admitted, he would make himself at home among the new and old-time Creoles. He would show them his latest letter from the King of France, beginning "Mon cher Bernard." Yes, he was obviously still the Great One in society. It was only society that was becoming small. He died in 1868 from a fall on the newly-paved Rue Royale, where stone and cement had finally replaced the familiar board banquettes.

Governor Claiborne persisted in his verbal war with Andrew Jackson through letters, circulars, and through the press. He attempted to bolster his sagging reputation by bombarding Jackson's aides and officers, as well as his own associates, with questionnaires designed to elicit answers favorable to his conduct. The letters were uniform in composition, requesting replies to thirty-one points relating to his military services. An opening paragraph: "Have you at any time heard from me a Sentiment, expression, or wish indicating other feelings than those of the warmest attachment to my Country's interest, and the greatest solicitude for the safety, welfare and tranquility of this Section of the Union?"

The response was generally favorable, but it came too late to afford him any satisfaction. Claiborne died of a liver ailment in 1817, shortly after relinquishing his office to Jacques Villeré. His beauteous widow Sophronie, after a suitable interval, married John Randolph Grymes, legal defender of the Baratarian pirates whom her earlier husband had abhorred. Perhaps Sophronie found in the flamboyant Grymes a bit of the glamour she had succumbed to in her secret meeting with the pirate leader Jean Laffite, shortly before the Battle of New Orleans.

A postscript on the Baron Henri St. Gême, Captain of Dragoons, is recorded by Charles Gayarré:

> Shortly after the war, there was between two citizens of Louisiana an affair of honor [a duel beneath The Oaks] which produced considerable excitement. Pierre Laffite was the second of one of them, and St. Gême of the other. St. Gême had no superior in New Orleans as to social position. He had distinguished himself under General Jackson as the captain of one of our uniformed companies. . . . Would St. Gême have consented to meet Laffite in the capacity I have mentioned, if the latter had really been looked upon as a pirate?

Pirates or no, the Baratarians were, according to promise, granted a Presidential pardon for pre-war offenses and received from Jackson a citation praising their "gallant conduct" throughout the siege. And true to their character, most of them quickly returned to their former life of smuggling and piracy.

The renegade Vincent Gambi was first to resume the role of buccaneer. By ingenious subterfuge he seized the impounded vessel *Philanthrope,* which Patterson had captured in his raid on Grande Terre, and sneaked with her down the Mississippi to prey on Spanish commerce in the Gulf. He was shortly followed by Renato Beluché, who, however, pursued a more honorable course. After a brief stint of privateering, Renato joined with Simón Bolívar in the latter's campaign to free the South American colonies from Spanish rule. Rising to the rank of Admiral in Bolívar's navy, Renato died in 1860, a hero and citizen of Venezuela.

Jean and Pierre Laffite petitioned the United States Government for the return of their confiscated fleet and for financial compensation for the plunder seized by Patterson in his raid on Grande Terre. Though Grymes and Livingston pleaded their case, they received no money, and their captured vessels were put up for auction. Acting as an undercover front for the Laffites, Joseph Sauvinet bid for and purchased the impounded fleet and returned it to Pierre and Jean, who forthwith followed Gambi and Renato to the Gulf.

Barataria and Grande Terre, however, were no longer safe resorts for piracy, since the shaky peace between Spain and the United States made Spanish vessels theoretically immune from privateering. Adept at double-dealing, Pierre and Jean enlisted as spies in the Spanish secret service and, while still avowing loyalty to the United States, supplied the Spanish authorities with information on American intentions toward the Southwest territories.

But their true calling was piracy, and they shortly sought another refuge similar to Barataria. Haiti seemed a likely choice, and sailing thereto the Laffites crossed paths with Vincent Gambi's marauding vessel. The old rivalry reasserted itself, and in a two-hour battle Gambi's ship with all aboard was sunk.

At this point Dominique You broke with his brothers and returned to New Orleans where he joined a conspiracy to rescue Napoleon from St. Helena and bring the exiled emperor to the Crescent City. A house was prepared for Bonaparte at Chartres and St. Louis streets and a ship engaged for his liberation. But a few days before the expedition was to sail, word of Napoleon's death reached New Orleans, canceling the venture. Five years later, broken in health and bankrupt, Dominique died and was buried with miliary honors. Chiseled on his tombstone were the words of Voltaire, consecrating him as an *intrépide guerrier sur la terre et sur l'onde. . . ."*

Haiti refused sanctuary to Pierre and Jean Laffite, and they sailed in the Gulf to Galveston Island, which they renamed Campêche. Here Jean sought to re-create the fortress community of Grande Terre, and briefly succeeded. But the United States authorities were cracking down on piracy. In 1821 a brig-of-war appeared off Campêche, and its commander, Lawrence Kearny, demanded that Laffite and his men evacuate the island. With surprising docility Jean agreed, asking only time to load their possessions aboard his fleet. This granted and the loading accomplished, Jean put his island kingdom to the torch.

At this point, and perhaps appropriately, Jean Laffite's life evaporates in legend. One can take one's choice of subsequent conclusions. He was variously reported as having died of disease in Yucatán, as having lost his ship and his life in a tropical storm, as continuing a career of piracy as "the Dragon of the Gulf." Perhaps the strangest of all denouements is recorded in the state of Illinois, where he allegedly expired at the ripe old age of seventy-two. In a graveyard at Alton a tombstone bearing his name and supposedly erected by his offspring imparts the hopeful message, "Our father died . . . will be with Uncle Pierre in Heaven."

The island of Grande Terre today bears few mementos of its long-gone fame as one of the greatest pirate kingdoms in the western world. The poet Lafcadio Hearn, who professed to "the worship of the Old, the Queer, the Strange, the Exotic, the Monstrous," could not resist a visit there at the turn of the last century. He found the island "a wilderness of wind-swept grasses and sinewy reeds, speckled with drift and decaying things, wormriddled timber and dead porpoises. . . waves and clouds flying in one wild rout of broken gold. . . a whirling flower drift of sleepy butterflies." A bit of that far-out atmosphere remains. But essentially it is a tranquil, pleasant spot for visiting fishermen and tourists, and for government and college students of ecology.

The fate of the Negro troops following the Battle of New Orleans was a tragically familiar one in race relations. In the first flush of victory, words of praise were generously bestowed. Jackson proclaimed that they "had not disappointed the hopes that were formed of their courage and perseverance." The General also reported to Monroe that Captain Joseph Savary and his men had "manifested great bravery." Even the free colored nurses in the city were awarded verbal recognition for their care and solace of the wounded.

In a sense, surely, the colored troops deserved more credit for the victory at New Orleans than that accorded to the glamorized Baratarians. For one thing, there were more of them: ten percent of all the troops engaged. Their casualties were higher than other units in proportion to their numbers on the line. A news dispatch after the battle recorded: "The killed and wounded on our part were chiefly of the New Orleans colored regiment, who were so anxious for glory that they could not be prevented from exposing themselves. They fought like desperadoes and deserve distinguished praise."

But according to Rudolphe Desdunes, historian and spokesman for the black militia, "they were forced to be content with honeyed words and stately phrases." Pensions promised them by the federal government, bounties and land warrants pledged to them by Andrew Jackson, were delayed. Even more bitter than these initial disappointments were the renewed suspicion and resentment of white citizens and fellow soldiers. Now that the colored troops had served their purpose in the defense of New Orleans, the city was anxious to be rid of them.

Writing in French under an assumed name, a veteran Negro poet circulated a ballad reflecting the plight of the free men of color. One translated quatrain read:

> I fought with great valor
> With the hope of serving my country,
> Not thinking that for recompense
> I would be the object of scorn.

The pride which the blacks had felt in serving and fighting beside their white compatriots turned sour. In the middle of February, Daquin's colored volunteers were ordered outside the city to erect additional defenses on the Chef Menteur. This was manual labor akin, they felt, to slavery. The colored troops regarded the order as an insult and refused to go. A written protest delivered by Captain Savary declared that "they would be willing to sacrifice their lives in combat in defense of their country as had been demonstrated, but preferred death to the performance of the work of laborers."

This mutinous action enhanced the distrust of the black militia and in succeeding years the corps was allowed to deteriorate. No colored units were invited to share or to parade in subsequent anniversary celebrations of the Battle of New Orleans. Though the black battalions continued to drill twice weekly in the Place d'Armes, their numbers diminished and by 1834 the colored militia was virtually nonexistent.

One enduring human symbol of the black man's moment of glory in the battle for New Orleans was drummer boy Jordan B. Noble, who continued his military service through the War with Mexico in 1849 and who was a much-applauded feature of the city's military jubilees. In a less exalted role Noble became a one-man act on the vaudeville circuit throughout the South, billed as the drummer who inspired the troops to victory in the defense of New Orleans.

When pensions and land grants finally came through, largely through the efforts of the Louisiana Legislature, most of the colored troops sold their lands to Americans arriving from the North and emigrated to Cuba, Haiti, Mexico and other territories where the color line was less defined. The "brave Captain Savary," who had alienated himself by his refusal of the Chef Menteur assignment, took fifty of his men to the Gulf for a venture in privateering. Savary later aligned himself with Mexican insurgents seeking freedom from the yoke of Spain. His following grew and became an appreciable factor in weakening Spanish rule in South America.

It was not until 1851, when slavery had become a national issue and the attitude of blacks became a matter of concern, that the colored veterans, some ninety of them, participated in services commemorating the great battle. At that time the New Orleans *Picayune* waxed sentimental in its tribute:

> Who more than they deserve the thanks of the country and the gratitude of succeeding generations? . . . We look with feelings akin to veneration of their aged forms. We reflected that beneath their dark bosoms were sheltered faithful hearts susceptible to the noblest impulses, and we involuntarily asked if these could be the people whose arms defended their country in its hour of extremity, against whom now a fatuous fanaticism is arrayed.

Some ten years later such sentiments and tributes were forgotten. On the fiftieth anniversary of the Battle of New Orleans the white press failed to mention "a single word of the presence on the field and the gallantry of the black volunteers." Perhaps the aged soldiers were too old to care. Some of their descendants were at war again, fighting on the sides of North and South — none for the Confederacy, which would not accept them, but many for such Southern states as would.

As the vanguard of the returning British fleet approached the shores of England, Major Sir Harry Smith, still mourning the loss of his commanding general Pakenham, hailed a passing trawler.

"Ahoy!" he shouted to the skipper. "Any news?"

The man on the bridge regarded his accoster, and the majestic fleet, with signal lack of interest. "Naw," he said.

Then, as the two ships pulled apart, the phlegmatic skipper remembered something.

"Ho! Bonaparte's back on the throne of France," he shouted.

The tricolor floating over Brest confirmed the news. Napoleon had returned from Elba, and the Continent was once again at war. General Lambert, informed that he had been knighted for his gallant conduct in Louisiana, received at the same time orders to join Wellington at Waterloo. There he commanded the 10th Brigade, which suffered the heaviest casualties of any British unit in that battle. Lieutenant-Colonel Francis Brooke and his 4th regiment, or King's Own, also served at Waterloo, as did the 7th, 40th, and 43rd regiments which had fought at New Orleans. But the 21st Fusiliers, Mullins's 44th, Thornton's 85th and Dale's 93rd, though they arrived in time, had been too decimated at New Orleans to be sent to Belgium.

Harry Smith also rejoined Wellington at Waterloo, glad, after New Orleans, to be contrastingly engaged in "humane warfare" and finding Wellington's command "delightful." But at the height of the action "with every moment a crisis," he found the noise and smoke confusing.

"Bring your people forward," Wellington shouted to him in the heat of the battle.

"In which direction, my lord?" Smith asked.

The Iron Duke solved Smith's dilemma with a pointing finger. "Straight ahead!" he said.

After recovering from his neck wound, General Keane, later Lord Keane, was appointed Lieutenant-Governor of Jamaica. Upon leaving that post for service in India he was succeeded by General Lambert, who survived the dreadful slaughter of his 10th Brigade at Waterloo. General John Burgoyne, as chief of fortifications at Sevastopol in 1854, did no better in protecting British troops and blasting enemy ramparts than he had on the fields of Chalmette. As a strange consequence of this he was made a baronet in 1856, then promoted to field marshal, and finally elected to Parliament.

The 93rd Highlanders returned to Plymouth, their point of departure, "a dreary, shattered band. . . with ragged tartans that had long since lost their original colours, haggard faces, skeleton figures! . . . many on crutches, some with their arms in slings, and the faces of others marked with ghastly scars." In their barracks hung their only consoling souvenir of the battle of New Orleans, Declouet's regimental colors captured on the right bank of the Mississippi.

Colonel Mullins was made the scapegoat for the English defeat at New Orleans. Tried by court-martial in Dublin in the summer of 1815, with Lieutenant Knight and Colonel Debbeig testifying against him, he was dismissed from the army on charges of having failed, on January 8, to bring forward the fascines and ladders so essential for scaling the American ramparts. The 44th Infantry, which came in for its share of castigation, partially redeemed itself in subsequent service in India.

Quartermaster Surtees, after serving undistinguishedly at Waterloo, was finally relieved, by mortal illness, of the wife he had sought to escape through service in the army. His own health rapidly failed, however, and he received a medical discharge in 1827, retiring on full pay after twenty years of service. The ever-disgruntled Sergeant Cooper finally received the discharge that had been due him before sailing for New Orleans and became a rural teacher in the north of England. He petitioned the War Department for a pension and received instead a medal with nine combat ribbons. None was for the Battle of New Orleans, which the government was not inclined to recognize.

The expedient of shipping to England the bodies of Pakenham and Gibbs, preserved in kegs of rum, gave rise to a grisly morsel of apocrypha. Reportedly the barrels were mistakenly returned to Charleston, and thirsty sailors tippled on the rum throughout the voyage until they discovered the forbidding contents. Legend apart, life-size statues of the two generals, paid for by public subscription, were installed in the South Transept of London's St. Paul's Cathedral.

Lieutenant Gleig, renouncing the horrors of war after the Battle of New Orleans, took orders and became Chaplain General of the British Army. He continued to brood upon Pakenham's death, blaming it on Mullins and the 44th Infantry whose rout had brought the General on the field and forced him to expose himself. Some of Sir Edward's peers, however, regarded Pakenham's fate as far from insupportable. "The death of the General was a fortunate event," observed one British officer. "His character was irretrievably ruined if he did not take New Orleans or perish in the attempt."

Such, however, was not the opinion of the Duke of Wellington, who had maneuvered his kinsman to New Orleans in the first place. Writing to Sir Edward's brother in May of 1815, he observed:

> We have one consolation, that he [Pakenham] fell as he lived in the honourable discharge of his duty, distinguished as a soldier and a man. I cannot but regret however that he was ever employed on such a service or with such a colleague [Cochrane] who had plunder as his object. . . . The American fortifications still would have been carried if the duties of others, that is of the Admiral, had been as well performed as that of him whom we lament.

Such comments, even the defeat at New Orleans, did not injure the career of Vice Admiral Alexander Cochrane. Though he saw no future action on the high seas, he was moved up the naval ladder to full admiral in 1819 and commander-in-chief at Plymouth in 1821, after which, with no higher to go, he died in honor and retirement in 1832.

Colonel Edward Nicholls, who had worked so assiduously at persuading the Creeks to join in the siege of New Orleans, not to mention backing Lockyer's efforts to enlist the Baratarians, never gave up. He remained in Florida, hopeful still of promoting an anti-American alliance with the expatriated Indians, and did, in fact, return to England in August with a treaty, signed by Creek and Seminole chiefs, which he presented to Lord Bathurst for approval.

Bathurst was understandably indignant, refusing to ratify a treaty which Nicholls ("a very wild fellow") had had no authority to negotiate, and which was "offensive to both Spain and the United States with which Great Britain is at peace." The fruitless incident served, however, as a springboard for future events in the career of Andrew Jackson, overnight hero of the Battle of New Orleans.

Arriving back in Nashville in mid-May of 1815, General Jackson wanted nothing more than quiet retirement, breeding and racing horses, being with Rachel, his adopted son, and friends, growing and selling cotton and tobacco. But adulation was not to be denied. He had become not only a national hero but a major military figure round the world. Both Wellington and Napoleon, reportedly, now studied his battle tactics at New Orleans, and the Iron Duke remained a professed and lifetime admirer of the Tennessee commander.

Though as early as 1815 Jackson's name was mentioned for the presidency, he wholeheartedly supported Monroe for that office, to which the latter acceded in 1816. Monroe's administration, firm but reasonable, launched the "Era of Good Feeling" which carried the President to a second term in 1820.

One of Monroe's last acts as Secretary of War had been to divide the military districts of the country into simply North and South, with Jacob Brown, hero of Niagara and Fort Erie, in command of the Northern District and Jackson commanding in the South. Along with this, to Jackson's distress, went a limitation of the standing army to 10,000 Regulars. Monroe's new Secretary of War, John C. Calhoun, perhaps indiscreetly made it known that General Jackson would have full powers to conduct what military operations he deemed best. It was the sort of carte blanche that the General relished.

Due to the efforts of Colonel Nicholls, whom Jackson had always hoped to catch and hang, the Peace of Ghent had brought no change to the troublesome situation in the Floridas. Sporadic Indian raids continued along the border. General Hayne, commanding this area under Jackson, reported in January 1818 that there were some 2,700 Seminoles, Creeks and Negroes in West Florida, well-organized, well-armed, and posing a threat to the United States. Jackson wrote to Monroe requesting permission again to invade Florida, which he had "conquered" in thirty days in 1814.

Billy Phillips, normally Jackson's express courier between the Hermitage and Washington, had settled down in Nashville as a prosperous planter. As a result, Monroe's reply, though generally approving, did not reach the General before he assumed that silence meant consent. With eight hundred Regulars and 1,200 Volunteers from Tennessee and Georgia (two-thirds of the Tennesseans were veterans of New Orleans), Jackson easily took possession, in April, of Fort St. Marks on Apalachee Bay. In this operation he had naval support from Lieutenant Isaac McKeever, Catesby Jones's second in command at the gunboat defense of Lake Borgne.

The General then marched his forces over a hundred miles of "impassable" swampland to occupy the Seminole stronghold of Suwannee. Satisfied that he had shown sufficient military strength without overcoming any real resistance, he returned to Fort St. Marks in May, executed two British-Indian collaborators, Ambrister and Arbuthnot, and proceeded west to Pensacola, where he again forced surrender of

that city by a show of force. Leaving McKeever in charge of the
Southern coast, the General forthwith returned to Nashville. His per-
sonal "Florida War," launched without written approval from the
President, was over.

Though a subject of bitter dispute in the Capitol (ignored by Jackson: "Washington is a poor place to find out what people think"), the
unauthorized invasion of Florida was upheld by Monroe and approved
in the House by a vote of two to one. It led to Spain's cession of the
Territory, two years later, to the United States.

Back at the Hermitage, Jackson resigned from the army in May of
1821, and on the same day—with apparently no connection—was
appointed Governor of Florida. It was not an office congenial to the
gritty warrior (his only significant act was to throw the ex-Governor
into his own *calabozo*) and six months later he resigned and returned
to Nashville, firmly resolved "to quit public life for good and all."

But he could not escape destiny. He was now, in spite of himself, an
acclaimed candidate for the presidency, supported in the West by the
stalwart political muscle of William Carroll and in Washington by
Congressman Edward Livingston of Louisiana. Try as he might to
remain a passive candidate, the "thunderbolt" of his victory at Chalmette had reverberated through the Union, to every state and to every
section, including once-recalcitrant New England, even to granite-
ribbed New Hampshire, where publisher-editor Isaac Hill proclaimed
him as "the people's hero!"

As a first step towards the White House, Tennessee again sent him to
the Senate (where he had first served in 1797–98) in December 1823.
Before his term was up the General was swept by a mighty tide of
national sentiment into the presidential race of 1824. Officers of his
New Orleans army promoted his candidacy in every state—Coffee,
Overton, Carroll, Butler, Adair, even the gallant Creole commander
Jean Baptiste Plauché. "You are the favorite in New England," re-
ported his former inspector general Arthur Hayne.

He was opposed by a formidable quartet: John Quincy Adams,
William Crawford, Henry Clay and John Calhoun—but Adams himself
almost conceded defeat. All the Jackson people had to do, he said, was
shout "8th of January and the Battle of New Orleans" and the General
was a shoo-in. What other candidate could boast such qualifications as
were carried on the General's campaign banner?

*"Under Washington our independence was achieved;*
*"Under Jackson our independence has been preserved!"*

It was a strange election. Jackson won ninety-nine electoral votes and eleven states, Adams eighty-four votes and seven states, with the other two candidates trailing badly. Since none, however, received a majority, the choice fell, by a still-surviving defect in the Constitution, to the House of Representatives, crowded with pro-Adams members elected two years previously. Out of the running altogether, Clay threw his thirty-one votes to Adams and the punctilious, uninspiring former peace commissioner at Ghent became sixth President of the United States, rewarding Clay with the post of Secretary of State.

While cries of corrupt bargaining, "sellout," and treason rose loud and clear—Jackson himself ever afterwards referred to Clay and Adams as "those damned rascals"—the General returned to his creature comforts and personal interests in Nashville. His health improved with Rachel's care, his uncertain wealth increased with rising prices for cotton and tobacco. He was visited by Judge Ballard of Kentucky, the Morgan Ballard who had "snuffed the candle" of British Major Whitaker from the ramparts of Chalmette's. The Judge reported that he had "never seen the General so well-fed and well-groomed."

Another visitor to the Hermitage was the Marquis de Lafayette, whom Jackson had admired in his youth. The aging French hero of America's War for Independence compared Jackson's victory at New Orleans with Wellington's triumph at Waterloo, a comment, wrote Rachel Jackson, "very gratifying to the General."

Jackson was back in full fighting spirit by 1828, ready for one of the dirtiest campaigns in American presidential history. This time the outcome was in little doubt. The results, which reached Nashville on November 21, showed Jackson with fifty-six percent of the popular vote and 178 electoral votes against eight-three for Adams. That evening Rachel Jackson complained of feeling faint. Two days later she was dead, shrouding in grief the General's last great victory.

There is too much of a story in Jackson's two-term administration to be covered here. Suffice it to say that he restored to the office of the presidency, which had reached its nadir under Madison, a new authority. He was a people's President, popularly elected, giving new meaning to democracy throughout the subsequent "Jacksonian Age."

But even in the White House he never seemed far removed, in spirit or companionship, from the days of New Orleans and Chalmette's. Edward Livingston was appointed his Secretary of State; John Henry Eaton, who had finished Reid's biography of Jackson, was for a while his Secretary of War, until Eaton's "scandalous" marriage to Peggy O'Neil blew the Cabinet apart. "Bill" Carroll and Colonel Butler, and the two "Jacks," Coffee and Adair, were trusted counselors. Even his only Caucasian servitor at the White House, a stableman named Malloy, had served with Peter Ogden's company of Dragoons at New Orleans.

The White House door was ajar to all of these and many others. When an aging, salt-bitten sailor showed up, he was readily shown to the President's office, where Jackson studied him a moment.

"I remember you," the President said with brightened eyes. "You were at the Battle of New Orleans."

"Yes, sir, with the *Carolina*'s crew."

"And afterwards you fought on my line at Battery Number Two. What are you doing now?"

"Getting a little along in years, General, and the sea's too hard for me these days."

Jackson told an aide: "Tell Dickerson [Secretary of the Navy] to fix this man up with a position at the navy yard."

Later the President remarked, "Old sailors of the *Carolina*'s crew are not so plentiful now, but they remain a special breed." He might have said the same for the crew of the *Louisiana,* still anchored idly in the Mississippi. She was there almost half a century later when Commodore David Farragut sailed up the river in April of 1862 to take possession of New Orleans in the War Between the States. But the tired old lady, deprived by age of fighting spirit, hovered for safety beneath Fort St. Philip and did not try to intervene.

Even on the streets the New Orleans veterans would approach the President.

"General, I was with you at New Orleans."

"You must be a Kentuckian, then, because I knew personally every man from Tennessee. What command were you in?"

"I was a regular, sir, with Humphrey's battery."

"Indeed! A great battery, my friend, and a most excellent commander. Give me your hand again."

As they clasped hands a second time, the veteran artillerist felt an eagle gold-piece pressed against his palm.

"Please keep it, sir," said the President, "as a token of my friendship. It's good to have a little something laid by for a rainy day."

It was because of such impulsive generosities that Jackson himself had often suffered, and would suffer again, from financial worries.

The President's last year in office was brightened by the overthrow of Mexican rule in Texas, concluded by the battle at the San Jacinto river, which Jackson compared with his fight to save New Orleans. "There my army behind the breastwork defeated an enemy three times their number. At San Jacinto the attacking Americans defeated a well-entrenched enemy three times *their* number! There was never anything like it in modern warfare!"

The General arrived back in Nashville in the Spring of 1837 after having all but personally appointed his Vice President, Martin Van Buren, to succeed him in the White House. He was returning to a life of waning health and rising debt. There were offers of financial help from many sources, but the ex-President refused to "travel as a pauper." One, however, overcame his pride. From New Orleans came a check for $8,000 signed by Jean Baptiste Plauché, with a note begging the General to accept it for old times' sake. Jackson did and promptly amended his will to include a bequest to his much-loved Creole officer.

Some time later he received another small but heartening windfall, when the following poster appeared in metropolitan areas on February 14, 1844:

JUSTICE TO THE BRAVE
Judge Hall's Sentence on
ANDREW JACKSON
Repudiated by the Nation!

He had been refunded Judge Hall's fine by the Baratarians in 1815. Now he received a check from the Treasury Department with, more rewardingly, belated vindication of the charges made against him after "The Glorious 8th of January." The restitution was timely. "My lamp is nearly burned out," he had said. "There is but a glimmer left."

The glimmer faded on June 6, 1845. Gathered around him on that final evening of his life were Andrew Jr., John Henry Eaton, and a Negro slave in whose arms Rachel Jackson had succumbed. To them Jackson addressed his last and inconclusive words. "We shall meet. . ."

Then his voice and eyes wandered, uncertain only where and when that meeting might take place. Two hours before sundown he was dead.

New Orleans would never forget the General, although it was not until 1850 that an equestrian statue of the wartime commander was erected in the Place d'Armes, which was renamed "Jackson Square." However, Jackson himself paid several sentimental visits to the city. The first was a brief one, on his way to Florida in July of 1816. At a private banquet in his honor on the Fourth, his former colonel, Michel Fortier, proposed the toast: "In the hour of danger, our country was fortunate in finding a second Washington." Also present at the gathering was Judge Dominic Hall, who had tried and sentenced the General for abuse of power and who now offered him his hand. "I took it," Jackson wrote, "and my conscience tells me I did right. The hatchet is buried."

Again, in 1827, almost on the eve of his first election, he and Rachel attended the Thirteenth Anniversary of the Battle of New Orleans. This time, erasing the bitterness engendered on his first arrival in December 1814, the Jacksons stayed with Bernard de Marigny, who, by his own report, "was able to give them some pretty entertainment." It was a warm, enthusiastic welcome he received in the Crescent City, hearing again the deep-hearted cry of *Vive Jackson!,* renewing old loyalties and friendships assayed by the crucible at Chalmette's.

But one familiar face was missing: that of his one-time guide and counselor and unofficial aide, Pierre Denis de la Ronde. Pierre had died at age fifty-eight in 1820, seven years before, apparently of a heart too freighted with crushed hopes and disillusionment. With him perished the centuries-old name of de la Ronde, since his only son had never married. Versailles had been sold for $140,000 to a real estate promoter named Warburg, who was developing the estate as a *faubourg* of New Orleans.

The Faubourg de Versailles was a far cry from de la Ronde's vision of two glittering twin cities rising on the Mississippi and the lakes. But the promoter had retained one symbolic artery of that idyllic dream. On Warburg's map of the development, edging the south side of de la Ronde's canal and arcing like a gull's wing to Lake Borgne, was a delineated highway with the haunting name of *Chemin à Paris* — Road to Paris — the end of a rainbow that had vanished over the plains of Chalmette-de la Ronde in the January dawn of 1815.

# Epilogue

So ended America's second war with England, not with a whimper but a bang.

It is not irrelevant to hark back to the statement made by Benjamin Rush at the close of the Revolutionary conflict. "The American war is over," wrote Rush in 1783, "but this is far from being the case with the Revolution."

As one of the younger and more perceptive signers of the Declaration of Independence, Rush foresaw a hard row to hoe before the volatile conditions of freedom and independence congealed into an orderly and self-sufficient Union.

His thought was echoed some thirty-two years later by a less-known figure in history, Captain Henry Garland, a French-born patriot serving under General Coffee at the Battle of New Orleans. At a banquet given by officers on the eve of the disbandment of Jackson's army, Garland was singled out to express the feelings of his countrymen. He concluded his farewell address:

Most people say that our American Republic was born the Fourth day of July, 1776, in Philadelphia. This is not true. It was only begotten then. It was never confirmed until the 8th of January last.

In time historians came to agree, referring to the War of 1812 as the

331

Second War for Independence. It is a fair definition, applying not only, however, to the independence which Washington had fought for — freedom from British rule and severence of the ties which bound the Colonies to the Crown. There was another species of freedom at stake. For the new United States, both psychologically and economically, had remained a dependency of Europe, modeling its policies and government with an eye to European policies and governments, fearful and uncertain of its destiny.

Now that was over and, with the Battle of New Orleans, America had found itself. On the fields of Chalmette a new confidence was born. The nation was prepared to stand on its own feet, answerable to none. Europe and the Western World were forced to recognize that fact.

Wrote the hardheaded Secretary of the Treasury, Alexander James Dallas, the "holy war" of 1812 had "advanced the nation a century in power and character." Observed Samuel Eliot Morison in modern times, "The United States was never again denied the treatment due to an independent nation." Fletcher Pratt attributed the burgeoning of national spirit to that moment on January 8 when the troops at the ramparts stood up and cheered as the British troops withdrew.

"In that shout, confused and triumphant," Pratt declared, "the American nation was born."

It had not been a costly war, in terms of lives and money. Of a total of 286,730 men involved — army, navy and marines — there were only 2,260 battle deaths, half the number who died in the Revolutionary War, in which far fewer men were under arms.

But the gains had been great, though they were not reflected in the treaty signed at Ghent. Almost overnight, sectionalism vanished, however temporarily, and a new sense of nationalism was born to take its place. No one was deceived by the Treaty of Ghent, which John Quincy Adams, its major architect, admitted "adjusted nothing, settled nothing."

Yet outcries against the treaty and its terms were merely a letting-off of steam. It was enough that peace had been established, and the nation was relieved of one of its most hateful wars in history. Now the country could look forward to an unprecedented period of development and territorial expansion. There were no shackles, economic or psychological, binding it to Europe. More important, there were no fences at home dividing the country and blocking the path of peaceful progress.

Wrote Morison and Commager in *The Growth of the American Republic,* "Most of the difficulties under which the young republic had labored since the War of Independence now dropped out of sight. With national union achieved, a balance between liberty and order secured, and a virgin continent awaiting the plow, there opened a serene prospect of peace, prosperity, and social progress."

There would be those to argue that the triumph at New Orleans was of little significance, had no effect upon the outcome of the war since the Treaty of Ghent had been signed two weeks before. Such was not the case. A state of war continued to exist. The Treaty had been signed, not ratified. Lord Bathurst's instructions to Pakenham stated specifically that, regardless of any agreement achieved at Ghent, hostilities should continue until both nations had ratified the Treaty.

At the close of his last term in the White House, Jackson was visited by Congressman William Allen — known as "Earthquake Allen" for his explosive attitude in those explosive times — who posed the question: "What did the battle amount to, in value as a victory, other than the triumph of American soldiers over British veterans?" As Allen recorded the General's answer:

> If General Pakenham and his ten thousand matchless veterans could have annihilated my little army, as he expected to do, he would have captured New Orleans and sentried all the contiguous territory, though technically the war was over. It was the purpose of Great Britain to have held that territory. She would immediately have abrogated the Treaty of Ghent and would have ignored Jefferson's transaction with Napoleon.

In other words, it was Jackson's belief that had the ramparts yielded below New Orleans on January 8, "the Louisiana Purchase would have been lost to this country, irrevocably and forever." Practically every acre of land between the Mississippi River and the Pacific Ocean would have fallen into Britian's sphere of influence, and the great American West would have been denied to the United States. If it were not to be denied, if the English lion kept its claws on the Mississippi Valley, stifling the young republic, it might well have taken another war with England to dislodge him.

It is idle, of course, to speculate on what might have happened if the British had won at New Orleans, if the Treaty of Ghent had not in consequence been validated, and the war had continued with a greatly strengthened British expeditionary force. One theory holds that the New England states might then have made their own peace with the enemy, as they had threatened to do at the Hartford Convention in December, 1814. Subsequent years might then have seen New England militia fighting with British allies to dismember the Union. America would have been split by civil strife some forty years before the War Between the States.

As it was, Jackson's victory at New Orleans was like a fresh and stimulating wind from the Louisiana lakes and bayous, clearing the air of its clouds of discontent, dispelling previous dissension. New England celebrated as if it had never opposed the war, while the compromise-minded Federalists were discredited as a party politic. New England, in fact, glorified in the gallant performance of the navy based so largely on its shores. The minds and hearts of much of the country's youth were fired by the names of Perry and Decatur, and the great age of American seafaring spread the Stars and Stripes around the globe.

While there was no rise of militarism as a consequence of victory — the authorized peacetime army was limited to ten thousand Regulars — there was a new spirit of adventure, exploration and discovery across the land. The name of Andrew Jackson and the exploits of the Tennesseans and the better part of the Kentuckians helped turn the eyes of young America towards the West. The great caravans began their treks across the Appalachians and the Mississippi; the forests fell; the plains were sown with wheat; and the opening of the American West began.

In England, where failure to gain a decisive victory was the equivalent of defeat, the Battle of New Orleans and the War of 1812 were unfortunate events to be forgotten. Hopefully, the troops returning to rejoin Wellington's campaign against Napoleon were unaware of public outcries at the stigma of New Orleans, the Treaty of Ghent and the government itself. In London the *Public Advertiser* proclaimed:

### ADVERTISEMENTS EXTRAORDINARY

*Wanted:* The spirit which animated the conduct of Elizabeth, Oliver, and William.

*Lost:* All idea of national dignity and honour.

*Found:* That every insignificant state may insult THAT which used to call herself MISTRESS OF THE SEAS.

But the British catastrophe at New Orleans was quickly overshadowed by the victory at Waterloo, and English histories and school-books chose to ignore or slight the War of 1812. The Duke of Wellington was known to have privately expressed his esteem for General Jackson, while Lord Castlereagh was willing to forget and forgive and to urge his government to act in such a way as "to smooth all asperities between the two nations, and to unite them in sentiments of good will as well as of substantial interest, with each other."

Yet one always comes back to the question: what did the battle amount to, of and by itself? — other than ending the war in what Samuel Eliot Morison refers to as "a blaze of glory." Perhaps there is significance in this strange fact: that, since 1776, the Declaration of Independence had never seen the light of day, remaining as mute and secluded as if independence had not truthfully existed.

For most of the time the parchment scroll was hidden in darkness in the War Department Building; then secreted for safety in a parsonage at Leesburg, Virginia, during the War of 1812. Only after the Battle of New Orleans was the document brought to light. Not only brought to light, but engraved and publicly distributed that all who cared might read:

*"We hold these truths to be self-evident . . ."*

# Bibliography

ADAMS, CHARLES FRANCIS, *Studies Military and Diplomatic*. New York, Macmillan, 1911.

AINSWORTH, WALDEN L., *An Amphibious Operation that Failed: The Battle of New Orleans*. Annapolis, U.S. Naval Institute Proceedings, February 1945.

ARMSTRONG, ORLAND KAY, *15 Decisive Battles of the United States*. New York, Longmans-Green, 1961.

ARTHUR, STANLEY CLISBY, *Jean Laffite, Gentlemen Rover*. New Orleans, Harmanson, 1952.

ARTHUR, STANLEY CLISBY, *The Story of the Battle of New Orleans*. New Orleans, Louisiana Historical Society, 1915.

ASBURY, HERBERT, *The French Quarter*. New York, Knopf, 1936.

BROOKS, CHARLES B., *The Siege of New Orleans*. Seattle, University of Washington Press, 1961.

BROWN, WILBURT S., *The Amphibious Campaign for West Florida and Louisiana, 1814–1815*. University (Ala.), University of Alabama Press, 1969.

BUELL, AUGUSTUS C., *History of Andrew Jackson* (2 vols.). New York, Scribner's, 1904.

CABLE, GEORGE W., *The Creoles of Louisiana*. New York, Scribner's, 1884.

CARTER, HODDING, *The Lower Mississippi*. New York, Farrar and Rinehart, 1942.

337

CASEY, POWELL A., *Louisiana in the War of 1812*. Baton Rouge, published by the author, 1963.

CASTEL, ALBERT, *The Battle for New Orleans*. Gettysburg, American History Illustrated, August, 1969.

CASTELLANOS, HENRY C., *New Orleans as it Was*. New Orleans, Graham, 1895.

CASTELLANOS, HENRY C., *The Invasion of Louisiana*. New Orleans, Times-Democrat, May 7–28, 1893.

CHIDSEY, DONALD BARR, *The Battle of New Orleans*. New York, Crown, 1961.

CHRISTIAN, MARCUS, *Negro Soldiers in The Battle of New Orleans*. New Orleans, Louisiana Landmarks Society, 1965.

CLAIBORNE, W. C. C., *Official Letter Books,* Vol. VI. Jackson, Miss., State Department of Archives and History, 1917.

COLES, HARRY L., *The War of 1812*. Chicago, University of Chicago Press, 1965.

*Contemporary Account of the Battle of New Orleans* by a soldier in the ranks. New Orleans, Louisiana Historical Quarterly, Vol. IX, 1926.

*Courrier de la Louisiane,* New Orleans. News reports in the weekly issues of July, August, September, 1814.

CRANE, STEPHEN, *Great battles of the World*. Philadelphia, Lippincott, 1900.

DART, HENRY P., *Jackson and the Louisiana Legislature, 1814–15*. New Orleans, Louisiana Historical Quarterly, Vol. IX, 1926.

DE GRUMMOND, JANE L., *The Baratarians and the Battle of New Orleans*. Baton Rouge, Louisiana State University Press, 1961.

DICKSON, SIR ALEXANDER, *The Expedition Against New Orleans, in North America, 1814–1815*. London: Journal of the Society for Army Historical Research, Vol. VIII, 1929.

DIXON, RICHARD R., *The Battle on the West Bank*. New Orleans, Louisiana Landmarks Society, 1965.

DUFOUR, CHARLES L., *Ten Flags in the Wind*. New York, Harper & Row, 1967.

ELLER, E. M., MORGAN, W. J., AND BASOCO, R. M., *Sea Power and the Battle of New Orleans*. New Orleans, Louisiana Landmarks Society, 1965.

ENGELMAN, FRED L., *The Peace of Christmas Eve*. New York, Harcourt, Brace & World, 1962.

EVERETT, DONALD D., *Emigres and Militiamen: Free Persons of Color in New Orleans, 1803–1815*. Washington, Journal of Negro History, Vol. XXXVIII, October, 1953.

FAYE, STANLEY, *The Great Stroke of Pierre Laffite*. New Orleans, Louisiana Historical Quarterly, Vol. XXIII, No. 3, July, 1940.

FORTESCUE, J. W., *A History of the British Army,* Vol. X. London, Macmillan, 1920.

FORTIER, ALCÉE, *A History of Louisiana,* Vol. III. New York, Goupil of Paris, 1903.

FOSTER, ALBERT A., *New Orleans, The Glamour Period, 1806–1840.* Natchez, Plantation Bookshop, 1957.

GAYARRÉ, CHARLES, *A History of Louisiana,* Vol. III, Part 1. New York, Widdleton, 1866. New Orleans, Armand Hawkins, 1885.

GLEIG, GEORGE ROBERT, *A Narrative of the Campaigns of the British Army at New Orleans, etc.* London, John Murray, 1821.

HANDLIN, OSCAR, *The Americans.* Boston, Little, Brown, 1963.

HANDLIN, OSCAR, *This Was America.* Cambridge, Harvard University Press, 1949.

HITSMAN, J. MACKAY, *The Incredible War of 1812.* Toronto, University of Toronto Press, 1965.

HORSMAN, REGINALD, *The War of 1812.* New York, Knopf, 1969.

HUBER, LEONARD V., *New Orleans as it Was in 1814–1815.* New Orleans, Louisiana Landmarks Society, 1965.

HUNT, CHARLES HAVENS, *Life of Edward Livingston.* New York, Appleton, 1864.

JACKSON, ANDREW, *Correspondence of Andrew Jackson,* edited by John Spencer Bassett, Vol. II. Washington, Carnegie Institution, 1927.

JACKSON, ANDREW, *Journal of Major General Jackson at the Battle of New Orleans.* Manuscript at the Library of the Louisiana State Museum, New Orleans.

JACOBS, JAMES R., *Tarnished Warrior.* New York, Macmillan, 1938.

JAMES, MARQUIS, *The Life of Andrew Jackson.* New York, Bobbs-Merrill, 1938.

JENKINS, JOHN S., *Life and Public Services of Gen. Andrew Jackson.* Buffalo, G. H. Derby, 1850.

KANE, HARNETT T., *Deep Delta Country.* New York, Duell, Sloan & Pearce, 1944.

KANE, HARNETT T., *Plantation Parade.* New York, Morrow, 1945.

KANE, HARNETT T., *Queen New Orleans.* New York, Morrow, 1949.

KENDALL, JOHN SMITH, *History of New Orleans,* Vol. I. Chicago, Lewis Publishing Co., 1922.

KING, GRACE, *Creole Families of New Orleans.* New York, Macmillan, 1921.

KING, GRACE, *New Orleans: The Place and the People.* New York, Macmillan, 1896.

LATOUR, MAJOR A. L., *Historical Memoir of the War of West Florida and Louisiana.* (Facsimile reproduction of the 1816 edition.) Gainesville, University of Florida Press, 1964.

LONGFORD, ELIZABETH, *Wellington: The Years of the Sword*. New York, Harper & Row, 1969.

LOSSING, BENSON J., *Field Book of the War of 1812*. New York, Harper & Brothers, 1868.

MARIGNY, BERNARD DE, [Memorandum] *To the Inhabitants of Louisiana and the United States*. Manuscript at the Library of the Louisiana State Museum, New Orleans.

MARTIN, FRANÇOIS-XAVIER, *The History of Louisiana*. New Orleans, Gresham, 1882.

MAYHEW, THADDEUS, *A Massachusetts Volunteer at the Battle of New Orleans*. New Orleans, Louisiana Historical Quarterly, Vol. IX, 1926.

MCCLELLAN, EDWIN N., *The Navy at the Battle of New Orleans*. Annapolis, U.S. Naval Institute Proceedings, December, 1924.

MCCONNELL, ROLAND C., *Negro Troops of Antebellum Louisiana*. Baton Rouge, Louisiana State University Press, 1968.

MORGAN, DAVID B., *General Morgan's Defense of the Louisiana Militia in the Battle on the West Bank of the River*. New Orleans, Louisiana Historical Quarterly, Vol. IX, 1926.

MORISON, SAMUEL ELIOT, *The Oxford History of the American People*. New York, Oxford University Press, 1965.

MORISON, S. E., AND COMMAGER, H. S., *The Growth of the American Republic*. New York, Oxford University Press, 1962.

MORISON, S. E., MERK, F., AND FREIDEL, F., *Dissent in Three American Wars*. Cambridge, Harvard University Press, 1970.

MULLER, CHARLES G. *The Proudest Day*. New York, John Day, 1960.

MULLINS, THOMAS, *Court Martial of Brevet Lieutenant Colonel Thomas Mullins*. Dublin, William Espy, 1815.

*Nile's Weekly Register*, Vols. VI, VII, VIII. Baltimore, news dispatches received from New Orleans from September, 1814 to April, 1815.

NOLTE, VINCENT, *Fifty Years in Both Hemispheres*. New York, Redfield, 1854.

OLMSTEAD, FREDERICK LAW, *The Slave States*, New York, Putnam's, 1959.

PARSONS, EDWARD ALEXANDER, *Jean Lafitte in the War of 1812, a Narrative Based on the Original Documents*. Worcester, Mass., American Antiquarian Society, Proceedings, Vol. 50, 1940.

PRATT, FLETCHER, *The Heroic Years*. New York, Smith & Haas, 1934.

RANKIN, HUGH F., ed., *The Battle of New Orleans, a British View* (Journal of Major Charles R. Forrester). New Orleans, Hauser, 1961.

ROBINS, C. C. *Voyages de la Louisiane*. Paris, Buisson, 1807.

ROOSEVELT, THEODORE, *The Naval War of 1812*. New York, Putnam's, 1889.

ROWLAND, MRS. DUNBAR, *Andrew Jackson's Campaign against the British*. New York, Macmillan, 1926.

SAXON, LYLE, *Fabulous New Orleans.* New York, Century, 1928.

SAXON, LYLE, *Lafitte the Pirate.* New Orleans, Crager, 1930.

SAXON, LYLE, *Old Louisiana.* New York, Century, 1929.

SCOTT, VALERIE M. (Lady Pakenham), *Major-General Sir Edward M. Pakenham.* New Orleans, Louisiana Landmarks Society, 1965.

SEEBOLD, HERMAN DE BACHELLE, *Old Louisiana Plantation Homes,* Vol. II. New Orleans, privately printed, 1941.

Sesquicentennial Celebration Commission, *The Battle of New Orleans.* Washington, D.C., Report to the Congress, 1965.

SINCLAIR, HAROLD, *The Port of New Orleans.* New York, Doubleday, Doran, 1942.

SURTEES, WILLIAM, *Twenty-five Years in the Rifle Brigade.* Edinburgh, William Blackwood, 1833.

TALLANT, ROBERT, *The Romantic New Orleanians.* New York, Dutton, 1950.

TATUM, MAJOR HOWELL, *Major H. Tatum's Journal.* Northampton, Mass., Smith College Studies in History, 1921–22.

WALKER, ALEXANDER, *Jackson and New Orleans.* New York, J. C. Derby, 1856.

WATSON, ELBERT L., *Tennessee at the Battle of New Orleans.* New Orleans, Louisiana Landmarks Society, 1965.

WELLINGTON, FIELD MARSHALL ARTHUR WELLESLEY, DUKE OF, *Letter of the Duke of Wellington on the Battle of New Orleans.* New Orleans, Louisiana Historical Quarterly, Vol. IX, 1926.

WELLMAN, PAUL I., *The House Divided.* New York, Doubleday, 1966.

WILSON, SAMUEL JR., *Plantation Houses on the Battlefield of New Orleans.* New Orleans, Louisiana Landmarks Society, 1965.

YEO, JAMES LUCAS, *Observations Relative to New Orleans.* New Orleans, Original 1812 manuscript in the private collection of Edward A. Parsons.

# Index

343

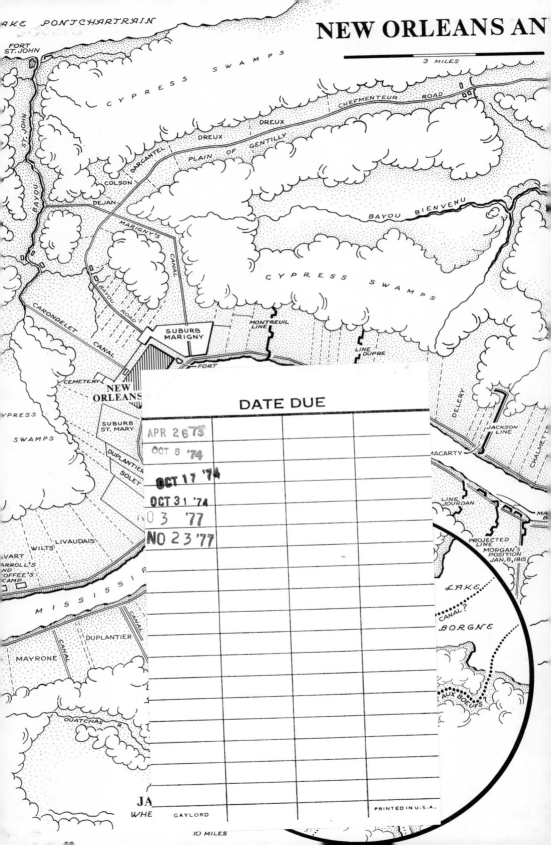

# NEW ORLEANS AN